SHAKESPEARE AND BECKETT

'The danger is in the neatness of identifications,' Samuel Beckett famously stated, and, at first glance, no two authors could be further distant from one another than William Shakespeare and Samuel Beckett. This book addresses the vast intertextual network between the works of the two writers and explores the resonant correspondences between them. It analyses where and how these resonances manifest themselves in their aesthetics, theatre, language and form. It traces convergences and inversions across both œuvres that resound beyond their conditions of production and possibility. Uncovering hitherto unexplored relations between the texts of an early modern and a late modern author, this study seeks to offer fresh readings of single passages and entire works, but it will also describe productive tensions and creative incongruences between them.

CLAUDIA OLK is Professor of English at Ludwig-Maximilians-University in Munich, and Director of the Munich Shakespeare Library. Her monographs include *Travel and Narration* (1999) and *Virginia Woolf and the Aesthetics of Vision* (2014). Her edition of unpublished Virginia Woolf manuscripts, *The Charleston Bulletin Supplements*, appeared in 2013. She is the president of the German Shakespeare Association.

SHAKESPEARE AND BECKETT

Restless Echoes

CLAUDIA OLK

Ludwig-Maximilians-University, Munich

Shaftesbury Road, Cambridge CB2 8EA, United Kingdom

One Liberty Plaza, 20th Floor, New York, NY 10006, USA

477 Williamstown Road, Port Melbourne, VIC 3207, Australia

314–321, 3rd Floor, Plot 3, Splendor Forum, Jasola District Centre, New Delhi – 110025, India

103 Penang Road, #05–06/07, Visioncrest Commercial, Singapore 238467

Cambridge University Press is part of Cambridge University Press & Assessment, a department of the University of Cambridge.

We share the University's mission to contribute to society through the pursuit of education, learning and research at the highest international levels of excellence.

www.cambridge.org
Information on this title: www.cambridge.org/9781009077200

DOI: 10.1017/9781009082402

© Claudia Olk 2023

This publication is in copyright. Subject to statutory exception and to the provisions of relevant collective licensing agreements, no reproduction of any part may take place without the written permission of Cambridge University Press & Assessment.

First published 2023
First paperback edition 2025

A catalogue record for this publication is available from the British Library

Library of Congress Cataloging-in-Publication data
NAMES: Olk, Claudia, author.
TITLE: Shakespeare and Beckett : restless echoes / Claudia Olk, Ludwig-Maximilians-University, Munich.
DESCRIPTION: Cambridge ; New York, NY : Cambridge University Press, 2022. | Includes bibliographical references and index.
IDENTIFIERS: LCCN 2022030157 (print) | LCCN 2022030158 (ebook) | ISBN 9781316514030 (hardback) | ISBN 9781009077200 (paperback) | ISBN 9781009082402 (epub)
SUBJECTS: LCSH: Shakespeare, William, 1564-1616–Criticism and interpretation. | Beckett, Samuel, 1906-1989–Criticism and interpretation.
CLASSIFICATION: LCC PR2976 .O4 2022 (print) | LCC PR2976 (ebook) | DDC 822.3/3–DC23/eng/20220707
LC record available at https://lccn.loc.gov/2022030157
LC ebook record available at https://lccn.loc.gov/2022030158

ISBN 978-1-316-51403-0 Hardback
ISBN 978-1-009-07720-0 Paperback

Cambridge University Press & Assessment has no responsibility for the persistence or accuracy of URLs for external or third-party internet websites referred to in this publication and does not guarantee that any content on such websites is, or will remain, accurate or appropriate.

Contents

Acknowledgements	*page* vi
List of Abbreviations	viii

	Introduction	1
1	Shakespeare and Beckett on the Edges	12
2	Molecular Shakespeare – Beckett Reading Shakespeare through Joyce	38
3	'Some remains': Beckettian and Shakespearean Echoes	73
4	Purgatory and Pause – Shakespeare, Dante and the Lobster	97
5	'[It is] winter/Without journey' – Still Lifes in Beckett and Shakespeare	123
6	Endgames	152
7	Theatres of Sleep	181
	Conclusion	209
	Bibliography	216
	Index	236

Acknowledgements

I should like to express my gratitude to the many people and institutions whose support was crucial during the process of writing this book. Many chapters were written at Oxford and I am much indebted to Exeter College, Oxford, for appointing me a visiting fellow. My special thanks goes to Andrew Allen, Philip Bullock, Frances Cairncross, Marguerite Dupree, Chris Fletcher, Jane Hiddleston and Sir Richard Trainor. Jeri Johnson, Emma Smith and Helen Watanabe O'Kelly accompanied many stages of my work and I will always be grateful to them.

I thank the Alexander von Humboldt-Foundation for providing me with a research grant. The Bodleian Library, the British Library and Widener Library at Harvard University, as always, provided outstanding resources and help.

For the opportunity to present work in progress I am immensely grateful to Brian Cummings, Michael Dobson and Nicola Watson, Paul Edmondson, Ewan Fernie, Gordon McMullan, Sir Stanley Wells and Richard Wilson. Andreas Höfele, Thomas and Susan Kohut, Joachim Küpper, Christopher Pye and James Simpson read drafts of single chapters and I am deeply grateful for their encouragement throughout.

For generous help, comments and discussion I warmly thank Homi Bhaba, Christoph Bode, Janet Clare, Hans Walter Gabler, Stephen Greenblatt, Anselm Haverkamp, Diana Henderson, Dirk van Hulle, Avi Lifschitz, Paul Nolte, Martin Puchner, Erika Tophoven, Roland Weidle and Susanne Zepp. I also thank Nicholas Shakespeare, the recipient of one of Beckett's last letters, who told me that Beckett would not have replied if his name had not been Shakespeare.

It was a pleasure to work with Emily Hockley at Cambridge University Press, and I thank her for her guidance and exceptional proficiency. Also, I wish to thank the two anonymous readers for their sensitive reading and deft reviews. I thank my doctoral and postdoctoral students in Berlin and Munich for their dedication, particularly Nikolina Hatton, Annegret

Schäffler and Marlies Zwickl for their care and diligence in assisting with the preparation of the text for publication.

Invaluable advice came from Sarah Stanton, and from Christian unfailing support and good cheer – to both of you my heartfelt thanks!

I would like to acknowledge permission from the following sources of Samuel Beckett's works:

George Craig, Martha Dow Fehsenfeld, Dan Gunn and Lois More Overbeck, *The Letters of Samuel Beckett*, © The Estate of Samuel Beckett, published by Cambridge University Press, reproduced with permission.

Quotations from the works of Samuel Beckett by permission of Faber & Faber LTD.

Claudia Olk, Berlin, September 2021

Abbreviations

Works by Samuel Beckett:

CDW	*The Complete Dramatic Works of Samuel Beckett*
CSP	*The Complete Shorter Prose of Samuel Beckett*
Disjecta	*Disjecta: Miscellaneous Writings and a Dramatic Fragment*
Dream	*Dream of Fair to Middling Women*
EB	*Echo's Bones*
HII	*How It Is*
Letters	*The Letters of Samuel Beckett*
MPTK	*More Pricks Than Kicks*

Works by William Shakespeare:

AC	*Antony and Cleopatra*
AYL	*As You Like It*
Cym	*Cymbeline*
Ham	*Hamlet, Prince of Denmark*
H 5	*King Henry V*
R II	*King Richard II*
R III	*King Richard III*
KL	*The Tragedy of King Lear*
Mac	*Macbeth*
MM	*Measure for Measure*
MV	*The Merchant of Venice*
MND	*Midsummer Night's Dream*
Oth	*Othello*
RJ	*Romeo and Juliet*
T	*The Tempest*
TC	*Troilus and Cressida*
Tim	*Timon of Athens*

TN   *Twelfth Night, or What You Will*
WT   *The Winter's Tale*

Works by other authors:

MD   Virginia Woolf, *Mrs Dalloway*
PL   John Milton, *Paradise Lost*
Portrait James Joyce, *A Portrait of the Artist as a Young Man*
TL   Virginia Woolf, *To the Lighthouse*
U   James Joyce, *Ulysses*

Introduction

In 1922, a year that saw the publication of landmark works such as James Joyce's *Ulysses*, Virginia Woolf's *Jacob's Room* and T.S. Eliot's *The Waste Land*, the sixth-form student Samuel Beckett read plays by William Shakespeare. His copies of editions of Shakespeare's plays like the one of *Macbeth*[1] contain many underlined or marked passages, but the reading trace very often found in their margins is: 'Learn by heart'.[2]

Reading the text as an actor would study it perhaps best describes Beckett's early encounters with Shakespeare: slowly absorbing the lines, concentrating on the words and memorizing them through many repetitions until passages can be delivered without any conscious effort. Bibliographical evidence such as this documents Beckett's initial and highly attentive responses to the works of Shakespeare.

A few years later, as a student of the Arts at Trinity College Dublin, Beckett continued to study a number of Shakespeare's works and when reading and rereading them[3] seemed to harbour a preference for the poems and the tragedies.[4] Unsurprisingly, he approached any kind of bardolatry with tongue-in-cheek irreverence and, as James Knowlson records, when he visited Stratford-upon-Avon in 1935, found it unspeakable.[5] Yet, Beckett was to remain a lifelong reader of Shakespeare. Even though he never devoted a single essay to Shakespeare as he did to Dante or Proust, his works abound with references, allusions, echoes and themes from the Shakespearean œuvre.

At first glance, perhaps no two writers could be more distant from one another: Shakespeare, who has an enormously rich language at his command, who creates the most eloquent and complex characters, whose vocabulary has shaped the *Oxford English Dictionary* and to whom it seems possible to express everything; and Beckett, who professes poverty and reduction, who longs for silences and 'black pauses', striving for a 'a literature of the non-word',[6] a writer who seems to be operating on the

1

basis that there is 'nothing to express' and still finds himself under 'the obligation to express' (*Disjecta*, 139).

On closer examination, however, commonplaces like these appear all too convenient and schematic. Instead, Beckett presented and also invented his works in relation to Shakespeare. Porter Abbott writes that 'Beckett was constantly reinventing his entire oeuvre'[7] in a sense in which he became author of himself. His vast and intense reading of French, German, Italian and English literature was part of this reinvention, in which texts recreate themselves in the light of each new reference. He was continuously drawn to Shakespeare the dramatist and the poet, an interest that was nurtured by his limitless and passionate fascination with poetry and language. Not only did Shakespeare's language creations inspire the young Beckett when in his early short stories he inserted Shakespearean usages such as 'whirligig' but also more generally in Shakespeare's works Beckett found a poetic language that first of all creates what it represents, a language that incarnates the very thing it expresses, (*Disjecta*, 27–8), in which form and content have become inseparable.

This book aims to explore the resonant correspondences between the works of the two writers. It analyses where and how these resonances manifest themselves in their aesthetics, theatre, language and form. It traces the convergences and inversions of both œuvres that resound beyond their conditions of production and possibility. Both writers share a profound scepticism about the mimetic functions of their art, and their productive interrelationship reveals both a critique of representation and the creative formation of something unrepresentable. Through their interactions and interanimating resonances Shakespeare's and Beckett's texts become part of the literary history that they generate.

This study, however, decidedly refrains from reducing historical distance and smoothing over existing differences. Steven Connor duly cautions us that comparing Shakespeare to Beckett can also be the result of the force of a tradition that makes Beckett into a classic in spite of himself, leading to an over-ardent embrace of both writers as exemplifying 'the eternal human spirit': 'And like Shakespeare, Beckett is the representative of a whole cultural patrimony, an inherited tradition that, despite Beckett's disgusted turn away from his "mother" tongue, is identified with the power and prestige of "English" as a language.'[8]

Beckett himself, who was always careful to list his sources in the extensive production notebooks of his plays, urges the readers of his early essay 'Dante...Bruno.Vico..Joyce' to refrain from drawing hasty conclusions and famously warns them that: 'The danger is in the neatness of identifications' (*Disjecta*, 19). He had little patience with the kind of scholarship that 'neatly' stifles its object by grafting fashionable theories onto a text and imposes a retrospective pattern of single analogy. A memorable instance of such 'analogymongering', as he called it, that concerns Beckett's relation to Shakespeare, occurred in March 1961, during one of Beckett's many visits to Germany, where he was honoured at a symposium organized by his German publisher Suhrkamp in Frankfurt. Before the event, the publisher Siegfried Unseld hosted a lunch for Beckett and Theodor Adorno. Knowlson records Unseld's account of the occasion:

> Adorno immediately developed his idea about the etymology and the philosophy and the meaning of the names in Beckett. And Adorno insisted that 'Hamm' [in *Endgame*] derives from 'Hamlet'. He had a whole theory based on this. Beckett said 'Sorry, Professor, but I never thought of Hamlet when I invented this name'. But Adorno insisted. And Beckett became a little angry ... In the evening Adorno started his speech and, of course, pointed out the derivation of 'Hamm' from 'Hamlet' [...]. Beckett listened very patiently. But then he whispered into my ear [...][:] 'This is the progress of science that professors can proceed with their errors!'.[9]

Even though Adorno had not intended anything of the kind, Beckett was concerned that his play and its characters were being reduced to the model provided by Shakespeare.[10] This book will not endorse Beckett's caricature of scientific progress when it explores some of the intricate connections between Shakespeare and Beckett. Neither will I try to tell a story of straightforward influence between two static entities nor delineate a teleological process in which Shakespeare emerges as the monolithic original and Beckett as a derivative end product.

Instead of merely demonstrating the rich and resilient afterlife of Shakespeare, I will address the connections and correspondences between major works of both writers. This concerns the explicit footholds, but more importantly also the more latent and oblique connections. Uncovering correspondences and suggestive relations between the texts of an early modern and a late modern author, this study seeks to offer fresh readings of single passages and entire works, but it will also describe productive tensions and creative incongruences between them. The study will not provide a genealogy of modernity from the sixteenth to the late twentieth century; it will rather shed light on both cultural moments.

The generative and constitutive role of intertextual relations has been prominently addressed by Julia Kristeva's development of Mikhail Bakhtin's model of intertextuality as dialogue that ranges between 'absorption and transformation' and by Roland Barthes' understanding of the poem as an echo chamber in which citations freely oscillate.[11] When considering these influential notions of intertextuality, however, it is useful to note that Kristeva, Foucault and Barthes were also readers of Beckett. Foucault's quoting from Beckett's *Texts for Nothing* in 'What is an author?'[12] is a further example of the creative interaction between theories of intertextuality and their object of scrutiny. Likewise, as Janet Clare reminds us, intertextuality was inherent in early modern theatre culture: 'Shakespeare was a supreme dramaturg *avant la lettre* – adapting, re-shaping, and re-conceptualizing borrowed materials to make them stage-worthy.'[13] Moving away from intertextuality as a study of mere citational influence, Elizabeth Bronfen has introduced the term 'crossmapping' to describe the analogies between two œuvres: 'Crossmapping thus entails using the historically later texts as the starting point for a speculation on their cultural origin and, in so doing, it looks at Shakespeare through the lens of his subsequent refiguration by authors who succeeded him.'[14] 'Crossmapping' is very relevant to my approach in that it includes the discussion of specific cultural moments and critical interrelations between a text and its antecedent. In this study, however, I use the term 'echo', which I discuss in Chapter 3, to describe a conceptual approach, which, more than a palimpsestic layering or a double exposure, foregrounds the dynamic aspect of transformation that concerns the relation between voice and matter, the performative, material and immaterial conditions of Shakespeare's and Beckett's texts in relation to one another. I also extend intertextuality beyond Kristeva's 'mosaic of quotations'[15] and analyse not only how the works of two authors connect laterally but also how they examine the nature of their very medium.

Central to my argument is the assumption that Shakespeare and Beckett interact in ways that are both representative and performative. Shakespeare's and Beckett's texts exhibit their aesthetic strategies and reflect on them at the same time. They investigate the foundations of artistic creation and comprehension and reveal the shifting foundations on which hermeneutic habits sometimes rely. In the works of both writers, self-reflection often becomes its own form of creation and offers insights into the constructive and critical role of art.

While Shakespeare held a firm place among the moderns,[16] Beckett has been considered as a 'Great Shakespearean'. Dan Gunn's illuminating article in the eponymous series interprets particular instances where Shakespeare's work opens on to a Beckettian perspective. Apart from Jan Kott's early notion of an existentialist Shakespeare, which will be discussed at some length in Chapter 1, Beckett and Shakespeare scholarship has always been aware of the many levels on which the works of the two writers interrelate. There is, however, no monograph extant that studies the creative connections between the two writers.

James Knowlson's groundbreaking biography *Damned to Fame* demonstrates Beckett's continuous engagement with Shakespeare in its many detailed observations. Like Knowlson, Anne Atik in *How It Was: A Memoir of Samuel Beckett* describes multiple instances of Beckett referring to Shakespeare.[17] Mark Nixon and Dirk van Hulle in *Beckett's Library* have shown how plays such as *King Lear* were 'at the core of Beckett's creative endeavours in the 1980s, as a cluster of quotations in the "Sottisier" Notebook suggests'.[18] The *Samuel Beckett Archive* at Reading and Nixon and van Hulle's invaluable *Samuel Beckett Digital Manuscript Project* contain Beckett's copies of Shakespeare's plays.

Allusions and intertextual references to Shakespeare's works are mentioned in most critical works on Beckett. Early on, Ruby Cohn had identified numerous links between the two writers and stated that 'Beckett and Shakespeare are reciprocally reactive.'[19] Additionally, her later works continuously address the links between them that exist on the page and on the stage.[20] Annotated editions and companions to Beckett's works list and explain their many references to Shakespeare.[21]

In terms of method, the works of Stanley E. Gontarski are pertinent to my approach of comparative reading. From different angles, his monographs *The Intent of Undoing* and *Creative Involution*[22] trace Beckett's processes of composition and expound the paradoxical progress of creative undoing in his texts that also affects his relation to his antecedents. A number of articles such as Gontarski's 'Literary Allusions in *Happy Days*', Werner Habicht's 'Becketts Baum und Shakespeares Wälder' or John Russell Brown's 'Mr. Beckett's Shakespeare'[23] examine the role of intertextual traces, quotations and references in specific plays or genres. Charles Lyons, in 'Beckett, Shakespeare, and the Making of Theory', explores the 'nexus of theory, writing, and performance'.[24]

The role of the comic and the relevance of Shakespeare's clowns and fools for Beckett's plays has constantly been emphasized.[25] Anne Marie Drew's dissertation *Tragicomic Fools in Shakespeare and Beckett* further explores this link. Her edited volume *Past Crimson, Past Woe: The Shakespeare–Beckett Connection* brings together a number of articles that, in the vein of Jan Kott, analyse Beckett's and Shakespeare's works as representing the human condition and offer perspectives on crucial moments of the existential absurd.[26]

Lines from Shakespeare have become emblematic for Beckett's aesthetics, and hence articles such as R.A. Foakes' on '*King Lear* and *Endgame*' or Andrew Fitzsimons' 'What wretches feel': Lear, Edgar and Samuel Beckett's *Worstward Ho*' evince the persistent connection between *King Lear* and Beckett's plays.[27] Dirk van Hulle explores further nuances of the notion of nothingness in Beckett and Shakespeare.[28] Caroline Patey's essay 'Beckett's Shakespeare, or, Silencing the Bard' compares Beckett to Racine and refers to the French translations of Beckett's plays. It also analyses semantic areas and images in which selected plays of Shakespeare appear in Beckett's works. Whereas Patey looks at a Shakespeare in Beckett who is '[d]ismembered, neutralized and variously ill-treated', 'a *corpse morcelé* ... dumped all over Beckett's works', whose shadows 'still linger on',[29] my approach considers the more productive tensions and parallels between the works of the two writers.

The overall architecture of this book, the diptych of Shakespeare and Beckett, is structured around metaphorical tropes that address key aspects of aesthetics, and it reviews models of intertextual exchange rather than offering a chronological or canonical approach. The seven chapters of this study will focus on the dramatic works of both writers, they will also analyse selected Shakespeare sonnets and attempt a comprehensive treatment of Beckett's work including more neglected and posthumously published works. This book will mainly consider Beckett's English texts, but where relevant, it will also refer to their French and German versions.

Chapter 1, 'Shakespeare and Beckett on the Edges', looks at modernity from its margins in the sixteenth and the late twentieth century and discusses Shakespeare's and Beckett's works in periods that were conceived of as inherently transformational. The chapter will address the early links between Shakespeare and Beckett that were established in British theatre history. The second part of this chapter will read the scenes on Dover cliff in Act IV of *King Lear* as a metaphor for the theatre in which both Beckett and Shakespeare explore the edges of their very medium. This latter part examines Beckett's 'variations on rise and fall' in many of his plays, which, in dialogue with *King Lear*, dramatize the experience of blindness, crawling and falling.

Building on the dialogue between early modernity and late modernism, Chapter 2 discusses how literary heritage and authorial legacies are addressed, reflected on and performed in Beckett's reconfigurations of Shakespeare. 'Molecular Shakespeare – Beckett Reading Shakespeare through Joyce' regards Beckett's encounter with Shakespeare by way of Joyce's use of language and his performative reworking of literary heritage.

I argue that, interacting with Joyce, Beckett also found an early model of how to engage with literary history in a way that is both creative and destructive. The chapter illustrates the processes by which Joyce and Beckett not only record various received paradigms of literary lineage, authorship and national heritage but also inscribe their works into these traditions, taking a stance that is both metahistorical and performative. I shall study the metaphorical functions of the 'mole', drawing on its treatment in Hamlet scholarship (Hegel, Marx), and particularly in Margreta De Grazia's reading of Hamlet's 'Old Mole',[30] to analyse Beckett's metaleptic use of the mole as a marker of genealogy on the level of character, and, on a conceptual level, to describe the embeddedness of the subject in objective conditions and its sometime blindness in using language. The second part of this chapter traces Beckett's inversions of Joycean and Shakespearean paradigms. Shakespeare becomes part of the creative matrix of Beckett's works such as *Murphy*, in which the very richness of his material emerges in the use of minute details and the attention to the mole-cular level of languages and ideas that form the minimal components of his work.

Chapter 3, '"Some Remains" – Beckettian and Shakespearean Echoes' considers the conceptual function of the echo as a metaphor for processes of intertextual dialogue and transformation. Instead of terms such as adaptation, quotation or association, it is the notion of the echo that aptly describes Beckett's ways of engaging with his predecessors and materializing this engagement in the theatrical performance. This chapter regards the echo both as a principle of composition, and as an immanent figuration that emerges in the theatrical performance. Matter and materiality, stones and bones, in Beckett's works very often become a metonymy for the text itself in that they expose its opacity and resistance, and, at the same time, render it immortal as a kind of petrified *lacuna*. I consider Beckett's use of the materiality of stones and bones and read *Happy Days* with *Romeo and Juliet*, *Cymbeline* and *Hamlet*. The chapter argues that in *Happy Days* Beckett materializes the tragic dilemma of being held captive, unable to move, buried alive, through the means of scenery and props.

Liminal spaces of waiting and expectation are at the centre of Chapter 4, 'Purgatory and Pause – Dante, Shakespeare and the Lobster', which focuses on *Hamlet*, *Waiting for Godot* and Beckett's short story 'Dante and the Lobster'. The chapter draws on Stephen Greenblatt's study *Hamlet in Purgatory* and on Daniela Caselli's *Beckett's Dantes*, but it also uses the idea of purgatory to describe a dynamic, permeable space for intertextual dialogue.[31] A main part of the chapter is devoted to reading 'Dante and the

Lobster' in dialogue with *Hamlet*, *King Lear* and also with the poetry of Thomas McGreevy, from which many of its themes derive. 'Dante and the Lobster' and *Hamlet* converge on the element of pause, and the chapter examines the ways in which both works become mutually interanimating in their reflections on the incongruous.

Not unlike the idea of purgatory, many of Beckett's works are built around the paradoxical notion of the still life. Suspended between motion and standstill, between destruction and creation, a still life conveys the state of a being that is simultaneously lifeless and alive. Chapter 5, '"[It is] winter/Without Journey" – Still Lifes in Beckett and Shakespeare' discusses the relation between visual, textual and dramatic still lifes. Beckett's line 'winter/Without journey' (*CDW*, 476) will be regarded in the context of Shakespeare's transformations of the artistic image in *The Winter's Tale* in which Hermione's statue fixes a transitional space where death and immortality become inseparable, and where the work of art restlessly aspires towards life-likeness. The emergence of ghostly 'Doppelgangers' will be addressed by way of Franz Schubert's *Winterreise*, a work that resonates through Beckett's late plays. Journeys of dispossession and shrinking as well as moments frozen in time that approach the condition of a still life will be analysed in *Timon of Athens*, 'The End', *King Lear*, 'Texts for Nothing', Sonnets 55, 18 and 81 and, finally, in *Breath*.

Rather than looking at the link between *Endgame* and *King Lear*, Chapter 6, 'Endgames', considers the reciprocal productivity between Beckett's *Endgame* and Shakespeare's late romance *The Tempest*. It examines the settings of both plays, their dialectics of making and unmaking, their dynamics of confinement and release, the materiality of air and earth in each, and their variations on ending. In both plays, the game of chess figures as a structural and thematic component and reflects on the art of the playwright. The chapter analyses the brief scene in which Prospero discovers Ferdinand and Miranda playing chess, a scene that functions as a *mise-en-abîme*, as a play-within-the-play, and, like Beckett's eponymous *Endgame* becomes a metaphor for the play itself.

Chapter 7, 'Theatres of Sleep', analyses the idea of sleep and closure in *The Tempest*, *Waiting for Godot*, *The Winter's Tale*, *A Midsummer Night's Dream*, *Macbeth*, 'Cascando', 'Nacht und Träume', *Footfalls* and *Rockaby*. The rhythm of sleeping and waking pervades the diurnal structure of *Waiting for Godot*, and many of Beckett's characters sleep waking or wake sleeping. Likewise, sleep, awakening and insomnia are ubiquitous in the structure and poetics of Shakespeare's works. This chapter regards sleep as a liminal state that generates a meta-dramatic stance, in which

Shakespeare's and Beckett's theatre experiments with the creation of stage presences that also affect the experience of seeing a play.

This study will trace distinct connections between the works of Shakespeare and Beckett, surveying their characteristic aesthetic operations, thematic concerns, historical figurations and poetic principles. In examining the continuous resonances, the restless echoes between both œuvres, I would like to demonstrate the creative and generative effect these writers have upon one another, and suggest that reading Beckett enhances our reading of Shakespeare and vice versa. This study therefore pursues a double focus. On the one hand, it will ask which aspects of Shakespeare's works were particularly relevant and productive for Beckett's aesthetic strategies. On the other, it seeks to discover ways of reading Shakespeare through Beckett's works by examining their metonymical uses of words, images and materiality, and their relentless precision in demanding a renewed attention to literal meaning.

Like Shakespeare before him, Beckett, who advised his actors to '[s]peak with the tone of moonlight in [their] voices',[32] remained also a listener, intensely aware of his embeddedness in other voices and restlessly connecting to them. He would write down texts from memory and recite poetry until the end of his life. Among the polyphony of echoes reverberating through Beckett's works, Shakespeare's plays and poetry were a constant point of departure and return.

Notes

1. William Shakespeare, *Macbeth*, ed. by A.W. Verity, M.A. (Cambridge University Press, 1922), 52. Cf. Dirk van Hulle and Pim Verhulst, *The Making of Beckett's* En attendant Godot/Waiting for Godot (London: Bloomsbury, 2017), 24–5.
2. Beckett Digital Library module © 2016 Samuel Beckett Digital Manuscript Project. Editors: Dirk Van Hulle, Mark Nixon and Vincent Neyt. Student Library edited by Veronica Bălă. Back leaf verso cover and page of Samuel Beckett's copy of *Macbeth* written in blue-black ink. William Shakespeare, *Macbeth* (Cambridge University Press, 1922), ed. by A.W. Verity, M.A., 19. Beckett's copy of *The Works of William Shakspeare* (London/New York: Frederick Warne and Co, n.d., p. 1087) for instance also contains his correction of a typing error in Sonnet 30. © 2017 Samuel Beckett Digital Manuscript Project. Editors: Dirk Van Hulle, Mark Nixon and Vincent Neyt. Student Library edited by Veronica Bălă. I wish to acknowledge the invaluable work of Dirk van Hulle and Mark Nixon in the *Samuel Beckett Digital Manuscript Project,* which holds the facsimiles of Beckett's copies of Shakespeare's plays.

3 James Knowlson, *Damned to Fame: The Life of Samuel Beckett* (London: Bloomsbury, 1996), 54.
4 *Letters* I, 240, 1.1.1935 to Thomas McGreevy.
5 Knowlson, *Damned to Fame*, 203.
6 *Letters* I, 519; 520, 9.7.1937 to Axel Kaun. Dan Gunn, 'Samuel Beckett' in Adrian Poole (ed.), *Joyce, T.S. Eliot, Auden, Beckett. Great Shakespeareans*, vol. XII (London: Continuum, 2012), 149–97.
7 Porter Abbott, *Beckett Writing Beckett: The Author in the Autograph* (Ithaca: Cornell University Press, 1996), 20.
8 Steven Connor, *Samuel Beckett: Repetition, Theory and the Text* (Oxford: Blackwell, 1988), 198–9.
9 Knowlson, *Damned to Fame*, 479. A section of Adorno's later published essay 'Versuch, das *Endspiel* zu verstehen' was delivered as a lecture in Beckett's presence in Frankfurt am Main on 27 February 1961.
10 Dirk von Hulle, 'Adorno's Notes on *Endgame*', *Journal of Beckett Studies*, 19.2 (2010), 196–217, 204.
11 Julia Kristeva, 'Word, Dialogue and Novel' in Toril Moi (ed.), *The Kristeva Reader* (New York: Columbia University Press, 1986), 34–61, 37; Roland Barthes, 'The Death of the Author' in Roland Barthes (ed.), *Image – Music – Text*, selected and trans. by Stephen Heath (London: Fontana Press, 1982), 142–8, 146. Roland Barthes, *Roland Barthes [by Roland Barthes]*, trans. by Richard Howard (New York: Hill and Wang, 1977), 74–6.
12 Michel Foucault, 'What is an Author?' in James D. Faubion (ed.), *Aesthetics, Method and Epistemology*, transl. by Robert Hurley et al. (New York: The New Press, 1999), 205–22, 205: '"What does it matter who is speaking," someone said.' Alastair Hird, '"What does it Matter Who is Speaking": Beckett, Foucault, Barthes', *Samuel Beckett Today/Aujourd'hui*, 22 (2010), 289–99. Hird reads Barthes and Foucault's theories of authorship in conjunction with Beckett, focusing on an 'understanding of paradoxical Beckettian authorship: the deliberate creation of a text devoid of the authorial presence', 290.
13 Janet Clare, *Shakespeare's Stage Traffic: Imitation, Borrowing and Competition in Renaissance Theatre* (Cambridge University Press, 2014), 23.
14 Elizabeth Bronfen, 'Afterword', in Tobias Döring and Ewan Fernie (eds.), *Thomas Mann and Shakespeare: Something Rich and Strange* (London: Bloomsbury, 2015), 246–56, 247.
15 Kristeva, 'Word, Dialogue and Novel', 37. Julia Kristeva, 'Bakhtine, le Mot, le Dialogue et le Roman', *Critique*, 23.4 (Avril 1967), 438–65, 440: 'tout texte se construit comme mosaïque de citations'.
16 Richard Halpern acutely addresses the intersection of early modern and modern discourses on representational crises in Richard Halpern, *Shakespeare among the Moderns* (Ithaca, London: Cornell University Press, 1997), 34.
17 Ann Atik, *How It Was: A Memoir of Samuel Beckett* (London: Faber & Faber, 2001), 53–9.
18 Dirk van Hulle and Mark Nixon, *Samuel Beckett's Library* (Cambridge University Press, 2013), 27.

Introduction 11

19 Ruby Cohn, 'Beckett and Shakespeare', *Modern Drama*, 15 (1972), 223–30, 223.
20 The present study is much indebted to Cohn's works, especially *Modern Shakespeare Offshoots*, Princeton, 1976; *A Beckett Canon*, 2001; and *Samuel Beckett: The Comic Gamut* (1962).
21 John Pilling, *More Pricks Than Kicks* (2004); John Pilling, *Dream of Fair to Middling Women* (2004); Chris Ackerley, *Murphy* (2004).
22 S.E. Gontarski, *The Intent of Undoing in Samuel Beckett's Dramatic Texts* (Bloomington: Indiana University Press, 1985); *Creative Involution: Bergson, Beckett, Deleuze* (Edinburgh University Press, 2015). Likewise, Gontarski's collection of essays, *Beckett Matters: Essays on Beckett's Late Modernism* (Edinburgh University Press, 2017) lays the foundation for discussions of Beckett as a late modernist, emphasizing the dynamic and digressive character of Beckett's works.
23 S.E. Gontarski, 'Literary Allusions in *Happy Days*' in S.E. Gontarski (ed. and intr.), *On Beckett* (London: Anthem Press, 2012), 232–44; Werner Habicht, 'Becketts Baum und Shakespeares Wälder', *Shakespeare Jahrbuch*, 106 (1970), 77–98; Russell Brown, 'Mr. Beckett's Shakespeare', *Critical Quarterly*, 5 (1963), 310–26.
24 Charles R. Lyons 'Beckett, Shakespeare, and the Making of Theory' in Enoch Brater and Ruby Cohn (eds.), *Around the Absurd: Essays on Modern and Postmodern Drama* (Ann Arbor: University of Michigan Press, 1990), 97.
25 Jean Jacques Mayoux, 'The Theatre of Samuel Beckett', *Perspective*, Autumn (1959), 142–55.
26 Anne Marie Drew (ed.), *Past Crimson, Past Woe: The Shakespeare-Beckett Connection* (New York, London: Garland, 1993), xv–xvi.
27 R.A. Foakes, '*King Lear* and *Endgame*', *Shakespeare Survey*, 55 (2002), 153–8; Andrew Fitzsimons, '"What Wretches Feel": Lear, Edgar and Samuel Beckett's *Worstward Ho*' in Tetsuo Kishi (ed.), *The Shakespearean International Yearbook 7. Special Section, Updating Shakespeare* (Aldershot, England: Ashgate, 2007), 256–71.
28 Dirk van Hulle, 'Beckett and Shakespeare on Nothing, or, Whatever Lurks behind the Veil', *Limit(e) Beckett*, 1 (2010), 196–217.
29 Caroline Patey, 'Beckett's Shakespeare, or, Silencing the Bard' in Giovanni Cianci (ed. and intr.) and Caroline Patey (ed.), *Will the Modernist: Shakespeare and the European Historical Avant-Gardes* (Oxford: Lang, 2014), 223–50, 227; 234.
30 Margreta De Grazia, Hamlet *without Hamlet* (Cambridge University Press, 2008). 23–44 (Chapter 2).
31 Stephen Greenblatt, *Hamlet in Purgatory* (Princeton University Press, 2001); Daniela Caselli, *Beckett's Dantes: Intertextuality in the Fiction and Criticism* (Manchester, New York: Manchester University Press, 2005).
32 Cf. e.g. Lawrence Graver, *Waiting for Godot* (Cambridge University Press, 2004), 52.

CHAPTER 1

Shakespeare and Beckett on the Edges
Restless Moderns

The history of modernity is a record of inherent restlessness. Modernity is not a stable condition established in perpetuity. It is always on the edges, verges towards historical, discursive and aesthetic thresholds and reaches beyond them. Equally, the discourse of modernity is by necessity incomplete and in need of constant revision and readjustment.[1] Historian Neil MacGregor speaks about 'Shakespeare's restless world',[2] and from the sixteenth century onwards, the sense of experiment, the transcending of limits and emphatic novelty have been conceived as intrinsic to the idea of a modern age that does not aspire towards an unchanging *status quo* but implies its own continuous demise in an inbuilt dynamic of self-supersession. Modernity foregrounds transitoriness and represents it at the same time, making it part of its condition. Jürgen Habermas describes this continuous emphasis on becoming rather than being as a 'dynamic of restless attempts, continued into our time, to arrest themselves'.[3] Fulfilment and closure, are, if at all, only temporarily achieved.

While the historical frame of this study is to look at 'modernity' from the edges, from its margins in early modernity and late modernism, it yet resists to endorse binarisms or to reconstruct the seemingly typical. Samuel Beckett and William Shakespeare wrote in periods of transition, periods that could no longer gain legitimacy by relying on a metaphysical ontology, and their works present their own contingency and develop their own immanent discursive validity in the absence of such foundations.[4] Both the sixteenth and the mid-twentieth centuries were periods of prolific literary production and reflection, phases in which literature itself, its representational practices, functions and effects became an object of scrutiny and reinvention. Stanley Cavell counters the notion of 'autonomous art' often claimed for modernity:

the trouble is that the genuine article – the music of Schoenberg and Webern, the sculpture of Caro, the painting of Morris Louis, the theatre of Brecht and Beckett – really does challenge the art of which it is the inheritor and voice. Each is, in a word, not merely modern, but modernist. Each, one could say, is trying to find the limits or essence of its own procedures.[5]

In both periods literature not only illustrated representational crises and challenged sets of expectations but also helped to shape notions of 'modernity' and narratives of the Renaissance, Humanism, Existentialism or the Absurd.

'The fact is that we create our own precursors,' writes Jorge Luis Borges in his short story 'Kafka and his Precursors', and he describes the anachronistic dynamics of writers interacting with their forebears.[6] Both modernism and the Renaissance rely on a productive interrelationship with the past. In the Renaissance, part of what Hans Blumenberg has discussed as a process of early modern self-assertion[7] is also a process of self-classicization in which philosophy, the sciences and literature reconnected themselves to classical antiquity.[8] Modernity thus instals its own generative dynamics in marking both the euphoria of a departure and the indebtedness to that from which it departs. It partakes in narratives of progress and of rupture at the same time. Stephen Connor notes that 'any emergent historical condition that breaks with a prior condition itself adds something to what it breaks from'.[9] By gesturing towards something beyond itself, modernity edges on a faith in newness and originality, in which the search for new forms of expression verges on the exhaustion of the possible,[10] and where renewal is often reinvention, or, as S.E. Gontarski argues, 'a struggle towards the new only to find the familiar yet again'.[11] The forceful thrust towards newness and the future that is accompanied by the imperative to always go on – often subsumed under epithets like innovation, evolution, progress and emancipation – hence also reflects back on and defines a past that 'retroactively becomes what it was',[12] as Slavoj Žižek observes when he considers Beckett's relation to Shakespeare.

Modernity needs tradition to assert itself and tradition needs modernity to continue. 'The historical sense,' T.S. Eliot writes in 'Tradition and the Individual Talent', shapes the present and 'involves a perception, not only of the pastness of the past, but of its presence.'[13] The paradoxical yet constitutive verticality of modernity does not follow a pattern of continuation through reiteration, renewal through the mythological return of the same; nor does it level historical distance.[14] Rather, it characterizes modernity as a necessarily incomplete and unfinished project, as Habermas and

Lyotard perceived it, a project in which every moment of the present both asserts itself and generates its own transgression in marking the provisional character of the present as modern.[15]

In twentieth-century modernism, conceptions of temporality are guided by the antithetical impulses of rupture and continuation. T.S. Eliot's *Four Quartets* considers the 'moment in and out of time',[16] describing modernist temporality as both centring on the revelatory stasis of an intense moment of being and as embedded in the linear and procedural condition of becoming. From Eliot's notion of the 'historical sense', in which the past is not merely 'a heap of broken images'[17] but a creative resource – 'a sense of the timeless as well as of the temporal'[18] – to Marcel Proust's foregrounding of the past as memory created in and through the text and Virginia Woolf's metaphor of 'the platform of time',[19] which conceives of the present as encoded in the past, modernists have always emphasized their indebtedness to literary history. The imperative to 'make it new' associated with Ezra Pound and his 1934 collection of essays of the same name does not instal a linear model of evolution but rather coincides with a recognition, even a reinvention of the past within a regenerative movement that centres on the semantic, rhetorical and performative potentiality of literary texts.

Shakespeare's works, for many writers of the twentieth century, became a privileged ground where they sought inspiration and examined their own creative processes. Joyce, Eliot and Woolf resorted to Renaissance texts to review and enhance their own works and to enter into a dialogue with the past as present. As Richard Halpern observes: 'what struck Eliot too about Renaissance culture was its essential *modernity*, which allowed him to read in that period's "anarchism, dissolution, and decay" a reflection of his own times. ... As a result ..., his awareness of historical difference is always transected by the sense of an eternal present which renders the past directly contemporaneous.'[20]

Shakespeare criticism, however, has become increasingly sensitive to the ambiguities that govern his works and make them speak to the persistent and sometimes also conflicting concerns of different ages. The extensive and varied reception of his plays and poems over the centuries bears ample witness to phases of euphoric bardolatry in which he was heralded as the epitome of original genius, or the eternal human spirit. Concomitant attempts to adopt Shakespeare as 'our Shakespeare' have produced versions of the dramatist that are closer to home, more familiar and tamer, emphasizing similarities between the twentieth century and the sixteenth and seventeenth centuries that make the Middle Ages seem even more distant and alien looking. Nonetheless, Shakespeare makes a reluctant Renaissance humanist. His plays configure elements of sources such as the ancient novel and medieval literature, a process that challenges conceptual boundaries between literary periods.[21] Above all Shakespeare's tragedies offer a contrasting perspective on an all-too-optimistic view on human potentialities professed by received ideas of early modernity as a period of progress and novelty, a perspective that Beckett retrospectively is to confirm. Macbeth's characterization of life as 'a tale/Told by an idiot, full of sound and fury/Signifying nothing' (*Mac* 5.5.25–7) could indeed serve as a motto for many of Beckett's works.

Correspondingly, Beckett makes a reluctant modernist. He increasingly refrains from embracing the euphoria about stylistic experiments and the sheer infinite possibilities of expression professed by classical modernism in the 1920s and 1930s. Beckett occupies shifting territory and is conceived as the last modernist or a postmodernist *avant la lettre*.[22] Both Foucault and Derrida acknowledge their indebtedness to Beckett,[23] and Julia Kristeva praises his works as models of a new kind of writing.[24] Richard Begam reads Beckett through postmodernity and postmodernity through Beckett, and shows how Beckett's novels 'anticipate' the critical approaches towards subjectivity later professed by de Man and Derrida.[25] S.E. Gontarski describes Beckett as a 'late or belated arrival' on the modernist scene, a second-generation modernist who retained and discarded some of its characteristics. He considers Beckett both as an insider and an outsider: 'Samuel Beckett seemed, almost from the first, simultaneously here and there, within and without, of his time and beyond it, always somehow elsewhere, or rather between there and elsewhere, simultaneously rooted and rootless, historical and ahistorical.'[26] The 2012 issue of *Samuel Beckett Today/Samuel Beckett Aujourd'hui* is devoted to 'Early Modern Beckett' and unfolds the vast network of early modern connections within Beckett's œuvre. From his early poetry and prose and his dialogue with the philosophy of Descartes, Geulincx, Pascal and Leibniz through his structural and thematic links to the works of Milton and Bunyan, up to his study of Ronsard, Corneille, Rabelais, Molière and Racine, Beckett's works are suffused with resonances to early modern texts.[27] The productive correspondences between early modernity and modernism are vital to Stanley Cavell's essays on Shakespeare and Beckett. Cavell illuminates the ways in which their plays interact with, present and transform contemporary philosophical issues.[28]

This study resists the celebration of Shakespeare and Beckett as iconic figures who represent or exclusively define the periods in which they wrote.

Their works rather help us to rethink our notions of periods as strictly delineated entities, to discern parallels and correspondences between them and to recognize patterns of cultural generation. The temporal verticality inherent in this comparative analysis is intended neither to establish nor affirm unidirectional hierarchies or structural teleologies, in which the optimism inherent in an early modern history of progress gives way to the fatalism of the late twentieth century, or in which Shakespeare holds the place of an uncontested classic and Beckett merely dismantles the classic canon through tragicomedy and parody. Created in periods traditionally conceived of as historical thresholds, Beckett's and Shakespeare's works also present such thresholds and margins when they write on the edges of conventional representation, test out the boundaries of their respective media and explore the limits of humanity or venture beyond them.

In considering characteristic constellations in which the works of Shakespeare and Beckett converge, this book is also about the dialogue between early and late modernity, and its implications for our contemporary understanding of cultural production and processes of reception. This study refrains from reducing historical distance or the forced synchronizing of otherwise disparate works. It rather offers comparative analyses that are founded on distinct issues that lie latent in the works of Samuel Beckett and William Shakespeare, and through which they interact and produce resonant correspondences that draw new attention to the poetic dimension of art and the theatre.

'A Pilgrim from Mars' – Stages of Shakespeare and Beckett

If Shakespeare's theatre can be linked to the beginnings of the theatre that would later be conceived as a mass medium, Beckett's theatre, from the 'arrival' of Godot, was regarded by some contemporaries as synonymous with 'the end of the theatre as we know it',[29] while at the same time new forms of popular entertainment were becoming more widely available.[30] '*Waiting for Godot* frankly jettisons everything by which we recognise theatre,' writes Kenneth Tynan on 7 August 1955 in his review of the play's opening night in London.[31] Whereas Shakespeare was conventionally associated with the glories of the Elizabethan Age, the flowering of Renaissance culture and the rise of imperialism, Beckett, the Irishman who chose to live in Paris, was met initially with some reserve, if not aggression.[32]

Famously, on the opening night of *Godot* in 1955, single members of the audience went so far as to hold him accountable for nothing less than the Fall of the British Empire: 'This is why we lost the colonies!'[33] Tynan describes the unprecedented character of Beckett's drama: 'It arrives in the custom house as it were with no luggage, no passport, and nothing to declare. Yet it gets through as might a pilgrim from Mars. It does this, I believe by appealing to a definition of drama much more fundamental than any in the books,' and he concludes, 'It forced me to re-examine the rules which have hitherto governed the drama, and, having done so, to pronounce them not elastic enough.'[34]

Beckett's theatre of subtraction and elimination reconfigured the dramatic tradition and ruffled the feathers of the well-made play; some of the lines of dialogue in *Waiting for Godot* lend themselves to describing the very experience of watching the play in metatheatrical terms:

> VLADIMIR   Charming evening we're having.
> ESTRAGON   Unforgettable.
> VLADIMIR   And it's not over.
> ESTRAGON   Apparently not.
> VLADIMIR   It's only the beginning.
> ESTRAGON   It's awful.
> VLADIMIR   It's worse than being at the theatre. (*CDW*, 33)
>
> VLADIMIR   This is becoming really insignificant.
> ESTRAGON   Not enough. (*CDW*, 63)

Plays such as *Waiting for Godot* operate at the limits of representation and dispense with conventional action, character and causality. S.E. Gontarski summarizes: 'From *Play* onward and despite the Tynans of British theatre, Beckett's stage images would grow increasingly dehumanized, reified and metonymic, featuring dismembered or incorporeal creatures as Beckett's became a theatre of body parts and spectres, a theatre striving for transparency rather than solidity, a theatre, finally, trying to undo itself.'[35] David Pattie argues that the climate in British theatre was ripening towards accepting the necessity of change: '*Godot*, then, arrived in a theatrical environment in which the idea that a fundamental change in the nature and structure of British theatre was imperative was already gaining traction.'[36]

After the war, the 1950s, according to Peter Hennessy in *Having it So Good*, tell a 'story of easement tinged with anxiety, a paradox which, in a way, captures Britain in the Fifties as a whole'.[37] In spite of the tangible improvement of social conditions, reforms and progress in many walks of life, cumulative anxieties remain as the 'security of the welfare state is crossed by the radical insecurity of a world that might be suddenly blown to bits'.[38] The early 1950s indeed present an amalgamation of remarkable political, social and scientific events that shape world history until the present.[39]

From its margins, the late-modern post-war period can be seen as a time capsule between two endings of history, in which the traumatic experience of the Second World War and the end of the master narratives of old Europe were still vividly present while the anticipation of another, yet more deadly and annihilating, nuclear war was constantly looming. Beckett's works emerged on this threshold between hot and cold, real and possible wars. Some of them are set in a potentially post-apocalyptic world, such as *Endgame* or *Happy Days*; others, such as *Waiting for Godot*, exist in expectation of a possible apocalypse in which the future weighs heavier than the past: '[T]he British Ministry of Defence issued instructions as to what we should do in the event of a nuclear attack. Their advice was to stay indoors and wait. Was Godot the bomb?'[40]

Beckett's works, however, cannot be exclusively read in light of the interwar period. He remained deeply interested in political issues well into the 1980s. In 1983, Beckett dedicated *Catastrophe* to the then still imprisoned Václav Havel,[41] and in November 1989, shortly before his death on 22 December 1989, Beckett witnessed the Fall of the Berlin Wall.[42] Tony Judt regards the years between 1945 and 1989 'not as the threshold of a new epoch but rather as an interim age: a post-war parenthesis, the unfinished business of a conflict that ended in 1945 but whose epilogue had lasted for another half century'.[43] Frank Bies considers German *angst* in the aftermath of the war not as a specifically national pathology; rather, it resulted from the omnipresent, continuously changing and dynamic memory of a catastrophic past, that precipitated a fear-ridden and sometimes apocalyptic anticipation of the future.[44] The possibility of a man-made end of the world, of humanity, of culture and any significant human act had more than ever become a realistic option with which to be reckoned.[45]

No tradition of thought has attempted to redefine the human more radically than the literature and philosophy of existentialism. Not least in the aftermath of the catastrophes of the twentieth century, the turn away from emphatically affirmative models of rationality and euphoric postulations of subject autonomy occurred side by side with the struggle to explore the breadth and limitations of traditional paradigms, and to open up new ways of interpreting and presenting the human, which were among the foundations of the philosophical anthropology and the aesthetics of the twentieth century. Yet Beckett's works are not readily subsumed under contemporary philosophies of nihilism or existential humanism.[46] Richard Begam notes: 'The so-called nihilism of Beckett, the cliché tag that the popular consciousness has attached to him, can thus be seen as no more than the necessary outcome of Beckett's refusal to deal in generalizations and abstract truths.'[47] Moreover, as Martin Esslin continues, Beckett deflates abstract and generalizing notions of existentialism:

> Beckett's writings, it might well be argued, are more than mere illustrations of the point-of-view of existentialist philosophers like Heidegger and Sartre; they constitute the culmination of existential thought itself, *precisely because they are free of any abstract concepts or general ideas*, and thus escape the inner contradiction of existentialist statements that are couched in the form of generalizations.[48]

Existentialism, however, provided one of the first contact zones in the reception of Shakespeare and Beckett – above all, in the influential notion of an existentialist Shakespeare. In the 1950s and beyond,[49] *King Lear*, in particular, was seen by many as the chief example of the theatrical experience of nothingness, radical meaninglessness and a way of imagining the worst, qualities that invited many convergences with the so-called theatre of the absurd and questions of existentialism.[50]

A central strand of research that explores thematic links between Shakespeare and Beckett goes back to the work of Jan Kott in *Shakespeare our Contemporary* (1964). In his essay on '*King Lear*, or *Endgame*'[51] Kott was among the first to expound a seemingly ahistorical existential trait in both Shakespeare and Beckett. Kott and many others after him[52] identify *King Lear* as Beckett's main Shakespearean source, which emerges in his many derelict, 'unaccomodated characters', on stage and in narrative, such as Molloy, who like Lear, the Fool, Gloucester or Edgar is exposed unprotected to the elements as an example of the human condition, of man as being thrown upon an empty stage. In Kott's account, *King Lear* likewise presents a pre-Beckettian reduction when at the end of the tragedy, 'just four beggars [are left] wandering about in a wilderness'.[53] Reading *King Lear* through an existentialist lens, Kott views the tragedy as an absurdist scheme severed from a metaphysical order of things emptied of providential design.

Kott, however, was not the first to note the absurdity of some of Lear's actions. The division of Lear's kingdom, for instance, is not only a breaking of basic cultural codes but moreover an act of de-creation, the annihilation of a world by its creator, an act that releases the excessive spiral of reduction that governs the rest of the plot. It was no lesser author than Johann Wolfgang von Goethe who noticed the irrational and ambivalent character of the first scene of *King Lear* and commended contemporary directors who omitted it from their productions: 'In this scene Lear appears so absurd that one cannot subsequently disagree with his daughters. The old man is execrable, but one does not feel pity for him.'[54]

Peter Brook, whose landmark production of *King Lear* in 1962 underlined the link between Beckett and Shakespeare, regards *Lear* as 'the prime example of the Theatre of the Absurd, from which everything in good modern drama has been drawn'.[55] Brook himself promoted the relation between both dramatists in his essay '*Endgame* as *King Lear*, or How to Stop Worrying and Love Beckett', where he writes that 'his [Beckett's] are the most positive works we've got.'[56] Brook acknowledges the inspiration he gained from reading Kott's writings:

> I read his writings with passionate interest and at the time of preparing *King Lear* it took just one phrase, one image amongst so many, to open a thousand doors. Gloucester hurls himself in despair off a cliff and in his mind his act is totally real: for the audience it is just an actor making an absurd little jump on a bare stage. The theatre allows us to enter into a passionately held belief and exposes to us its absurdity.[57]

Like Peter Brook, interpreters of Beckett cannot but find Beckettian moments in Shakespeare. Kott, for instance, referred to Beckett's mode of tragicomedy, where one of Beckett's mottos is taken from Edgar's lines in *King Lear*: 'The worst is not/So long as we can say "This is the worst"' (*KL* 4.1.27–8).[58] Edgar's lines have inspired Beckett's works, above all *Worstward Ho*, which Akra Chattopadhyay interprets as 'a minimalist distillation of Shakespeare's text'.[59] Beckett's working title was 'Better Worse', and in lines from *Lear* such as: 'Nothing will come of nothing, speak again' (*KL* 1.1.85), Shakespeare to some interpreters sounds like a Beckett before Beckett.[60] This effect is achieved by the process of reduction and magnification that we often find in Beckett's dialogue with Shakespeare. Single words and phrases are taken out of their initial context and acquire metonymical significance for entire works. These then reflect back on Shakespeare's texts and allow us to see them unfolding through the lens of Beckett's literalism.

From the late 1950s onwards, the link between Shakespeare and Beckett became firmly established in England's theatre culture.[61] Important productions such as George Devine's at the Royal Court Theatre, Roger Blin's world premieres of *Waiting for Godot* (1953) and *Endgame* (1957) in Paris and Alan Schneider's American premiere of *Waiting for Godot* (1956) paved the way for a wider reception of Beckett's plays. As early as the 1950s, the theatrical works of Beckett and Shakespeare became intertwined on a number of levels, and, in the history of British theatre, converged in the eminent figure and enduring legacy of Sir Peter Hall.[62]

In August 1955, the then 24-year-old Peter Hall, who, according to his diary, was summoned from Spain, where he had intended to read all twelve volumes of Proust's *À la recherche du temps perdu*, directed the English-language premiere of *Waiting for Godot* at the London Arts Theatre.[63] Five years later, he was appointed the first director of the RSC (1960–8),[64] and subsequently director of the National Theatre (1973–1988), where he, twenty years later, would often direct plays by Shakespeare and Beckett, if not simultaneously, then in close temporal proximity to each other, such as *Happy Days* (1974) and *Hamlet* (1975). Overall, as Charles Lyons remarks:

> in the early 1960s important productions at the newly retitled Royal Shakespeare Company used selected visual techniques of the epic theatre ... to develop self-consciously Beckettian images of the isolated subject. ... Shakespearean production assimilated aspects of each [the Epic Theatre and the Theatre of the Absurd] as the Royal Shakespeare Company marked out its aesthetic course in the 1960s and 1970s.[65]

From early on in his career, Peter Hall admired Samuel Beckett, whom he once referred to as 'Le Grand Sam',[66] and in Beckett's works he found a continuous source of inspiration.[67] After attending the Royal Court's Production of Beckett's German Schiller-Theater production of *Godot* in 1976, Hall thought it magnificent and uplifting: 'It revived my shaken faith in the theatre,'[68] he notes in his diary. Beckett likewise held Peter Hall in great esteem and worked closely with him on several occasions, most intensely during the production of *Happy Days* with the Shakespeare actress Dame Peggy Ashcroft as Winnie. When attending Hall's London production of *Waiting for Godot*, however, he reportedly clutched Alan Schneider's arm and inimitably whispered: 'It's ahl wrahng! He's doing it ahl wrahng!'[69] In a letter to Desmond Smith on 1 April 1956, he explains that: 'There were, I thought, good things in the London production, in particular some good playing by Estragon and Lucky, but the set was quite wrong, and the timing, which is all important, I mean the giving full value to the silences.'[70]

After George Devine retired from the Royal Court, Peter Hall requested that Beckett's works become a permanent part of the RSC's repertoire.[71] Later, in 1997, he directed both *Waiting for Godot* with Alan Howard, who also played Lear in the same year, as Vladimir and Ben Kingsley as Estragon, and *King Lear*, deliberately initiating a dialogue between the two plays that went beyond the mere domains of theme and included the dimension of performance by casting actors of his company in both productions: 'The value and resonance of such programming can be seen in the reception of the Peter Hall Company's *King Lear* in 1997, where uncanny links to the company's *Godot* were felt especially strongly in Gloucester's suicide but reverberated throughout.'[72] Sos Eltis summarizes,

'Hall's 2005 anniversary production of *Godot* both drew upon and cemented his reputation as England's foremost director of Beckett,'[73] and it also exemplifies the eminent role of the theatre in fostering and enhancing the dialogue between Shakespeare and Beckett.

'look with thine ears' – Theatre in the Rough

> *Listen! you hear the grating roar*
> *Of pebbles which the waves draw back, and fling,*
> *At their return, up the high strand,*
> *Begin, and cease, and then again begin,*
> *With tremulous cadence slow, and bring*
> *The eternal note of sadness in*
> Matthew Arnold, from: *Dover Beach* (1867)

Recalling lines from Sophocles and from Shakespeare's Sonnet 60 'Like as the waves, make towards the pebbled shore', Matthew Arnold's poem 'Dover Beach', in its theme and metaphors, is set on the edges – spatial, historical and personal. Arnold's poem also evokes a culminating moment of early modern theatre: the scenes on Dover cliff in *King Lear* are perhaps some of the most prominent Beckettian scenes of Shakespeare's plays. Marking a threshold between life and death, between catharsis and miracle, between the creation and destruction of illusion, they can be taken as a metaphor for the theatre at large in that it shows, rather than explains, how performative reality can be created. The Dover-cliff-scenes present a self-conscious theatrical experience in which the perspective of the blind Gloucester and that of the audience intersect.

The two scenes in Act IV of *King Lear* encapsulate a theatrical moment that reveals many levels of the encounter between Shakespeare and Beckett. Edgar and Gloucester, father and son with their roles almost reversed, find themselves on the verge between life and death.[74] Both men are broken. Edgar, disguised as the beggar 'poor Tom' and posing as a madman to protect himself from the reach of the likes of Regan and Goneril, sees his blinded father Gloucester led by an old man. He is denied any self-pity. Rather, the sight of his much-harmed father becomes more unbearable than anything he could have imagined. Edgar articulates his grief in the lines that Beckett often used: 'And worse I may be yet. The worst is not/So long as we can say "This is the worst"' (*KL* 4.1.27–8).[75] Edgar's insight that, with his own state of affairs being bad enough, there might be no end of misery and things will continue to get worse *ad infinitum* is paralleled by Gloucester's loss of faith in a fate that he deems arbitrary: 'As flies to wanton boys are we to the gods;/They kill us for their sport' (*KL* 4.1.36–7).[76]

Gloucester is resolved to end his life in a spectacular way. He intends to make his way to Dover, where he had earlier sent the distraught Lear in the hope of witnessing Cordelia's salutary arrival from France. At this stage, however, Dover is no longer a safe haven of escape to him. He intends to die by climbing onto the edge, 'the very brim' (*KL* 4.1.70) of Dover cliff and taking a leap: 'From that place/I shall no leading need' (*KL* 4.1.72–3). Unlike Edgar, who chooses to divest himself of everything he owns in order to survive, Gloucester is driven to his desperate state partly by his own tragic mistake of placing his trust in the villain Edmund. In an almost Beckettian kind of reduction, and analogous to Lear's predicament, everything has been taken from him: his liege, his status, his children, his home. In one of the cruellest scenes on the Shakespearean stage, he is lastly deprived of his eyesight and reduced to an animal state of being when Regan maliciously casts him out of his own castle to 'let him smell/His way to Dover' (*KL* 3.7.92–3). The thus expelled Gloucester enacts Lear's initial wish to '[u]nburdened crawl toward death' (*KL* 1.1.36) in a bitterly literal way.[77]

The encounter between Edgar and his blind father evokes the beginning of Beckett's late piece *Company*: 'A voice comes to one in the dark. Imagine' (*Company*, 7). Edgar's voice comes to Gloucester 'in the dark', and *Company* likewise parallels the crescendo and decrescendo of the approaching voice with the ebb and flow of the sea, suggesting the nexus of time, death and art that pervades Shakespeare's Sonnet 60: 'A faint voice at loudest. It slowly ebbs till almost out of hearing. Then slowly back to faint full. At each slow ebb hope slowly dawns that it is dying. He must know it will flow again. And yet at each slow ebb hope slowly dawns that it is dying' (*Company*, 22).

Similar to Edgar and Gloucester, in *Company*, father and son occasionally walk side by side: 'You are an old man plodding along a narrow country road. [...] Halted too at your elbow during these computations your father's shade. In his old tramping rags. Finally on side by side from nought anew' (*Company*, 18–19). In some passages of *Company*, the roles of Shakespeare's characters seem reversed, for example, when it is the father who encourages the boy to jump into the sea: 'You stand at the tip of the high board. High above the sea. In it your father's upturned face. Upturned to you. You look down to the loved trusted face. He calls to you to jump. He calls, Be a brave boy' (*Company*, 23).[78]

Edgar guides the helpless and blind Gloucester, who resembles the 'crawling creator' in *Company*: 'The crawling creator. Might the crawling creator be reasonably imagined to smell? Even fouler than his creature. Stirring now and then to wonder that mind so lost to wonder' (*Company*, 72). Even though Gloucester often wonders whether the voice he hears does not deceive him, Edgar does not reveal himself to his father. He is torn, and in an aside confesses, 'Bad is the trade that must play fool to sorrow' (*KL* 4.1.38). Yet, Edgar goes on, and like many of Beckett's characters, who in the face of utter adversity decide to continue in spite of themselves, says,: 'I can't go on, I'll go on' (*The Unnamable*, 418). He struggles to keep up his disguise: 'I cannot daub it further ... And yet I must' (*KL* 4.1.55; 57).

Like *Waiting for Godot* which repeatedly insists that there is 'nothing to be done', the Dover-cliff-scenes in *King Lear* explores ways of facing nothingness both in the sense of 'nothing to be done' and as nothingness to be countered and, if not defeated, at least deferred. The scenes are characterized by the paradoxical desire for death and the desire to keep it at bay by speech, action and theatrical performance. Edgar is driven by equally paradoxical impulses in creating and maintaining a double illusion. When Gloucester repeatedly voices doubt about Edgar's disguise: 'Methinks thy voice is altered' and 'Methinks y'are better spoken' (*KL* 4.5.7; 10), he upholds his dissimulation precisely by speaking the truth: 'Y'are much deceived. In nothing am I changed/But in my garments' (*KL* 4.5.9–10).

Although Gloucester appears not to be entirely convinced that the ground gets steeper and that one can actually hear the sea, he is gradually persuaded by Edgar's detailed and vivid description of the view from the cliff, which creates the three-dimensional reality of the steep ground on a two-dimensional surface, demanding a leap of faith from both Gloucester and the audience. Edgar is both cruel and kind and seeks to ward off the worst by means of lesser harm. The theatre he creates deceives and saves Gloucester: 'Why I do trifle thus with his despair/Is done to cure it' (*KL* 4.5.33–4). Edgar stage-manages Gloucester's leap like a microplay within the play and reveals to the audience the mechanisms with which he creates his desired effect.[79]

The Dover-cliff-scenes, which take theatrical experience to the extreme, have proved most perplexing to critics across the ages. A.C. Bradley considers the scenes not 'in the least absurd' and highlights their intricate working upon the 'imagination and the feelings',[80] whereas G. Wilson Knight famously claims, 'The core of the play is an absurdity, an indignity, an incongruity. In no tragedy of Shakespeare does incident and dialogue so recklessly and miraculously walk the tight-rope of our pity over the depths of bathos and absurdity.'[81]

The scenes indeed take theatre to the verge of its own capacities. Gloucester wants to make an end, but is not allowed to do so, and yet the vicarious theatrical experience he undergoes may be no less real for him: 'Is wretchedness deprived that benefit/To end itself by death?' (*KL* 4.5.61–2). Theatrical illusion is built up and undercut by the reality that the event carries for Gloucester. Edgar stages both an ending and a new theatrical beginning. Waiting for the promised end is juxtaposed with the realization that the end has already happened. Edgar takes his father and the theatre through this experience of finality in order to restart from where the catastrophe has taken place. *Company* likewise explores the threshold of the '[b]ourneless dark' (*Company*, 69), a phrase that recalls Hamlet's notion of death as '[t]he undiscovered country from whose bourn/no traveller returns' (*Ham* 3.1.79–80) as a source of the imagination.

Acousmatic, disembodied voices emerging from the dark are the raw material of many of Beckett's dramatic experiments. Lear advises Gloucester to 'look with thine ears' (*KL* 4.5.145), referring to inward knowledge and an imagination that does not depend on what is visible. Like Edgar's art, which stages the imaginative creation of theatrical reality, *Company* traces the workings of the imagination in its own fictional construction, the potential invention of an other's voice for company:

> The fable of one with you in the dark. The fable of one fabling of one with you in the dark. And how better in the end labour lost and silence. And you as you always were.
>
> Alone (*Company*, 88–9).

'variations of rise and fall'

Crawling and falling, standing on the precipice and taking the imagination beyond the end become metaphors for the artistic processes that reflect on the acts of writing and performance as explorations of the limits of representation. Analogous to the Dover-cliff-scenes in *King Lear*, in Beckett's works blindness and uncertainty constitute the theatrical experience of his audiences and actors. As Billie Whitelaw describes to James Knowlson, Beckett made his actresses and actors live through the experience of sensory deprivation and physical constraint. Whitelaw recounts a terrifying rehearsal of *Not I*: 'The very first time I did it, I went to pieces. I felt I had no body; I could not relate to where I was; and, going at that speed, I was becoming very dizzy and felt like an astronaut tumbling into space . . . I swore to God I was falling, falling . . .'[82]

Beckett's short piece 'Imagination Dead Imagine' explores 'variations of rise and fall' (*CSP*, 183) that are rhythmically paired with light and darkness and the grey zone in between. The piece evokes characters who find themselves on the verge of death, and draws on Lear's desperate wish that Cordelia might still be alive: 'Hold a mirror to their lips, it mists' (*CSP*, 184). Indeed, many of Beckett's father and son constellations present variations on Lear and Gloucester. The blind Hamm in *Endgame* that Adorno regarded as 'true gerontology'[83] insults his battered father as his 'accursed progenitor' (*CDW*, 96) and blames him for his existence.[84] In a way similar to *King Lear*, old age is not necessarily linked to wisdom but to frailty and senile confusion. 'A wet night' in *More Pricks than Kicks* uses the storm scene in *King Lear* to illustrate the futile rage of the protagonist: 'It was now, beating his bosom thus bared to the mean storm vaguely with marble palms, that he took leave of himself and felt wretched and sorry for what he had done' (*MPTK*, 78). In *Waiting for Godot*, the master-and-servant hierarchy between Pozzo and Lucky is reversed in the second act, when Pozzo has become blind and is led by Lucky, presenting a version of Gloucester's remark: ''Tis the time's plague when madmen lead the blind' (*KL* 4.1.47). However, Lear's metadramatic pathos – 'When we are born, we cry that we are come/To this great stage of fools' (*KL* 4.5.174–5) – is undercut by Estragon in *Waiting for Godot*: 'We are all born mad. Some remain so' (*CDW*, 75).

The notion of inescapability, of characters desiring to move but being confined to stasis in *Waiting for Godot* and *King Lear* is emblematically expressed in the use of boots. When Beckett wrote to the Irish director Alan Simpson thanking him for the photographs of his production of *Waiting for Godot*, he takes special note of the boots, and likens them to a Hamlettian pose: 'I liked particularly that of Vladimir looking at the boot as if it were an early 17th century skull.'[85] Lacking, ill-fitted or stubbornly unremovable boots create practical impediments preventing characters from walking or leaving. The two lines in which King Lear asks Gloucester to help him take off his boots – 'Now, now, now, now./Pull off my boots. Harder, harder! So.' (*KL* 4.5.164–5) – are alluded to at the beginning of *Waiting for Godot*. Vladimir and Estragon resemble Gloucester and Lear, when after some dialogue, Estragon exhaustedly struggles to take off his boot, until he in a slapstick manner – 'with supreme effort' – manages to do it:[86] 'Vladimir: What are you doing?/ Estragon: Taking off my boot. Did that never happen to you?' (*CDW*, 12). *Waiting for Godot* expands the moment from *King Lear* and provides room for the actors to improvise on their dilemma, in which the tragic inability to move on is translated into a seemingly inconspicuous act.

Falling or jumping to one's death is at the centre of *Rough for Theatre II*. In the triangular setting of the play, the two characters Bertrand and Morvan, abbreviated as A and B, contemplate whether they should have Croker, or C, who stands mute and motionless facing the window with his back to the audience, jump out:

> A   Let him jump.
> B   When?
> A   Now.
> B   From where?
> A   From here will do. Three to three and a half meters per floor, say twenty-five in all. (*CDW*, 238)

They adopt Edgar's stance, and, in a manner that is bureaucratic and investigative at the same time, they review fragments of C's life from a number of files and testimonials, all rather miserable: 'art and nature, heart and conscience, health, housing conditions, God and man, so many disasters' (*CDW*, 238). However, like Edgar, they have seen worse: 'A: Seen worse dumps. [*Turning towards window.*] Worse outlooks' (*CDW*, 239). A and B are as sinister as they are disinterested. They are neither dead nor 'sufficiently alive' (*CDW*, 248). C, likewise, is left in an undead state, and paralleled to a songbird that A and B find dying in a cage: 'A: [. . .] Oh you pretty little pet, oh you bonny wee birdie! [*Pause. Glum.*] And to think all that is organic waste! All that splendour!' (*CDW*, 248). The associations with Gloucester's fall and Lear and Cordelia in prison further reinforce the pervading sense of indifference and futility: 'Lear: No, no, no, no! Come, let's away to prison./We two alone will sing like birds i'th'cage' (*KL* 5.3.8–9).

Rough for Theatre II, however, remains on the threshold as C is left in limbo, and the dying bird continues to sing. A and B wonder 'How end?' (*CDW*, 249) and decide to leave since there 'is nothing we can do' (*CDW*, 249). Just before the end, A lights a match to C's face and, like a miniature theatrical curtain, raises his handkerchief towards it. *Rough for Theatre II* aligns itself to scenes from *King Lear*, and it foregrounds the staging of those scenes by interchangeable figures, commenting on the potential aloofness and cruelty of the theatre director.

It is above all in his radio plays that Beckett experiments with the effects of voices and sound in ways that leave the audience in the dark, their imagination dependent on what sound suggests to it. Gontarski elucidates

Beckett's use of contemporary technology to create disembodied voices and memories:

> Beckett's exploration of voice is consonant with one of the century's technological signatures, the projection, transmission and reception of not just coded data ..., but of the human voice itself, wireless, voice separated from presence or source. The twentieth was the first century to confront such separation and then to store the results for retrieval and repetition in a form of electronic, disembodied memory.[87]

Embers (1959), Beckett's piece for the radio, is set on the border between land and sea, fire and water. The main character, Henry, dwells in-between space and time and tries in vain to remember the past to build a consistent narrative from it. Similar to Krapp, Henry is haunted by his failures in the past, his thwarted attempts at storytelling and his inability to finish anything. Prompted by the voice of his wife, Ada, he incoherently recalls scenes from his past, and Ada reminds him of his own troubled family history. His sister intended to 'throw herself off the cliff' (*CDW*, 262), and his father possibly died at sea: 'that evening bathe you took once too often' (*CDW*, 253).

Henry's initial monologue is addressed to his drowned father, who evokes not only the blind Gloucester but also the ghost of Hamlet's father and Lear, the 'foolish, fond old man' (*KL* 4.6.57): 'Who is beside me now. [...] An old man, blind and foolish. [...] My father, back from the dead, to be with me' (*CDW*, 253). Sounds of the sea and 'boots on shingle' suggest that Henry finds himself on a beach. Like Edgar, he creates his own fictional reality, and addressing both the audience and his father, insists: '[T]hat sound you hear is the sea. [...] I say that sound you hear is the sea, we are sitting on the strand' (*CDW*, 253). He further emphasizes the reality of the sea by considering his listeners' inability to see it: 'I mention it because the sound is so strange, so unlike the sound of the sea, that if you didn't see what it was you wouldn't know what it was' (*CDW*, 253). The audience becomes a sounding board for Henry's attempts to create a world out of his memories, but, by evoking Gloucester on the imaginary cliff, the play, at the same time, calls into question whether a world outside of his imagination and remembrance exists at all.

Like embers, offering last glimpses of a fire on the verge of dying, Henry, despite his attempts to rekindle the fire of his life and his past, remains on the threshold between past and present and between life and death. The final scene of the play returns to its initial setting when Henry moves towards the sea and the last stage direction says: '*He halts at water's edge*' (*CDW*, 264). His last words, 'Not a sound' (*CDW*, 264) release him into a soundless void. His presence, which to the listeners consisted only of sounds, and his voice vanishes. *Embers* builds on *King Lear* to depict life on the threshold, where sound carries the potential to create reality and remembrance.

The liminal states between motion and standstill, climbing and falling, blindness and sight are at the centre of *All that Fall* (1956). The allegorical dimension of the radio play, the fallen state of mankind in general, is referred to when the two protagonists, Mr and Mrs Rooney, are bemused at the title of the next day's sermon – 'The Lord upholdeth all that fall and raiseth up all those that be bowed down' from Psalm 145:14. They break into wild laughter pointing to the lines as a cynical reflection of their predicament.

In their village, named Boghill,[88] life is at a grotesquely fallen, paralysed state, verging towards death. Characters long for death by pulverization, 'oh to be in atoms, in atoms! [*Frenziedly*.] ATOMS!' (*CDW*, 177), realize that they are 'not half alive' (*CDW*, 176), or 'buried [...] alive' (*CDW*, 194), or, with reference to their own medial construction, tell the listeners that they do not exist at all: 'Mrs Rooney: [...] Don't take any notice of me I do not exist. The fact is well known' (*CDW*, 179). Schubert's 'Death and the Maiden' is heard twice emerging from the house of a dying old woman. The Boghill community is ageing, ill and of ill-temper. Most women are childless, men are grandchildless and some of the few children that are still alive, like Tommy and Jerry, are orphaned.

On a horizontal level, movement and standstill, and on a vertical level, climbing and falling, are central structural and metaphorical operations of the play. Blind Mr Rooney does not know which direction he is facing on the road and suggests Mrs Rooney move forwards while he goes backwards 'Like Dante's damned, with their faces arsy-versy' (*CDW*, 191). On her way to the station to pick up her husband from the train, Mrs Rooney stops and goes, and the sound most heard in the radio play is that of dragging feet: 'How can I go on, I cannot' (*CDW*, 174).

All movement in the play leads to standstill and doom. The three men Mrs Rooney meets on her way are each associated with means of transportation that become either dysfunctional or suggest a major cataclysm. Christy and his hinny is a version of Christ on his way to his death in Jerusalem, Mr Tyler's bicycle runs flat and the name of Mr Slocum, who finally takes her to the station with his car running over a hen, alludes to the steamboat *General Slocum*, which caught fire on the East River in New York on 15 June 1904[89] and created one of the worst maritime disasters of the early twentieth century. Mrs Rooney further mentions both the sinking of the *Lusitania* and the *Titanic* (*CDW*, 184), and wonders what songs people were singing on the brink of disaster.

Horizontal movement is a challenge for the characters in the play and so is walking uphill. Mrs Rooney tells Christy not to walk but to climb his dunghill instead: 'Why do you not climb up on the crest of your manure and let yourself be carried along? Is it that you have no head for heights?' (*CDW*, 173). The scene implicitly evokes Gloucester's climb and his humiliation in *King Lear* when Cornwall orders: 'Turn out that eyeless villain. Throw this slave/Upon the dunghill' (*KL* 3.7.95–6). References to climbing imply the danger of falling and bring back past memories. Mr Tyler tells Mrs Rooney about having saved the life of his friend Hardy, the incumbent preacher, once: 'Whom are you meeting, Mr Tyler? Mr Tyler: Hardy. [*Pause.*] We used to climb together. [*Pause.*] I saved his life once. [*Pause.*] I have not forgotten it' (*CDW*, 175). Mrs Rooney compares the steps to the station to the Matterhorn, one of the highest mountains in the Alps and the one that claimed the most lives of those who climbed it: 'This is worse than the Matterhorn, were you ever up the Matterhorn, Miss Fitt, great honeymoon resort' (*CDW*, 184).

Mrs Rooney clings to other people in fear of falling and refers to the steps as the face of a cliff: 'Mrs Rooney: If you would help me up the face of this cliff, Miss Fitt' (*CDW*, 183). Mrs Rooney climbing the steps of the station prefaces the climax of the play, the long-awaited and unusually belated arrival of the 12:30 train. The Rooneys dramatize their predicament, but, like Gloucester, they overcome all obstacles without literally falling. Rather, they already live in a fallen state from which they try to escape, but cannot do so.

The catastrophe of the play is the fatal fall of a child from the train and onto the line. It remains uncertain whether Mr Rooney is in any way responsible for this, but some suspicion remains when he avoids being questioned about it, grumpily claims that the little ball that Jerry presents him with is something that he carries about with him, and when he asks Mrs Rooney if she has ever wanted to kill a child (*CDW*, 191). The death of children and young life is ubiquitous in *All that Fall* in its symbolism and its references to children that have not been born; its allusions to Schubert and *Effi Briest*, but also to *Romeo and Juliet*, recall untimely deaths, when Mr Tyler uses Mercutio's line to tell the time: '[a]t the bawdy hour of nine' (*CDW*, 186).

Not unlike Lear and the Fool, the Rooneys make their way home through the wind and rain, but the rainfall that ends the play does not bring about a cathartic turn. *All that Fall* focuses on blindness and the role of sounds in conveying dramatic reality. Its characters are led towards the edges of their existences, but they remain trapped and do not take the final leap. In the light of *All that Fall*, Kent's lines about Lear's resilience – 'The wonder is he hath endured so long./He but usurped his life' (*KL* 5.3.290–1) – carry more ominous overtones by highlighting that it is the old who survive and the young who die.

Beckett's variations on rising and falling experiment with edges, limitations of expression and perception, and they set themselves on the boundaries of their very medium. *Rough for Theatre II* and *Embers* present a ghostly, unending world in suspension that reflects on the condition of the theatre, whereas *All that Fall* is situated on the other side of the Fall, in an unredeemable gerontocracy. The scenes on Dover cliff from *King Lear* are one example of how Beckett, in dialogue with Shakespeare, concentrates on single images or scenes and expands them, turning them into metaphors for the dramatic experience. As such they release associations that reflect back on Shakespeare's works, changing and enhancing our reading of them.

Notes

1 Cf. Wilhelm Schmidt-Biggemann, 'Tradition und Legitimation' in Andreas Höfele, Jan-Dirk Müller, Wulf Oesterreicher (eds.), *Die Frühe Neuzeit. Revisionen einer Epoche* (Berlin, Boston: De Gruyter, 2013), 47–83.
2 Neil MacGregor, *Shakespeare's Restless World* (London: Allen Lane, 2012).
3 Jürgen Habermas, 'Das Zeitbewußtsein der Moderne und ihr Bedürfnis nach Selbstvergewisserung' in Jürgen Habermas, *Der Philosophische Diskurs der Moderne. Zwölf Vorlesungen* (Frankfurt a. M.: Suhrkamp, 1989), 9–33, 16.
4 According to Richard Begam, Beckett's five major novels represent the end of literary modernity. Richard Begam, *Samuel Beckett and the End of Modernity* (Stanford University Press, 1996), 3.
5 Stanley Cavell, 'A Matter of Meaning It' in Stanley Cavell, *Must We Mean What We Say?: A Book of Essays*, 2nd edition (Cambridge University Press, 2015) 202–3.
6 Jorge Luis Borges, *Labyrinths: Selected Stories and Other Writings* (Harmondsworth: Penguin, 1970), 201.
7 Hans Blumenberg, *Die Legitimität der Neuzeit* (Frankfurt a. M.: Suhrkamp, 1988), 75–200.
8 Claudia Olk, *Reisen und Erzählen: Studien zur Entwicklung von Fiktionalität in Narrativen Reisedarstellungen des Englischen Spätmittelalters und der Frühen Neuzeit* (Trier: WVT, 1999).
9 Steven Connor, *Beckett, Modernism and the Material Imagination* (Cambridge University Press, 2014), 6.

10 Jacques Derrida, '"This Strange Institution Called Literature": An Interview with Jaques Derrida', in Jacques Derrida, *Acts of Literature*, ed. by Derek Attridge (New York: Routledge: 1992), 33–75, 61.
11 S.E. Gontarski, *Beckett Matters: Essays on Beckett's Late Modernism* (Edinburgh University Press, 2017), 13–14.
12 Slavoj Žižek, 'The Minimal Event: Subjective Destitution in Shakespeare and Beckett' in Russell Sbriglia (ed.), *Everything You Always Wanted to Know about Literature but were Afraid to Ask Žižek* (Durham: Duke University Press, 2017), 290–316, 290: 'it is not that the past events are secretly directed by a hidden force steering them toward a predetermined future. The point is rather that the future is open, undecided – *but so is the past*. The past retroactively becomes what it was.'
13 T.S. Eliot, 'Tradition and the Individual Talent', *The Sacred Wood: Essays on Poetry and Criticism* (London: Faber & Faber, 1920), 49.
14 According to Habermas, Hegel was among the first to conceptualize this critical, reflexive quality of modernity that correlates abstract categories of time, the finite and the infinite, within the modern subject. Jürgen Habermas, 'Hegels Begriff der Moderne' in Jürgen Habermas, *Der Philosophische Diskurs der Moderne* (Frankfurt a. M.: Suhrkamp, 1989), 34–58, 46.
15 Jürgen Habermas, 'Das Zeitbewußtsein der Moderne', 9–34, 15.
16 T.S. Eliot, 'Four Quartets' in T.S. Eliot, *Collected Poems 1909–1962* (London: Faber & Faber, 2002), 177–213, 199.
17 T.S. Eliot, 'The Waste Land' in T.S. Eliot, *Collected Poems 1909–1962* (London: Faber & Faber, 2002), 53–77, 53.
18 Eliot, 'Tradition and the Individual Talent', 49.
19 Virginia Woolf, *The Diary of Virginia Woolf Volume 5*, ed. by Anne Olivier Bell and Andrew McNeillie (New York: Harcourt Brace Jovanovich, 1980), 281.
20 Richard Halpern, *Shakespeare among the Moderns* (Ithaca, London: Cornell University Press, 1997), 44, note 78; T.S. Eliot, *Elizabethan Essays* (New York: Haskel House, 1964), 18.
21 Cf. the important essays in: Ruth Morse, Helen Cooper and Peter Holland (eds.), *Medieval Shakespeare: Pasts and Presents* (Cambridge University Press, 2013). David Bevington's essay, for instance, argues that Shakespeare adapted medieval forms of history to his purposes: David Bevington, 'Conclusion The Evil of "Medieval"', 232–7.
22 Cf. e.g. Laura Cerrato, 'Postmodernism and Beckett's Aesthetics of Failure', *Samuel Beckett Today/Aujourd'hui*, 2 (1993), 21–30, 21.
23 'Beckett has decisively influenced the work of poststructuralism's two leading practitioners, Foucault and Derrida. In separate interviews, both philosophers have acknowledged the importance of Beckett to their own development.' Begam, *Samuel Beckett and the End of Modernity*, 185.
24 Julia Kristeva, 'Postmodernism?', *Bucknell Review*, 25 (1980), 141; Begam, *Samuel Beckett and the End of Modernity*, 27.
25 Begam, *Samuel Beckett and the End of Modernity*, 70.

26 Gontarski, *Beckett Matters*, 2.
27 Angela Moorjani, 'Beckett's Racinian Fictions: "Racine and the Modern Novel" Revisited', *Samuel Beckett Today/Aujourd'hui*, 24 (2012), 41–55; Danièle de Ruyter, 'Fascination de la Tragédie Racinienne: Resonances dans *Oh les beaux jours*', *Samuel Beckett Today/Aujourd'hui*, 24 (2012), 57–71; Julie Campbell, 'Allegories of Clarity and Obscurity: Bunyan's *The Pilgrim's Progress* and Beckett's *Molloy*', *Samuel Beckett Today/Aujourd'hui*, 24 (2012), 89–103.
28 Stanley Cavell, *Disowning Knowledge in Seven Plays of Shakespeare* (Cambridge University Press, 2003). Cavell's analyses centre on philosophical scepticism in Shakespearean tragedy, which he regards e.g. as 'an interpretation of what skepticism is itself an interpretation of', 5–6.
29 Robert Morley to Peter Bull. Peter Bull, *I know the Face. But…* (London: Peter Davis, 1959), 177 (quoted in David Pattie 'The Arrival of *Godot*: Beckett, Cultural Memory and 1950s British Theatre' in David Tucker and Trish McTighe (eds.), *Staging Beckett in Great Britain* (London, Oxford, New York: Bloomsbury Methuen Drama, 2016), 3–20, 9.
30 Pattie, 'The Arrival of *Godot*', 12: Pattie records that 'even though the war had devastated London, the theatre industry survived through to the post-war period in reasonably good health'. John Russel Taylor *Anger and After: A Guide to the New British Drama* (London: Methuen, 1962) and Dan Rebellato, *1956 and all that: The Making of Modern British Drama* (London: Routledge, 1999) argue for a narrative of rupture in British theatre history between the 1940s and the 1960s.
31 Kenneth Tynan, 'New Writing', *The Observer*, 7 August 1955, 11. Eugène Ionesco's 'The Lesson' premiered in London in the same year as *Godot*.
32 Godot arrived in a theatrical world that was already shakespearized. Peggy Ashcroft suggests that "playing Shakespeare for many years before encountering Beckett" may well account for her strong response to the rhythms of Beckett's language. Linda Ben-Zvi, *Women in Beckett: Performance and Critical Perspectives* (Urbana: University of Illinois Press, 1990), 11.
33 'This is why we lost the colonies!' James Knowlson, *Damned to Fame: The Life of Samuel Beckett* (London: Bloomsbury, 1997), 415.
34 Tynan, 'New Writing', 11.
35 S.E. Gontarski, '"I Think This does Call for a Firm Stand": Beckett at the Royal Court', in David Tucker and Trish McTighe (eds.), *Staging Beckett in Great Britain* (London, Oxford, New York: Bloomsbury Methuen Drama, 2016), 21–36, 32.
36 Pattie, 'The Arrival of *Godot*', 15.
37 Peter Hennessy, *Having It So Good: Britain in the Fifties* (London: Penguin, 2007 [2006]), 7.
38 Hennessy, *Having It So Good*, 132.
39 *Waiting for Godot* was written in 1952, the year in which Elizabeth II was proclaimed Queen, when the first British atomic bomb detonated off the coast of Australia, the US tested its first hydrogen bomb in the Pacific, and

Eisenhower won the US presidency. The play premiered in Paris the next year, 1953, which is characterized by incidents such as the death of Stalin, the unveiling of the structure of DNA by Watson and Crick, the first climbing of Mount Everest by Hunt, Hilary and Tenzing, the coronation of Queen Elizabeth II, the workers' uprising in East Berlin and Winston Churchill winning the Nobel Prize for Literature.

40 John Elsom, *Cold War Theatre* (London, New York: Routledge, 1992), 50.
41 *Letters*, IV, 612–14. On Beckett's engagement in political issues from the late 1970s onwards cf. Knowlson, *Damned to Fame*, 641f.
42 Godot and Beckett's plays were not performed inside the Soviet Union for thirty years. Elsom, *Cold War Theatre*, 49.
43 Tony Judt, *Postwar: A History of Germany since 1945* (London: Random House Vintage, 2010), 2.
44 Frank Bies, *Republik der Angst: Eine andere Geschichte der Bundesrepublik* (Reinbek: Rowohlt, 2019), 19: 'deutsche Angst – das ist eine Kernthese dieses Buches – war keine nationale Pathologie. Sie resultierte vielmehr aus einer stets präsenten, sich permanent verändernden und dynamischen Erinnerung an eine katastrophale Vergangenheit, die eine angstvolle und zuweilen apokalyptische Zukunftsantizipation nach sich zog.'
45 Leonard Cheshire, one of the pilots who flew close to Nagasaki when the atomic bombs fell, addressed the Oxford Air Squadron soon afterwards in 1946, and succinctly states: 'Realise this, that if these bombs are ever going to be used there is not much point in anything that you are doing now.' Tony Benn, *Years of Hope: Diaries, Paper and Letters 1940–1962*, ed. by Ruth Winstone (London: Hutchinson, 1994), 97–8.
46 Richard Begam summarizes these two major strands of Beckett scholarship until the 1980s: 'The criticism on Beckett ... identif[ies] two approaches that were especially influential during the 1950s, 1960s, and 1970s. The first approach, which treats Beckett as a mimetic nihilist, argues that his literature mirrors the fragmentation and alienation of modern life by giving us works that are paradoxical, confusing, absurd. The second approach, which views him as an existential humanist, maintains that he acknowledges the "nothingness" of human existence but celebrates man's freedom to choose himself as an *être-pour-soi*. Both approaches have proven valuable, not only because they shed light on difficult and obscure texts, but also because they established important affiliations between Beckett's work and such movements as existentialism and absurdism.' Begam, *Beckett and the End of Modernity*, 7–8.
47 Martin Esslin, 'Introduction' in Martin Esslin (ed.), *Samuel Beckett. A Collection of Critical Essays* (Englewood Cliffs: Prentice Hall, 1965), 1–15, 8.
48 Esslin, 'Introduction', 4–5.
49 David Wheatley, '"Nothing will come of nothing": Zero-Sum Games in Shakespeare's *King Lear* and Beckett's *Endgame*' in Janet Clare (ed.), *Shakespeare and the Irish Writer* (University College Dublin Press, 2010) 166–78; Andrew Fitzsimons, '"What Wretches Feel": Lear, Edgar and Samuel Beckett's *Worstward Ho*' in Graham Bradshaw and Tom Bishop (eds.), Tetsuo

Kishi (special guest ed.), *The Shakespearean International Yearbook 7. Special Section, Updating Shakespeare* (Aldershot, London: Ashgate, 2007), 256–71. Arka Chattopadhyay, '"Worst in Need of Worse": *King Lear, Worstward Ho* and the Trajectory of Worsening', *Samuel Beckett Today/Aujourd'hui*, [*Early Modern Beckett/Beckett et le début de l'ère moderne*] (Amsterdam, New York: Rodopi, 2012), 73–87.

50 Dan Gunn, 'Samuel Beckett' in Adrian Poole (ed. and intr.), *Joyce, T.S. Eliot, Auden, Beckett: Great Shakespeareans Volume XII*, vol. 7 (New York: Continuum, 2012), 149–97, 156. Gunn argues that Cohn is also influenced by 'the work of Jan Kott in which *King Lear* is read through Beckettian spectacles darkened by the catastrophe of the Second World War, the inhumanity of the Holocaust, the bleakness of the Cold War, the threat of nuclear annihilation'.

51 Jan Kott, *Shakespeare our Contemporary*, transl. by Boleslaw Taborski, pref. by Peter Brook (London: Methuen, 1965), 100–33.

52 Anne M. Drew, *Past Crimson, Past Woe: The Shakespeare-Beckett Connection* (New York: Garland, 1993), xiv.

53 Kott, *Shakespeare our Contemporary*, 122.

54 Johann Wolfgang Goethe, 'Shakespeare und kein Ende', *SämtlicheWerke nach Epochen seines Schaffens*, ed. by Karl Richter et al., vol XI.ii, ed. by Johannes John et al. (Munich: Hanser, 1998), 173–86.

55 Brook, Peter, *The Shifting Point: Forty Years of Theatrical Exploration 1946–1987* (London: Bloomsbury Methuen Drama, 1989), 89.

56 Peter Brook, '*Endgame* as *King Lear*, or How to Stop Worrying and Love Beckett', *Encore*, 12.1 (Jan–Feb 1965), 8–12, 9.

57 Peter Brook, 'For Jan Kott', *New Theatre Quarterly*, 10 (1994), 303–4.

58 All references to Shakespeare's works are taken from the New Cambridge Shakespeare editions listed in the bibliography.

59 Arka Chattopadhyay, '"Worst in need of worse": *King Lear, Worstward Ho* and the Trajectory of Worsening', *Samuel Beckett Today/Aujourd'hui*, 24 (2012), 79.

60 Andrew Fitzsimons, '"What Wretches Feel". Lear, Edgar and Samuel Beckett's *Worstward Ho*', in *The Shakespearean International Yearbook 7, Special Section Updating Shakespeare*, 259.

61 Gregorio DaSilva examines selected adaptations of Shakespeare's plays from the 1960s until the 1980s, in which dramatic elements of Beckett's plays were used. Gregorio DaSilva, *Intersections between Shakespeare and Beckett on Stage, Screen and Page* (Dissertation, University of Birmingham, 2017).

62 Gontarski, '"I Think This does Call for a Firm Stand"', 22.

63 David Pattie describes the chequered memories of Peter Bull, who played Pozzo in Hall's production. Pattie, 'The Arrival of *Godot*', 9. See also Knowlson who records comments of members of the audience such as 'This is why we lost the colonies!' Knowlson, *Damned to Fame*, 415.

64 Sos Eltis summarizes the significance Beckett held for Hall's life and career: 'Directing *Godot* changed Hall's life: Harold Pinter and Tennessee Williams

approached him to direct their plays; he was appointed the first director of the Royal Shakespeare Company; Leslie Caron asked him to direct her in *Gigi* – and he married her (Hall 1977).' Sos Eltis, '"It's All Symbiosis": Peter Hall Directing Beckett', in David Tucker and Trish McTighe (eds.), *Staging Beckett in Great Britain* (London, Oxford, New York: Bloomsbury Methuen Drama, 2016), 87–104, 87.
65 Charles R. Lyons, 'Beckett, Shakespeare, and the Making of Theory', *Around the Absurd: Essays on Modern and Postmodern Drama* (Ann Arbor: University of Michigan Press, 1990), 97–127, 99.
66 *Peter Hall's Diaries*, ed. by John Goodwin (London: Oberon, 2000 [1983]), 233, 11.05.1976.
67 *Peter Hall's Diaries*, 100, 08.06.1974. 'New writing is the only way one can hear the voice of the present. [...] It was the same excitement as I have had in the past with John Whiting, Beckett, Osborne, Pinter. A voice which makes you revalue your own attitudes.'
68 *Peter Hall's Diaries*, 230, 24.04.1976.
69 Alan Schneider, 'Waiting for Beckett. A Personal Chronicle', *Chelsea Review*, 2 (September 1958), 3–20, 8.
70 *Letters*, II, 610, 01.04.1956.
71 Gontarski, '"I Think This does Call for a Firm Stand"', 33. Gontarski records the exchange between Beckett, Devine and Calder on the matter. Cf. Letter of 17.03.1965; 09.04.1965: 'After correspondence with George and Peter Hall I have decided that my commitment to the former ends in September when he leaves and not to commit myself to the Royal Shakespeare, though welcoming any proposal from them' (*Letters*, III, 664).
72 Eltis, '"It's All Symbiosis"', 103.
73 Eltis, '"It's All Symbiosis"', 100. 'The critical and box-office success of Hall's productions clearly played a central role in establishing Beckett's plays as a vital part of the English dramatic landscape, but Hall's role as director of the RSC, the NT, and then his own repertory company has also been crucial in promoting and integrating Beckett's drama.' Eltis, '"It's All Symbiosis"', 102.
74 Stanley Wells explains the pivotal and cathartic nature of the scenes: 'The Dover beach scene shows the play's central characters at the nadir of their fortunes; yet it shows them, too, in spite of their afflictions, as in some senses wiser and better men than they had been at the beginning of the action.' Stanley Wells, '*The Taming of the Shrew* and *King Lear*: A Structural Comparison', *Shakespeare Survey*, 33 (1980), 55–66, 64.
75 Knowlson, *Damned to Fame*, 674; Gunn, 'Samuel Beckett', 155.
76 In August 1976, Beckett, while working on the rehearsals of *Endgame* at the Schiller-Theater, writes to Barbara Bray from Berlin: 'Dear B. Can you get me: "the gods, like wanton boys with flies...?....for their sport" – complete quotation and reference. [...] Forget about it if too much of a nuisance. Not at all important.' (*Letters*, IV, 85).

77 In December 1987, Beckett describes his own state of affairs to Jocelyn Herbert: "...The worst is not/So long as we can say, This is the worst." To myself, as Edgar to the Fool. *Letters*, IV, 696, 12.12.1987.
78 This episode can be linked to an episode in Beckett's childhood at Forty-Foot beach. Knowlson, *Damned to Fame*, 652.
79 Derek Peat, '"And that's true too": *King Lear* and the Tension of Uncertainty', *Shakespeare Survey*, 33 (1980), 43–53, 47: 'the working of the scene depends on our remaining confused about the existence of cliff and sea'.
80 A.C. Bradley, *Shakespearean Tragedy* (London: Macmillan and Co. 1904), 249.
81 G. Wilson Knight, *The Wheel of Fire* (London: Routledge, 2001 [1930]), 191.
82 James Knowlson, 'Practical Aspects of Theatre, Radio and Television: Extracts from an Unscripted Interview with Billie Whitelaw', *Journal of Beckett Studies*, 3 (1978), 85–91, 87.
83 Theodor W. Adorno, 'Versuch, das Endspiel zu verstehen', *Noten zur Literatur II* (Frankfurt a. M.: Suhrkamp, 1961), 201.
84 Angela Moorjani discusses Beckett's use of vision and blindness: 'Many generational pairs are split into one blind and one seeing party, as in Gall Senior and Junior, Pozzo and Lucky, Hamm and Clov, Dan and Jerry, with the blind half pictured as an ironic image of the artist (looking inward) while acting out an imperious form of neediness and dependence on the seeing half (looking outwards).' Angela Moorjani, 'Peau de Chagrin. Beckett and Bion on Looking not to See', *Samuel Beckett Today/Auhourd'hui*, [*After Beckett/D'après Beckett*], 14 (2004), 25–38, 30.
85 *Letters*, II, 569, 20.11.1955.
86 Edward Bizub, 'Beckett's Boots: The Crux of Meaning', *Samuel Beckett Today/Aujourd'hui*, 25 (2013), 267–78. Bizub draws a parallel between Estragon's struggle with his left boot and the thief on the left of Christ who was damned. He also mentions that Beckett puns on his own name, bequjée, as 'hobnail', used in bootmaking.
87 Gontarski, *Beckett Matters*, 22.
88 Somewhat ironically, today the Boghill Centre is a holistic living centre in Co. Clare on the edge of the Burren that advertises its rural setting, including an orchard and a chicken coop.
89 The incident happened a day before Bloomsday, 16 June, and *Ulysses* in the 'Wandering Rocks' episode refers to the disaster: 'Terrible affair that *General Slocum* explosion. Terrible, terrible! A thousand casualties. And heartrending scenes' (*U*, 196), cf. also (*U*, 149).

CHAPTER 2

Molecular Shakespeare – Beckett Reading Shakespeare through Joyce
The poetics of the hieroglyph and 'the insurrection of molecules'

Beckett's œuvre engages significantly with the works of other writers. Enoch Brater observes: 'Every work by Samuel Beckett is likely to strike its reader as the discovery of some rich archaeological find.'[1] This find encapsulates an array of relations and associations to other artefacts, and the reader-archaeologist trying to unearth this treasure has to dig carefully through layers of material, taking away just as much as necessary to discover the hitherto hidden work of art that apart from its own novelty also reveals the 'familiar network [Beckett] has made so authentically his own'.[2] Dante and Proust are part of this network, as are more generally, literature, music, art and philosophy within and beyond the European tradition.[3]

Beckett himself encourages this kind of archaeological reading. In his essay on Proust, he claims: 'the only fertile research is excavatory, immersive, a contraction of the spirit, a descent. The artist is active but negatively, shrinking from the nullity of extracircumferential phenomena, drawn into the core of the eddy' (*Proust*, 48). The work of both artist and researcher consists of mining their material, as they immerse themselves more and more into their object, a process Beckett describes as a descent into the 'core of the eddy'.[4] This plunge into the heart of the matter is quite different from a tamed, antiquarian mode of interpretation that merely delights in tracing influences of the most straightforward, quotational kind instead of revealing the function of these references and allusions within and for the text.

Interpretations of his works have to acknowledge Beckett's productive dialogue with the literary and artistic past, with contemporary writing and with the many connections and continuities among his own texts. Beckett's life and his works, many of which are at least bilingual, are remarkable for their transnational outlook. Early on, in his travels through Europe, in Paris and later also in Hamburg, Berlin and Munich, Beckett was introduced to influential figures of the artistic scene, and he quickly found access to and became part of a group of friends, artists, painters and writers.[5] In Paris, he met Thomas McGreevy, who like Beckett was a lecturer at the École Normale and with whom he shared a keen interest in art, music and poetry. In November 1928, McGreevy introduced Beckett to James Joyce, which marked the beginning of a long-standing collaboration and friendship.[6]

Joyce both challenged and inspired Beckett. He suggested that Beckett contribute a chapter to 'Our Exagmination Round His Factification For Incamination of Work in Progress' and was pleased with the result.[7] He also encouraged Beckett's academic writing in the role of mentor and as an object of study when Beckett proposed a doctorate on Proust and Joyce that materialized as his short study on *Proust* (1931), which, together with his essay on 'Dante...Bruno.Vico..Joyce', was to be one of the few academic writings that Beckett ever published. Together with Alfred Péron he was trusted with the translation of the Anna Livia Plurabelle section of *Finnegans Wake*. Even though Peggy Guggenheim claimed that Joyce 'loved Oblomov [a nickname for S.B.] as his son',[8] and many of Beckett's works such as his poem 'Home Olga' (homo logos) display an unmitigated admiration for Joyce, it would be inaccurate to regard their relationship in terms of an artistic or even Oedipal hierarchy:[9] 'Joyce was a major force, but Beckett's response to the maestro may be defined as much in terms of resistance as influence.'[10] Beckett's encounter with Joyce proved formative in numerous ways for both writers. *Finnegans Wake* is known for its references to *Murphy*,[11] and Beckett, who in 'Dante...Bruno. Vico..Joyce' dubs Joyce 'His Contemporary Holiness' (*Disjecta*, 32), was intimately familiar with Joyce's entire œuvre.[12]

Apart from the wealth of material that Joyce's works encompass, Beckett, along with many of his contemporaries, was fascinated and inspired by Joyce's inventive use of language. In 'Dante...Bruno.Vico..Joyce', he analyses and defends Joyce's capacity to create a language that is both representative and also performative. This twofold quality of language is central to Joyce's poetics and Beckett compares it to Giambattista Vico's conception of 'direct expression', where 'form and content are inseparable' (*Disjecta*, 25). Likewise, in Joyce's use of language, not only do word form and meaning converge and constitute what the text is about, but this textual entity also includes the visual impact of the written word, as well as the aural impact of its performative rendition: 'Here form *is* content, content *is* form. You complain that this stuff is not written in English. It is not written at all. It is not to be read – or rather it is not only to be read. It is to be looked at and listened to. His writing is not *about* something; *it is that something itself*' (*Disjecta*, 27).[13] Joyce and Vico, however, were not the first to create this kind of language that incarnates the very thing it expresses, and Beckett compares Joyce to Shakespeare who 'uses fat, greasy words to express corruption' in *Hamlet* (*Disjecta*, 27).[14] Not unlike Shakespeare's plays, Joyce's writing, according to Beckett, is an 'extraction of language and painting and gesture' in which the words 'are alive' (*Disjecta*, 27).

Eugène Jolas likewise speaks about Joyce giving 'his words odors and sounds that the conventional standard does not know. ... In this supertemporal and multispatial composition, language is born anew before our eyes.'[15] This animation of language, according to Beckett, involves 'an endless verbal germination, maturation, putrefaction, the cyclic dynamism of the intermediate' (*Disjecta*, 29). Jolas refers to Joyce's use of language as 'verbal decomposition',[16] and Beckett describes Joyce's poetics as a 'reduction of various expressive media to their primitive economic directness, and the fusion of these primal essences into an assimilated medium for the exteriorization of thought' (*Disjecta*, 29). Analogous to a chemical experiment, Joyce's text presents this process of reduction, fusion and remediation. The textuality, the language and structure of his works, as well as their metaphors and images, become poetic manifestations of the epistemology they negotiate.

Beckett shared with Joyce the fascination for 'a primitive economic directness', for minimal units of expression that encapsulate a maximum of potential signification. In further analogy to the natural sciences, the model of a molecule as the 'smallest identifiable unit, into which a pure substance can be divided and still retain the composition and chemical properties of that substance',[17] can serve to metaphorically describe the representational dynamics of both Joyce's and also Beckett's experiments with language. Beckett describes these restless dynamics when discussing the paintings of Bram van Velde: 'Here everything moves, swims, flees, returns, gets undone, redone. Everything ceases, ceaselessly [Tout cesse, sans cesse]. This looks like the insurrection of molecules, the inside of a stone one millionth of a second before it disintegrates. This is literature' (*Disjecta*, 128).

Inside the exploding stone of literature, the 'particular and the universal' (*Disjecta*, 24) do not contradict, but mutually shape one another. Beckett takes the idea of antithetical equivalence from the early modern philosopher Giordano Bruno:

> There is no difference, says Bruno, [...] between the infinite circle and the straight line. The maxima and minima of particular contraries are one and indifferent. [...]. The principle (minimum) of one contrary takes its movement from the principle (maximum) of one another. Therefore not

only do the minima coincide with the minima, the maxima with the maxima, but the minima with the maxima in the succession of transmutations. Maximal speed is a state of rest. (*Disjecta*, 21)

Minimal units of expression can produce maximal interpretive possibilities. Concentration and reduction inspire a process of reading as deciphering and expanding the scope of possible meanings and of forming new relations. Beckett again turns to archaeology to describe the simultaneity of expressive concentration and expansion when he describes Joyce's use of language as 'the savage economy of hieroglyphics' (*Disjecta*, 28). Language in Joyce's works constitutes a textual entity that *is* what it *can* be, that is inherently productive as a representation containing its performative dimension. Expression is encoded into its irreducible essence from which new combinations and associative syntheses can be formed to inspire new readings.[18] As Peter Hall would later say about Beckett, 'There is no decoration. And by this economy, Beckett regains a total philosophy of the theatre, where the words and action fuse.'[19]

Reduction, contraction and a word-perfect literalism that emulates its object in order to expand its scope of meaning and to multiply the ways in which a text can be read are central operations of Joyce's poetics. Both Joyce's and Beckett's virtuosity in word-formation, their immersion into other languages and their creation of new modes of expression also guides their transformational dialogue with other writers.

Dialectical Afterlives: Beckett – Joyce – Shakespeare

Next to T.S. Eliot, it was perhaps Joyce who, among Beckett's contemporaries, most deeply and extensively explored Shakespeare's works and integrated them into his own. Laura Pelaschiar argues that: 'Joyce needed Shakespeare more and more for and within his creative process. This is why *Ulysses* and *Finnegans Wake* are more Shakespearean than his earlier texts.'[20] Apart from his own extensive study of Shakespeare and Renaissance literature, which began as early as when Beckett was a student at Portora Royal School and continued at Trinity College Dublin in 1924–1925 to become a lifelong commitment,[21] in Joyce Beckett also found an early model of how to engage with literary history in a way that is both creative and destructive. Along with *The Waste Land*, *Ulysses* became a major modernist example of how the works of one's predecessors such as Shakespeare can be made resonant within one's own writing through one literary permutation to the next. Richard Halpern summarizes the modernist reception of Shakespeare in similar terms: 'By unleashing a conflicted, dialectical interplay between past and present, they construct a Shakespeare who is at once "our contemporary" and our bracing Other.'[22] With and through Joyce, therefore, Beckett not only reflected on and refined his own writing but also explored the European literary tradition, above all Dante[23] and Shakespeare.

Both Shakespeare the author and his works pervade *Ulysses* on many levels. Most directly, Shakespeare makes a cameo appearance in 'Circe', prompted by Stephen's and Bloom's Hamlet-like gaze into the mirror: 'Lynch (*points*) The mirror up to nature. [...] The face of William Shakespeare, beardless, appears there, rigid in facial paralysis, crowned by the reflection of the reindeer antlered hatrack in the hall' (*U*, 463). Stephen and Bloom conjure Shakespeare's ghostly image through an unsheeted mirror,[24] which shows him as a hunting trophy and both alludes to him as a horned husband and the son of an alleged poacher. When he eventually starts to speak, Shakespeare's temper ranges from dignified ventriloquy when he mentions '[his] Oldfellow Iagogogo!' (*U*, 436) to a 'paralytic rage' when he rants 'Weda seca whokilla farst' (*U*, 464).

Apart from this dramatic *mise-en-abîme*, in *Ulysses* the relation between the contemporary artist and Shakespeare is nowhere dealt with more intricately than in the ninth episode that Joyce in a letter to Ezra Pound in 1917 referred to as 'the Hamlet-chapter',[25] which is itself a creative reworking of the Shakespearean text and its various traditions of criticism and reception. The ninth episode of *Ulysses*, 'Scylla and Charybdis', if one adheres to the Homeric terminology, forms the middle part of the novel and indeed creates one of its culminating moments: it takes place at 2 p.m., halfway through the novel's timeline, and in it, Stephen Dedalus' aesthetic reflections reach a climax before he as a character gradually recedes from the main plot.

The episode's dense network of references to Platonic and Aristotelian philosophy, to theology and literature, opens a vast interpretive horizon as it investigates dialectical configurations of life and art, tradition and literary creation. 'Scylla and Charybdis', the rock and the whirlpool, demarcate a narrow strait through which Ulysses and his companions must sail and metaphorically summarize the episode's antithetical structure. It delineates a Western tradition of thought, which relies on binary oppositions as it juxtaposes and subsequently interweaves Aristotelian notions of materiality, flesh and the feminine, maternal principles of creation with male legacies and paternal ideals of immateriality mostly derived from Plato. From there it rehearses theories of emanation, entelechy and transubstantiation to scholastically inquire into the interdependence of form and matter.

These inquiries prominently include questions of authorship, of national heritage and identity; the episode not only records various received paradigms of literary lineage and reception and reflects on them but also inscribes itself into these traditions in a stance that is both metahistorical and performative. In its dialogic form, its scenic units and its theatrical entrances and exits, the chapter fashions itself as an animated afterlife of the tradition of afterlives that it so carefully rehearses. *Ulysses* thus confidently embraces T.S. Eliot's argument in 'Tradition and the Individual Talent' that each new work, instead of merely adding to an existing canon, shapes it anew, enters into a dialogue with its predecessors, questions, revises or reinvents them: 'the *whole* existing order must be, if ever so slightly, altered; and so the relations, proportions, values of each work of art toward the whole are readjusted; and this is conformity between the old and the new'.[26]

In the ninth episode of *Ulysses*, the legacy of William Shakespeare and particularly of *Hamlet* is the tradition with which the characters predominantly engage in their dialogues, their theories and eventually in their staging of a play. Set in the National Library of Ireland, the chapter renders a discussion between Stephen Dedalus, librarians and various members of the Irish Literary Revival who epitomize different approaches to the issues of biographical criticism and national tradition.[27] The library furthermore provides the space where the material presence of a literary work, its history and the virtual presence of its author encounter readers, artists and critics. As a national and cultural institution, the library preserves materialized knowledge and memory and provides access to it. The National Library is therefore not only a vast treasury of knowledge and heritage but also a model of the cultural dynamics that determine traditions of reading and enable the discovery, reinvention and resurrection of single works and authors. The library hence facilitates processes of reception, interpretation and canonization that can assume a quasi-autonomous life and are beyond the control of an author, who, compared to the material presence of his or her works, leads an absent and almost spectral mode of existence.

The episode comments on these tendencies of recuperation and appropriation and engages with Shakespeare scholarship since the eighteenth century. Alluding to Stephen Dedalus' return from Paris,[28] the episode briefly draws on the French tradition of 'Hamletisme' in referring to Mallarmé's 'Hamlet et Fortinbras' (1896) and mocks the 'French point of view' as 'distressingly shortsighted' (*U*, 154).[29] Joyce's reflecting on traditions of Shakespeare scholarship can also be regarded as a literary reaction to the kind of Shakespeare criticism that is tied to national and imperial interests, and more specifically to the surge of Shakespeare biographies and the general fascination with life-writing in the nineteenth century.

'Scylla and Charybdis' therefore begins with what is already a retrospective on an influential tradition in Shakespeare reception. Stephen refers to it as 'Shakespeare made in Germany' (*U*, 197), a way of reinventing and appropriating Shakespeare that stems from the hypothesis that there is an unparalleled and almost archaic affinity between Germany and Shakespeare, who subsequently became naturalized by the canonical Schlegel-Tieck translation and was firmly embedded in German classicism, swiftly occupying the rank of the third 'German' classic next to Goethe and Schiller. As the chapter illustrates, Shakespeare became a crucial force in the literary and intellectual history of Germany from the eighteenth century onwards, a tradition that was seconded by the enthusiasm of the German *Sturm und Drang*, by German classicism's intense engagement with *Hamlet* and, among others, by Gottfried Herder's proprietorial claim, founded on rather elaborate linguistic observations, that Shakespeare was in fact German.[30]

The widespread appeal that Shakespeare enjoyed throughout German classicism was manifest in numerous ways of popularizing his works. Joyce alludes to this rich tradition, which comprised translations such as Wieland's and later prominently Schlegel's and Tieck's, and drew on the idealistic conception of Shakespeare as an original genius, which manifested itself in the rampant 'Hamlet fever' that succeeded and fed on an earlier 'Werther fever' as well as in the many creative interactions with his works in Goethe, Schiller and Kleist.[31] To illustrate Shakespeare's prominence in the German tradition and beyond it, the episode explicitly draws on Goethe's eponymous character Wilhelm Meister, who is both successor and kindred spirit to Hamlet.[32] In Goethe's *bildungsroman*, *Wilhelm Meisters Lehrjahre* (1795), the protagonist praises Hamlet's excellence as the ideal to which he himself aspires when he becomes both director and actor in a performance of *Hamlet*.[33]

In *Ulysses*, the assistant librarian John Eglinton, who uses this example, maintains that Goethe, in fraternal attachment to Shakespeare, creates Wilhelm, the German equivalent to William (or Master Will), as a brother to the sensitive soul of Hamlet, and both characters share similar problems related to romantic melancholia: 'The beautiful ineffectual dreamer who comes to grief against hard facts' (*U*, 176). The universal lifelikeness that

Eglinton attests to Hamlet's and Wilhelm's personal issues in his view does not dampen but rather enhance the poetry of both works: 'And we have, have we not, those priceless pages of Wilhelm Meister? A great poet on a great brother poet. A hesitating soul taking arms against a sea of troubles, torn by conflicting doubts, as one sees in real life' (*U*, 176).

'Scylla and Charybdis' approaches the relations between art and life, and art as a form of afterlife, on a number of levels. Thomas William Lyster, who had translated Dunster's *Life of Goethe* in 1883, becomes the model for Joyce's Quaker librarian of the National Library of Ireland, and not only does *Wilhelm Meister* emerge as a literary manifestation of *Hamlet*'s afterlife but Shakespeare and Goethe become looming presences that recurrently emerge in the many discussions about the links between an author's life and his works, about processes of canonization, paternal and maternal legacies. 'Hamlet's musings about the afterlife of his princely soul' (*U*, 178) therefore take shape in the various conceptions of afterlives on which Joyce reflects, in the many dialectical oppositions that constitute 'Scylla and Charybdis' and also in the literary afterlife that the chapter itself presents.

The discussion in the library circles around the real and ideal, the material and immaterial contributions of Shakespeare to national literatures, be they German, English, French or Irish, and the ways in which he becomes the backdrop against which art and the artist constitute themselves. National heritage, or rather the lack of it, is a concern of John Eglinton, who sees his own country in an inferior position to England and deplores the pitiful state of Ireland whose 'young bards' have not 'yet create[d] a figure which the world will set beside Saxon Shakespeare's Hamlet' (*U*, 177). Russell, by contrast, inclining more towards Platonism, dismisses any probing into the life of the poet as grossly irrelevant and considers attempts at determining whether Shakespeare was James I or the Earl of Essex as fruitlessly petty and bureaucratic: 'interesting only to the parish clerk' (*U*, 181). He rather holds that 'Art has to reveal to us ideas, formless, spiritual essences' (*U*, 177) through which idea *Hamlet* emerges as a source of eternal wisdom and 'the plays, and the poetry of King Lear' as 'immortal' (*U*, 181).

Stephen Dedalus, by contrast, adheres to an Aristotelian view, seeks to reconcile work and context, life and art, and proposes that a work of art is also an imaginative reworking of an author's life. In his view, Shakespeare casts himself into the role of Hamlet's ghost, having once allegedly impersonated old Hamlet's ghost in the play's first performance at the Globe Theatre in 1602. Shakespeare, as Stephen holds, is thus not only the author who conceived of the play and character of Hamlet in his imagination but also the bodily father of his own aptly named son Hamnet. *Hamlet*, the play, and Hamlet, the character, therefore partake in a twofold nature as emanations of both 'son of his soul, [...] son of his body' (*U*, 181). The life and art of an author, as well as his bodily and mental conception, a son in real life and his dramatic equivalent, intersect: 'A triple analogy is at work here. Shakespeare is to his son, Hamnet, as the ghost is to Hamlet as Stephen's father is to Stephen.'[34] Stephen illustrates his theory and metaphorically equates both the material body and also the image of the artist with a text when he states:

> we or mother Dana weave and unweave our bodies, Stephen said, from day to day, their molecules shuttled to and fro, so does the artist weave and unweave his image. And as the mole on my right breast is where it was when I was born, though all my body has been woven of new stuff time after time, so through the ghost of the unquiet father the image of the unloving son looks forth (*U*, 186).

Stephen conflates mother Dana, the character in Irish mythology who symbolizes the land, with the 'Moirai', the goddesses of fate who in classical mythology incessantly weave and eventually cut the threads of life. For Stephen, the process of 'weaving and unweaving of the artist's image' has both a temporal and a spatial dimension. He relates himself to Hamlet, the son of an unquiet ghostly father who is both present and absent from what he has created. This dialectic of presence that underlies the artist's image is configured in analogy to metabolic processes of renewal and disintegration, of familiarity and alienation and of spatial fixity and temporal flux. The comparatively static mole becomes a marker of the filial connection, a 'hieroglyph' in which indelible ancestry and the uneasy lineage of the 'unloving son' become encoded. Stephen conceives of textual and artistic heritage in terms of a father-son relation and alludes both to the Holy Trinity and also to *Hamlet*. Father and son, the author and his work, literary heritage and its singular manifestations become mutually dependent.

Beckett had characterized Joyce's use of language in terms of creation and destruction as a continuous dynamism of 'germination, maturation, putrefaction' (*Disjecta*, 29), and an 'inner elemental vitality' that 'imparts a furious restlessness to the form' (*Disjecta*, 29). In Stephen's view, the body is comparable to such a text – that is subject to continuous material renewal and destruction and becomes a 'restless form'. As an apparently static and unchanging signifier of filial inheritance, the mole, at the same time, denotes its opposite – an identity that is a work in progress and consists of the dynamic process of becoming and undoing, of dealing with the legacy of an 'unquiet father'.

Whereas the mole, the outward sign of one's ancestry, remains unchanged to the observer and to its bearer, its component molecules are in flux, in a continuous process of destruction and renewal: 'Wait. Five months. Molecules all change. I am other I now' (*U*, 156). In these processes of becoming and undoing, the 'unquiet father' remains a latent presence. This kind of ghostliness hence becomes an immaterial condition of both fatherhood and authorship that remains materially present in Stephen's birthmark: 'That mole is the last to go, Stephen said, laughing' (*U*, 160). Stephen's pun on 'mole-cule' illustrates this mutual pervasiveness of opposites, of the smallest unit that retains properties of a larger substance. The verticality of paternal legacy to Stephen conveys a state of simultaneous difference and sameness, in which the whole is present in its irreducible parts.

In *Ulysses*, as well as in some of Shakespeare's plays, the mole becomes a synecdochal marker of an identity in flux. Like Hamlet, Stephen is a son in mourning, and the mole on his right breast is not only an allusion to the subterranean dwelling of old Hamlet's ghost, whom Hamlet flippantly addresses as 'Well said old mole, canst work i'th'earth so fast?' (*Ham* 1.5.162). Margreta De Grazia discusses the catachrestic nature of the mole in *Hamlet* that signifies the embeddedness of the subject in objective historical and material conditions and refers to both Hegel and Marx, who prominently refer to this passage to describe the progress of world history.[35] Both draw on the mole in *Hamlet* to express the progress of spirit and to describe the future-oriented movement of revolution. Martin Harries, who analyses Marx's *Eighteenth Brumaire*, unravels some of the complexities resulting from Marx's and Hegel's focus on the mole's historical activity as 'grubbing, digging and undermining': 'In alluding to *Hamlet* Marx engages a play whose concerns are in many ways those of the Brumaire: legitimacy, usurpation, ghostly intervention, theatrical and historical repetition.'[36] In *Hamlet*, the mole is ambivalent and not only mocks the ghost in comparing him to a benign creature burrowing away but also denotes a potentially evil flaw that remains with some men regardless of their virtues: 'So, oft it chances in particular men,/That for some vicious mole of nature in them,/... the stamp of one defect' (*Ham* 1.4.23–31).

As an indelible and tenacious stamp of one's heritage, the mole in *Twelfth Night* becomes a sign of identification when Sebastian and Viola are reunited as they both quite literally re-member their father's mole:

Sebastian: 'My father had a mole upon his brow./... And so had mine' (*TN* 5.1.226–7). Contrary to this joyful reunion at the end of *Twelfth Night*, in *Cymbeline*, Imogen's 'cinque-spotted' (*Cym* 2.2.38) mole on her left breast becomes a mistaken token of her infidelity, which thus separates her from her husband Posthumus. At the end of *Cymbeline*, however, Guiderius is recognized as one of her lost brothers by his 'mole, a sanguine star;/It was a mark of wonder' (*Cym* 5.6.364–5). As it does for Stephen Dedalus, the mole in *Twelfth Night* and even more so in *Cymbeline* ambiguously denotes crises of identity and their concomitant sexual tensions. Viola as Cesario is protected by her male guise, until the mole reveals her true identity and reunites her to her brother. Imogen's truthfulness, by contrast, is called into question by the sight of her birthmark, and it is only at the end of the play that she is reconciled to Posthumus.

While indicating the descent and identity of a character, the mole becomes instrumental in the overall pattern of a play, the resolution of its plot, the separation, recognition and reunion of father and son, brother and sister, husband and wife. 'There can be no reconciliation, Stephen said, if there has not been a sundering' (*U*, 187), and the mole signifies both. It becomes a *pars pro toto* that represents the textual strategies in which *Ulysses* engages with its predecessors, above all Shakespeare. It illustrates the transformative processes of the body that by analogy also constitute the artist's image as a text that is intricately woven to be creatively undone, a 'molecule' in which the substance of earlier narratives and future possibilities lies latent and where it is virtually present: 'that which I was is that which I am and that which in possibility I may come to be' (*U*, 186).[37]

The mole's German equivalent 'Muttermal' illustrates the gendered dimension that it acquires for Stephen more vividly than does the English 'birthmark'. For Stephen, the mole that connects him to Shakespeare is charged with sexual anxiety: 'Ravisher and ravished, what he would but would not, go with him from Lucrece's bluecircled ivory globes to Imogen's breast, bare with its mole cinquespotted' (*U*, 189). By invoking the rape of Lucrece, Stephen is wavering between the roles of victim and perpetrator, he 'would, but would not', and shares Hamlet's anxieties about 'the lustful Queen' (*U*, 198), hence alluding to Gertrude's position between two conflicting male characters within an Oedipal triangle.

For Stephen the genealogy of the artist and gender-configurations in Shakespeare are linked to traditional imperatives of matrilineal and patrilineal forms of self-replication that result in conflicts:

> Fatherhood, in the sense of conscious begetting, is unknown to man. It is a mystical estate, an apostolic succession, from only begetter to only begotten. [...] On that mystery [...] the church is founded and founded irremovably because founded, like the world, macro and microcosm, upon the void. Upon incertitude, upon unlikelihood (*U*, 199).

Stephen reveals the narrative of a linear, paternal genealogy in theology and in theories of authorship as a myth that Shakespeare's heroes and heroines likewise render problematic. Hamlet has to come to terms with conflicting impulses. He is 'too much i'th'sun' (*Ham* 1.2.67), struggles to fulfil his revenant father's command and has trouble in managing his affection towards his mother. Likewise, Perdita in *The Winter's Tale*, to whom Stephen refers alongside other Shakespearean daughter-figures such as Marina ('a child of storm') and Miranda ('a wonder'), returns as a lost likeness of her mother, and Stephen asks himself: 'Will any man love the daughter if he has not loved the mother?' (*U*, 188),[38] pointing to an inner conflict that is related to incestuous feelings.

In Shakespeare and in Joyce, straightforward narratives of succession, self-replication and influence become complicated, potentially incestuous or end in betrayal. Stephen finds himself in a similar dilemma to Shakespeare's 'children'. Unlike Imogen's mole, however, Stephen's is placed on his right breast, which denotes paternity, the biblical place of the son at the 'right hand side of the father' according to the Apostolic Creed.[39] Yet, like Hamlet, he is torn between fatherly authority and love for his mother: '*Amor matris*, subjective and objective genitive, may be the only true thing in life. Paternity may be a legal fiction' (*U*, 199). For Hamlet, *amor matris* can indeed work both ways and paternity has undeniably become a legal fiction, since with Claudius' usurpation of the Danish throne, Hamlet's hereditary claim to kingship within a patrilineal line of succession has been irrevocably suspended, the paternal promise broken.

Like Shakespeare, who travelled between Stratford and London, and like Odysseus, who navigated between the poles of Scylla and Charybdis, Stephen moves between Dublin and Paris. He is able to steer between the extremes, and from this position theorizes about the multiple dialectical transformations that art is able to perform. The chapter emulates this movement in its wealth of formal variations and transformations, in which it reflects on models of literary creation, and, in the process, creates itself. Single expressions, like moles and molecules, become indicative of the vertical and formative processes behind them. *Ulysses* only stresses the Cleopatra-like, 'infinite variety' (*U*, 204) of these transformations, and resorts to Coleridge's romantic idea of Shakespeare as a 'myriadminded man' (*U*, 197), who '[a]fter God [...] has created most' (*U*, 204), but in its language and theme, it presents an 'entelechy of forms' in its creative re-formations of ideas, characters and references within a densely associative texture.

The episode does not merely stage dogmatic disputes about the apostolic succession or the hierarchy of matter and spirit, nor does it merely engage in theoretical debates about authorship, adaptation and transformation – it also materializes the emergence of these ideas in its experiments with form and language, and it places itself at the end of the multiple entelechies and metamorphoses it has incorporated in its combinations of words and themes. In the texture of 'Scylla and Charybdis', Shakespeare emerges as a molecular presence through word-formation and implicit characterization.

The chapter is suffused with references to Shakespeare's plays and vocabulary that are being re-contextualized in new dialectic syntheses. The famous Joycean composite 'Rutlandbaconsouthamptonshakespeare' (*U*, 199),[40] condenses in one compound the ever-increasing number of theories of authorial ascriptions; the direct quotation from *Love's Labor's Lost*: 'honorificabilitudinitatibus' (*U*, 172), ironically comments on the attachment to one's name; 'Puck Mulligan' who thinks that Shakespeare is 'the chap that writes like Synge' (*U*, 190) characterizes Buck Mulligan's boisterous deftness in relation to Shakespeare's defiant sprite from *A Midsummer Night's Dream*, who, like Mulligan, dressed 'blithe in motley' (*U*, 162), gradually takes over the course of events. In instances like these, Joyce's text blends in early modern techniques of word-formation with his style and weaves references to Shakespeare into his own text. The alliteration 'Dan Deasy's ducats' (*U*, 190) recalls Solanio reporting Shylock's divided grief over his money and daughter in *The Merchant of Venice*: "My daughter! O my ducats! O my daughter!' (*MV* 2.8.15), and it further underlines the materialism of Mr. Deasy's sinister character. The almost proverbial '[a] quart of ale is a dish for a king' (*U*, 196), is a repetition of Autolycus' song in *The Winter's Tale* (*WT* 4.3.9), and it also resonantes with Enobarbus in *Antony and Cleopatra*, who refers to Cleopatra as the 'Egyptian dish' (*AC* 2.6.123) as well as with the clown who, in Act V, brings in the basket of snakes, arguing with Cleopatra that 'a woman is a dish for the gods' (*AC* 5.2.268–9).[41]

These embedded references to Shakespeare multiply interpretive possibilities, create analogies and release chains of associations between *Ulysses* and Shakespeare's plays, and they enable readings in which both

Shakespeare's works themselves and their reception histories and traditions can be conceived through the lens of *Ulysses*. Joyce's use of direct quotation, allusion and amalgamation expands the breadth of associations that imaginatively reverberate back on his own text and add further hermeneutic dimensions to it.

Apart from the semantic and lexical exuberance displayed in Shakespeare's works, which *Ulysses* seeks both to emulate and to surpass, it is Shakespeare's art of anachronism, of combining, even uniting contraries that John Eglinton finds remarkable: 'That was Will's way, John Eglinton defended. We should not now combine a Norse saga with an excerpt from a novel by George Meredith. [...] He puts Bohemia on the seacoast and makes Ulysses quote Aristotle' (*U*, 203). *Ulysses*' textual travels in Shakespeare's works reveal them as unquiet, molecular presences that manifest themselves not only in theories of national heritage but also on the micro-levels of linguistic permutation and morphological combination.

Furthermore, 'Scylla and Charybdis' both invokes and obliterates these presences in its theatrical dimension, which includes the transformation of the narrative dialogue into a play. The episode, at many instances, verges on becoming a play when characters such as Bloom briefly appear and disappear and when the library increasingly becomes a stage onto which major and minor characters make their entries and exits: 'Enter Magee Mor Matthew, a rugged rough rugheaded kern, in strossers with a buttoned codpiece' (*U*, 189). Mr Magee is characterized in terms of a Renaissance image of an Irish or Scottish foot soldier (*Mac* 1.2.30; *R II*, 2.1.155–6), and together with him, Stephen, Best, Mulligan and the Quaker librarian stage a miniature music-hall type of play that involves 'the trinity of black Wills, the villain shakebags, Iago, Richard Crookback, Edmund in *King Lear*' (*U*, 201).

Stephen's casting of the unholy trinity of Shakespeare's worst villains takes up the theme of treason and brotherly conflict, in which he connects the Trinitarian dogma to Shakespearean as well as biblical contexts of inheritance and betrayal. Pairs such as Cain and Abel, Jacob and Esau, Claudius and old Hamlet as well as the usurpers 'nuncle Richie and nuncle Edmund' (*U*, 202–3) set the scene for Stephen's drama of treachery and usurpation. He compares himself both to Esau, who gave away his birthright for a bowl of pottage, and to Richard III, who loses his kingdom through his manipulations: 'I'm tired of my voice the voice of Esau. My kingdom for a drink' (*U*, 203).[42]

Time and again, Shakespeare becomes a model for how the artist weaves and unweaves his image in and through his works. Apart from

Shakspeare's reportedly casting himself into the role of the ghost, the chapter plays with his habit of punning on his name:[43] Will, William or simply the letter 'W' become molecular signifiers in which further allusions to the plays, proverbial wisdom and puns intersect. Likewise, 'will' literally contains a temporal dimension alluding to one's heritage and legacy. Shakespeare's Sonnet 135 is one of the 'Will' sonnets that combines liturgical speech with allusions to mercantilism[44] and to an amorous desire that seeks to unite with the beloved's will as it performs the copious abundance of wills it addresses:

> Whoever hath her wish, thou hast thy Will,
> And Will to boot, and Will in overplus;
> More than enough am I that vex thee still,
> To thy sweet will making addition thus.
> Wilt thou, whose will is large and spacious,
> Not once vouchsafe to hide my will in thine?
> Shall will in others seem right gracious,
> And in my will no fair acceptance shine?
> The sea, all water, yet receives rain still,
> And in abundance addeth to his store;
> So thou being rich in Will add to thy Will
> One will of mine to make thy large Will more.
> Let no unkind no fair beseechers kill;
> Think all but one, and me in that one Will.

The profusion of multiple wills, however, at the end of the sonnet is condensed into the 'all but one [...] Will' and forges unity between the whole and its component parts. *Ulysses* likewise dissects 'will' into segments when, for instance, Stephen who had commented on the resourcefulness of Shakespeare's wife – 'If others have their will, Ann hath a way' (*U*, 183) – plays with the letter 'w' when he quotes Richard III's boast 'Was ever woman in this humour wooed? Was ever woman in this humour won?' (*R III* 1.2.231–2) to describe Ann Hathaway as a version of both Penelope and Lady Ann ('Wait to be wooed and won' (*U*, 202)) and who, he speculates, betrayed Shakespeare in an adulterous relation with his brother Richard, which then allegedly served Shakespeare as a model for the marriage of Gertrude and Claudius.[45]

Shakespeare's habit of leaving traces and images of himself in his poetry and his plays inspires Stephen to compare him to a painter, in this case Fra Lippo Lippi, who creates his own afterlife by including his image in 'dark corners of the canvas':

> Stephen (stringendo.) He has hidden his own name, a fair name, William, in the plays a super here, a clown there, as a painter of Old Italy set his face in a dark corner of his canvas. He has revealed it in the sonnets where there is Will in overplus. [...] greatest shakescene in the country. What's in a name? That is what we ask ourselves in childhood when we write the name that we are told is ours. A star, a daystar, a firedrake, rose at his birth. It shone by day in the heavens alone, brighter than Venus in the night, and by night it shone over delta in Cassiopeia, the recumbent constellation which is the signature of his initial among the stars. His eyes watched it, lowlying on the horizon, eastward of the bear, as he walked by the slumberous summer fields at midnight returning from Shottery and from her arms. (U, 172)[46]

Like the mole, the author's initial becomes a synecdochal marker of identity. It is part of the name arbitrarily given to him at birth, which he then can weave into his texts, but it also partakes in a larger tapestry and emerges in a stellar image of himself, the five-spotted constellation of Cassiopeia, a message in the sky that becomes legible in the great leaning letter 'W'. The walker in the night is confronted with this external sign denoting the self, a birthmark as a signature written by the stars.

In Stephen's interpretation, a star, not unlike the star of Bethlehem, appears at William's birth and marks his identity. Indeed, in the winter of 1572, the schoolboy Shakespeare would have been able to view a newly emerging natural phenomenon that shattered traditional hermeneutics as well as the dominating Aristotelian philosophy of the spheres. On 11 November 1572, Tycho Brahe, the Danish astronomer and disciple of Johannes Keppler, observed a very bright star in the constellation of Cassiopeia.[47] This new star had been viewed at various places in Europe, and Holinshed mentions it in his *Chronicles* (1587). Stephen connects this new stellar image with Shakespeare as the manifestation of an identity that is part of a larger, potentially salutary, providential design. In Elizabethan England, 'Tycho's star' indeed provided room for much speculation and was taken as a sign to indicate that the second coming of Christ was imminent.[48] As we know today, the star that Tycho Brahe studied was a supernova that did not denote the end of the world in eschatology, but rather the end of the life cycle of a star.

The scene that Stephen imagines, of young William being confronted by his initial written by the stars, both signifies the transgression of the self into the infinity of the universe and denotes a finite existence, the death of a star in a supernova, which shines all the brighter while on the brink of extinction. Goethe prominently figured Shakespeare's afterlife in similar stellar terms in his poem 'Zwischen beiden Welten' ('Between both worlds') when he addresses Shakespeare as 'William! Stern der schönsten Höhe' ('William! Star of the fairest height').[49]

Like Goethe, who expresses his debt to Shakespeare in this poem and elsewhere, Stephen conflates several notions of the author as creator, 'the playwright who wrote the folio of this world and wrote it badly' (*U*, 175), and he also alludes to the absent presence of a ruler or author of the play with reference to Shakespeare's 'old fantastical Duke of dark corners' (*MM* 4.3.147–8) in *Measure for Measure*. Similar to the world of *Measure for Measure* and to that of all of Shakespeare's plays, the world of Joyce's *Ulysses* is replete with traces that can be read, interpreted and related to other signs to create new interpretive patterns and networks. Stephen's description of William Shakespeare's nightly walk hence also includes Prospero, who is an expatriate like Ulysses, and it evokes the epiphanic presence of the God of Israel that led his wandering people from Egypt through the desert to the Promised Land. In this context, the five-spotted star denotes the Star of David, marking Leopold Bloom's perambulatory Jewish ancestry. Bloom, who has lost a son, is contrasted to Hamlet, who has lost a father, and Bloom, at the end of *Ulysses*, unites with Stephen in a bond that comes close to that of father and son.

Shakespeare, whom John Eglinton summarizes in the phrase 'He is all in all' (*U*, 174), pervades the chapter as a manifestation of the ideas of entelechy and metamorphosis, and also as a presence in the material, everyday world of *Ulysses*, a pun on the German expression of 'All-Tag', the all-inclusive universe of the everyday.[50] When Stephen describes the dramatic structure of life as 'It doubles itself in the middle of his life, reflects itself in another, repeats itself, protasis, epitasis, catastasis, catastrophe' (*U*, 174), this quasi-dramatic structure governs the chapter itself, the midpoint of *Ulysses* that reflects itself in and through the works of Shakespeare as its other. For Stephen the entelechy of forms hence also materializes in the many roles that the individual can assume in the imagination. He describes this imaginative simultaneity of difference and similarity as a journey: 'We walk through ourselves, meeting robbers, ghosts, giants, old men, young men, wives, widows, brothers-in-love, but always meeting ourselves' (*U*, 175).

The semiotic texture of *Ulysses* is composed of 'the signatures of all things' that Stephen had contemplated in the Proteus-chapter (*U*, 31). With and also through Shakespeare, the exuberant totality of Joyce's text is built on dialectic correspondences that include individual and larger patterns, in which star-shaped moles and constellations of stars mutually reflect on and define one another. The pattern of Cassiopeia represents the potential universality that lies latent in the individual's origin, 'the name given to him at birth'. Within the many antithetical constellations the chapter explores, 'Scylla and Charybdis' also becomes a metonymy for Stephen's encounter with Shakespeare: 'My will: his will that fronts me. Seas between' (*U*, 209). Stephen's 'will' in defiantly confronting William's will, however, encompasses another's will, that is Goethe's, in a hitherto unnoticed reference to his drama *Prometheus*. The first lines of Goethe's *Prometheus* are:

> Ich will nicht, sag es ihnen! Und kurz und gut, ich will nicht!
> Ihr Wille gegen meinen!
> [Mich dünkt es hebt sich!]
> (I will not, tell them, in short, I will not! Their will against mine!)

When Mercurius tries to alleviate Prometheus's adamant determination by referring to his parental heritage,[51] Prometheus only becomes all the more incensed and flouts his father and mother:

> PROMETHEUS
> Was Vater! Mutter!
> Weißt du woher du kommst?
> (What, father! Mother! Do you know where you come from?)[52]

Stephen's Promethean attempt to liberate himself from predecessors such as Shakespeare at the same time becomes a Sisyphean procedure that entails further restless navigations between the seas, between Scylla and Charybdis, between the artists Shakespeare and Dedalus and between Goethe's two worlds.

'Shakespeares were as common as Murphies' – Beckettian Inversions

Between 22 and 24 January 1937, Beckett visited Weimar on his way to Dresden and stayed in the 'White Swan' hotel next to Goethe's house, where he took extensive notes on the houses of both Goethe and Schiller.[53] In the 1930s, Beckett intensely studied the literature of German classicism and read and copied out excerpts from a great number of Goethe's works.[54] Yet perhaps it was not so much the idea of a Promethean/Oedipal revolt against one's elders that interested the young Beckett as the Faustian idea of innate restlessness. The desire to fulfil itself in itself is a category that Beckett uses to describe the poetry of Denis Devlin:

On the one hand the 'Unbefriedigt jeden Augenblick', the need to need ('aimant l'amour') the art that condenses as inverted spiral of need that condenses in intensity and brightness from the mere need of the angels to that of the seraphims, whose end is its own end in the end and source of need. And on the other the gogetters, the gerrymandlers [...] There seems no other way in which this miserable functionary can hope to achieve innocuity. Unless of course he is a critic.[55]

Beckett describes art as a restless movement of inverse approximation that never becomes one with its object, but instead finds an end and a beginning in itself, generating its own existence. The convergence of opposites, their antithetical correspondences and chiastic interrelations are aesthetic operations immanent within Beckett's works. As Beckett had noted early on, the individual and the universal can be one and the same thing in Vico and Joyce.[56] Like Joyce, Beckett's aesthetics explores the at times paradoxical, mutual pervasiveness of the universal and the singular, the fusion of form and matter and the ways in which ideas take shape: 'I am interested in the shape of ideas, even if I do not believe in them ... It is the shape that matters,' Beckett told Harold Hobson in an interview in 1956.[57] Shakespeare becomes part of the creative matrix of Beckett's works where the very richness of his material emerges in his use of minute details and attention to the molecular level of languages and ideas that form the minimal components of his work. Gilles Deleuze defines writing with regard to Beckett as an inherently creative and assimilative process: 'Writing is inseparable from becoming: in writing, one becomes-woman, becomes-animal or vegetable, becomes-molecule to the point of becoming-imperceptible.'[58]

In Shakespeare, Beckett finds a productive source to engage with the dialectical dynamics of reduction and fusion, of weaving and unweaving that characterizes his aesthetics. The creative and destructive process of writing and unwriting is described in S.E. Gontarski's analyses of Beckett's works in *The Intent of Undoing*, and more recently in *Creative Devolution*: 'Beckett's theatre is always a theatre of becoming, a decomposition moving towards a recomposition, itself decomposing.'[59]

Whereas Joyce's poetics in his hieroglyphic use of language represents what it can be and multiplies significance in relating itself to another, in Beckett's aesthetics language and its intertextual echoes undergo a continuous process of making and unmaking, a rhythm of contraction and expansion that rather finds its being in the dynamics of becoming. In Joyce, Shakespeare is 'all in all', including the smallest and the largest parts, moles and stellar constellations that afford sheer infinite possibilities of reading: 'He found in the world without as actual what was in his world within as possible' (*U*, 175). In Beckett, Shakespeare rather lies latent and becomes part of the destructive and generative processes of his art.

S.E. Gontarski describes Beckett's relation to literary tradition as one of belonging and resistance that necessitates a more radical kind of unweaving of the artist's image than Joyce's characters are capable of: 'As much as Beckett might resist the notion, he finds himself already written into the text of Western literature. In much of his creative process, he struggles to undo himself.'[60] Undoing in Beckett can be seen as the reverse of reinventing himself. H. Porter Abbott analyses Beckett's novels as projects of both 'narratricide' and continuous reinvention, and in this respect he regards them as an ongoing autographical project.[61] The structural appeal of chiasmic thinking for Beckett's poetics is discussed by Dirk van Hulle: 'from a Beckettian perspective the idea of "self-undoing" corresponds with a poetics based on a principle of reversibility that has left its mark on many of his works and on his writing method'.[62] Like Joyce, who 'had succeeded in creating an art without end. Work forever in progress',[63] Beckett also creates a work that 'must go on', even in spite of itself.

Stephen Dedalus states that 'Shakespeares were as common as Murphies. What's in a name?' (*U*, 578), and yet Joyce's use of names is by no means arbitrary. With Beckett he shared a preference for character names beginning with the letter 'M' as in the three prominent women of *Ulysses*: Molly, Milly and Martha. Beckett, who apparently liked Fritz Lang's film 'M',[64] links the thirteenth letter of the alphabet to his birthday on 13 April, and thereby subtly inscribes himself into his characters such as Murphy, Molloy, Malone, Moran, Mercier, Mahood, Maddy or May, which was also the name of Beckett's mother, who died a year before *Molloy* was published.[65]

Beckett both evokes biographical and intertextual connections and destabilizes them at the same time.[66] This gesture of negation and inversion can also be found at the end of 'Scylla and Charybdis' and characterizes Stephen Dedalus' 'Hamlet theory'. When John Eglinton asks Stephen: 'Do you believe your own theory? No, Stephen said promptly' (*U*, 175). Stephen's almost Beckettian reaction negates that which it had previously elaborated. Fiction reveals its own fictional ontology in denying reference to systems of belief or objective reality. Instead, the narrative unwrites itself. This textual strategy of metanarrative self-denial is prominent at the end of *Molloy*: 'Then I went back into the house and wrote. It is midnight. The rain is beating on the windows. It was not midnight. It was not raining' (*Molloy*, 176). In *Molloy*, fictions of origin and heritage are established and dissolved. At the beginning, the protagonist finds himself in his mother's room, but cannot remember how he got there. When he is taken to the police station and questioned about his name and ancestry, he is equally perplexed:

> Is it your mother's name?' [...] Molloy, I cried, my name is Molloy. Is that your mother's name? said the sergeant. What? I said. Your name is Molloy, said the sergeant. Yes, I said, now I remember. And your mother? said the sergeant. I didn't follow. Is your mother's name Molloy too? said the sergeant. I thought it over (*Molloy*, 23).

Molloy is left puzzled, having earlier contemplated his relation to his mother, in which he to her was both husband and son: 'She never called me son, fortunately, [...] but Dan, I don't know why, my name is not Dan. Dan was my father's name perhaps, yes, perhaps [...] I took her for my mother and she took me for my father' (*Molloy*, 17).

The names and properties of Beckett's characters are fluid and the boundaries between them become permeable. Ironically, it is the 'Unnamable' who, assuming an exhausted metanarrative stance, states this palimpsestic texture of his own being: 'All these Murphys, Molloys and Malones do not fool me. They have made me waste my time, suffer for nothing, speak of them when, in order to stop speaking, I should have spoken of me and of me alone' (*The Unnamable*, 297). 'Me alone', a pun on 'M-alone', illustrates the interpretive possibilities of expansion, contraction and variation that can be derived from single letters, and it emphasizes the continuity of single works, between which, as Estragon in *Waiting for Godot* has it, 'everything oozes', and where some characters keep each other company precisely in their solitude.

'In the beginning was the pun' (*Murphy*, 65), states the narrator of *Murphy*, and many of Beckett's wordplays take their starting point from the quasi-molecular level of the single letter. *Company* ends on the word 'alone', which can also be read as 'all-one'. The permutations of letters, their inversions and the ensuing semantic properties that emerge as they branch out into words fascinated Beckett. 'M' stood on its head turns into 'W' and characters such as Watt, Worm, Winnie and Willie or entire works such as *Waiting for Godot* are christened accordingly. The narrator of *Company* (59) refers to himself as 'W' and to his 'hearer' as 'M' as if they were two sides of the same coin. Letters in Beckett metonymically represent characters, narrators and listeners or readers in a way that foregrounds the metadramatic or metafictional artifice of the presentation. In his early novels such as *Murphy* and *Dream of Fair to Middling Women*, Beckett plays with Shakespeare in an inverted way, invoking references to Shakespeare to illustrate and comment on his own narrative.

Before he goes to London and takes up work at the mental institution MMM, Murphy starts out as a student at Neary's Pythagorean Academy in Cork, and yet continuously adduces dualisms derived from Cartesian thought. To him the world is a world of binaries: 'The issue therefore, as lovingly simplified and perverted by Murphy, lay between nothing less fundamental than the big world and the little world' (*Murphy*, 178).[67] Murphy is solipsistically in love with this little world and describes it as a self-contained, all-inclusive universe: 'Murphy's mind pictured itself as a large hollow sphere, hermetically closed to the universe without. This was not an impoverishment, for it excluded nothing that it did not itself contain' (*Murphy*, 107). He contrasts his autopoetic world of the mind, which does not have a referent from which it can be judged as right or wrong to 'the time ... out of joint' (*Ham* 1.5.189) that Hamlet speaks about: 'This system had no other mode in which to be out of joint and therefore did not need to be put right in this' (*Murphy*, 11).

He decides to dwell in the little world of his mind, but is prevented from doing so entirely by his bodily needs, 'his deplorable susceptibility to Celia' (*Murphy*, 179) and his appetite for ginger biscuits. Alluding to the lovers' pursuits in *A Midsummer Night's Dream*, Murphy, who himself is chased by Miss Counihan, meets Celia on midsummer night (*Murphy*, 14–15)[68] and proposes to her the very next day (*Murphy*, 16).

When going about his daily routines, Murphy, other than meditating in his room, spends time in Hyde Park and organizes his assorted biscuits[69] in 'the Cockpit', a green plot in the park (*Murphy*, 96),[70] where he likes to recline: 'on Maundy Thursday late afternoon, supine on the grass, in the Cockpit in Hyde Park, alone and plunged in a torpor' (*Murphy*, 50). Murphy's little theatre, that faintly echoes the 'cockpit' in *Henry V*,[71] holds the world at large, which he speculates about: 'Murphy fell forward on his face on the grass, beside those biscuits of which it could be said as truly as of the stars, that one differed from another' (*Murphy*, 97). His reverie, however, is interrupted by the arrival of Rosi Dew asking him to look after her dog while she tries to feed the sheep. Captivated by what he calls her 'argonautic' endeavour (*Murphy*, 100), Murphy's world of the mind clashes with the real world when he finds out that in the meantime Mrs Dew's dog Nelly has eaten all his biscuits.

For Murphy, the world elsewhere is presented by astrology as a mechanistic system that is outside individual consciousness and governed by the laws of a *deus absconditus*, and he initially places his faith in the determinism suggested by this cosmic design in which the planets follow their predestined courses.[72] It is part of the novel's irony that a number of quotations and allusions to the stars are taken from *Romeo and Juliet*. Murphy abides by the horoscopic wisdom of the treatise 'Thema Coeli' that takes its fatalistic motto 'I defy you, stars' (*RJ* 5.1.24) from one of Romeo's final speeches.[73] Like Romeo, Murphy avoids the sun: 'The sun shone, having no alternative, on the nothing new. Murphy sat out of it, as though he were free' (*Murphy*, 1), and like the multifaceted Mercutio, his planet is Mercury: '"Because mercury," said Murphy, "god of thieves, planet par excellence and mine, has no fixed colour"' (*Murphy*, 31–2).

Murphy's doomed relation to the at least allusively celestial Celia is envisaged in terms of the 'star-crossed-lovers' Romeo and Juliet, who similarly disregard their ill-fated destiny: 'they walked off happily arm-in-arm, leaving the star chart for June lying in the gutter' (*Murphy*, 15). Likewise, his meeting with the shady figure of Ticklepenny, who helps him into the MMM and installs the gas burner that eventually kills Murphy, gains tragic significance in alluding to *Romeo and Juliet*. Ticklepenny mentions a performance of *Romeo and Juliet* at the Gate Theatre in Dublin in 1932, where he recalls meeting Murphy: '"Didn't I have the dishonour once in Dublin," he said. "Can it have been at the Gate?" "Romiet," said Ticklepenny, "and Juleo. 'Take him and cut him out in little stars ...' Wotanope!" Murphy dimly remembered an opportune apothecary' (*Murphy*, 85–6). Whereas Ticklepenny remembers Juliet's line about Romeo, but crosses their names in the cut-and-paste fashion to which he alludes – 'Romiet and Juleo' – , Murphy only vaguely recalls the apothecary, who provides the poison.

In the course of the novel, the outside world increasingly loses its hold on Murphy. Whereas he initially tries to gaze at the stars through the skylight in his garret at the MMM, which is 'ideal for closing against the sun by day and opening by night to the stars' (*Murphy*, 162), in the end, the stars and the system of belief inherent in them fails him – 'He did not see the stars any more' (*Murphy*, 188) – and towards the end of the novel one senses his utter dereliction: 'He raised his face to a starless sky, abandoned' (*Murphy*, 251).

Murphy's doom, like Romeo and Juliet's, is rendered in metaphors of day and night as well as stars, and is foreshadowed by the absence of nightingales. Not only has his sky become a starless void but also his night has grown silent: 'The cackle of a nightingale would have been most welcome, to explode his spirits towards its nightingaleless night. But the season seemed over' (*Murphy*, 240). Even though Shakespeare's tragedy provides recurrent themes and a structure for the plot of *Murphy*, these elements gradually desert Murphy. Their disappearance reveals the tragicomic dimension of the novel, in which Beckett pares away layers of meaning that could serve as possible points of reference. Hence the accident that ends Murphy's life leaves behind 'superfine chaos' (*Murphy*, 253), and the novel ends in a theatrical blackout: 'She closed her eyes. *All out*' (*Murphy*, 282).

Among the many minutely ironical instances in the novel in which Beckett subtly refers to both Joyce and Shakespeare, is its quasi-molecular beginning and end. In the first scene in which Celia and Murphy appear together, she is enthralled by Murphy's birthmark: 'A huge pink naevus on the pinnacle of the right buttock held her spellbound' (*Murphy*, 29). After his death, it is by this very birthmark that Celia is able to identify Murphy's remains: 'Here he had a big birthmark' (*Murphy*, 266).

Unlike Stephen's mole on his right breast, Murphy's mole on his right buttock is not a sign of procreative or genealogical continuation. Even though it marks the last sign of his identity, it, like 'the body, mind and soul of Murphy [that] were freely distributed over the floor of the saloon' (*Murphy*, 275), profanely vanishes. Instead of being both a forward- and backward-pointing emblem of one's heritage, the mole in *Murphy* is part of a cyclical dynamic that is both generative and destructive: '"How beautiful in a way," said the coroner, "birthmark, deathmark, I mean rounding off life somehow, don't you think, full circle ..."' (*Murphy*, 267).

In Beckett's early prose, Shakespeare and particularly *Romeo and Juliet*, *A Midsummer Night's Dream* and *Hamlet* become part of the process of writing and unwriting, of an intertextual dialogue with the past in which the literary work constitutes itself with and against its predecessors. Beckett sometimes compares his writing, which both performs its artistic processes and simultaneously traces them, to the foraging of a mole. In a passage of *Dream of Fair to Middling Women*, he describes Belacqua stargazing 'like Mr Ruskin in the Sistine':

> The night firmament is abstract density of music, symphony without end, illumination without end, yet emptier, more sparsely lit, than the most succinct constellations of genius. Now seen merely, a depthless lining of hemisphere, its crazy stippling of stars, it is the passional movements of the mind charted in light and darkness. The tense passional intelligence, when arithmetic abates, tunnels, skymole, surely and blindly (if we only thought so!) through the interstellar coalsacks of its firmament in genesis, it twists through the stars of its creation in a network of loci that shall never be

co-ordinate. The inviolable criterion of poetry and music, the non-principle of their punctuation, is figured in the demented perforation of the night colander (*Dream*, 16).

The lover of art, the musician and the reader are attracted to the stellar patterns of the firmament, trying to make sense of its boundless interplay of light and darkness. Not unlike Stephen Dedalus' description of Shakespeare's nightly stroll across the Shottery plain, Beckett's Belacqua is confronted with the immateriality and infinity of constellations that in the 'abstract density' of the non-referential music of the spheres provide possibilities for poetry and artistic creation. From early on, Beckett was fascinated by music's non-referentiality, which he explored in reading Schopenhauer and Proust: 'music is the Idea itself, unaware of the world of phenomena, existing ideally outside the universe, apprehended not in Space but in Time only, and consequently untouched by the teleological hypothesis' (*Proust*, 92).[74] For Belacqua, it is not the clear-cut image of a constellation such as Cassiopeia that figures as an objective correlative to the poet's identity, but rather the 'non-principle' of the uncontrolled, arbitrary and 'demented perforation' of the night sky that art needs to approach. Beckett's artist stresses the necessity of non-referentiality, of non-principles, blindness and working in the dark, aware of the impossibility of finding neat patterns of significance. The passage not only recalls Stephen Dedalus' self-assertion when facing a vast literary heritage but also alludes to the productive impossibility of capturing a reliable referent.

Stargazing and wishing to apprehend the inaudible music of the spheres is at the centre of the first scene in Act V of *The Merchant of Venice*, when Lorenzo elaborates on the inaudible, airy and immaterial music of the angelic spheres. Alongside Belacqua's more domestic imagery of the 'interstellar coalsacks' and the 'night colander', Lorenzo describes the night sky in more exalted terms:

> Look how the floor of heaven
> Is thick inlaid with patens of bright gold
> There's not the smallest orb which thou behold'st
> But in his motion like an angel sings,
> Still choiring to the young-eyed cherubins.
> Such harmony is in immortal souls,
> But whilst this muddy vesture of decay
> Doth grossly close it in, we cannot hear it. (*MV* 5.1.58–65)

The nightly splendour that is merely visible to human eyes is infinitely richer in its audible qualities. The motion of the 'smallest orbs' carries angelic song, which like the harmony of immortal souls remains inaudible to human ears.[75] The scene explores the dialectics of materiality and the immaterial, when Lorenzo, in keeping with musical theory of the sixteenth century, refers to the musico-mathematical perfection of the universe and implies that the world is a musical creation.[76] He, however, contrasts the Platonic idea of the immateriality of the soul with the fragile and mortal materiality of the body: 'this muddy vesture of decay', as Lorenzo explains to Jessica, holds the soul captive and prevents it from hearing the music of the spheres.

For Lorenzo and Jessica, as for Belacqua, the sound resonating from universal harmonies lacks a precise referent. Beckett's 'skymole', by contrast, tunnels through the sky as if it were excavating geological matter. The non-Platonic 'passional intelligence' of the skymole artist tunnels through the darkness ('the interstellar coalsacks')[77] of the sky as the mole tunnels its way through the earth. As a 'skymole' he is also at home in the heavenly spheres and creates new stellar constellations in an act of 'genesis', and finds new combinations between the stars that do not follow a preordained, intelligent design. Poetry and music, as Beckett insists, are founded on this non-principle of creation. Instead, the 'passional movements of the mind' create new patterns in a textual universe. Its continuous permutations and combinations are reminiscent of the poet as 'freely ranging onely within the Zodiack of his own wit' as Sir Philip Sidney describes artistic freedom in the *Apology for Poetry*.[78]

To Beckett and his character Belacqua, the mole is not only a metaphor for one's vertical heritage and its ever-changing potential, but it also describes a literal experience denoting the performative activity of the writer himself in digging through textual matter and carving out passages for himself. Analogous to another creature living in tunnels underground, he describes himself as the 'insistent, invisible rat, fidgeting behind the astral incoherence of the art surface' (*Dream*, 17) and, in doing so, refers to Hamlet who mistakes Polonius, hiding behind the arras (the art surface), for Claudius and exclaims: 'How now, a rat? Dead for a ducat, dead' (*Ham* 3.4.24). In Beckett's works, most prominently in *How It Is*, there is no shortage of rats and the narrator ironically states: 'every rat has its heyday I say it as I hear it' (*HII*, 6), alluding to Hamlet's proverbial expression of hope before the end: 'the cat will mew, and dog will have his day' (*Ham* 5.1.259).

In *Company* he calls the writer a 'crawling creator' (*Company*, 52), and in an interview with Charles Juliet, he refers to himself as an author as 'a mole in a molehill',[79] a creature burrowing in the dark that carves out new passages and works through layers of age-old matter. Like an archaeologist or a sculptor, he both finds and unearths hitherto unseen treasures and also clears away matter – sculpting his own work by ridding it of superfluous and encumbering stuff. Frederik Smith and many others have noted the 'Genesis situation in which something – in this case a literary work – is being shaped out of the mud of one's own experience'.[80] As a token of experience, the mud also denotes language. Beckett recurrently uses the image of 'mud in the mouth'[81], which metaphorically also refers to the malleability, the at once creative and destructive potential of language, literary traditions, precursors and intertexts.

Genesis, creation and birth are all associated with the mud, but are at the same time paired with death, unmaking and ending: *How It Is* literalizes the narrator's experience of digging through the mud, which is both his life element, the 'warmth of primeval mud' (*HII*, 11), and also that which threatens to bury him alive. Processes of composition and creation are at the same time a work in progress and a 'work in regress', a retracing of one's steps and a moving backward in the creative process.[82] *How It Is* is not a linear or teleological view of genealogy, but a cyclical dialogue of the voice with itself, moving forward and backward at the same time, speaking and listening to the murmurings in the mud (*HII*, 1).[83] The creative word of the maker fuses with the matter of creation.

Whereas bodily and textual matter become interwoven with the artist's image in Stephen Dedalus' reflections on Shakespeare, Beckett's narrator in *How It Is* rather traces the progression and regression of writing and conflates body, matter and text.[84] Matter, the ubiquitous mud, however, becomes ambivalent, and in Beckett, it is both creative and destructive. In *Happy Days*, Winnie is slowly buried in a mound of sand and addresses the earth as 'the old extinguisher' (*CDW*, 153). More generally, graves and graveyards abound from Beckett's early prose onwards.

In the short story 'Echo's Bones', as Mark Nixon observes, the main literary dialogue is with Shakespeare's *Hamlet*, which haunts 'Echo's Bones',[85] where both Lord Gall of Wormwood in his grotesque armour and the protagonist Belacqua, recently risen from his grave, appear as caricatures of old Hamlet's ghost: 'clad in amaranth caoutchouc cap-à-pie, a cloak of gutta percha streaming back from the barrel of his bust' (*EB*, 15).

Whereas 'Echo's Bones' parodically alludes to *Hamlet*, *How It Is* approaches the ambivalence of matter and largely dispenses with puns and direct quotations. Yet analogous to *Hamlet*, it foregrounds the body and matter that denote both creation and fall. Gertrude chides Hamlet not to forever seek 'for [his] noble father in the dust' (*Ham* 1.2.71), and yet dust is the substance from which Adam in Genesis 1:4 was fashioned in a creative act of self-repetition, *adamah*, the Hebrew word for clay. Hamlet puns on the ambivalence of creation when he refers to man as that clayey 'piece of work' (*Ham* 2.2.286) and a 'quintessence of dust' (*Ham* 2.2.290).[86] To Ophelia the 'muddy death' (*Ham* 4.7.183) that Gertrude laments becomes the fate that meets her in the river and in her grave. The gravedigger exemplifies the cycle of creation and death when he says that he became a gravedigger on 'the very day that young Hamlet was born' (*Ham* 5.1.123–4).

The earth, mud and matter to Beckett become the ground through which and against which he shapes his works. During the war, Beckett was no stranger to the many shapes of 'muddy death'. On 19 August 1945, Beckett writes to Thomas McGreevy from St. Lô:

> St. Lô is just a heap of rubble, la Capitale des Ruines as they call it in France. Of 2600 buildings 2000 completely wiped out, 400 badly damaged and 200 'only' slightly. It all happened in the night of the 5th to the 6th June. It has been raining hard the last few days, and the place is a sea of mud.[87]

In the middle of the deadly sea of mud that surrounded the hospital in which Beckett worked, where the boundary of land and water had become indistinct, life and history had almost become extinguished. In 'The Capital of the Ruins', written for Radio Éireann in June 1946, he concludes: 'I mean the possibility that some of those who were in Saint-Lô will come home realising that they got at least as good as they gave, that they got indeed what they could hardly give, a vision and sense of a time-honoured conception of humanity in ruins' (*CSP*, 278).

Beckett's well-known phrase of a 'humanity in ruins' does not necessarily call for a humanist reading of his relation to authors such as Shakespeare as a safe and salutary ground from which to start and to which to return. His writerly, mole-cular movements of subtraction and expansion, his relentless digging through the mud and slowly making progress rather takes its starting point from this vision of humanity in ruins. From there he engages with the work of his predecessors without pathos and remains deeply sceptical of the human ability to have ever learnt from the catastrophes of the past. Yet the ruins, both spatial and human, that his works explore infuse them neither with debilitating fear nor with euphoric haste. Beckett's excavations of humanity and humanism are guided by a profound knowledge about the inevitable, and yet they are at the same time inspired by a sense of freedom.

Waiting for Godot presents this stance towards predecessors such as Shakespeare in a manner that is both reflective and performative. When Vladimir asks 'What are we doing here, *that* is the question?' (*CDW*, 74), he conceives of their predicament by reiterating Hamlet's question about being and non-being and yet rephrases it with regard to theatrical action, which in their case is the non-action of waiting. Rather than Hamlet's neo-Stoic contemplation of being, Vladimir and Estragon emphasize doing and resolve the question in a dramatical paradox through their performance of non-action. Their non-action, or inaction, on the other hand, makes them accomplices of Hamlet, who also tries to resolve the question of who murdered his father dramatically, by putting on an antic disposition and by staging 'The Mousetrap'. Unlike Hamlet, Vladimir and Estragon become the true Stoics through their persistence in spite of themselves, which makes them heroes of endurance for whom the mere act of getting up is a 'Simple question of will-power' (*CDW*, 78).

Notes

1 Enoch Brater, 'The *Company* Beckett Keeps: The Shape of Memory and One Fabulist's Decay of Lying' in Morris Beja, S.E. Gontarski and Pierre Astier (eds.), *Samuel Beckett. Humanistic Perspectives* (Columbus: Ohio State University Press, 1983), 157–71, 157.
2 Ibid.
3 C.J. Ackerley, *Demented Particulars: The Annotated Murphy* (Edinburgh University Press [Journal of Beckett Studies Book], 2010 [2004]), 15; Frederik N. Smith, *Beckett's Eighteenth Century* (Palgrave: Macmillan, 2002); Anthony Uhlmann (ed.), *Samuel Beckett in Context* (Cambridge University Press, 2013); Dirk van Hulle and Mark Nixon, *Samuel Beckett's Library* (Cambridge University Press, 2013); S.E. Gontarski (ed.), *The Edinburgh Companion to Samuel Beckett and the Arts* (Edinburgh University Press, 2014).
4 Beckett describes the way in which his work is different, almost 'diametrically opposed' to Joyce's: 'I take away all the accidentals because I want to come down to the bedrock of the essentials.' James Knowlson, *Damned to Fame. The Life of Samuel Beckett* (London: Bloomsbury, 1997), 47.
5 Knowlson, *Damned to Fame*; Erika Tophoven, *Becketts Berlin* (Berlin: Nicolai, 2005); Mark Nixon, *Beckett's German Diaries 1936–1937* (London: Continuum, 2011).
6 Peter J. Murphy, *Beckett's Dedalus: Dialogic Encounters with Joyce in Beckett's Fiction* (University of Toronto Press, 2009). Murphy examines Beckett's early fiction in relation to Joyce's aesthetics and demonstrates the vital role it played in the formation of Beckett's own theories. Murphy takes *Portrait* to be the most influential text, references to which occur, among others, in 'Assumption' and *Dream of Fair to Middling Women*.

7 Sam Slote, 'The Joyce Circle' in Anthony Uhlmann (ed.), *Samuel Beckett in Context* (Cambridge University Press, 2013), 150–9, 152–3.
8 Peggy Guggenheim, *Out of this Century: Confessions of an Art Addict* (London: Deutsch, 2005), 199.
9 H. Porter Abbott argues against a narrative of this kind. Cf. H. Porter Abbott, *Beckett Writing Beckett: The Author in the Autograph* (Ithaca, London: Cornell University Press, 1996), 19.
10 Ackerley, *Demented Particulars*, 16; Ruben Rabinovitz, *The Development of Samuel Beckett's Fiction* (Urbana, Chicago: University of Illinois Press, 1984), 3.
11 Barbara Reich Gluck, *Joyce and Beckett* (Lewisburg, London: Bucknell University Press/Associated University Presses, 1979), 72.
12 Ibid., 20.
13 Claudia Olk, '"A Matter of Fundamental Sounds"– The Music of Beckett's *Endgame*', *Poetica* 43 (2011), 391–411. Cf. also Daniel Albright, *Beckett and Aesthetics* (Cambridge University Press, 2003).
14 Beckett here refers to the words of old Hamlet's ghost when he imparts the story of his murder to his son: 'I find thee apt/And duller shouldst thou be than the fat weed/That rots itself in ease on Lethe wharf,/Wouldst thou not stir in this' (*Ham* 1.5.31–4). See also Thomas McGreevy, 'A Note on Work in Progress', *transition*, 12 (September 1928), 216–19, 217: 'the author of *Ulysses* will have justified himself again as a prose writer who combines a well-nigh flawless sense of the significance of words with a power to construct on a scale scarcely equalled in English literature since the Renaissance, not even by the author of *Paradise Lost*.'
15 Eugène Jolas, 'The Revolution of Language and James Joyce', *transition*, 11 (Febuary 1928), 109–16, 113.
16 Ibid., 110.
17 *Encyclopedia Britannica*: britannica.com. Adorno uses the term 'molecule' to describe Beckett's construction of meaninglessness in language: 'Solche Konstruktion von Sinnlosigkeit hält auch nicht inne vor den sprachlichen Molekülen'. Theodor Adorno, *Versuch, das Endspiel zu Verstehen*, 169.
18 Claudia Olk, '"Ah the soap": Objekt und Materie im *Ulysses*', *Poetica*, 40 (2008), 169–88.
19 Peter Hall, *Exposed by the Mask: Form and Language in Drama* (London: Oberon Books, 2010), 129.
20 Laura Pelaschiar, 'Introduction' in Laura Pelaschiar (ed.), *Joyce/Shakespeare* (Syracuse University Press, 2015), viii.
21 Knowlson, *Damned to Fame*, 47–51. 'At Trinity, Beckett's passion for words, literature and art developed under the influence of his Professor of French, Thomas Rudmose-Brown, who passed on his deep love of and witty irreverence of the texts he taught [...] This integration of past and present, long before Beckett had heard of Eliot's "Traditon and the Individual Talent", would henceforth characterize his way of reading.' Ackerley, *Demented Particulars*, 15.

22 Richard Halpern, *Shakespeare among the Moderns* (Ithaca, London: Cornell University Press, 1997), 14.
23 Daniela Caselli, *Beckett's Dantes: Intertextuality in the Fiction and Criticism* (Manchester, New York: Manchester University Press, 2005).
24 Cf. *U*, 156: 'Mother's deathbed. Candle. The sheeted mirror. Who brought me into this world lies there, bronzelidded, under few cheap flowers. *Liliata rutilantium.*'
25 James Joyce, *The Letters of James Joyce*, ed. by Stuart Gilbert (London: Faber and Faber, 1957) vol. I, 101.
26 T.S. Eliot, 'Tradition and the Individual Talent' in Frank Kermode (ed. and intr.), *Selected Prose of T.S. Eliot* (London: Faber and Faber, 1975), 37–45, 38–9.
27 In 1912 Joyce had delivered twelve lectures on *Hamlet*, from which, according to John McCourt, Stephen Dedalus's Hamlet theory was derived. John McCourt, 'Joyce's Shakespeare: A View from Trieste' in Pelaschiar (ed.), *Joyce/Shakespeare*, 72–88, 72.
28 'Elizabethan London lay as far from Stratford as corrupt Paris lies from virgin Dublin' (*U*, 154).
29 David Spurr, *Joyce and the Scene of Modernity* (Gainesville: University Press of Florida, 2002), 84–5.
30 Johann Gottfried Herder, *Von deutscher Art und Kunst. Einige Fliegende Blätter* (Hamburg: Bode, 1773), 92; Johann Gottfried Herder, 'Shakespear' in Hansjürgen Blinn (ed.), *Shakespeare-Rezeption: Die Diskussion um Shakespeare in Deutschland I: Ausgewählte Texte von 1741–1788* (Berlin: Erich Schmidt, 1982), 104–19.
31 Andreas Höfele, *No Hamlets: German Shakespeare from Nietzsche to Carl Schmitt* (Oxford University Press, 2016); Roger Paulin, *The Critical Reception of Shakespeare in Germany 1682–1914: Native Literature and Foreign Genius* (Hildesheim: Olms, 2003). Claudia Olk, '*Prinz Friedrich von Homburg* – Kleists Märkischer *Hamlet*', *Kleist Jahrbuch*, (2017), 23–37.
32 Vike Martina Plock, 'Made in Germany: Why Goethe's Hamlet Mattered to Joyce' in Pelaschiar (ed.), *Joyce/Shakespeare*, 89–106. Plock argues that in 'Scylla and Charybdis', Joyce sought to 'challenge, surpass, and negate Goethe's Hamlet interpretation' in *Wilhelm Meister* and that 'Goethe becomes the true opponent in Joyce's literary sparring match,' 92.
33 Johann Wolfgang Goethe, *Sämtliche Werke*, ed. by Hans-Jürgen Schings, vol. V [*Wilhelm Meisters Lehrjahre*], (Munich: Hanser, 2006), 253.
34 Spurr, *Joyce and the Scene of Modernity*, 80.
35 Margreta De Grazia, *Hamlet without Hamlet* (Cambridge University Press, 2008), 29: 'There is, it has to be said, something catachrestic about the use of the old mole's tunnelling as a figure for the trajectory of world history and the action of Prince Hamlet.'
36 Martin Harries, *Scare Quotes from Shakespeare: Marx, Keynes, and the Language of Reenchantment* (Stanford University Press, 2000), 82.

37 Critics such as Barbara Reich Gluck attribute a Trinitarian structure to *Ulysses* as a whole: '[P]art 1 deals with the son, part 2 with the father, and part 3 is the word made flesh. Molly Bloom.' Gluck, *Joyce and Beckett. Friendship and Fiction*, 157.
38 In Robert Greene's *Pandosto*, one of Shakespeare's sources of *The Winter's Tale*, the father indeed falls in love with the daughter.
39 *Ulysses* alludes to the Creed and pinpoints some of its peculiarities: 'there these nineteen hundred years sitteth on the right hand of His Own Self but yet shall come in the latter day to doom the quick and dead when all the quick shall be dead already' (*U*, 189).
40 The Rutland-Theory is further alluded to when Karl Bleitreu, a German poet, is mentioned. In his work: *The Solution of the Shakespeare Question* (1907) Bleibtreu claims that the fifth earl of Rutland, Roger Manners had written Shakespeare's plays.
41 The passage also recalls Hamlet's ironical claim that he feeds on air 'the chameleon's dish' (*Ham* 3.2.83).
42 Cf. Murphy: 'the science that had got over Jacob and Esau' Ackerley, *Demented Particulars*, 56. Cf. 'sheep and goats': The Goat, Capricorn, tenth sign of the zodiac, ruled by Saturn. Ackerley, *Demented Particulars*, 62.
43 Stanley Wells, 'My Name is Will: Shakespeare's Sonnets and Autobiography', *Shakespeare Survey*, 68 (2015), 99–108.
44 Helen Vendler, *The Art of Shakespeare's Sonnets* (Cambridge, MA, London: Harvard University Press, 1997), 574. Cf. also Sonnets 136 and 143.
45 Cf. also the alliterative use of m's and w's in: 'Richard, a whoreson crookback, misbegotten, makes love to a widowed Ann (what's in a name?), woos and wins her, a whoreson merry widow' (*U*, 203).
46 For further references to characters named William in Shakespeare's plays cf. Gifford and Seidman, 244–5.
47 Tycho Brahe, *De Nova Stella* (1573).
48 *Holinshed's Chronicles of England, Scotland, and Ireland* (London: J. Johnson et al, 1807–1808), Vol. 4, 321: 'The eighteenth of Nouember in the morning was seene a star northward verie bright and cleere, in the constellation of Cassiopeia, at the backe of hir chaire, which with three cheefe fixed stars of the said constellation made a geometricall figure losengwise, and of the learned men called Rhombus. This starre in bignes and at the first appeering seemed bigger than Iupiter, and not much lesse than Venus when she seemeth greatest. ... (by the skill and consent of the best and most expert mathematicians, which obserued the state, propertie, and other circumstances belonging to the same starre) it was found to haue beene in place celestiall far aboue the moone, otherwise than euer anie comet hath beene seene, or naturallie can appeere. Therefore it is supposed that the signification therof is directed purposelie and speciallie to some matter not naturall, but celestiall, or rather super-celestiall, so strange, as from the beginning of the world neuer was the like.' Cf. also A. Hall, 'Tycho Brahe's New Star', *Science* 1, 23 (1880), 274–5.

49 Johann Wolfgang von Goethe, 'Zwischen beiden Welten', *WA* I, 3, 45.
50 Eckhard Lobsien, *Der Alltag des Ulysses. Die Vermittlung von ästhetischer und lebensweltlicher Erfahrung* (Stuttgart: J.B. Metzler, 1978).
51 MERKUR: 'Deinem Vater Zeus das bringen?/Deiner Mutter?'
52 Johann Wolfgang Goethe, *Prometheus*, HA 4, 176.
53 Beckett tried to encourage Thomas McGreevy to join him on his trip to Germany: 'I know you don't want Germania, unless maybe Weimar' (*Letters, I*, 100, 20.12.1931); Cf. also: 'I still hope to have a look at Weimar, Naumburg & Leipzig on the way to Dresden' (*Letters, I*, 432, 18.01.1937); 'I was in Weimar for the week-end, in a pub in the Frauenplan.' (*Letters, I*, 438, 25.01.37).
54 Dirk van Hulle and Mark Nixon, *Samuel Beckett's Library*, 87–90.
55 Samuel Beckett, 'Commentaries: Denis Devlin', *transition*, 27 (April–May 1938), 289–94. 290.
56 Richard Begam, *Samuel Beckett and the End of Modernity* (Stanford University Press, 1996), 33: 'in Vico and Joyce the individual and the universal are treated as one: Homer, the author of the Iliad and the Odyssey, and Homer the archetype of all poets are identical.'
57 Chris J. Ackerley and S.E. Gontarski (eds.), *The Grove Companion to Samuel Beckett* (New York: Grove, 2004), 593.
58 Gilles Deleuze, *Essays Critical and Clinical*, transl. by Daniel W. Smith and Michael A. Greco (London, New York: Verso, 1998), 1.
59 S.E. Gontarski, 'Introduction', *The Edinburgh Companion to Samuel Beckett and the Arts* (Edinburgh University Press, 2014), 10.
60 S.E. Gontarski, *The Intent of Undoing in Samuel Beckett's Dramatic Texts* (Bloomington: University of Indiana Press, 1985), xiii.
61 Abbott, *Beckett Writing Beckett*, 20–2.
62 Dirk van Hulle, 'Beckett's Principle of Reversibility: Chiasmus and the "Shape of Ideas"', *Samuel Beckett Today/Aujourd'hui*, 21 (New York, Amsterdam: Rodopi, 2009), 179–92, 188.
63 Ibid., 19.
64 James Knowlson and John Pilling, *Frescoes of the Skull. The Later Prose and Drama of Samuel Beckett* (London: John Calder, 1979), 119.
65 Cf. C.J. Ackerley and S.E. Gontarski (eds.), *The Grove Companion to Samuel Beckett* (New York: Grove, 2004), 332. 'E' is M rotated 90 degrees as in *Endgame*, 'The Expelled', 'The End'.
66 Lois Oppenheim notes Beckett's deliberate dismantling of previously created material. Cf.: 'The Uncanny in Beckett' in Colleen Jaurretche (eds.), *Beckett, Joyce and the Art of the Negative* (Amsterdam, New York: Rodopi [*European Joyce Studies* 16], 2005), 125–40, 130.
67 Cf. Ackerley, *Demented Particulars*, 156: '*Werther* (1774) which Beckett had been reading: "Ich kehre in mich selbst zurück und finde eine Welte!"'.
68 Cf. Ackerley, *Demented Particulars* (46) for a further reference to *MND* in *Malone Dies* (179): 'Shakespeare's night of love and the feast of St. John the Baptist, which Malone hopes to survive.'

69 'He took the biscuits carefully out of the packet and laid them face upward on the grass' (*Murphy*, 96).
70 *Demented Particulars*, 74: 'a natural amphitheater'.
71 'Can this cockpit hold the vasty fields of France?' (*HV*, Prol); 'Skinner's was the cockpit of the M.M.M. and here the battle raged most fiercely' (*Murphy*, 165).
72 Begam, *Samuel Beckett and the End of Modernity*, 105.
73 Rabinovitz, *The Development of Samuel Beckett's Fiction*, 218–19.
74 Claudia Olk, '"A Matter of Fundamental Sounds" – The Music of Beckett's *Endgame*', *Poetica*, 43 (2011), 391–411.
75 Murphy, the student of Platonic-Pythagorian thought refers to 'the brightness of the firmament', 'to invest his own with a little of what Neary, at that time a Pythagorean, called the Apmonia' (*Murphy*, 17). 'Apmonia' is derived from the Greek spelling of Harmonia αρμονια. On Beckett reading Greek philosophy cf. *Demented Particulars*, 33. In Augustine's *Confessions* (13.15, 402–5), the firmament is God's book, stretched over us like a skin, as in *Dream* (26). Also in *Dream* (16) there is a scintillating rhapsody to the night firmament. *Demented Particulars*, 47.
76 Claudia Olk, 'The Musicality of *The Merchant of Venice*' in Christina Wald (ed.), *Medieval Shakespeare* (London, New York: Routledge, 2012), 386–97.
77 Cf. Murphy: 'that most dismal patch of night sky, the galactic coal-sack, which would naturally look like a dirty night to any observer in Murphy's condition' (*Murphy*, 188).
78 Sir Philip Sidney, 'An Apology for Poetry' in G. Gregory Smith (ed.) *Elizabethan Critical Essays* I (Oxford University Press, 1971), 148–207, 156.
79 Charles Juliet, *Conversations with Samuel Beckett and Bram van Velde*, transl. by Tracy Cooke and Axel Nesme (London: Dalkey, 2009).
80 Frederik N. Smith, 'Fiction as Composing Process: *How It Is*' in Morris Beja, S.E. Gontarski and Pierre Astier (eds.), *Samuel Beckett: Humanistic Perspectives*, 107–21. 108.
81 Abbott, *Beckett Writing Beckett*, 103.
82 When sending John Calder a piece of *How It Is* in English he referred to the enclosed material as a 'work in regress' (Letter 17 March 1960) HRC University of Texas at Austin. Cf. Smith, 'Fiction as Composing Process', 118: 'That is how it was. Quite literally, Beckett's progression forward into this new novel was turning out to be a regression backward into the composing proc
83 'I hear them murmur in the mud' (*HII*, 1).
84 Édouard Magessa O'Reilly notes that earlier versions of *How It Is* contained more explicit references to moles, which interfered with Beckett's gardening in Ussy. 'Preface', *How It Is*, vii–viii. On 4 February 1959 Beckett writes to Ethna Maccarthy-Leventhal: 'Losing battle with the moles, la pelouse n'est plus qu'une plaie'. *Letters, III*, 197. Cf. also Knowlson, *Damned to Fame*, 460–1.

85 Mark Nixon (ed.), 'Introduction', *Echo's Bones* (New York: Grove, 2014), xix. Cf. also Chapter 3 of this study.
86 The phrase is part of the Ash Wednesday liturgy: 'dust thou art and to dust thou shalt return'.
87 *Letters*, II, 18. Hugh Kenner, *Flaubert, Joyce and Beckett: The Stoic Comedians* (London: W.H. Allen, 1964).

CHAPTER 3

'Some remains': Beckettian and Shakespearean Echoes

> *Not the intense moment*
> *Isolated, with no before and after,*
> *But a lifetime burning in every moment*
> *And not the lifetime of one man only*
> *But of old stones that cannot be deciphered.*
>
> T.S. Eliot, 'East Coker', *Four Quartets*[1]

Beckett's works resonate with the many contexts they draw on and establish. Echoes from his own works, most perceptibly in his self-translations, as well as from numerous literary, musical and philosophical voices resound in his texts. In these interanimating correspondences, the notion of the echo becomes both a principle of composition and an immanent figuration. Like the old stones in Eliot's poem, from early writings like *Echo's Bones* onwards, works that fashion themselves as material remnants in which immaterial voices are residually present, Beckett explores the relation between voice and textual being.[2]

Krapp's Last Tape is built around the incongruence of recognition and variation when the recorded voice of young Krapp is revived by old Krapp's acts of *memoire volontaire*, contrasted and paralleled to his present speech. Beckett's Watt senses a harmony between the outside world and his inner being 'the earth trodden the earth treading, and all sound his echo' (*Watt*, 32). His late piece *Company* consists of a speaker's interchange with the 'voice that comes to one in the dark' and it not only recapitulates scenes of his lifetime, but includes parts of earlier works as main constituents, companions, as it were, of his textual life. Beckett considered plays such as *Endgame* to be 'full of Echoes, answering one another',[3] and yet, as Stephen Connor observes, even though the many verbal echoes and repetitions in the play convey a sense of closure and unity, many of its features refuse to endorse such unity, completion and 'the consummation of the ending that its form and title suggest'.[4]

An echo is not merely an imitation or repetition. It can be traced back to a source, however indeterminate it may be. The echo's sound, however, is different from its source and produces variants of it. In literature and drama, the echo is not just synonymous with intertextuality. More than terms such as adaptation, quotation or association, the echo becomes a heuristic means that conceptualizes and metaphorically describes processes of transformation and modification when texts engage with the works of contemporaries and predecessors. The echo becomes a representative practice that reflects on its own operations.

Beckett named both his early short story (1933)[5] and poems *Echo's Bones* after the nymph Echo in Ovid's *Metamorphoses*, who after she was rejected by her beloved Narcissus pined away in a cave where her bones were turned into stone, leaving only her voice to resonate the endings of phrases that reach her. An echo creates a divided presence. It is not an exact repetition, a recurrence of the same, but rather a critique of the idea of mere repetition or sameness. In an echo the sound waves that are reflected back to the listener from some distant surface suggest familiarity and closeness, yet they harbour the notion of difference and deferral. The reflection is never complete or mimetically congruent with the origin. An echo creates secondary presences that produce semblances and yet are marked by difference. In an echo, an original source undergoes changes as its content and quality acquire different nuances. Faint traces can be foregrounded and amplified through iteration, louder noises, or more straightforward references can be subdued and dispersed.

Echoes include and exhibit nuances of meaning that they have gained on their travels through literary history. In her essay 'Craftsmanship', Virginia Woolf writes: 'Words, English words, are full of echoes, of memories, of associations – naturally. They have been out and about, on people's lips, in their houses, in the streets, in the fields, for so many centuries.'[6] Fragments of texts return like the 'dead voices' (*CDW*, 58) that Vladimir and Estragon contemplate in *Waiting for Godot*, and they become alive in the voices and the dialogue and the performance on stage that highlight or magnify an intertextual connection or let it fade and disappear. Beckett's works play with these echoing effects when they engage with texts of antecedents like Dante's *La Divina Commedia*, Shakespeare's plays and poetry or the Bible. They integrate fragments and variants of other works, including his own, to create multiple relations through resemblance and difference. Beckett's language and the composition of his works produce this kind of musical resonance that imitates the acoustical phenomenon. In this process, the text itself as well as the sources with which it interacts are transformed and constitute an echoing chamber that enables new combinations through resonance.

Echo and Narcissus

The story of Echo and Narcissus from Ovid's *Metamorphoses* unites the conceptual processes of transformation and reflection with a cyclical dynamic of death, metamorphosis and the afterlife. It describes an etiological model, an original scene, as it were, that presents a paradigm of self-differentiation, and at the same time stages a doubling of the self into material and immaterial component parts. Echo's voice becomes an invisible presence that constitutes itself by insistently foregrounding its material remains, bones and stones, as forms of visible absence. An echo creates a presence that is established and obliterated at the same time.

Echo's Bones becomes a metaphor for the text as an aesthetic object that emerges out of the poetic interaction with its predecessors, and Ovid's metamorphosis provides an example for this interaction. Echo and Narcissus present two antithetical impulses: they perform the withdrawal into the self to the point of disappearance and the need to seek an other that is driven by the futile desire to reach unity with it. It describes a dilemma of writing when relating to the past: the kind of literature that, like Echo, exclusively desires an other – the past, or tradition – and tries to imitate it, disappears, loses itself and remains equally fated to be the kind of literature that in a narcissistic gesture of self-reflection imitates only itself.

John Hollander in *The Figure of Echo* (1981) and Jonathan Goldberg in *Voice Terminal Echo* (1986) unfold the mythography of Echo and discuss its significance for English literature. This chapter follows Hollander, who distinguishes between echo and resonance in acoustic theory, but uses the terms echo, reverberation and resonance figuratively and often synonymously. It is also indebted to Goldberg in that it traces reconfigurations of the Ovidian myth, but instead of presenting exemplary readings from the English Renaissance, I focus on intersections between modern and early modern drama.[7]

Shakespeare's texts assume a variable and metamorphic character in Beckett's œuvre, but Beckett's transformative use of Shakespeare leads out of this dilemma between imitation and self-reference. His works reflect back on their sources and transform the texts with which they engage in a kind of inverse metamorphosis. Without being mere reverberations, they foreground traces and residues in metonymic correlations between voice, language and the materiality of the performance.

Nicolas Poussin, Echo et Narcisse (c. 1630–1637), Paris, Musée du Louvre

Matter and materiality, bones and stones, in Beckett's works, very often become a metonymy for the text. Chris Ackerley describes the poems in *Echo's Bones* as 'calcified and petrified remnants of what once was, a voice that is no more'.[8] Stones and bones materialize the opacity of a text and turn it into a kind of petrified lacuna. As Julie Bates has shown, stones fascinated Beckett and appear throughout his œuvre.[9] Beckett was fond of collecting stones.[10] His characters keep them in their pockets, or, like Molloy, have taken on the habit of sucking stones like sweets. They thus demonstrate the resistance of textual materiality and ironically comment on the incessant and futile attempts of criticism to dissolve it: 'Suck is not suck that alters,'[11] writes Beckett in 'Sanies II', the second of the thirteen poems titled *Echo's Bones* in a pastiche on Shakespeare's Sonnet 116 'Let me not to the marriage of true minds admit impediments.'

The very moment in which the metamorphosis takes place seems to be statically arrested in Nicolas Poussin's painting 'Echo and Narcissus' (1629–30) in the Louvre that Beckett loved very much.[12] It is remarkable that Poussin ostentatiously avoids picturing the moment that is most popular in paintings such as Caravaggio's oil painting of Narcissus, who falls in love with his reflection on the water's surface the very moment he looks at it. Poussin's painting, by contrast, both captures the moment of metamorphosis and presents it in a retrospective way. In the background of the painting, Echo, who is languidly leaning on a stone, almost starts to transform herself into it. The body of the sleeping Narcissus in the foreground with the eponymous flower already growing out of his hair, resembles a marble statue and seems to slip away out of the painting, betrayed by the transient reflection. What is and what is to come, life and death and the transformations between them are presented simultaneously. Echo metamorphoses into stone in the background at the same time as her beloved, who appears as a stony sculpture, is about to turn into the flower in the foreground, and Eros, who is standing between both of them, looks in the direction of the viewer and stoutly holds the torch of a love that will never be fulfilled.

Poussin's painting shows the metamorphosis as it is virtually happening, and it simultaneously comments on painting as an art of transformation and metamorphosis. Jonathan Unglaub in his analysis of pictorial narrative goes back to Alberti, according to whom it was Narcissus who discovered painting, and he argues that 'Poussin transfers the Narcissistic fascination exclusively to the beholder.'[13] The lure of the painting's surface, analogous to the mirror-like surface of the stream, instigates the spectator's desire. Yet the image also interprets its function for the viewer when, in 'Echo and Narcissus', it presents two ways in which Cupid's dart becomes misdirected into selfless and self-consuming desire that both prove equally fateful. Commenting on the artistic transformation of its mythological subject matter, the metamorphosis of Echo and Narcissus, the painting becomes a self-performing metaphor.

This double role of the echo that is both a presentation and a reflection of what it presents, is important for Beckett's manner of engaging with Shakespeare. In Beckett's œuvre, the metamorphosis of Echo and Narcissus reflects on ways of transforming the past. At the same time, it expands the resonance of the metamorphosis and enters into a diachronic dialogue that reaches beyond modernism and evokes an older and specifically early modern paradigm of relating to antiquity, in which Ovid's *Metamorphoses* held a paradigmatic status as an example of *imitatio veterum*, a paradigm that served as a major reference point for Shakespeare.[14]

In both its theme and in its compositional structure, the metamorphosis of Echo and Narcissus describes the interplay of presences and absences. As a metaphor for processes of textual transformation, the metamorphosis presents the text not as a static entity but as a changeable being that interacts with the past in ways both destructive and regenerative. This process also describes a text's inherent ability to transform into its opposite. Materiality can dissolve into immaterial, imaginary presences, and latent, immaterial voices acquire a material presence on stage. In Beckett's narratives and plays, fragments, voices, the material body and objects on stage undergo this transformative process that exemplifies and produces an inherently generative structure of text and theatre.

Echo's Bones

Beckett had initially written his short story 'Echo's Bones' to be included in the collection *More Pricks Than Kicks*. However, the piece was excised from the work by Chatto & Windus on the grounds that, as editor Charles Prentice explained: '*It is a nightmare*', it '*would . . . lose the book a great many readers . . . [and] depress sales considerably*'.[15] Beckett, although dismayed by this harsh verdict, proceeded to write a poem of the same name and used the title again for his first collection of poems *Echo's Bones and Other Precipitates* (1935).[16]

The short story was published for the first time only in 2014, but the conceptual dualism of the immaterial 'echo' and its material counterpart 'bones' remained embedded in Beckett's entire œuvre, an œuvre that instead of progressing from one stage of development to another can be seen in spatial terms as an echo chamber in which his own works resonate with each other as well as with those of his many contemporaries and predecessors. The story playfully draws on issues of death, resurrection and the production of offspring by presenting itself as a product of resurrected fragments that combines plot elements from, among others, Dante's *La Divina Commedia* and a number of Shakespeare's plays.

'Echo's Bones' refers to itself as a 'fagpiece' (*EB*, 3), a 'little triptych' (*EB*, 4), and self-consciously creates both a structural analogy to Dante's *La Divina Commedia* and plays on variations of the Holy Trinity. The first part narrates the resurrection of its Dantean protagonist Belacqua Shuah and his brief encounter with the prostitute Miss Zaborovna Privet. The second part is about Belacqua's purgatorial confrontation with the childless giant, Lord Gall of Wormwood,[17] who takes him on an aerial journey that resembles a medieval dream vision and recalls both Dante's *Purgatorio* and Chaucer's *The House of Fame*. Belacqua learns that Lord Gall cannot have children and is about to lose his estate to his wife's lover, the Baron Extravas (German for something extra). Belacqua helps out, becomes a lover of Lady Gall himself, but only adds to the family drama when he fathers a girl. In the last part of the story, the ghostly Belacqua is found sitting on his own headstone in a graveyard and watches the gravedigger Doyle rob his grave.

The story is flamboyantly charged with references to a number of works. According to Beckett: 'The major influences are Grock, Dante, Chaucer, Bernard de Mandeville and Uccello.'[18] Yet, some of its main structural, verbal and thematic echoes are taken from *Hamlet* and *A Midsummer Night's Dream*. In 'Echo's Bones', Beckett conflates tragedy and comedy, and combines elements from fairy tales and dream visions with notions of death, Purgatory, resurrection and the afterlife. Resurrection becomes both a continuous element of the plot and part of Beckett's self-reflexive narrative practice in which he engages with his sources in a way that is indeed procreative and reviving. References to Shakespeare's works are both evoked and dispersed; they emerge and subside and become part of the process in which the text continuously recreates itself.

Having recently resurrected from his death in the story 'Yellow', the protagonist Belacqua, whose 'troubles are over' (*EB*, 3), in 'Echo's Bones' sits on a fence, 'puff[ing] away at his Romeo and Juliet', his Cuban cigar (*EB*, 3). As the reference to the Shakespearean couple immaterializes in smoke, Belacqua meets the very material prostitute, a humble version of Beatrice, and to her announces that he is 'a corpse in torment' (*EB*, 8): 'I am' said Belacqua, 'restored for a time by a lousy fate to the nuts and balls and sparrows of the low stature of animation' (*EB*, 6). Dissatisfied with his karmic disposition, Belacqua combines father, son and ghost, when he poses both as Hamlet, who suffers 'the slings and arrows of outrageous fortune' (*Ham* 3.1.58), and as old Hamlet's ghost, who is '[D]oomed for a certain term to walk the night' (*Ham* 1.5.10) until he has to yield to the 'sulph'rous and tormenting flames' (*Ham* 1.5.3) of Purgatory. He then follows his new mistress like a Faerie in *A Midsummer Night's Dream* 'up hill and down dale, to her lodging' (*MND* 1.5.13).

The hilarious theatricality of the scene is further brought out when the pair becomes associated with Bottom and Titania as well as with Pyramus and Thisbe. Unlike the separated lovers Pyramus and Thisbe in *A Midsummer Night's Dream* who meet by Ninus' tomb, Belacqua and his mistress consummate their passion 'after the manner of Ninus the Assyrian' (*EB*, 14), a style 'that she [Miss Zaborovna] afterwards described to a bosom pal as the dream of the shadow of the smoke of a rotten cigar' (*EB*, 14). Like Hamlet, who thinks that 'A dream itself is but a shadow' (*Ham* 2.2.247), and Puck's suggestion to think of the play as but a dream in case the 'shadows have offended' (*MND* 5.1.401), the first part of the story self-consciously de-materializes itself.

In the middle part, Lord Gall of Wormwood, whose name also alludes to 'wormwood', the bitter herb that Hamlet repeatedly mentions when the player queen has revealed the murder during the 'Mousetrap', appears as yet a further caricature of old Hamlet's ghost, who is 'Armèd at point exactly, cap-a-pe' (*Ham* 1.2.200): 'clad in amaranth caoutchouc cap-à-pie, a cloak of gutta percha streaming back from the barrel of his bust' (*EB*, 15). Like Hamlet's father, he finds himself in a purgatorial dilemma. He has no heir and there is no escape from this predicament, or as he puts it: 'Possibility of issue is extinct' (*EB*, 15). He instinctively adopts Belacqua, dubbing him Adeodatus after St Augustine's son, and sees in him the solution to his problem: 'I don't know who you are, but that you will do me the hell of a lot of good I have little doubt' (*EB*, 16). The ghostly Belacqua becomes a son who is about to become a father in replacing the father who himself has become a ghost. He however breaks the unity suggested by the model of the Holy Trinity and ends the line of male heirs.

Lord Gall transports Belacqua to 'Eden of Wormwood, one of the few terrestrial Paradises outstanding in this country' (*EB*, 21), where he trusts him to accomplish 'a Moby Dick of a miracle' (*EB*, 24), that is to secure his offspring with Moll, his wife and 'partner of [his] porridge days' (*EB*, 27), alluding to Melville, Dickens and in a more British vein to Cleopatra who spent her 'salad days' (*AC* 1.5.76) with Julius Caesar. Belacqua, who is not to judge Moll as Hamlet is not to judge Gertrude ('Leave Moll to me' (*EB*, 31)/'Leave her to heaven' (*Ham* 1.5.86)), does as he is told, but fails to produce a boy. Like the usurped crown of Denmark, the rotten world of Eden of Wormwood will remain without a male heir.

Belacqua instead returns to his own headstone in the graveyard, where he sits with the 'moon shining' (*EB*, 36) and encounters his old friend 'Mick', the groundsman Doyle, who is about to open and rob Belacqua's grave. In a state worthy of the desperation of old Hamlet's ghost who urges Hamlet to remember him (*Ham* 1.5.111), Belacqua states that '[his] memory has gone to hell altogether' (*EB*, 42) and calls the cemetery 'a cockpit of comic panic' (*EB*, 51), an epithet for the stage used in the Prologue of *Henry V*: 'Can this cockpit hold/The vasty fields of France' (*H5* Prol.11–12). The empty grave, in the end, however, only holds a handful of stones, 'Echo's Bones' into which Belacqua subsequently metamorphoses, returning to the irreducible materiality from which he originated.

This reverse metamorphosis in the open grave mirrors the scene in *Hamlet* where Hamlet wonders why his father has risen from the grave and asks the ghost: 'Why thy canonized bones, hearsèd in death,/Have burst their cerements' (*Ham* 1.4.47–8). It also comments on the gravedigger scene, the gravediggers' dialogue on processes of decomposition and Hamlet's reflection on the difference between the living body of a human being and its mortal remains: 'Why, e'en so, and now my Lady Worm's, chopless, and knocked about the mazard with a sexton's spade. ... Did these bones cost no more the breeding but to play at loggets with'em? Mine ache to think on't' (*Ham* 5.1.74–8).

Beckett's story verges upon drama and gains its performative dimension through condensed echoes from Shakespeare's plays. These become assimilated to Beckett's work, and yet undergo metamorphosis and variation, marking both similarities and differences to the plays they evoke. 'Echo's Bones' in itself creates a resonance chamber when the three parts of the story become each other's echoes as they change shape and place. The cyclical course of the story, its departure from and return to the grave is complemented by its composition. Like a triptych, the three parts of the story can be viewed simultaneously and related to one another. One thing can be more than merely itself and transform into its opposite. Each of the three parts of the story is at once Paradise, Purgatory and Hell, each of the two male characters at once father, son and ghost. The story is both a comedy and a tragedy. In Beckett's plays, this tragicomic mode when interacting with Shakespeare, together with the notion of the echo and metamorphosis becomes perhaps most apparent in his later play *Happy Days* (1961).

'There always remains something [...] Of everything. [...] Some remains' (*CDW*, 161)

Happy Days interacts with many of Shakespeare's tragedies and sonnets. In his production notebook and also in his correspondence with his friend and director Alan Schneider,[19] Beckett lists a number of references to Shakespeare's works that he inserted into the play, and thus deliberately aligns his work with that of precursors such as Shakespeare and Milton.

We encounter the two characters, Winnie, a woman of about fifty, and Willie, whom Adorno would have perhaps interpreted as a short form of William, a man of about sixty, in a desert-like landscape, an 'expanse of scorched grass' (*CDW*, 138) under blazing light. Unlike Willie, who is able to crawl into and out of his cave, Winnie cannot move and is mercilessly exposed to the scorching sun. In the first act, she is buried up to her waist in a mound of earth, behind which Willie is lying asleep. The categories of time and space seem to be suspended, and yet time seems to be inexorably progressing. Day and night are introduced by the sound of a bell, and in Act II, Winnie, as if she were imprisoned in an hourglass, is buried up to her neck. The progression of time between the two acts is also a progression of Winnie's life from being buried up to the middle of her body in mid-life to becoming almost entirely interred in Act II. The passing of time, indicated by Winnie's sinking into the ground, is not shown on stage; night never falls and Winnie is no longer certain if time still exists: 'May one still speak of time?' (*CDW*, 160). The audience encounters her in two states, and the change between them has happened during the break between the acts.

From the beginning of the play, the notion of a linear progression of time intersects with that of a potentially infinite recurrence of the same. Although Winnie greets 'Another heavenly day' (*CDW*, 138), and starts her daily routine as usual, she is confronted with a sense of finitude, when she notices that her provisions, her medicine, her lipstick and her toothpaste, 'another of those old things' (*CDW*, 139), are fast becoming exhausted. Winnie's dwindling supplies and the increasingly finite world in which she is less and less able to move is contrasted to the vast desert-like non-space around her that presents an anachronistic hybrid of different historical and literary traditions. Reduction equals expansion as the scenery invites numerous projections. The desert can be a liminal space, a space of temptation, a place of contemplation or conversion, where tragic stasis as well as mystical ek-stasis find their spatial equivalent. Yet, the utopian no-place is a carefully orchestrated, finite theatrical space, which according to Beckett's stage direction is to convey a '*Maximum of simplicity and symmetry*' (*CDW*, 138).

When Winnie starts the play with her inaudible prayers and ends them with the liturgical expression 'world without end' from the *Book of Common Prayer*, this phrase comments on her own situation. At the beginning of Act II, she wonders if she could speak to herself or to 'the wilderness' (*CDW*, 160) like 'the voice of one crying in the wilderness' that in Isaiah 40:3 commands its listeners to 'Prepare the way of the LORD; Make straight in the desert A highway for our God' and prophesies the redemption of Jerusalem. In the New Testament, John the Baptist becomes Isaiah's echo when he takes up the phrase in John 1:23 and identifies himself with the voice that was to announce the coming of Christ. The desert-like setting evokes this main trajectory of salvation history, and Winnie alludes to its typological frame but she smilingly denies that her voice could be the prophetic voice in the wilderness: 'But no. [...] No no' (*CDW*, 160). In Winnie's world, the teleological Christian hope of eternal life is no longer yet to be fulfilled, but instead 'the world without end' is already there, the eschaton has arrived as a lasting and potentially endless misery. Winnie examines herself and confirms this static notion of eternity: ' – no better, no worse – [...] no change' (*CDW*, 139; 141).

The fundamental changelessness she encounters in the sunlit desert echoes the verse from *Ecclesiastes*: 'What has been will be again, what has been done will be done again; there is nothing new under the sun' (1:9). The passage from which this verse is taken opens a context relevant to *Happy Days*, describing a cyclical model of sameness. It explains how the works of creation follow their preordained course from the beginning of time, how the sun rises and sets at its appointed times, and that what appears to be new is in fact old and has happened before. Novelty is dependent on forgetting. *Happy Days* both affirms and challenges the notion of changelessness; it produces the sense of a here and now, of something that happens, repeats itself and produces variants of itself. The present moment on stage, however, is embedded in literary and biblical reflections on presence, on newness and on creation and decay. It is through these dialogical relations that the performance creates a presence that is at the same time a representation.

The predestined course of the 'nothing new under the sun' also marks the beginning of Beckett's first novel *Murphy*: 'The sun shone, having no alternative, on the nothing new.'[20] In *Happy Days* as in *Ecclesiastes*, the paradox of changeless change, of an immediacy that appears in mediated form, is linked to the ephemerality of human vanity. In the Hebrew Bible, the word for 'vanity' or 'futility', *Hävāl*, the wisp of wind or breath, also refers to the fleeting nature of a presence that eliminates itself in the face of eternity. Correspondingly, Winnie comments on her situation by quoting lines from Milton's *Paradise Lost*, that she cannot remember in their entirety: 'O fleeting joys/Of Paradise dear bought with lasting woes!' (*PL*, 10.741–2).[21]

The chiasmic coupling of 'fleeting joy' and 'lasting woe', of the ephemeral moment of happiness and the endurance of agony, indeed sets the scene for the entire play in which the first direct Shakespearean reference is to *Hamlet* – 'what are those wonderful lines [...] – woe woe is me [...] – to see what I see' (*CDW*, 140) – recalling the first scene of Act III, where Ophelia elegizes her lover Hamlet: 'Oh, what a noble mind is here o'erthrown! ... Oh, woe is me,/T'have seen what I have seen, see what I see' (*Ham* 3.1.144–55).[22] Winnie wipes her eyes and has 'seen enough'

(*CDW*, 139). The 'woe' that she sees in her sunlit world also resonates with the Prince's lines that end *Romeo and Juliet*, where the sun no longer shines for woe: 'The sun for sorrow will not show his head ... For never was a story of more woe/Than this of Juliet and her Romeo' (*RJ* 5.3.306–10).

Fragments of, as she calls them, 'wonderful lines', 'immortal lines', from Milton and Shakespeare surface in Winnie's memory and constitute imaginary points of reference that characterize her, comment on her situation and make it possible for the audience to reflect on her actions in a context that resonates with traces from literature, the Bible and music. Winnie quotes these sources and also reflects back on them, adding to them and placing her performance into the temporal continuum she seeks to retrieve.

Whereas Willie is seen holding a newspaper in front of him and seldom speaks, Winnie longs to speak in the 'sweet old style', Dante's *dolce stil novo*, but like Echo's reverberation, her memories remain incomplete: 'One loses one's classics. [...] Oh not all. [...] A part [...] A part remains. [...] That is what I find so wonderful, a part remains, of one's classics, to help one through the day' (*CDW*, 164).[23] To Winnie 'There always remains something' (*CDW*, 161), and she contributes to its continuation. Like an actress who vaguely recalls passages from her repertoire, or like the faintly recognizable sound of an echo, she reverberates parts and incomplete lines from earlier texts and becomes herself a creation of language, pointing to the difference between the source and its variant.

Daylight and Happiness

Winnie's and Willie's world is a world of eternal daylight and an indefinite present, which is only punctuated by the shrill sound of the hellish bell. There is no night; instead, everything is subjected to 'this hellish sun' (*CDW*, 147). The semantic link between the fiery underworld, 'hell', and the blazing light above them is established by the German word 'hell' for a light that shines brightly. The sun carries multiple connotations and can be seen as an instrument of torture, the all-seeing eye of Heaven, or a source of life-giving energy. Light like the sun is configured into a metatheatrical and intertextual phenomenon when Act II opens with a further reference to Milton's *Paradise Lost*: 'Hail, holy Light, offspring of Heav'n first born' (*PL*, 3.1).[24]

Even though Winnie's apostrophe alludes more to the fact that she and Willie are living in a lost paradise, or rather in a paradise that they had never gained in the first place, Beckett undermines the traditional

Daylight and Happiness 85

interpretation of light as a symbol of life and tells the story of creation as one that is immanent in the practice of theatre, a process in which the spotlights create the world of the stage, give life to it for the actors and the audience and make visible a scenery that is arranged by the perspective, the all-seeing eye of the director. The 'hellish' light is life-giving, but it also condemns the actors, like victims, to act.[25] The technical and performative reality of the theatre becomes part of the dramatic fiction.

In Beckett, as often in Shakespeare, the sun is an ambivalent symbol, and love often suffers from too much sun, from a superficial and conventional life by daylight. In *Romeo and Juliet*, the world of Verona is one of such daylight, shaped by the public interaction of a feudalistic society that sentences its members to conform to predetermined roles. Already lovesick and melancholic at the beginning of the play, Romeo avoids the sun. Old Montague confirms this and describes the paradoxical movements of the sun and of his son in a chiastic verse structure: 'But all so soon as the all-cheering sun/Should in the farthest east begin to draw/The shady curtains from Aurora's bed/Away from light steals home my heavy son' (*RJ* 1.1.125–8). In a much more sarcastic vein, Hamlet, wearing his 'nightly cover', expresses his loathing for Claudius' complacent and patronizing display of avuncular affection when he remarks to Gertrude: 'I am too much i'th'sun' (*Ham* 1.2.67).[26] In *Happy Days* as in *Romeo and Juliet*, the midday heat proves to be destructive. Mercutio ridicules: 'the bawdy hand of the dial is now upon the prick of noon' (*RJ* 2.4.92–3), an expression that inspired Beckett's short story collection *More Pricks than Kicks*, but Mercutio also ignores Benvolio's warning that '[in] these hot days, is the mad blood stirring' (*RJ* 3.1.4) that foreshadows his own death during the heated quarrel with Tybalt.

Reading Shakespeare with Beckett, however, is not only to discover the ambiguities of traditional symbolism. Like the sun, the light of day, that can bring life as well as death, the idea of 'happiness' itself is highly ambiguous in the works of both authors. After reading *Happy Days*, Shakespeare's use of the word 'happy' carries more and more ambivalent overtones, and one is also reminded of its more literal meaning, which refers back to the Middle English *hap* or *happe* as 'coincidence, destiny or fate' – that which happens on stage. In *Macbeth*, 'happiness' becomes an expression of dramatic irony when King Duncan shares his joy about Macbeth's success in the war by exclaiming 'Great happiness!' (*Mac* 1.2.58). In *A Midsummer Night's Dream*, having subjected Hippolita, Theseus eagerly waits for 'four happy days [to] bring in/Another moon' (*MND* 1.1.2–3), so that nothing may stand in the way of his wedding anymore. A quick look at the concordance reveals another 'Beckettism': the drama in which the combination of the words 'happy' and 'days' appears most often is *Richard III*, where, in Act I Scene iii, for instance, Queen Margaret lays what might be one of the cruellest curses in Shakespeare on Richard: 'Long die thy happy days before thy death' (*R III* 1.3.205).

Consequently, one cannot but anticipate sombre events when Paris in *Romeo and Juliet* greets Juliet with the phrase: 'Happily met, my lady and my wife' (*RJ* 4.1.18). A similarly ambiguous idea of 'happiness' appears in the scene in which Friar Laurence tries to cheer up the depressed Romeo: 'What, rouse thee, man! thy Juliet is alive,/For whose dear sake thou wast but lately dead:/There art thou happy. Tybalt would kill thee,/But thou slewest Tybalt: there art thou happy./.../A pack of blessings light upon thy back,/Happiness courts thee in her best array,' (*RJ* 3.3.135–42). In an equally benevolent yet more poignant way, the Nurse wistfully bestows her motherly blessing on Juliet's meeting with Romeo: 'Go, girl, seek happy nights to happy days' (*RJ* 1.3.106). Both the Friar's and the Nurse's emphasis on happiness, however, merely point all the more to the unhappy prospects that await the lovers.

Metamorphic States

Just as Romeo and Juliet, who cannot live their love, are constrained by custom and appear as a proto-Beckettian couple, so Winnie and Willie, who can no longer reach each other, present themselves as a post-Shakespearean couple. Like Winnie and Willie, Romeo's and Juliet's 'star-crossed love' is doomed to failure. Romeo and Juliet may have recognized the creative power of language that can build the world, but they are also painfully aware of the barriers against life that language can erect once it is fixated as convention.

Juliet essentially longs for an almost Beckettian kind of liberating nothingness that questions conventional meaning and rather creates significance by disclosing habitual and arbitrary ascriptions when she realizes ''Tis but thy name that is my enemy' (*RJ* 2.1.38), and asks herself: 'What's in a name?' (*RJ* 2.2.43). At the same time, she is conscious of the fact that she remains dependent on her family, trapped by heritage and convention and is doomed to stay silent: 'Bondage is hoarse, and may not speak aloud,/Else would I tear the cave where Echo lies,/And make her airy tongue more hoarse than mine/With repetition of my Romeo's name. Romeo!' (*RJ* 2.2.160–7). Earlier in the play, Juliet voices her distress:

'O Romeo, Romeo, wherefore art thou Romeo?' (*RJ* 2.2.33), and from this passage from the ending of the first balcony scene onwards, she literally becomes her own echo by repeating the name of Romeo. Juliet seeks to escape the imprisonment caused by her family's pointless feuds by subjecting herself to a much more extreme imprisonment in her family's crypt. In a scene that is exceptional on early modern stages, she takes the Friar's sleeping potion, is pronounced dead and buried alive.

At various instances, *Romeo and Juliet* refers to characters being caught in an impasse from which they cannot free themselves. Romeo, at the beginning of the play, describes himself as stuck to the ground, immobilized by his unrequited love for Rosalind: 'You have dancing shoes/With nimble soles, I have a soul of lead/So stakes me to the ground I cannot move' (*RJ* 1.4.14–16). Later on, Mercutio plans to 'drive him from the mire of love wherein he sticks up to the ears'.[27] These metaphorical expressions of confinement and incarceration culminate in the staging of Juliet's death and burial and the final, tragic reunion of the lovers in the crypt. Like Echo in her cave, Juliet metamorphoses into a lifeless state in the stony vault. Paris, shortly before his own death, mourns for her: 'O woe, thy canopy is dust and stones' (*RJ* 5.3.13), and Friar Laurence describes her as a 'thing like death' (*RJ* 4.1.74), a 'Poor living corse, closed in a dead man's tomb' (*RJ* 5.2.29).[28] Life and death have become indistinguishable and their likeness prompts Romeo's deadly mistake. Desperately going to his own death, he approaches the crypt and addresses it as 'thou womb of death' (*RJ* 5.3.45) linking love and death, beginning and end. Earlier in the play, the Friar, while foraging, describes the cyclical course of nature in similar terms: 'The earth that's nature's mother is her tomb;/What is her burying grave, that is her womb' (*RJ* 2.3.9–10). Beckett, from *Dream of Fair to Middling Women* on, often alludes to the reciprocity between birth and death in his composite 'wombtomb', which combines morphological difference with phonological and semantic similarity.[29]

Like Juliet, who in the end stabs herself with the 'happy dagger' (*RJ* 5.3.169), Winnie is buried alive. She is a woman whose womb is already entombed at the beginning of the play, and later on, she ironically addresses the earth: 'Ah earth you old extinguisher' (*CDW*, 153). The sunlit setting of *Happy Days* recalls the inside of the tomb, that to Romeo is being lit by Juliet's beauty: 'For here lies Juliet, and her beauty makes/This vault a feasting presence full of light' (*RJ* 5.3.85–6). Lady Capulet takes the sight of her dead daughter as a sign of warning, a bell indicating her own death, her own motherly womb returning to its tomb: 'O me!

This sight of death is as a bell/That warns my old age to a sepulchre' (*RJ* 5.3.206–7).

When Winnie puts on her lipstick, she speaks parts of Romeo's lines 'Ensign crimson. [...] Pale Flag' (*CDW*, 142) from the scene when he finds Juliet in the crypt and incredulously describes her appearance: 'Thou art not conquered, beauty's ensign yet/Is crimson in thy lips and in thy cheeks,/And Death's pale flag is not advancèd there' (*RJ* 5.3.94–6).[30] Winnie further alludes to the first meeting of Romeo and Juliet, when she reminisces about her own first and her second ball and her first kiss (*CDW*, 142). Shakespeare's colour 'crimson' for Winnie becomes a prop. Wearing 'crimson' on her lips asserts that she is still beautiful and alive and not yet 'conquered' by death. She echoes those fragments of Romeo's lines that contrast life and death and mark the transition between them, which characterizes Winnie's own liminal state.

Winnie begins her day as if she were changing into the role she plays in front of the audience. Playing Winnie, however, is also to play Juliet; and in relating to her Winnie participates in a temporal continuity of the theatre, in which the fleeting moment of the performance is both unique and potentially infinitely variable.[31] Winnie's performance reflects on its own metamorphosis of Shakespeare's tragedy. Her physical in-between state, in which she is half visible and half embedded in the mound, becomes a reflexive, metatheatrical space, in which Beckett stages what lies latent in Shakespeare.

In *Happy Days*, traces from *Romeo and Juliet* are taken to materialize the tragic dilemma of being held captive, unable to move, buried alive through the means of scenery and props. Beckett's drama focuses on the framework, 'the bare bones', the skeleton of the tragedy. He only uses two characters, pares away subplots and distils the main plot down to elementary components: characters that are paralysed by conventions and circumstances in an unremitting course of events and a couple that cannot be united. Form and content converge. The notion of the tragic is turned into a metaphor that constitutes itself in a performance, in which theatrical materiality and dramatic fiction are combined.

'Fear No More'

In the midst of the symmetries and resonances that constitute *Happy Days*, extremes define each other. Joy and pain, stasis and movement, sleep and wakefulness, presence and absence, speech and silence mutually evoke one another. Winnie and Willie eventually become each other's echo in a resonance chamber created by Shakespeare's *Cymbeline*:

WINNIE   [*Same voice.*] Fear no more the heat o'the sun. [*Pause.*] Did you hear that?
WILLIE   [*Irritated.*] Yes.
WINNIE   [*Same voice.*] What? [*Pause.*] What?
WILLIE   [*More irritated.*] Fear no more.
WINNIE   [*Same voice.*] No more what? [*Pause.*] Fear no more what?
WILLIE   [*Violently.*] Fear no more! (*CDW*, 148)

In need of reassurance that she is being heard, Winnie performs a sound-check in which Willie grudgingly takes part. Even if she prompts him on the second half of Shakespeare's line, Willie's answer remains incomplete and more general, omitting the sun as the cause of fear.

'Fear no more the heat o'th'sun' (*Cym* 4.2.257) is the beginning of a song that accompanies the solemn rites during Imogen's burial in *Cymbeline*. Imogen, disguised as the page Fidele, escapes to the Welsh wilderness, where she meets Belarius and his two young companions, who are known to the audience to be her brothers, the king's stolen sons. Feeling weary and unwell, she takes a sleeping potion that was given to her as a medicine. Like Juliet, she assumes a deathlike state, on which Guiderius later comments: 'The same dead thing alive' (*Cym* 5.6.123). When she is laid into a cave by Belarius, Guiderius and Arviragus, their dirge commences:

> Fear no more the heat o'th'sun,
> Nor the furious winter's rages.
> Though thy worldly task hast done,
> Home art gone and ta'en thy wages.
> Golden lads and girls all must,
> As chimney sweepers, come to dust. (*Cym* 4.2.257–62)

Imogen's living death is a state between the extremes of heat and cold, summer and winter. Virginia Woolf uses 'Fear no more the heat of the sun' as one of her *leitmotifs* in *Mrs. Dalloway* (1925) to emphasize the equanimity of her heroine Clarissa Dalloway,[32] and to contrast her serenity with her doppelganger, the young Septimus Smith, who has returned traumatized from the war. Yet Clarissa also senses herself being entombed when she returns home at midday, finds '[t]he hall of the house [was] cool as a vault' (*MD*, 31), and anticipates: 'Narrower and narrower would her bed be' (*MD*, 33–4). Winnie's range of action has indeed narrowed, and yet she, like Clarissa, does not step out of her role but rather keeps her composure between the extremes.[33]

Happy Days resonates with *Cymbeline* and *Romeo and Juliet* and it transforms central scenes and metaphors of both plays into an onstage reality. In the dirge from *Cymbeline*, '[g]olden lads' is a term in Warwickshire dialect for the dandelion, whereas 'golden girls' implies the golden blonde hair of a Petrarchan beauty. Winnie casts herself as such a beauty when she remembers: 'Golden you called it, that day, when the last guest was gone' (*CDW*, 146). When Imogen disguises herself as Fidele, Pisanio advises her to renounce her courtly complexion and tan her skin: 'Nay, you must/Forget that rarest treasure of your cheek,/Exposing it … to the greedy touch/Of common-kissing Titan' (*Cym* 3.4.158–62). Winnie, who is exposed to the sun, considers herself beautiful both in Petrarchan and also in anti-Petrarchan, more Shakespearean terms, when she looks at her cheeks and compares them to damask roses: 'cheek … no … [*eyes right*] … no … [*distends cheeks*] … even if I puff them out … [*eyes left distends cheeks again*] … no … no damask' (*CDW*, 162). Her lines recall Imogen's appearance as Fidele and they also refer to Shakespeare's Sonnet 130 'My mistress' eyes are nothing like the sun', where the speaker praises the beauty of his beloved through what she is not: 'I have seen roses damasked, red and white,/But no such roses see I in her cheeks'.

Winnie's character and her performance offer themselves to be read in correspondence with Shakespeare's plays and poetry, but *Happy Days* also makes Shakespeare's works resonate with each another, offering synoptic interpretations of his heroines Juliet and Imogen, reflecting on conventions of female beauty, incarceration and the necessity of role play. The link between *Happy Days*, *Romeo and Juliet* and *Cymbeline* is further supported by performance history: Peggy Ashcroft, among many other roles, played Juliet under John Gielgud in the 1930s, Imogen with the RSC in 1957 at Stratford-upon-Avon and Winnie in 1976 at the National Theatre, directed by Peter Hall.

Echo Chambers and Musical Echoes

In *Cymbeline*, the setting in Imogen's bedchamber becomes a *mise-en-abîme*, a visual and verbal echo chamber of metamorphosis. The walls of the chamber are adorned with tapestries and ornaments showing auspicious meetings of heroic and mythological couples. Iachimo reporting to Posthumus is amazed by the splendour of an arras that presents Cleopatra about to meet Antony on Cydnus and the lifelikeness of a painting of the goddess Diana bathing. Like Diana, who in this scene is spied upon by Actaeon, who later metamorphoses into a stag, is hunted down by his own hounds and transforms into a flower, Imogen is spied upon by Iachimo, who also compares himself to the ravisher Tarquin.

Before she falls asleep, Imogen reads Ovid's *Metamorphoses*, and Iachimo notices that 'She hath been reading late,/The tale of Tereus: here the leaf's turned down/Where Philomel gave up' (*Cym* 2.2.44–6). Iachimo evokes two stories of rape, which contextualize his breaking into the privacy of the bedchamber and his own false story of Imogen's infidelity. The moment of Imogen's surrender to sleep is paralleled with Philomela's yielding to Tereus. The story of Tereus and Philomela who, being mutilated and condemned to silence, weaves her tale into a tapestry and when she is transformed into a nightingale sings it over and over, contrasts the grandeur of the tapestry that shows Cleopatra, juxtaposing love and violence.

Imogen is spared the cruel fate of Philomela. Yet, her waking up unaware of what happened and her later transformations from life to death and from death to life, are presented in the context of birds and their song. She awakes to the song of the musicians: 'Hark, hark, the lark at heaven's gate sings, And Phoebus' gins arise' (*Cym* 2.3.17–18). Disguised as Fidele, she is pronounced dead by Arviragus – '[t]he bird is dead' (*Cym* 4.2.196) – and ironically, it is Iachimo, who at the beginning anticipates her resurrection, describing her as the Phoenix: 'She is alone th' Arabian bird' (*Cym* 1.6.17).

Like the bird Philomela, who can only sing, Winnie must speak. She needs an opposite and is made distraught by the silence that surrounds her: 'nothing to break the silence of this place' (*CDW*, 145). She tries but fails to stop herself from talking incessantly: 'Something says, Stop talking now, Winnie, for a minute, don't squander all your words for the day, stop talking and do something for a change, will you?' (*CDW*, 155). For Winnie, as this passage also reminds her, there is not much left to do. Similar to Echo, who has nothing left but her voice and whom Arthur Golding in his translation of the *Metamorphoses* (1567) called 'the babbling nymph', Winnie is 'babbling away' (*CDW*, 148). Winnie transforms into Echo not only linguistically and meta-theatrically, but also through her progressing physical absence.

Like Echo, Winnie becomes more and more disembodied over the course of the play and, as Poussin's Echo illustrates, she is transformed into the matter that surrounds her. Her increasing physical absence correlates with the growing presence of earth and stones, and consequently in the end only her voice and her gaze remain to communicate with the world around her. Beckett's scenery materializes her disembodiment and Winnie describes her disintegration as an echo of Hamlet's words: 'O that this too too solid flesh would melt, /Thaw and resolve itself into a dew' (*Ham* 1.2.129–30), to which she refers twice: 'and wait for the day to come [...] the happy day to come when flesh melts at so many degrees' (*CDW*, 144) as well as 'Shall I myself not melt perhaps in the end, or burn, oh I do not mean necessarily burst into flames [...] all this [...] visible flesh' (*CDW*, 154). Winnie not only metamorphoses into the material around her like Echo, but she also becomes the echo of Juliet and Imogen and voices Hamlet's longing for a transformative finality while being unable to act.

At the end of the play, the echo is not only employed as a structural-linguistical, metaphorical and theatrical device but also becomes a part of the performance when music, the acoustic dimension of the echo, is included. Music becomes a signature of transformation in Beckett and Shakespeare and is used to transcend limitations. It is therefore only at the end of *Happy Days*, after her previous, failed attempts, that Winnie is able to sing: 'How often I have said, in evil hours, Sing now, Winnie [...] Could not' (*CDW*, 155). Winnie compares her song to that of a thrush or '[t]he bird of dawning' (*Ham* 1.2.160), which Marcellus mentions in the first scene of *Hamlet*. In *Hamlet*, the cock, the 'bird of dawning' announces the day and makes 'extravagant and erring spirit[s]' (*Ham* 1.1.154) disappear. Marcellus has heard it said that before 'that season comes/Wherein our Saviour's birth is celebrated' (*Ham* 1.1.158–9), the 'bird of dawning singeth all night long' (*Ham* 1.1.160). In Winnie's world, however, there is no saviour imminent, no holy season to be announced and no night whose end the birdsong could mark. Apart from the reference to *Hamlet*, contemporary audiences might also have recalled the popular song 'Happy days are here again' (1929), and Beckett was indeed toying with the idea of adding a song such as 'When Irish Eyes Are Smiling' before he chose the waltz duet from Léhar.[34]

Winnie ultimately sings her swansong, 'Love unspoken', a part of the waltz song that is the ending to Franz Léhar's light opera *Die Lustige Witwe* (1905), *The Merry Widow*. Recalling *The Merry Wives of Windsor*, the song also alludes to the transition between life and death, when Romeo reminds himself: 'How oft when men are at the point of death/Have they been merry!' (*RJ* 5.3.88–9). Speech transforms into song when Winnie sings about love unspoken and strings that are able to speak:

> Love unspoken, Faith unbroken,
> All life through.
> Strings are playing, Hear them saying – 'Love me true'.
> Now the echo answers – 'Say you want me too'.
> All the world's in love with love
> And I love you.[35]

Winnie's song about the echo becomes her own echo, and yet the play finally reaches beyond this self-referential moment when, at the end, Winnie and Willie are looking at each other in silence in a kind of visual echo of the text 'love unspoken'. In this visual echo, the gaze of the characters is reciprocated. Instead of contemplating their own images in narcissistic absorption or searching for each other in vain, Winnie and Willie, unlike Echo and Narcissus, are brought together in this last look as music transforms into the domain of silence.

Analogous to Hamlet, the rest, the end of *Happy Days* is silence: 'Words fail, there are times when even they fail' (*CDW*, 147), Winnie concedes, and as so often in Beckett's plays, the last things remain unspoken. Language rather becomes its other: silence. It thereby conveys a latency that is preserved in silence and in the end, it leads back to the beginning of theatre, to the Greek 'theatron' – a place for viewing. This includes the resonance chamber of the silent audience, which Beckett in *Happy Days*, using a pun on the German words *schauen* or *gucken* (to watch or to look) has alluded to as 'Shower' or 'Cooker': 'Shower – does the name mean anything – to you, Willie – evoke any reality' (*CDW*, 156).[36]

In its correspondence with its predecessors, Beckett's theatre intimates a passing through speechlessness. His is also a theatre that is not unfamiliar with the experience that the catastrophe or the apocalypse has already happened. From there, it engages with its predecessors in a dialogue that enables new creation and relies on a way of thinking that knows how to forget its traditions without denying them: a way of thinking that can hold on to them, but does not necessarily have to do so, a way of thinking that, being conscious of the possibilities that have been gained by interacting with tradition, can release itself into freedom from it.

The speaker of Shakespeare's Sonnet 71 'No longer mourn for me' addresses this conversation with posterity when he anticipates his passing from one world to the next.

> No longer mourn for me when I am dead
> Than you shall hear the surly sullen bell
> Give warning to the world that I am fled
> From this vile world with vilest worms to dwell:
> Nay, if you read this line, remember not
> The hand that writ it, for I love you so
> That I in your sweet thoughts would be forgot
> If thinking on me then should make you woe.
> O, if, I say, you look upon this verse
> When I perhaps compounded am with clay,

> Do not so much as my poor name rehearse,
> But let your love even with my life decay,
> Lest the wise world should look into your moan
> And mock you with me after I am gone.

Imagining this posthumous setting, the speaker forbids his beloved to mourn for him or even to remember him because the beloved would only suffer ('make you woe') and be mocked by 'the world' for having been associated with the speaker. The speaker performs his vanishing from the world in a successive reduction of his persona, from the moment of his death that is announced by the 'sullen bell', his dwelling with 'vilest worms' and his being 'compounded with clay' until he is finally 'gone'. This regress is paralleled by his envisaged disappearance in the beloved's memory. He instructs the beloved not to 'mourn for me', then not to remember a part of him, 'the hand that writ it' and in the third quatrain, when the materiality of 'clay' has already 'compounded' him, not to rehearse his immaterial 'poor name'.

In asking the beloved not to do something, however, he all the more implores him or her to do precisely that. As Helen Vendler observes: 'its principal result in us is sympathy for the lover who must ask less and less, lest he find his least request callously refused'.[37] Not least of all, the desire to stay alive in the memory of posterity materializes in the sonnet, where the progressive dissolution of the speaker is contained and contrasted in the materiality of the text.

The material remains of the speaker's voice in the sonnet, or of the text of a play in Shakespeare, as in Beckett, cast themselves into a textual entity that to be kept alive depends on their readers, actors and audiences as their body of resonance. Beckett loved to recite Sonnet 71[38] and thought that someone should write a play about it. Perhaps this is precisely what he has accomplished in *Happy Days*.

Notes

1 T.S. Eliot, *Four Quartets* (New York: Harcourt, Brace and Company, 1943), 17.
2 S.E Gontarski, *Beckett Matters: Essays on Beckett's Late Modernism* (Edinburgh University Press, 2017). Gontarski views Beckett's use of disembodied voices as part of the author's late modernist practice.
3 Stephen Connor, *Samuel Beckett: Repetition, Theory and Text* (Oxford: Blackwell, 1988), 136.
4 Connor, *Samuel Beckett: Repetition, Theory and Text*, 137.

5 Samuel Beckett, *Echo's Bones*, ed. by Mark Nixon (London: Faber & Faber, 2014).
6 Virginia Woolf, 'Craftsmanship' in Virginia Woolf, *The Death of the Moth and other Essays* (London: The Hogarth Press, 1942), 126–32, 129.
7 John Hollander, *The Figure of Echo: A Mode of Allusion in Milton and After* (Berkeley: University of California Press, 1981), 4; Jonathan Goldberg, *Voice Terminal Echo: Postmodernism and English Renaissance Texts* (New York: Methuen, 1986).
8 Chris Ackerley, 'The Uncertainty of Self. Samuel Beckett and the Location of Voice', *Samuel Beckett Today/Aujourd'hui*, 14 (2004), 39–51, 40.
9 Julie Bates, *Beckett's Art of Salvage: Writing and Material Imagination, 1932–1987* (Cambridge University Press, 2017), 208.
10 James Knowlson describes this 'early fascination with the mineral, with things dying and decaying, with petrification'. James Knowlson, *Damned to Fame: The Life of Samuel Beckett* (London. Bloomsbury, 1997), 29.
11 Lawrence Harvey, *Samuel Beckett – Poet and Critic* (Princeton University Press, 1970), 106.
12 Knowlson, *Damned to Fame*, 186: 'In … 1934 he took a short trip to Paris with his brother, where he again made lists of pictures that captured his attention in the Louvre – Poussin and the Dutch primarily –.' Cf. Ibid.: 72, 113, 186, 236. Thomas McGreevy greatly admired Poussin and had given his book on the artist to Samuel Beckett and Suzanne. Thomas McGreevy, *Nicolas Poussin* (Dublin: The Domen Press, 1960), vi. Beckett owned Poussin's *Lettres et propos sur l'art: Textes réunis et présentés par Anthony Blunt* (Paris: Hermann, 1964).
13 Jonathan Unglaub, *Poussin and the Poetics of Painting: Pictorial Narrative and the Legacy of Tasso* (Cambridge University Press, 2006), 73.
14 Jonathan Bate, *Shakespeare and Ovid* (Oxford University Press, 1993), 148.
15 Mark Nixon, 'Introduction' in Samuel Beckett, *Echo's Bones*, ed. by Mark Nixon (London: Faber & Faber, 2014), xii.
16 Nixon, 'Introduction', xii. Beckett changed the title of his collection: 'Not poems after all, but: Echo's Bones, and Other Precipitates. C'est plus modeste.' *Letters*, I, to George Reavey, 15.03.1935, 264.
17 The character is a minor demon in C.S. Lewis, *The Screwtape Letters* (1942), and also an angel in the biblical Book of Revelation. Cf. Hamlet's comment aside on the player's revelation of the murder: 'That's wormwood, wormwood' (*Ham* 3.2.162).
18 *Letters*, I, to Nuala Costello, 10.05.1934, 208.
19 Maurice Harmon (ed.), *No Author Better Served: The Correspondence of Samuel Beckett and Alan Schneider* (Cambridge: Harvard University Press, 1998), 92–7; James Knowlson (ed.), *Happy Days: Samuel Beckett's Production Notebook* (New York: Grove, 1985).
20 Samuel Beckett, *Murphy* (New York: Grove, 1957), 1.
21 John Milton, *Paradise Lost*, ed. by Gordon Tesky (New York, London: Norton, 2005), 250.

22 An allegorical parallel to this passage can be found in Chaucer's 'The Knight's Tale': 'This world nis but a thurghfare full of wo,/And we ben pilgrimes, passing to and fro;/Deeth is an ende of every worldly sore,' Geoffrey Chaucer, 'The Knight's Tale' in Larry Benson (ed.), *The Riverside Chaucer* (Oxford University Press, 1987), ll. 2847–9.
23 Winnie continually attempts to remember the 'old style' that Ruby Cohn has identified with Dante's *dolce stil nuovo*, but she is unable to reconnect herself to a past and cannot find any consolation in it.
24 Milton, *Paradise Lost*, 56.
25 Hugh Kenner speaks about Beckett's 'Gestapo theme'. Hugh Kenner, *A Reader's Guide to Samuel Beckett* (London: Thames and Hudson, 1973), 153.
26 In *Romeo and Juliet*, the world of the lovers is the nightly world of stars and planets, where they become each other's sun and moon: 'Romeo: But soft, what light through yonder window breaks?/It is the east, and Juliet is the sun./ Arise fair sun, and kill the envious moon' (*RJ* 2.2.2–4).
27 Mercutio: 'If thou art Dun we'll draw thee from the mire/Of (save your reverence) love, wherein thou stickest/Up to the ears. Come, we burn daylight, ho!' (*RJ* 1.4.41–3).
28 Juliet: 'Or bid me go into a new-made grave/And hide me with a dead man in his shroud' (*RJ* 4.1.84–5).
29 Cf. e.g. *Dream of Fair to Middling Women*, ed. Eoin O'Brien and Edith Fournier (New York: Arcade, 1992), 125.
30 Cf.: 'but the livery of death, leaving aside its pale flag altogether, was too much for her' (*MPTK*, 198).
31 It is unclear whether Beckett was familiar with the photography of Angus McBean, whose surrealist photographs show actresses such as Frances Day or Beatrice Lillie buried to the waist or to the neck. Knowlson, *Damned to Fame*, 475–6.
32 Virginia Woolf, *Mrs. Dalloway* (London: Penguin, 1992), 10.
33 Ruby Cohn regards 'fear no more' as meaningless for both characters: 'In Beckett's world, death alone enables one to 'fear no more' – a meaningless trisyllable for Winnie and Willie, who are determinedly alive', Ruby Cohn, *Modern Shakespeare Offshoots*, 386; the implications of Imogen's liminal state, however, are constitutive for *Happy Days*.
34 Knowlson, *Damned to Fame*, 478–9.
35 Franz Lehár, *The Merry Widow* (London: Glocken, 2016), 96.
36 Ruby Cohn, *Back to Beckett* (Princeton University Press, 1973), 182; Maurice Harmon (ed.), *No Author Better Served*, 95.
37 Helen Vendler, *The Art of Shakespeare's Sonnets* (Cambridge, M.A.: Belknap, 1997), 329.
38 Anne Atik, *How It Was: A Memoir of Samuel Beckett* (London: Faber & Faber, 2001), 53.

CHAPTER 4

Purgatory and Pause – Shakespeare, Dante and the Lobster

In the late 1920 and early 1930s, during and after his stay in Paris, Beckett explored literary and critical genres, pondered whether he should enter academia and articulated aesthetic concerns and goals such as to 'obtain that inexplicable bombshell perfection' (*CSP*, 4). The wide scope of works he wrote during those years include the short story 'Assumption' (1929), the poem 'Whoroscope' (1930), his first critical essays 'Dante...Bruno. Vico..Joyce' (1929), and *Proust* (1931), and his first novel *Dream of Fair to Middling Women* (1932, publ. 1992).

Beckett takes the motto for *Dream of Fair to Middling Women* from Geoffrey Chaucer's dream vision *The Legend of Good Women* (1380s): 'A thousand sythes have I herd men telle,/That there is joye in hevene and peyne in helle,/But natheles, this wot I wel also.'[1] The quotation stops in mid-sentence. After demarcating Heaven and Hell as the two opposing locales of salvation history, and evoking the traditional associations of joy and pain linked to them, Chaucer's narrator and Beckett's quote end on the emphatic 'but' qualifying conventional beliefs by ironically confronting them with empirical evidence. Chaucer's narrator acknowledges the Christian narrative, but is quick to point out that he himself has never met anyone, at least in his home country, who had been either in Heaven or Hell to verify it: 'But natheles, yet wot I wel also,/That there ne is non dwelleth in this contre/That eyther hath in helle or hevene ybe'.[2] Beckett not only engages with Chaucer's *Legend* in his own dream vision, but both texts open an imaginary space, which holds the possibility that things could be otherwise than previously thought.

Aligning his work to Chaucer, Shakespeare and Dante, Beckett enters an intertextual dialogue that creates significance and challenges received hermeneutic habits. He places many of his works between binaries such as Heaven and Hell, between the extremes, in a way that foregrounds dualisms and also undermines them. His works thereby create intersections that refer to and elucidate paradoxes of Western thought. They both exhibit their indebtedness to literary traditions and reveal aporetic incongruences. These intertextual intersections take place in an intermediate realm that, analogous to the medieval idea of Purgatory, presents a space of the imagination. Whereas the parodic and subversive functions of Beckett's recourse to Dante have often been noted, Beckett's relation to Shakespeare regarding purgatorial literary spaces has not been studied in detail.

Imagining the Intermediary

T.S. Eliot famously considered Dante and Shakespeare the giants of modern literature: 'Dante and Shakespeare divide the modern world between them, there is no third.'[3] Beckett, from early on, draws on the works of both Dante and Shakespeare,[4] not least to explore the imaginary construction of third spaces. As products of the imagination and places that assert themselves in between traditional boundaries, purgatorial spaces fascinated Beckett, who was inspired by Dante's literary construction of the intermediary. Dante Alighieri's (1265–1321) monumental world-poem, *La Divina Commedia* (1307–21), relies on a threefold structure. Between *Inferno*, the place of eternal pain of the damned and *Paradiso*, a place of eternal bliss, lies *Purgatorio*, which, in keeping with medieval traditions of piety, is a place of purgation where the dead who had sinned moderately during their lifetime can expiate their minor and yet unatoned sins. Purgatory, located in between the two poles, constitutes a dynamic moment between the static and timeless states of damnation and heavenly bliss. In the *Commedia*, stillness and motion are fundamental categories that carry symbolic weight. When Dante strides through Hell, he passes through precisely charted zones that represent the different categories of sins, in which the damned remain forever spellbound, repeat mechanic motions and stay fixed to the place of their punishment. The places in Hell are reminiscent of the irreversibility of divine retribution and denote an abode where there is no mercy left for the souls. On Mount Purgatory, by contrast, the souls leave the place assigned to them as soon as they have accomplished their penance and are saved, and finally ascend to the summit. In contrast to the places in Hell, those on Mount Purgatory are places of expectation. They imply that movement is possible and, with upward movement, salvation. In Paradise, the souls are likewise bound to a place in the hierarchical order of the heavenly sphere. Unlike the souls in Hell, however, the souls in Paradise are not driven by the desire to leave their assigned place. In Paradise, the movement of the souls, like the movement of the heavenly wheels and the constellations of stars, suggests that individual freedom and divine will are identical.

The space of Mount Purgatory is closed and yet permeable. It is both a space for penance and a space of salvation, a space of immanence in which divine transcendence is virtually present. In its theological significance as a place of repentance and return, Mount Purgatory in Dante's *La Divina Commedia* is characterized as a transitional space of change. It constitutes an imaginary in-between space of mediation that makes it possible to establish connections between earthly life and the hereafter. Transcending the borderline of death, this new prospect promises that the boundary between this life and the hereafter is not entirely impassable, but penetrable. Purgatory as a denotation of a liminal meeting place between this world and the next was of great significance for the medieval imagination, and its immense attraction as a new symbolic space is documented in numerous works of art. Beckett's manifold uses of Purgatory explore how a transcendental abode in the Christian imagination can be turned into a literary space immanent to the text.

The eminence and the constitutive function of Purgatory for church history as well as for the history of thought in the Middle Ages and the Renaissance has been demonstrated by Jacques LeGoff.[5] In installing the intermediary space of Purgatory in the mid-twelfth century, medieval church doctrine multiplied possible locations of the dead and, apart from Heaven and Purgatory, also distinguished between the limbo for unbaptized infants and the limbo for the righteous patriarchs and prophets who had died before the incarnation of Christ.[6] In the doctrine of the 'Harrowing of Hell', to which a play in the medieval mystery cycles was dedicated, this limbo is emptied by the cleansing action performed by Christ. The term *purgatory* itself was not used until the twelfth century. However, in the context of far-reaching ecclesiastical reforms within the Roman Catholic Church in the sixth century, Pope Gregory the Great taught that the missal sacrifice during a service was to be conceived as a mass for the souls of the departed. For the faithful this created the possibility of getting into contact with, and even influencing the fate of, the sinful dead in the here and now. For the Catholic Church, it created numerous options to shape this transitional permeability by installing new practices of worship. Among the most prominent measures of intercession taken by church authorities was the selling of indulgences to alleviate punishment for souls in Purgatory. This provided the church with a major source of revenue and attracted significant reformist critique.

Early on, the reformers recognized the significance of the invention of Purgatory for the human imagination. Luther referred to it as an invented third space.[7] Reformers such as Bishop Hugh Latimer and translator William Tyndale wrote and preached about the illicit profit made by 'purging the purses' of the believers rather than the souls in Purgatory.[8] To them the doctrine of Purgatory lacked any scriptural foundation and presented a clerical fiction that was shamelessly and ubiquitously instrumentalized. It not only encouraged solidarity with the dead, but also enabled Christians to bargain with their fate in a proto-capitalist fashion. Since there was always the chance of making amends later, the final reckoning could easily be postponed and the wicked could continue to sin blithely: 'The doctrine of purgatory thus rationalized, equalized, and eventually commodified the relationship between human sin and its eternal consequences.'[9] In England, the notion of Purgatory was eliminated as an article of faith in the 'Forty Two Articles' of the Church of England in 1553, almost fifty years before *Hamlet* was written. In 1563 the Council of Trent, in reaction to the Reformation, affirmed the existence of Purgatory but rejected superstitions and for-profit practices such as the selling of indulgences.[10] Peter Marshall examines the *Doctrinal Treatises* of William Tyndale and demonstrates that the word often used to describe Purgatory is 'feign' or 'feigning'.[11] Purgatory hence was conceived of as a fictional space. Stephen Greenblatt draws on this definition of Purgatory as 'a poet's fable'[12] in *Hamlet in Purgatory*, where he studies the ways in which Shakespeare used and transformed the notion of Purgatory in *Hamlet*.

It is not certain whether Shakespeare ever studied Dante's works in the original, but he was acquainted with them by way of their reception in the works of many of his predecessors and contemporaries: e.g. Geoffrey Chaucer, John Gower, John Florio or Thomas Lodge.[13] The 'sulph'rous and tormenting flames' (*Ham* 1.5.3) that cause King Hamlet's horror, the 'kingdom of perpetual night' Richard III dreams about, seeing 'a thousand fearful wrecks' (*R III* 1.4.24) and not least the Porter in Macbeth comparing himself to the 'porter of hell-gate' (*Mac* 2.3.1–2) suggest that Dante's works were at least latently present in English literature between Geoffrey Chaucer and John Milton's more extensive and explicit evocation of the poet in *Paradise Lost* (1667–74).

The imaginative energy released by notions of the hereafter, its theatricality and spectacular significance, its interweaving of individual and social identity creates a *theatrum mundi*, a 'world theatre', which conceives of human history as a divine artefact that is the very subject of Dante's

Commedia. For poetry and literature, Purgatory indeed became a space for the imagination, a dynamic entity that materialized between the no longer and the not yet, between the present and the future, between the existential extremes of being and non-being that result in a state of waiting, of procrastination, pause and postponement.

The experience of waiting and expectation that characterizes the situation on Mount Purgatory can be compared to aesthetic experience, which Dante also portrays as pausing and dwelling in the presence of beauty and as an intense way of focusing on the aesthetic object. In the fourth canto of *Purgatorio*, Dante describes these states of deep concentration as a kind of lingering at a place: 'E però, quando s'ode cosa o vede/che tegna forte a sè l'anima volta,/vassene'l tempo e l'uom non se n'avvede'. (*Purgatorio*, 4, 7–9). (And therefore whenas aught is heard or seen,/That firmly keeps the soul toward it turned,/Time passes, and a man perceives it not (4, 7–9). Dante explains that in moments of intense experience, the soul is capable of concentrating entirely on its perceptive capacity, so that it loses its sense of time. Perception and the sense of time for Dante are two potentialities of the soul (*virtú*, *Potenza*) that diverge in states of deep concentration. Purgatory as a place of waiting thus affords an experience that is both embedded in a temporal continuum and yet exempt from it.

Waiting and Pause in *Hamlet*

In Shakespeare's plays, the condition of waiting and the expectation of hesitation and pause in relation to the notion of Purgatory, as has been prominently shown by Stephen Greenblatt, is nowhere more impressively presented than in *Hamlet*. Greenblatt explains the role of Purgatory as an influential cultural institution that allows the living to stay in contact with the dead.[14] For Greenblatt, Shakespeare's Hamlet, who is placed between earthly life and the finality of death, has inherited this cultural function of Purgatory, and he argues that in the play, the stage turns into a purgatorial space in which old Hamlet's ghost for a short time becomes his own revenant: 'the space of Purgatory becomes the space of the stage where old Hamlet's ghost is doomed for a certain term to walk the night'.[15]

Written in around 1600, *Hamlet* is not set in contemporary Elizabethan England but in ninth-century Denmark. From its very beginning, the play casts itself into an in between space. The guards are in place on the walls of Elsinore Castle, shortly before daybreak, just after midnight, at the dawn of a new day, expecting the arrival of a potentially hostile Norwegian army. 'Who's there?' (*Ham* 1.1.1) are the first words of the play as mistrust pervades the scene. The situation of profound uncertainty is further intensified by the appearance of King Hamlet's ghost. This is the ghost of the father, the old King, whose tale reveals that he was murdered by his own brother in a garden. From early on, the play introduces a number of biblical parallels and inverts them at the same time. Instead of calling his son to forgiveness or vicarious sacrifice as a more benign and charitable-minded ghost perhaps would, Hamlet's fatherly ghost presses his son to revenge. In some respect, *Hamlet* is more a tragedy about the revenge of the father on the son than otherwise.

Even if young Hamlet first obeys and elevates the ghost of his father to God's place when he promises him: 'thy commandment all alone shall live/ Within the book and volume of my brain' (*Ham* 1.5.102–3), he very soon is beset by doubt about the ghost's questionable shape. He mistrusts him, procrastinates in obeying his command, and uses the theatre, putting on 'an antic disposition' (*Ham* 1.5.172) and staging 'The Mousetrap', the play-within-the-play, in which he confronts his uncle with the murder scenario to convince himself of Claudius' guilt. This does not bring about the desired certainty and Hamlet hesitates yet again, remaining a sceptic and a spectator.[16] It is only at the very end of the play that he rashly accomplishes his father's will, which results in his own death. Stephen Greenblatt succinctly characterizes Hamlet's religious dilemma in *Hamlet in Purgatory*: 'a young man from Wittenberg, with a distinctly Protestant temperament, is haunted by a distinctly Catholic Ghost'.[17] Indeed, after the encounter with his father's ghost, Hamlet, the student from Wittenberg, swears by Saint Patrick, the patron saint of Purgatory, and Denmark to him becomes a prison from which he seeks to escape.

Even if apocalyptic thought thrived in England in the sixteenth and seventeenth centuries and the expectation that the end of the world was imminent was shared by Puritans, Anglicans and Catholics alike, the doctrine of Purgatory had become obsolete in Post-Reformation England and at the time of Shakespeare's writing of *Hamlet* was considered a mere residue of Catholic faith. Yet Shakespeare draws on the old faith when the ghost of the father explains to this son 'I am thy father's spirit,/Doomed for a certain term to walk the night' (*Ham* 1.5.9–10), interrupting his stay in Purgatory for a short while to request that his son revenge his murder. The fatherly expectation, however, is not fulfilled by the son, at least not straightaway. The entire arc of suspense of the play is determined by an in-between time, between the revengeful fatherly command and its fulfilment in the bloodbath that ends the play.[18] From the beginning, the end is immanent in the dramatic structure, but it remains postponed and protracted. When Hamlet, in Act V Scene ii, says 'It will be short. The interim's mine' (*Ham* 5.2.73), his theatrical metaphor describes his own position and realm of action as between the acts, which gives him room to play and enact different roles. Margreta De Grazia summarizes: 'The extremes are set, and the middle – the meantime – is all that remains. ... The play's multiple acts of revenge all conform to this structure. A pause invariably intervenes between the resolution to act and its execution.'[19]

Pause, the wavering and hesitancy before the completion of a task, is central to the structure of *Hamlet*. In his monologue 'To be, or not to be, that is the question –' (*Ham* 3.1.56), Hamlet envisions the consequences of his possible action and ponders several scenarios that make him hesitate to proceed in the revenge requested of him: 'For in that sleep of death what dreams may come,/When we have shuffled off this mortal coil,/ Must give us pause' (*Ham* 3.1.66–8). Hamlet comes closest to finishing his task and murdering Claudius when he finds him seemingly praying in the chapel and refrains from acting, causes further delay and, as Margreta De Grazia has shown, displays his roguishness rather than acting like a conscientious Christian: 'Its [the prayer scene's] conspicuous forestalling of the climactic action gives Hamlet the opportunity to show off his villainy, ratcheting it up to the point of devilry.'[20] Remarkably, all of the murderers in *Hamlet* pause before the execution of their intended action.[21] Hamlet himself delays, but also Lucianus in *The Mousetrap*, Laertes and Pyrrhus whose murdering of Priam is rendered in the speech of the First Player: 'for lo, his sword,/Which was declining on the milky head/Of reverend Priam, seemed i'th'air to stick./So, as a painted tyrant, Pyrrhus stood,/And like a neutral to his will and matter,/Did nothing' (*Ham* 2.2.435–40). This 'Pyrrhus pause' describes an instance that gains metonymical significance for the play as a whole: an action is performed in slow motion, abides suspended and postponed at a point of the plot from which the end is deferred, and yet remains inevitable.

The entire fourth act in which Hamlet is sent to England with Rosencrantz and Guildenstern creates such a structural pause in the play, and Claudius explains the purpose of his plan: 'To bear all smooth and even,/This sudden sending him away must seem/Deliberate pause' (*Ham* 4.3.7–9). Yet Hamlet, in the meantime, sends Rosencrantz and Guildenstern to the scaffold intended for him. He returns unscathed from his voyage, renounces hesitation and embraces 'rashness' (*Ham* 5.2.7), yet dies lingering in the 'not half an hour of life' (*Ham* 5.2.295) that is left to him. At the end, the English ambassadors arrive to 'tell him his commandment is fulfilled' (*Ham* 5.2.349), and Fortinbras calls for 'haste' to hear Horatio's report (*Ham* 5.2.365).

Beckettian and Joycean Purgatories

Hamlet resonates through modernism, from A.C. Bradley, Wilson Knight and F.R. Leavis to T.S. Eliot and W.B. Yeats[22] – and so does Dante. Piero Boitani even identifies an 'Irish Dante' in Yeats, Joyce and Beckett, and considers Purgatory the 'favourite dimension' of Joyce, Beckett and Heaney.[23] The purgatorial condition of in-between-ness – of waiting, hesitation and pause – gains further relevance in the works of Beckett's contemporaries.[24] Joyce's *A Portrait of the Artist as a Young Man* (1916) illustrates Stephen Dedalus' growing alienation from the church during his formative years at a Catholic boarding school, where he is taught about 'the prison of purgatory'[25] and confronted by the violent visions of Father Arnell, who takes sadistic pleasure in delivering sermons about excessive torment in Hell.

Waiting for Godot has become almost proverbial for describing the situation of waiting for the arrival of a potentially salvific power. The play has therefore often been read as a drama about the *condition humaine*, an allegory of the human search for meaning between the Christian hope for salvation and absurdity. Waiting invokes the unfulfilled promise of a presence yet to come and creates a space of potentially infinite anticipation, but also presents a space of non-action that fulfils itself in itself. Tom Stoppard's characters Rosencrantz and Guildenstern in his play *Rosencrantz and Guildenstern are Dead* (1967) have often been compared to Beckett's Vladimir and Estragon in *Waiting for Godot*: 'plot and characters from Shakespeare set in a Beckettian ambiance, or vice versa',[26] and the play has sometimes been conceived as 'Waiting for Hamlet'.[27] Famous examples from the performance history of *Waiting for Godot* underline the metaphorical significance the play acquired when it was staged, among others, in a prison in the German town of Wuppertal, in South Africa (1955 and 2010), and also in Sarajevo (1993) while it was under siege during the war in former Yugoslavia.[28] The settings of these performances not only dramatize the experience of waiting as an allegorical condition but also relate to the reality of Dantean visions of Purgatory and Hell. J.M. Coetzee's novel *Waiting for the Barbarians* (1980) places his protagonist, a magistrate and loyal administrator, on the margins of the Empire to explore the shifting boundaries between interior and exterior, victim and perpetrator, human being and its barbarian other. Coetzee draws on

Beckett's play and treats the theme of fearful anticipation within the political context of South Africa.

The importance of Dante for Beckett within his profound knowledge of European literature has been widely documented: 'He had at his ready command, even in his later years, not only all of Shakespeare, Dante, Milton, Petrarch, the King James Bible (not to mention the *Book of Common Prayer*), and much of English and German Romantic poetry (Goethe, Heine, and Hölderlin, in particular), but Sterne, Defoe, Flaubert, and Yeats, as well as Dr. Johnson and his commentators.'[29] Daniela Caselli in *Beckett's Dantes* explores the importance of Dante's works as a source for Beckett's imagination and also traces his ways of questioning the authority of Dante.[30] Michael Robinson and Phyllis Carey likewise examine individual aspects of Beckett's interaction with Dante and Joyce.[31] The intertextual connections between Beckett, the medieval world of Dante and their legacy in Shakespeare's works that this chapter addresses are not to be merely understood in terms of a literary influence that manifests itself in quotations and intertextual allusions in a comparative infernalism. Beckett's dialogue with Shakespeare and Dante rather creates paradigms of cultural generation and reflects on systems of creating symbolic and semiotic significance as intertextually determined.

In constellations like these, between authors as well as between traditions of thought, the idea of Purgatory as an intermediary space of movement is apt to describe a dynamic, permeable space for intertextual dialogue. The works of Beckett, Dante and Shakespeare do not appear as stable entities, but they are rather in flux and reciprocally resonate with one another. Beckett's recourse to Purgatory is therefore not only the metaphorical adaptation of a space that was constitutive for the imagination of medieval readers who stayed in touch with the departed, but also a means of reflecting on the processes in which literary space is constructed. Dante's *La Divina Commedia* is part of this culturally inherited repertoire of hermeneutic paradigms. The cathartic notion pertinent to purgation in Beckett's texts also metaphorically applies to his paring away and making readers aware of traditional ways in which meaning is constructed, and it informs as well as alters the perception of literature across the centuries. Beckett's purgatorial aesthetics also grants insights into the way in which aesthetic categories and hermeneutic models have become part of our epistemic and cultural repertoire, and how interpretive habits have been shaped by normative schemata that claim dogmatic inescapability.

One of Beckett's first scholarly pieces of writing was the essay 'Dante...Bruno.Vico..Joyce' (1929). It discusses the relation between

La Divina Commedia and Joyce's poetics in *Work in Progress*,[32] later known as *Finnegans Wake*. Beckett compares the specific presentation of Purgatory in Dante and Joyce: 'Dante's is conical and consequently implies culmination. Mr Joyce's is spherical and excludes culmination' (*Disjecta*, 33). Whereas in Dante's work it is possible to ascend Mount Purgatory, Joyce's Purgatory is issueless and constitutes the immanent space of the text.[33] Joyce's texts, however, are not conceived as stationary, but their immanent purgatorial condition is one of innate restlessness: 'This inner elemental vitality and corruption of expression imparts a furious restlessness to the form, which is admirably suited to the purgatorial aspect of the work. There is an endless verbal germination, maturation, putrefaction, the cyclic dynamism of the intermediate' (*Disjecta*, 29).

Beckett's texts have often been considered 'purgatorial', as allegories on the human condition, hence regarding them in categories similar to those of medieval theories of art that contained elements of allegory.[34] *How It Is* has been read as a literary Purgatory,[35] and 'The Lost Ones' describes a conical Purgatory 'a flattened cylinder fifty metres round and sixteen high for the sake of harmony' (*CSP*, 202), an '[ABODE WHERE LOST] bodies roam each searching for its lost one' (*CSP*, 202). Likewise, Beckett's theatrical works contain many allusions to Dante's *Purgatorio*. In Act II of *Waiting for Godot*, Vladimir and Estragon reminisce about the many dead and 'all the dead voices' rustling, whispering and murmuring, finding themselves in a purgatorial condition similar to the murmuring damned in Dante's fifth circle: 'Vladimir: To have lived is not enough for them./ Estragon: They have to talk about it./Vladimir: To be dead is not enough for them./Estragon: It is not sufficient' (*CDW*, 58).[36]

'Dante and the Lobster'

One of Beckett's best-known and most explicit literary references to the *Commedia* is his short story 'Dante and the Lobster'. It was published for the first time in the journal *This Quarter* (Winter 1932) and in 1934 it was used as the opening story of his collection of short stories *More Pricks than Kicks*.[37] The very title of the story is remarkable. How does the great Italian poet of the Trecento relate to the crustacean that in many parts of the world is considered a delicacy?[38] Does a lobster play any role in *La Divina Commedia*, or does it perhaps introduce a topic that has hitherto been overlooked by research?

The peculiar constellation of the title in which Beckett connects the creator of the medieval world epos to a creature of comparatively lower rank, is characteristic for the paradoxical construction of the entire story. In a similar vein to Chaucer's 'but' in Beckett's reference to *The Legend of Good Women*, the contrast between the real, everyday world, its practical and ethical problems and an idealized world of philosophical dimension becomes the story's formal as well as thematic principle of structure. The contrapuntal movement of the story follows the figure of a paradox in which the sacred and the profane, Paradise and Hell, salvation and damnation, creator and creature, human being and animal encounter one another in a realm of possibility that is afforded by the story itself. This place between the extremes of either-or, in Beckett, Dante and Shakespeare, can be considered purgatorial, located between Paradise and the Inferno. Beckett describes Purgatory with recourse to Joyce: 'In what sense, then, is Mr Joyce's work purgatorial? In the absolute absence of the Absolute. Hell is the static lifelessness of unrelieved viciousness. Paradise the static lifelessness of unrelieved immaculation. Purgatory a flood of movement and vitality released by the conjunction of these two elements' (*Disjecta*, 33.). The 'absolute absence of the Absolute', the lack of fixed ontological ascriptions and a univocal teleological direction towards salvation is what characterizes the space of Purgatory. Purgatory becomes a dynamic state in between the no longer and the not yet, and the finite zone of transition between the stasis of eternal bliss in Paradise and the similarly invariant perpetual state of eternal torment in Hell.

In its recourse to Shakespeare and Dante, Beckett's story, from the very beginning, establishes itself as an artefact that enters into intertextual dialogue. The richly allusive figure of Dante's Belacqua Shuah fascinated the early Beckett. In the first cantos of Dante's *Purgatorio*, the pilgrim Dante, led by the poet Virgil, meets a number of souls who cannot yet be admitted to Purgatory proper, but who find themselves in an ante-Purgatory in order to prepare themselves in a period of waiting for the penance of their sins.[39] Among them is Belacqua Shua, the Florentine lutemaker, whom Dante is said to have known, and whose most characteristic features were his indolence and apathy. Belacqua is not granted an immediate entry into Purgatory and has to remain waiting to be admitted for a time that equals the duration of his earthly life. The time of waiting is marked by repetition, and Belacqua, in waiting for Purgatory, is sentenced to repeat the time of his life. Shuah, whose initials B.S. are a reversal of S.B. (Samuel Beckett) also refers to figures in the Old Testament like the mother of Onan in Genesis 38, one of Abraham's sons and also one of Job's interlocutors, and becomes the prototype of many of Beckett's heroes or rather anti-heroes. He is the protagonist of *Dream of Fair to Middling*

Women as well as of a number of stories in *More Pricks than Kicks*.[40] In the short story 'Ding-Dong', Belacqua is described as 'Being by nature however sinfully indolent, bogged in indolence' (*MPTK*, 31). He leads an existence that is defined by pause: 'He did not fatigue himself, he said; on the contrary. He lived a Beethoven pause, he said, whatever he meant by that' (*MPTK*, 32). When he further explains his contradictory existence to the narrator of 'Ding Dong' – 'he gave me an account of one of these "moving pauses". He had a strong weakness for oxymoron' (*MPTK*, 32) – the narrator himself succumbs to an oxymoronic description of Belacqua.

Like Joyce's *Ulysses*, Beckett's story takes place on a single day in Dublin. Beckett's Belacqua, similar to Leopold Bloom, appears as an intertextually constructed figure that explicitly refers to its textual origins. In Beckett's story, Belacqua himself is first of all introduced as a reader and translator of *La Divina Commedia* who, at the very beginning of the story becomes stuck in the process of reading: 'It was morning and Belacqua was stuck in the first of the canti in the moon' (*MPTK*, 3). The story refers to the passage in *Paradiso* II, where Beatrice explains to Dante the structure of the heavens, and Dante notices shadow-like spots on the surface of the moon. He assiduously surmises that these are reminders of the mark of Cain and the first fratricide according to a common belief. Beatrice responds enigmatically, encouraging Dante to find his own answer and continues to elaborate on the dimensions of the spheres.[41]

In 'Dante and the Lobster', Belacqua, the reader of the *Paradiso*, therefore finds himself in a parallel situation of stasis to Dante himself and Dante's Belacqua in ante-Purgatory. He is stuck and can neither move forwards nor backwards. To both figures, the access to Paradise remains barred, physically and intellectually. Belacqua's fruitless hermeneutical endeavours to understand the fictional hereafter expounded in the *Commedia* are abruptly disturbed by the intrusion of the here and now, the ringing of the church bells at midday, which causes Belacqua to close the book in frustration: 'he slammed it shut' (*MPTK*, 3).

In analogy to *La Divina Commedia*, 'Dante and the Lobster' follows a tripartite structure. The stages *Inferno*, *Purgatorio* and *Paradiso* become inverted in rich variations and appear to Belacqua as 'Three large obligations ... First lunch, then the lobster, then the Italian lesson' (*MPTK*, 4). The story begins with Belacqua trying to read the *Paradiso* and ends in the kitchen of his aunt, which is described as a kind of underworld. Between these stations, the narration consists of a purgatorial process of postponement that metaphorically materializes in the fate of the lobster.

The mere accomplishment of Belacqua's first task, the preparation of his lunch that consists of toast and cheese, is by no means trivial, but demands the highest degree of precision and requires the entire focus of Belacqua, a pathological lover of order. A daily routine such as the toasting of bread is described in metaphors of crime and punishment in the Inferno, and it thus becomes both defamiliarized and metaphysically elevated. The everyday world and the world of ideas are paradoxically intertwined. It is through Belacqua's obsessive pedantry, devoting himself to the execution of his task as if it were a religious ritual, that the scene gains both comic effect and tragic inevitability.

In order to not be disturbed under any circumstances, Belacqua closes the door, and to cut his bread spreads a newspaper on the table where he spots the photograph of the murderer McCabe who has been condemned to death. The story then creates a context of associations in which the bread that is about to be eaten is related to the murderer who awaits his execution. Belacqua cuts the end of the bread over the face of McCabe. The decapitated loaf of bread ('the stump') is returned to the breadbox, which is described as 'the prison'. While Belacqua is toasting the bread, the kitchen turns into a kind of Inferno: 'Long before the end the room was full of smoke and the reek of burning' (*MPTK*, 5). Adding to the association of hellfire, the hot gas grill burns a sizeable mark into the wallpaper. Belacqua, however, takes this with equanimity: 'What the hell did he care?' (*MPTK*, 6). Similar to the stigmata of the 'branded moon' and Cain, the original murderer of his brother, who as an outcast is both marked and protected by the mark of Cain given to him by God, in Belacqua's world the wallpaper is also branded.[42] The scene makes possible a synoptic vision of profane actions in the narrative present and alludes to moments in salvation history that signify salvation or damnation. It does so by providing room for the interpretation of the everyday world in terms of *La Divina Commedia*, thus making the dimension of transcendence virtually present in the story.

In contrast to God, however, who bestows the mark of protection on Cain out of pity, Belacqua does not care about the damage he has done. He frenetically continues the preparations for his lunch and anticipates his meal in a violent fantasy: 'he would devour it with a sense of rapture and victory' (*MPTK*, 6). He appears as an agent of blind destruction. Whereas the bread, his victim, is characterized by human attributes 'soft ..., ... alive, ... face' (*MPTK*, 7), Belacqua compares his own frenzy of destruction to that of a wild animal: 'He would snap at it with closed eyes, he would gnash it into a pulp, he would vanquish it utterly with his fangs'

(*MPTK*, 6). Human being and animal, matter and animate being, change places and morph into one another in a parody of the eucharistic transubstantiation.

It is remarkable that Belacqua illustrates his rapture with a quotation from *Hamlet*: '[I]t would be like smiting the sledded Polacks on the ice' (*MPTK*, 6). This is a variation of Horatio's words from Act I, where he reports about King Hamlet and his warlike actions against Norway and confirms that the ghost wore the same frown as the late king: 'So frowned he once, when in an angry parle/He smote the sledded Polacks on the ice' (*Ham* 1.1.62–3). In the library-episode in *Ulysses*, Joyce draws on the editorial debate about this passage, which in Q1 and Q2 reads 'sleaded pollax' as opposed to 'sledded Pollax' in the First Folio. Whereas Horatio seems to be speaking about two incidents, one with the Norwegians and another with the Poles,[43] Stephen Dedalus refers to the weapon to describe Hamlet's rashness in the carnage that ends the play and that he compares to contemporary warfare: 'Not for nothing was he a butcher's son, wielding the sledded poleaxe and spitting in his palms. Nine lives are taken off for his father's one. Our Father who art in purgatory. Khaki Hamlets don't hesitate to shoot' (*U* 9, 154). 'Dante and the Lobster' resonates with Shakespeare's *Hamlet*, but also with Stephen Dedalus' 'Hamlet theory'. Like the slightly incorrect quotation from *Hamlet* in the story, the alliteration 'smitting, sledded' rhetorically expresses the violent act of destruction. In Belacqua's domestic setting, during the preparation of his lunch, this small-scale imitation of old King Hamlet's infernal fury in Shakespeare and that of young Hamlet in Joyce appears comical.

Apart from Beckett's fascination with Shakespeare's 'fat language' that constitutes its object through words, this quotation and its evocation of old Hamlet's ghost is not randomly chosen. Beckett's allusion leads as it were through Joyce and Shakespeare to Dante and from there back to his own text. The extremes of fire and ice that mark King Hamlet's predicament are even more vividly imagined in *Measure for Measure*, where Claudio describes his fear of Hell in Dantean terms: 'To bathe in fiery floods or to reside/In thrilling region of thick-ribbed ice' (*MM* 3.1.122–3). Fire and ice are put into a paradoxical relation when Dante, for instance in *Inferno* XXII (46–8), speaks about an icy Hell. In numerous passages of the *Inferno*, ice is mentioned to characterize the situation of the damned, such as the traitors in the ninth circle of Hell, who remain frozen in a lake of ice (*Inferno* XXXII, 22–4) and are stuck there, immobilized to such a degree that even their tears are frozen.[44] In 'Texts for Nothing 6', for instance,

Beckett's narrator explicitly connects the plight of the frozen damned to the undead state of the souls in Purgatory: 'I was, I was, they say in Purgatory, in Hell too, admirable singulars, admirable assurance. Plunged in ice up to the nostrils, the eyelids caked with frozen tears, to fight all your battles o'er again, what tranquillity, and know there are no more emotions in store, no, I can't have heard aright' (*CSP*, 124–5).[45]

While Horatio in *Hamlet* reports about the acts of war of old Hamlet on the ice, the latter, at this moment of the play already finds himself in Purgatory from where he intermittently returns. He, who was by no means a saint during his lifetime, is afraid that on account of his unatoned sins he will have to go to Hell: 'My hour is almost come/When I to sulph'rous and tormenting flames/Must render up myself' (*Ham* 1.5.2–4). The fratricide in the garden of Elsinore and the poison applied to King Hamlet's ear during his sleep, causing a 'lazar-like' (*Ham* 1.5.72) outbreak of his skin, on many levels evokes the Fall and the expulsion from the Garden of Eden. During the reign of Hamlet senior, however, Denmark was by no means a paradise, nor was he himself a pious figure like Lazarus who rose from the dead without taking a detour through Purgatory. Not least because of his many miserable sins, he is worried that he might not be granted eternal forgiveness. Next to forcing his son to take revenge, one of the overriding concerns of the ghost is that he was not given the sacrament of penance or extreme unction. After the murder of old Hamlet and the marriage between the usurper Claudius and Gertrude that swiftly followed it, the country is not a paradisiac Elysium, either; for Hamlet, it rather becomes Hell on earth. He characterizes his dilemma as that of a fellow 'crawling between earth and heaven' (*Ham* 3.1.125) and finds himself in a purgatorial predicament between the two extremes.

'Something is rotten in the state of Denmark' (*Ham* 1.4.90): *Hamlet* portrays a fallen world. The throne is usurped, and to Hamlet his father compared to Claudius is like 'Hyperion to a satyr' (*Ham* 1.2.140). Claudius himself calls his crime rancid and smelling: 'Oh my offence is rank, it smells to heaven;/ It hath the primal eldest curse upon't,/A brother's murder. Pray can I not,/Though inclination be as sharp as will./My stronger guilt defeats my strong intent,/And like a man to double business bound,/I stand in pause where I shall first begin,/And both neglect' (*Ham* 3.3.36–43). Like Hamlet, Claudius is tied to his dilemma, his 'double business', and like his nephew, he cannot act nor pray, but remains paralysed, in pause. The moral corruption of the state in *Hamlet* is juxtaposed in 'Dante and the Lobster' to the material rottenness of the cheese that Belacqua intends to buy. 'Rotten' – rancid, decomposed – is what the cheese has to be and for these qualities Belacqua cherishes a specific predilection: 'a good green stenching rotten lump of Gorgonzola cheese, alive, and by God he would have it' (*MPTK*, 7). For Belacqua, the cheese has to be rotten, dead to such a degree that it is alive again. The gravediggers in *Hamlet*, when asked how long it takes for a buried corpse to rot, also refer to a state of rottenness before death: 'Faith, if a be not rotten before a die, as we have many pocky corses nowadays that will scarce hold the laying in' (*Ham* 5.1.140–1). In his poem 'Casket of Pralinen for the Daughter of a Dissipated Mandarin', Beckett connects gorgonzola cheese with Purgatory as well as with *King Lear*, *Hamlet*, *All's Well That Ends Well* and *Macbeth*: 'Gloucester's no bimbo/and he's in Limbo/so all's well with the gorgonzola cheese of human kindness'.[46] The 'milk of human kindness' (*Mac* 1.5.15), which Lady Macbeth denounces her husband for possessing in abundance, has curdled into cheese in Beckett's poem – it invokes a purgatorial 'limbo' as potentially granting a humane and salvific ending. Belacqua, however, who finds the cheese still not rotten enough, dismisses the affirmations of the cheesemonger that '[i]n the length and breadth of Dublin [said the grocer] you won't find a rottener bit this minute' (*MPTK*, 7), and leaves the shop with his provisions. Like the loaf of bread before, the piece of cheese is characterized by human attributes and becomes anthropomorphic – 'the cadaverous tablet of cheese' (*MPTK*, 7–8). This allusion to the cadaver, the body of Christ, is further reinforced when the cheesemonger, who is described as a warm-hearted man, feels pity for Belacqua and spreads his arms in a gesture that is compared to that of the crucified (*MPTK*, 8). The cheesemonger himself is called Angelo, referring to the motif of the 'Bread of Angels' ('pan de li angeli') in *Paradiso* (II, v. 11) and the *Convivio*,[47] which, once again, hypostasizes the everyday world of Dublin in citing its Florentine subtext.

And yet, in spite of all its allusions to death on a monumental scale – the crucifixion and the Inferno – lunch, for Belacqua, finally becomes a paradisiacal experience: 'his teeth and jaws had been in heaven' (*MPTK*, 10). At the same time, however, he hears that a petition by the prisoner McCabe has failed, and that he is to be hanged the next day: 'the man must swing at dawn in Mountjoy and nothing could save him' (*MPTK*, 10). Mountjoy, the name of the main prison in Dublin, acquires paradoxical allegorical connotations in the context of *La Divina Commedia*. The 'mountain of joy' does not allude to heavenly bliss that awaits the prisoner after a Purgatory of waiting, but it stands for an inexorable earthly judgement that renders the purgatorial process hopeless. Beckett's friend

Thomas McGreevy sets his poem 'The Six Who Were Hanged', at Mountjoy in March 1921, and speaks about the six prisoners in similar terms as Belacqua: 'For these there is no uncertainty'.[48]

Belacqua's next task, his Purgatory, is to buy the lobster for his aunt on his way to his Italian lesson with his admired Professoressa Ottolenghi. The fishmonger bequeaths the animal to him, and emphasizes that it is 'lepping', which is old Scots for 'leaping', being alive, but which Belacqua merely interprets as 'fresh'. The expression 'to hand over' is ambiguous and it refers to the treason of Judas and creates yet another parallel to Hamlet who calls Polonius 'a fishmonger' (*Ham* 2.2.172), who betrays his own children and hands over Ophelia to the machinations of Claudius.

Belacqua becomes a creative misreader and mistranslator throughout, and, during the Italian lesson, he asks his teacher about the passage about the spots on the moon where he got stuck in the morning, the 'moon enigma', but she promises to deal with this question later. Another enigma to which Belacqua seeks the resolution in vain is the Dantean passage: '[q]ui vive la pietà quand' è ben morta' (*Inf* XX, 28). The term 'pietà' carries the double meaning of pity and piety and the passage could be translated as: 'here lives piety only when pity is already dead'. In the *Commedia*, Virgil admonishes Dante not to feel any pity for the souls in Hell, because their punishment expresses God's justice. In Hell, it is therefore pious to let pity die because the souls in Hell have been justly punished by God and deserve no pity. The line 'qui vive la pietà quand' è ben morta' is also used in Thomas McGreevy's poem 'Fragments', where it is referred to as the 'freezing comfort' one gains from the death of pity as the foundation of piety.[49]

The paradoxical configuration of life in death in 'Dante and the Lobster' is further extended with references to the central paradox of Christian doctrine, salvation through the death of Christ. Belacqua's reflection is once again interrupted by the sudden appearance of the French teacher, Mlle Glain, who asks about the content of the parcel in the hallway because her cat has already tackled it. Once again, the profane everyday world enters the world of transcendence that is inspired by reading the *Commedia*. Belacqua, for lack of the French word for lobster, calls the lobster a fish and returns to the relation between creator and creature, human being and animal: 'He did not know the French for lobster. Fish would do very well. Fish had been good enough for Jesus Christ, Son of God, Saviour. It was good enough for Mlle Glain' (*MPTK*, 12). The term 'fish' here refers to the symbolic substitution of the name of Christ with the acronym 'ichthys' (Jesus Christ, Son of God, Saviour).[50]

Belacqua has almost reached the third stage of his journey, his aunt's house, and yet the two most important questions, the significance of the spots on the moon and the relation between pity and piety, have remained unanswered. Also, the once again misinterpreted lobster, invisible in the parcel, retains its enigmatic quality. The beginning of the last part of the story evokes not only Dante's *Paradiso* but also the *Purgatorio* and the *Inferno*. On his way to the house of his aunt, Belacqua sees a few people by moonlight who are reminiscent of characters from the *Commedia* – a poorly dressed couple at a gate, for instance, recalls Paolo Malatesta and Francesca da Rimini. He further ponders the incongruity of justice and grace and asks himself: 'Why not piety and pity both, even down below? Why not mercy and Godliness together? A little mercy in the stress of sacrifice, a little mercy to rejoice against judgment. He thought of Jonah and the gourd and the pity of a jealous God on Nineveh. And poor McCabe ... He would relish one more meal, one more night' (*MPTK*, 13). The passage links the example of the prophet Jonah, who in the Old Testament resists God's command to warn the inhabitants of the town of Niniveh to abandon their sinful ways, and who is spared God's wrath and survives in the belly of a fish, to the Passion of Christ and to the fate of the murderer McCabe. McCabe has one last supper to look forward to, but other than the Eucharist, which celebrates Christian communion as the overcoming of death and access to life everlasting through God's grace in the sacramental sacrifice, for McCabe there seems to remain neither mercy nor pity.

An ambivalent communion is also performed at the end of *Hamlet*. Hamlet calls for 'judgement' (*Ham* 5.2.256) in his fight with Laertes and abstains from the drink Claudius offers him. Instead, it is Gertrude who drinks to her son from the poisoned cup. Hamlet, Laertes and Claudius die from the poisoned points of their swords. 'Is thy union here?' (*Ham* 5.2.305) are Hamlet's last words to Claudius before Horatio and Hamlet forgive one another and die. Death by poison frames the entire play. It marks the beginning, the murder of King Hamlet, and the poisoned swords and chalice lead to the end of the entire dynasty. In 'Dante and the Lobster', the allusion to the biblical meal that potentially brings no salvation to McCabe, at the same time, anticipates the very earthly supper at Belacqua's aunt's, in which the lobster is to furnish the main course.[51] Having arrived at his aunt's house, the third and last stage of his journey and of the story, what awaits Belacqua and the lobster is not the Paradise of the third part of the *Commedia*, but first of all a kind of descent into an underworld: 'together they went down into the bowels of the earth, into the kitchen in the basement' (*MPTK*, 13). There she unwraps the lobster-enigma, and the animal, to Belacqua's greatest surprise, is still alive: 'Christ!' he said 'it's alive' (*MPTK*, 13).

The story further explores the parallel between Christ and the lobster through the metaphor of the cross: 'They stood above it, looking down on it, exposed cruciform on the oilcloth' (*MPTK*, 13). The text puns on 'oilcloth' as 'loincloth' and later alludes to the legendary thirty years of the life of Christ: '[i]t had about thirty seconds to live' (*MPTK*, 14). It also suggests the imminent ending of Hamlet's life when Laertes refers to the less than thirty minutes that Hamlet can expect to live after he had been wounded by the poisonous blade: 'In thee there is not half an hour of life –' (*Ham* 5.2.295). Belacqua is shocked when he learns that lobsters, similar to the souls in Hell, are boiled alive; and he feels pity for the creature. His earlier indulging of violent fantasies when eating the burnt bread subsides when he is faced with the living flesh and fish. His summary of the fate of the lobster closes, rather than with a prayer, with a quotation from Keats's 'Ode to a Nightingale': 'In the depths of the sea it had crept into the cruel pot. For hours, in the midst of its enemies, it had breathed secretly. It had survived the French-woman's cat and his witless clutch. Now it was going alive into scalding water. It had to. Take into the air my quiet breath' (*MPTK*, 14).⁵² The closing of this passage recalls a further line from Keats's 'Ode to a Nightingale': 'to die upon the midnight with no pain' (l. 56) and implicitly expresses Belacqua's wishful thinking that the lobster may die with no pain. His aunt tries to allay his fear with the conventional wisdom that the lobster will not feel a thing: '"They feel nothing," she said' (*MPTK*, 14). The end of the story again condenses its many paradoxes and figures of contrast: Belacqua's initial cruel fantasy about the living bread in a kind of mock Eucharist, at the end of the story, is reflected in the cruelty of his aunt towards the living lobster, the fish and flesh that denote Christ. The execution of both actions is supplemented by references to the condemned murderer McCabe, the crucifixion of Christ and the more fundamental question about justice and grace that constitutes the realm of Purgatory. The thematic paradox becomes a structural paradox. But here, the story pauses.

It does not render the final death of the lobster, but it stops shortly before it: 'She lifted the lobster clear of the table. It had about thirty seconds to live. Well, thought Belacqua, it's a quick death, God help us all. It is not' (*MPTK*, 14). The lobster, the 'neuter creature' (*MPTK*, 13) as Belacqua has called it, remains, if only briefly, in an in-between state, between life and death. The term 'neuter' recalls Pyrrhus in *Hamlet*, who 'like a neutral to his will and matter,/Did nothing' while his sword seems to stick 'i'th'air' (*Ham* 2.2.437–40). The lobster remains stuck in the air, and the three words 'it is not' mark the end of the story and question a given commonplace. As Ruby Cohn has noted, Beckett, in an earlier version of the story, had planned to end it with the words 'like Hell it is'.[53] The final contraction of the paradox lies in a figure of double negative. 'It's a quick death' and its negation 'it is not' bring the extremes of life and death into a realm of significance, where they become mutually reflexive. The quick death is at the same time the living death, death while one is still alive, and it also alludes to the Last Judgement in the Apostolic Creed 'from there He will come to judge the quick and the dead'. Hamlet, when bantering with the gravedigger, puns: 'Thou dost lie in't, to be in't and say 'tis thine.'Tis for the dead, not for the quick, therefore thou liest' (*Ham* 5.1.106–7). The gravedigger replies: "Tis a quick lie' (*Ham* 5.1.108), and speaks about the untimely death of Ophelia in terms of a neutral being who is neither man nor woman. In a similar vein, Estragon, in *Waiting for Godot*, combines the notion of rash action with a living death: 'Estragon: Yes. And they crucified quick' (*CDW*, 51).

Again, parallels to the story can be found in the earlier poems of Thomas McGreevy. His poem 'De civitate hominum', written in the years 1917/1918, takes its title from the Augustinian distinction between the *civitas dei* and the *civitas terrena* or *hominum*. The poem describes a cold winter morning during the war as it is perceived by a soldier. The speaker looks at the blue morning sky of winter and sees the black spots of new shell holes in the otherwise snow-white earth. What he sees reminds him of 'A Matisse ensemble', and he refers to his and his fellow soldiers' predicament as one in a liminal state between life and death, war and peace:

> The model is our world,
> Our bitch of a world.
> Those who live between wars may not know
> But we who die between peaces
> Whether we die or not.[54]

The speaker's sense of himself as 'The *nature morte* accessory' is reflected in a scene in which life and death become paradoxically conflated: '*Morte* . . .!/'Tis still life that lives,/Not quick life –'.[55] The still life that constitutes the scenery around him, however, is disturbed when he hears the drone of an engine and sees an aircraft falling out of the clouds, the 'fleece-white flowers of death' catching fire: 'A delicate flame,/A stroke of orange in the morning's dress'.⁵⁶ The descent from Heaven into the Hell of a fearful death is reported by a sergeant:

> My sergeant says, very low, 'Holy God
> 'Tis a fearful death.'
> Holy God makes no reply
> Yet.⁵⁷

McGreevy's poem describes the *civitas terrena* in wartime as being suspended, waiting for a divine answer that may never come. The final word 'yet' gestures towards such an answer, which at present remains deferred. The last three lines of the poem create a direct analogy to the ending of 'Dante and the Lobster', where the intervention of an omniscient narrator – 'It is not'– unlike McGreevy's 'yet', concludes the story and contradicts 'it's a quick death', pronouncing a Last Judgement that puts an end to the hope for pity and mercy and confronts it with an unforgiving reality.

'Dante and the Lobster', Beckett's version of the *Commedia* with his many parallels to *Hamlet*, a story that evokes salvation history from the murder of Abel until the Last Judgement, does not end in a reassuring vision of universal salvation, but rather in fundamental uncertainty. It does not offer closure, neither salvation nor damnation, but, like the lobster, who has seconds to live, it remains in an in-between state, in limbo, 'where we were, as we were', as the Italian teacher put it. The end seems inevitable, yet its ultimate finality remains suspended.⁵⁸ Dante's *Commedia*, Shakespeare's *Hamlet* and Beckett's story create this space between being and nothingness. Their works enter into an intertextual polylogue that opens a realm of possibility that is not governed by dualisms but grants us the opportunity to view the one in terms of the other in a productive 'and as well' – Dante and the lobster, justice and grace, transcendence and immanence. Beckett, like Shakespeare and Dante, brings together the incongruous, through programmatic deferral of syntactic closure and through the element of pause. *Hamlet* and 'Dante and the Lobster' create imaginary third spaces that remain without the prospect of a pacifying gesture of closure or satisfactory salvation. Instead, they situate themselves in a realm that can be interpreted as a liminal, dynamic purgatorial space.

At the very beginning of *King Lear*, Lear refers to this space between the extremes that the play is to inhabit by introducing the notion of 'meantime': 'Meantime we shall express our darker purpose' (*KL* 1.1.31). Similarly, the French title of *Waiting for Godot*, 'En attendant Godot', 'while waiting for Godot' can be translated as 'meanwhile'. Reading 'Dante and the Lobster' with *Hamlet* and *La Divina Commedia* suggests the ways in which literature and drama create the imaginary spaces they inhabit. These intermediary realms set up the boundaries within and between which they restlessly operate. They represent and at the same time reflect on their status as finite yet permeable intertextual spaces.

Notes

1. Geoffrey Chaucer, 'The Legend of Good Women' in Larry Benson (ed.), *The Riverside Chaucer*, 3rd ed. (Oxford University Press, 1987), 588, ll. 1–2 Text G.
2. Chaucer, 'The Legend of Good Women', 588, ll. 4–6 Text G.
3. T.S. Eliot, *Dante* (London: Faber & Faber, 1929), 51.
4. Daniela Caselli, *Beckett's Dantes* (Manchester University Press, 2005).
5. Jacques Le Goff, *Un autre Moyen Âge* (Paris: Gallimard, 1999); Jaques Le Goff, *La naissance du Purgatoire* (Paris: Gallimard, 1981).
6. Unbaptized pagans inhabit Dante's first circle of Hell. Peter Marshall, 'The Reformation of Hell? Protestant and Catholic Infernalisms in England c.1560–1640', *Journal of Ecclesiastical History*, 61 (2010), 279–98, 280.
7. Paul Althaus, 'Luthers Gedanken über die letzten Dinge', *Luther Jahrbuch*, 23 (1941), 9–34, 22–8.
8. Peter Marshall, *Beliefs and the Dead in Reformation England* (Oxford University Press, 2002), 55.
9. Lori Anne Ferrell, 'Religion' in Bruce R. Smith (ed.), *The Cambridge Guide to The Worlds of Shakespeare* I (Cambridge University Press, 2016), 685.
10. The last session of the Council (Sessio XXV) was held in 1563 and defined the doctrine of Purgatory: 'Purgatorium esse, animasque ibi detenas, fidelium suffragiis, protissimum vero acceptabili altaris scarificio juvari: praecipit sanct Synodus episcopis, ut sanam de Purgatorio doctrinam, a sanctis Patribus et sacris Conciliis traditam, a Christi fidelibus credi, teneri, doceri et ubique praedicari diligenter studeant. … Ea ver, quae ad curiositatem quandam aut superstitionem spectant, vel turpe lucrum sapiunt, tanquam scandala et fidelium offendicula prohibeant'. Heinrich Denzinger, *Enchiridion Symbolorum et Definitionum, que de Rebus Fidei et Morum A Conciliis Oecomenicis et summis Pontificibus emanarunt*, 7th ed. (Würzburg, 1895), 231.
11. Marshall, *Beliefs and the Dead in Reformation England*, 57–64.
12. Stephen Greenblatt, *Hamlet in Purgatory* (Princeton University Press, 2001), 10–46.
13. Roland Weidle, '"If man were porter of hell gate". Dante in der englischen frühen Neuzeit und Shakespeares Hölle' in Stefanie Heimgartner and Monika Schmitz-Emans (eds.), *Komparatistische Perspektiven auf Dantes 'Divina Commedia'. Lektüren, Transformationen und Visualisierungen* (Berlin, Boston: de Gruyter, 2017), 183–206.
14. Greenblatt, *Hamlet in Purgatory*, 18.

15 Greenblatt, *Hamlet in Purgatory*, 257.
16 Christoph Menke, 'Tragödie und Skeptizismus. Zu *Hamlet*', *DVJS*, 75/4 (2001), 561–86, 578.
17 Greenblatt, *Hamlet in Purgatory*, 240.
18 Margreta De Grazia analyses the entire tradition of scholarship that has been preoccupied with the question why Hamlet procrastinates. Margreta De Grazia, *Hamlet without Hamlet* (Cambridge University Press, 2008), 158–204.
19 Margreta De Grazia, *Hamlet without Hamlet*, 196–7.
20 Margreta De Grazia, *Hamlet without Hamlet*, 193.
21 Margreta De Grazia also includes the biblical story of Jephtah (2, 2, 399–400) and Gertrude's narrative about the time between Ophelia's fall into the brook and her sinking down. *Hamlet without Hamlet*, 198–9.
22 Cf. e.g. A.C. Bradley, *Shakespearean Tragedy* (London: Macmillan, 1904); T.S. Eliot, 'Hamlet and his Problems', *The Sacred Wood: Essays on Poetry and Criticism* (London: Faber & Faber, 1920), 95–104; G. Wilson Knight, *The Wheel of Fire* (London: Routledge, 2001 [1930]).
23 Piero Boitani, 'Irish Dante: Yeats, Joyce, Beckett' in Manuele Gragnolati, Fabio Camilletti and Fabian Lampart (eds.), *Metamorphosing Dante: Appropriations, Manipulations, and Rewritings in the Twentieth and Twenty-First Centuries*, Cultural Inquiry, 2 (Vienna: Turia + Kant, 2011), 37–59, 37, 38. Boitani provides many examples of how references to Dante frame *Dubliners* and speaks about the 'para-Dantean' structure of *Ulysses* (44).
24 Wallace Fowlie, 'Dante and Beckett' in Stuart McDougal (ed.), *Dante among the Moderns* (Chapel Hill: University of North Carolina Press, 1985), 129–52.
25 James Joyce, *A Portrait of the Artist as a Young Man* (London: Jonathan Cape, 1964), 103. Father Arnell quotes Hamlet's monologue 'to be or not to be' when he describes Adam and Eve who 'knew not the ills our flesh is heir to' (*Portrait*, 108).
26 Jill L. Levenson, 'Stoppard's Shakespeare' in Katherine E. Kelly (ed.), *The Cambridge Companion to Stoppard* (Cambridge University Press, 2006), 158; 160.
27 Cf. e.g. Tony Adler, 'Waiting for Hamlet. Tom Stoppard's Early, Beckettian Play at Writers' Theatre', *Chicago Reader*, 5 November 2009.
28 'There was only one play for me to direct. Beckett's play, written over forty years ago, seems written for, and about, Sarajevo.' Susan Sontag, 'Waiting for Godot in Sarajevo', *Performing Arts Journal*, 16.2 (1994), 87–106, 88.
29 C.J. Ackerley and S.E. Gontarski (eds.), *The Grove Companion to Samuel Beckett* (New York: Grove, 2004), xii.
30 Caselli, *Beckett's Dantes*, 2.
31 Michael Robinson, 'From Purgatory to Inferno: Beckett and Dante Revisited', *Journal of Beckett Studies*, 5 (1979), 69–82; Phyllis Carey, 'Stephen Dedalus, Belacqua Shuah, and Dante's Pietà' in Phyllis Carey and Ed Jewinski (eds.), *RE: Joyce'n Beckett* (New York: Fordham University Press, 1992), 104–116.
32 Dirk van Hulle, 'Undoing Dante: Samuel Beckett's Poetics from a Textual Perspective', *Text*, 16 (2006), 87–95, 87.

33 Walter Strauss, 'Dante's Belacqua and Beckett's Tramps', *Comparative Literature*, 11.3 (1959), 250–61, 260.
34 Caselli, *Beckett's Dantes*, 2; R. Federman, 'Beckett's Belacqua and the Inferno of Society', *Arizona Quarterly*, 20 (1964), 231–41; P.N. Furbank, 'Beckett's Purgatory', *Encounter*, 22 (1964), 69–72.
35 Caselli, *Beckett's Dantes*, 5
36 On his journey, Dante often encounters the murmuring and whispering voices of the damned: Cf. Purgatorio XXXII:

> Onward had we moved, as far,
> Perchance, as arrow at three several flights
> Full winged had sped, when from her station down
> Descended Beatrice. With one voice
> All murmur'd 'Adam'; circling next a plant
> Despoiled of flowers and leaf, on every bough. (*Purgatory* 4, 33–38)

> Sì passeggiando l'alta selva vòta,
> temprava i passi un'angelica nota.
> Forse in tre voli tanto spazio prese
> disfrenata saetta, quanto eramo
> rimossi, quando Bëatrice scese.
> Io senti' mormorare a tutti: 'Adamo';
> poi cerchiaro una pianta dispogliata
> di foglie e d'altra fronda in ciascun ramo. (*Purgatorio* 32, 32–39).

37 Kay G. Stevenson, 'Belacqua in the Moon: Beckett's Revisions of "Dante and the Lobster"' in Patrick A. McCarthy (ed.), *Critical Essays on Samuel Beckett* (Boston: G.K. Hall & Co., 1986), 36–46, 37.
38 David Foster Wallace famously describes annual lobster festivities in Maine and contemplates the popular belief that lobsters do not feel any pain. 'Consider the Lobster', *Gourmet Magazine*, (August 2004), 50–64.
39 Michael Robinson, 'Belacqua' in Patrick A. McCarthy (ed.), *Critical Essays on Samuel Beckett* (Boston: G.K. Hall & Co., 1986), 30–36, 40.
40 Caselli, *Beckett's Dantes*, 57: 'he is not only an explicitly intertextual figure but also an intratextual one, in so far as he inherits many features of the *Dream* Belacqua'.
41 She somewhat smiled, then spake: 'If mortals err
   In their opinion, when the key of sense
   Unlocks not, surely wonder's weapon keen
   Ought not to pierce thee: since thou find'st, the wings
   Of reason to pursue the senses' flight
   Are short. But what thy own thought is, declare. (*Paradise* 2, 53–8)

> Ella sorrise alquanto, e poi: 'S'elli erra
> l'oppinïon", mi disse, 'd'i mortali
> dove chiave di senso non diserra,
> certo non ti dovrien punger li strali

d'ammirazione omai, poi dietro ai sensi
vedi che la ragione ha corte l'ali.
Ma dimmi quell che tu da te ne pensi" (*Paradiso* 2, 52–8)

42 Cf. Caselli, *Beckett's Dantes*, 60: 'Cain is mentioned in *Paradiso* II as a legend used to explain the presence of the spots on the moon; he is also referred to in *Inferno* XX, 126, where he is used as a periphrasis indicating the moon.'
43 *Ham* 1.1.63 note.
44 Ackerley and Gontarski (eds.), *The Grove Companion to Samuel Beckett*, 121. The allusion to the damned plunged in ice (*Inf* XXII. 46–8) recurs in *Ill Seen Ill Said* (27): 'The eye will return to the scene of its betrayals. On centennial leave from where tears freeze.' In a letter to Ruby Cohn Beckett explains: 'Bocca is among the traitors in the nethermost hell, up to their necks in ice', referring to Dante's *Inferno*, Canto 32. *Letters*, IV, 641, 28.06.1984.
45 The contrast between inner, emotional heat and external cold that causes the in-between state of Dante's damned can also be found in Schubert's song 'Frozen Tears' from *Winterreise*: 'Gefrorne Tropfen fallen/von meinen Wangen ab:/Ob es mir denn entgangen,/daß ich geweinet hab?/daß ich geweinet hab?/ Ei Tränen, meine Tränen,/und seid ihr gar so lau,/daß ihr erstarrt zu Eise,/wie kühler Morgentau?/Und dringt doch aus der Quelle/der Brust so glühend heiß,/als wolltet ihr zerschmelzen/des ganzen Winters Eis', Franz Schubert, *Franz Schubert. Neue Ausgabe sämtlicher Werke*, ed. by Internationale Schubert-Gesellschaft, comp. by Walter Dürr (Kassel, Basel, Tours, London: Bärenreiter, 1979), vol. IVa [Lieder], 118–19.
46 Samuel Beckett, *Poems 1930–1989* (London: John Calder, 2002), 197. The poem was first published in *The European Caravan* in 1934.
47 Gerhard Neumann, 'Inszenierung und Destruktion. Zum Problem der Intertextualität in Samuel Becketts Erzählung *Dante and the Lobster*', *Poetica*, 19 (1987), 278–301, 291. Cary and more recently, C.H. Sisson (2008) both translate 'pan de li angeli' as 'food of angles': *The Divine Comedy Being the Vision of Dante Alighieri*, transl. Henry Francis Cary (Oxford University Press, 1950); *The Divine Comedy*, transl. C.H. Sisson (Oxford University Press, 2008).
48 Thomas McGreevy, 'The Six Who Were Hanged', *Poems by Thomas McGreevy* (London: William Heineman Lt., 1934), 9.
49 Thomas McGreevy's poem 'Fragments' was written in the 1920s:

Qui vive la pietà quando è ben morta.
And that I might have
Freezing comfort, Dante said:
If you should go to hell like me,
You'll see,
All through eternity,
Him flayed with fiery rods beside
The Jew high priest who crucified
A Man in A.D. 33

For blasphemy
   And glad you'll be.
   There pity must be dead
   For piety to live.
   Thomas McGreevy, 'Fragments', *Poems by Thomas McGreevy*, 40.

50 In *Dream of Fair to Middling Women*, Beckett links fish and flesh in describing Belacqua: 'his hands were two clammy cadaverous slabs of cod in his lap' (*Dream*, 5).
51 James Knowlson mentions that Beckett and his friend Thompson read Keats' poem and learned it by heart. He also notes that the lobster incident occurred at Beckett's Aunt Cissie's house in Howth. James Knowlson, *Damned to Fame. The Life of Samuel Beckett* (London: Bloomsbury, 1997), 42.
52 In *Dream* Belacqua seeks to free himself from an uncomfortable encounter with the Smeraldina: 'All he wanted was to know a few good prods of compunction and consider how best his quiet breath, or, better still, his and hers mingled, might be taken into the air' (*Dream*, 107).
53 Ruby Cohn, *A Beckett Canon* (Ann Arbor: University of Michigan Press, 2001), 391, n11.
54 Thomas McGreevy, *Poems* (London: Wilhelm Heinemann, 1934), 4.
55 Ibid., 5.
56 Ibid.
57 Ibid.
58 John Murphy explains uncertainty as a pervasive feature in Beckett's works: 'his characters are trapped. In imagined vestibules of the afterlife, in which none know what lies beyond their urns, Beckett's figures are "partially purged"'. John L. Murphy, 'Beckett's Purgatories', in Colleen Jaurretche (ed.), *Beckett, Joyce and the Art of the Negative*, European Joyce Studies 16 (Amsterdam, New York: Rodopi, 2005), 109–24, 109.

CHAPTER 5

'[It is] winter/Without journey' – *Still Lifes in Beckett and Shakespeare*

> *vive morte ma seule saison*
> *lis blancs chrysanthèmes*
> *nids vifs abandonnés*
> *boue des feuilles d'avril*
> *beaux jours gris de givre*[1]

Samuel Beckett wrote this poem while he was staying at his brother's house near Dublin in 1954, shortly before Frank Edward Beckett's death. The temporal anachronism of the poem's structure and imagery defines life through lifelessness and suggests the coexistence of the two, as the speaker registers traces of natural life that transition towards lifelessness and death. With life having vanished, nests are abandoned, leaves decompose and once beautiful days have become greyed by frost. The first two lines capture the momentary state of living death of a single season that is symbolically adorned by white lilies and chrysanthemums signifying the innocence of the soul of the departed. The poem's imagery emulates the painterly rendition of a still life that is also indicated by the first two words *'vive morte'*. Like the painting of a still life, Beckett's poem captures the moment of grief and turns it into a poetic image in which vestiges of life converge into a deathlike state.

Many of Beckett's works are built around the paradoxical notion of the still life. Suspended between motion and standstill, destruction and creation, a still life conveys the notion of a being that is simultaneously lifeless and alive. In a state of quivering unrest that is driven towards finality and yet resists coming to an end, it describes a dialectical state approximating what Walter Benjamin called 'dialectics at a standstill'.[2] Still lifes are located at the intersection of life and death, of presence and absence, of the material and the immaterial dimension of a work of art. They consist of a perpetual interplay of dialectical oppositions, in which being and becoming are inseparably linked, and yet never coincide. As Steven Connor writes: '[F]or Beckett the condition of being is such that

Being as such can never be.'³ Stanley Gontarski identifies Beckett's theatre more generally as 'a theatre of becoming, a decomposition moving toward recomposition, itself decomposing. ... Even as it often appears stationary or static, even amid the Beckettian pauses, images move, flow, become other, not representing a world that we know, but perpetually creating new worlds. Bergson would call this "durée", Deleuze "becoming", Beckett simply "art".'⁴

For Beckett, as for Shakespeare, the still life is a figure that reflects on the temporal and ontological status of the work of art and marks its condition of being as one of inherent, residual unrest between composition and decomposition. In painting, the chiastic French epithets *nature morte* and *tableau vivant* express this double quality of a work of art that is both representation and presence, pointing to itself as self-conscious artifice and simultaneously an artefact and a synecdoche that presents what it is about. Lois Oppenheim observes that 'Beckett's art became increasingly self-conscious[,] ... [a] self-consciousness that resulted in the minimalist writing, and the collapse of genre, characteristic of all the late work.'⁵

Beckett, most notably in his later prose and drama, uses the still life as a reflection on the creation of a work of art while simultaneously performing this creative process as it were *in vivo*. It is therefore within and by means of literature and drama, or in relation to other art forms and media that Beckett develops his art and, at the same time, investigates its representational potentialities. Above all, he explores the nature, the breadth and the limits of representation in relation to the visual arts and to music. Ruby Cohn notes that 'Beckett comes close to painting still lives in movement',⁶ and Mary Bryden analyses ways in which Beckett's works 'undermine[ ] the notion that "to live is to move"'.⁷ She describes Beckett's characters as 'professional waiters, caught in the machinery of interrupted dynamics', and defines the intermedial potentiality inherent in the still life: '[it] draws into collocation two tendencies which, though *potentially* mutually exclusive, are in fact part of an uncomfortable continuum in Beckett's scenic world. As well as being an adjective, 'still' can be a noun. A 'still' denotes an image which, while not being cinematographic, may be applied to a frame, or series of frames, from an ongoing reel of pictures.'⁸ Still lifes continuously exceed the boundaries of the medium within which they are created – the canvas, the form of a poem or the theatrical stage – and precisely in doing so, they reinstate and affirm these artistic boundaries as their condition of becoming.

This chapter is concerned with the aesthetics of the still life in Beckett's and Shakespeare's works regarding their relations to painting, music and the theatre. Beckett admired the fine arts, and both his criticism and his literary and dramatic works were inspired by them, as he in turn inspired many artists.[9] His early reflections on painting, published in *Disjecta*, include dialogues with and essays on the works of his friends and acquaintances such as the painters Georges Duthuit, Bram van Velde and Avigdor Arikha.[10] As James Knowlson and others have shown, Beckett had a keen interest in painting throughout his life. Initially inspired by paintings in the National Gallery of Ireland, he continued to develop his expertise in the galleries of Paris, Berlin, London, Hamburg, Dresden, Leipzig and many other European cities. He took a serious interest in the Old Masters of the seventeenth century, as well as Dutch landscape painting, and was intrigued by peasant scenes that, as Knowlson argues, shaped some of the scenes of plays such as *Waiting for Godot* and inspired Beckett's stage imagery.[11] In his observations on art in *Disjecta*, Beckett was concerned with how time and space interact in a work of art, how temporality as past, present and future can be related to the two-dimensional space of a painting.[12] He asks: 'A quoi les arts représentatifs se sont-ils acharnés, depuis toujours? A vouloir arrêter le temps, en le représentant' (*Disjecta*, 126). Representation hence strives to bring time to a halt, to immortalize it in the condition of mortality.

Other than in painting and sculpture, temporal succession and causality are inherent characteristics of the symbolic system of literature. Even though a painting creates the impression of spatialized time in representing a single moment frozen in time, it is fraught with its own sense of provisional temporality. It presents a transient object, and self-consciously transforms this sense of finitude into art. Paradoxically, the object presented finds both continuous life in the very space of the painting as well as boundedness, preservation and arrest.

Still lifes, furthermore, like all images, are governed by an iconic paradox in that they create something that without them would not exist. They present a structural difference between the image and what it represents, their presence conveys an absence, and they present what is absent as present. Images create and appear as something other than themselves. As Gottfried Boehm has written: they establish negation as a condition of possibility. They suggest evidence and immediacy where there is no immediacy. Images make visible the invisible, but at the same time, they conceal what they represent.[13]

Beckett's works express an interest in the ways in which art captures this kind of non-existence and creates the conditions of lives that take on a life of their own. In 'First Love', he writes: 'But I have always spoken, no doubt always shall, of things that never existed, or that existed if you insist, no doubt always will, but not with the existence I ascribe to them' (*CSP*, 35). The artist Lily Briscoe in Virginia Woolf's *To the Lighthouse* defines her quest for the elusive substance of a reality not yet in being in similar terms as the 'very jar on the nerves, the thing itself before it has been made anything' (*TL*, 193). Beckett's aesthetics centres on the area where composition and decomposition are brought closest to each other, where language is on the verge of silence, where sight is on the verge of blindness, where time and movement approximate stasis, and where life is on the brink of death. Being remains linked to transcending itself towards an other and to becoming both 'I and Not I', a nameless or unnameable other, or as Molloy puts it, 'one is what one is, partly at least' (*Molloy*, 54).

The dynamics between the state of being and the process of becoming in a still life for Beckett finds an analogue in the process of writing, in its ambiguous moments of agony and necessity. In this respect, the restless dialectics of the still life is vital to Beckett's literary creations. His works operate on a threshold of representation where something needs to be seen in the light of its opposite. John Keats had conceived of this form of aesthetic resilience as 'negative capability'. On 22 December 1818, he writes to his brothers George and Tom Keats: 'several things dovetailed in my mind, and at once it struck me, what quality went to form a Man of Achievement, especially in Literature and which Shakespeare possessed so enormously – I mean *Negative Capability*, that is when a man is capable of being in uncertainties, Mysteries, doubts, without any irritable reaching after fact and reason.'[14]

Beckett's literary and dramatic still lifes exhibit representational uncertainty in a dynamics of transition, in which to understand language is also to experience silence, to study sight is to encounter blindness and to be oneself is also to become an other.[15] His investigation into the dialectics of the still life remains without synthesis and does not merely set up binaries that cancel each other out for the sake of doing so, but challenges received notions of representation in making readers and playgoers adopt a double perspective in which one thing can be seen in terms of an other such as 'Dante and the Lobster', 'Words and Music' and 'Winter without Journey'.

Tableaux Vivants: *A Piece of Monologue, Stirrings Still* and *What Where*

Many of Beckett's plays begin and end in brief theatrical *tableaux vivants*. *Endgame* starts and finishes with Hamm immobilized in his wheelchair, his face covered by a handkerchief while Clov is standing near the door. The handkerchief, the 'old stauncher' that Hamm addresses at the end, can be taken as a reference to the sudary of St. Veronica, producing the vestigial imprint of an invisible presence. It can also represent a miniature version of the curtain in the theatre. *Play* more iconically enacts the stasis of a lingering existence by placing three disembodied heads onto grey urns and only brings them to life when they are prompted to speak by the spotlight which is alternately directed at them. In *Rockaby*, the attitude of the protagonist in the rocking chair is described as 'Completely still till fade-out of chair. Then in light of spot head slowly inclined' (*CDW*, 433). Beckett's still lifes on stage create theatrical presences that foreground the material conditions of the theatre, the stagecraft that produces them and above all the lighting, which brings the stage to life by making it visible and indicating the existence of a creator, director or ruler who is in charge of the world of the play.

In *A Piece of Monologue*, written for David Warrilow in 1979,[16] the rising curtain reveals the ghostlike figure of Speaker, dressed in white on a stage equipped with only a few props such as a lamp with a skull-sized white globe and a bed. Other traces of life have vanished from the speaker's world and only some remnants of them remind the audience of what was once there: pictures of 'the loved ones' have been ripped from the wall with only the pins remaining, the ceiling was 'once white', the room that 'once was full of sounds' is now silent apart from the pouring rain. Before he starts with his monologue, Speaker remains silent in a theatrical *tableau vivant* for ten seconds. In the figure of Speaker, character and playwright, actor and spectator merge as he describes life paradoxically continuing as death. Yet Speaker is unable to end and his first words conflate birth and death: 'Birth was the death of him' (*CDW*, 425). Speaker then describes a scene of nightly waiting and watching: 'Up at nightfall. Every nightfall' (*CDW*, 425), '[s]o nightly' (*CDW*, 426) that resonates with the anxiety and unease of the night watch for the ghost at the beginning of *Hamlet*. Francisco in *Hamlet* reports that there is 'Not a mouse stirring' (*Ham* 1.1.10), and Speaker repeatedly states: 'Stock still staring out. Nothing stirring in that black vast' (*CDW*, 425). Speaker describes the appearance of several ghostly forms such as hands lighting the lamp, or 'Then slow fade up a faint form' (*CDW*, 427). He aligns himself to these apparitions, and like an actor about to speak comments on the first words in a play as giving birth to them: '[w]ait[ing] for first word … It gathers in his mouth. … Birth' (*CDW*, 428). Speaker reflects on the ghostly legacy of theatrical performances, which he conceives of shadowy presences in front of the curtain, the 'black veil': 'Thirty thousand nights of ghosts beyond. Beyond that black beyond. Ghost light. Ghost nights. Ghost rooms, Ghost graves. Ghost ... he all but said ghost loved ones. Waiting on the rip word. Stands there staring beyond at that black veil lips quivering to half-heard words' (*CDW*, 429).[17]

Referring to all the unquieted ghosts that once populated the stage, Speaker notes that they are still waiting to rest in peace, 'the rip word' that would also sever their link to the present. Their predicament is reminiscent of the purgatorial non-death of Hamlet's ghostly father who like the '[s]tarless moonless heaven. Dies on to dawn and never dies' (*CDW*, 427). The family that Speaker remembers resembles that of Hamlet, his father, 'the grey void', Gertrude and the 'smiling' (*Ham* 1.5.108) other, Claudius[18]: 'There was father. That grey void. There mother. That other. There together. Smiling. Wedding day. There all three' (*CDW*, 426). In *Hamlet*, Gertrude and Claudius' wedding follows all too swiftly upon the funeral of old Hamlet (*Ham* 1.2.180),[19] and Speaker's text also moves: 'From funeral to funeral' (*CDW*, 425). Like Hamlet, who from the funeral of his father, upon his second arrival in Denmark moves on to that of Ophelia, Speaker asks: 'Coffin out of frame. Whose?' (*CDW*, 428). He continues to describe a funeral scene from a ghostly vantage point above it: 'Umbrellas round a grave. Seen from above. Streaming black canopies. Black ditch beneath. Rain bubbling in the black mud. Empty for the moment. That place beneath. Which ... he all but said which loved one?' (*CDW*, 428). The scene recalls parts of Ophelia's funeral and Hamlet's dialogue with the gravediggers before it. Speaker repeats: 'Birth was the death of him. Ghastly grinning ever since' (*CDW*, 425). Similarly, Hamlet reminisces about his bygone childhood when he addresses Yorick's skull: 'Here hung those lips that I have kissed I know not how oft. Where be your gibes now? your gambols, your songs, your flashes of merriment that were wont to set the table on a roar? Not one now, to mock your own grinning? Quite chop-fallen?' (*Ham* 5.1.159–63). The analogy to the theatre and particularly to *Hamlet* is further evoked by Speaker's references to the globe of the lamp. Like Hamlet, who is isolated, melancholic and gloomy and seeks revenge 'whiles memory holds a seat/In this distracted globe' (*Ham* 1.5.96–7), Speaker mentions the 'Pale globe alone in gloom' (*CDW*, 427).

Monologues are central to Shakespeare's dramatic poetry and to the development of his main characters as they speak to themselves in front of an audience. Unlike Hamlet's monologues, which consider intricate existential dilemmas, raise doubts and inquire into what it means to be human, Beckett's *A Piece of Monologue* creates a condensed theatrical still life in which speech denotes action and where the interior equals the exterior when Speaker's introspection is directed towards an audience. Not least through its resonances with *Hamlet*, Beckett's *Piece* is reflexive of its own condition of being. The piece, the play itself, consists of a monologue that enters into a dialogue with itself as performance and reflection, encapsulating the position of the actor, the spectator and the audience. *A Piece of Monologue* responds to Hamlet's exclamation 'What a piece of work is a man' (*Ham* 2.2.286) – life, as it were, in theatrical terms. Anticipating the end of the play, Speaker compares its theme and its duration on stage to gradual leave-taking and death: 'Never but the one matter. The dead and gone. The dying and the going. From the word go. The word begone. Such as the light going now' (*CDW*, 429).

The stage life Speaker creates and performs for the audience is at the same time a meditation on the recurring yet ephemeral life of a play, in which he conjures the ghosts of his predecessors to reflect on the creation of a theatrical presence that finds itself surrounded from beginning to end in the symbolically charged space of 'the globe': 'Unnoticed by him staring beyond. The globe alone. Not the other. The unaccountable. From nowhere. On all sides nowhere. Unutterably faint. The globe alone. Alone gone' (*CDW*, 429). Beckett's *Piece* casts the theatre, the globe, into a place where a faint form of life, the actor, coming from nowhere and going nowhere, can be observed. Macbeth's final soliloquy combines reflections on the brief stage life of an actor, life in general and his own tragic predicament when he conceives of his present as fading into insignificance:

> Tomorrow, and tomorrow, and tomorrow
> Creeps in this petty pace from day to day
> To the last syllable of recorded time;
> And all our yesterdays have lighted fools
> The way to dusty death. Out, out, brief candle,
> Life's but a walking shadow, a poor player
> That struts and frets his hour upon the stage
> And then is heard no more. It is a tale
> Told by an idiot, full of sound and fury
> Signifying nothing (*Mac* 5.5.18–27).

Beckett's novella *Company* (published 1979), which was written around the same time as *A Piece of Monologue* (between 1977 and 1979), likewise pictures a divided self whose words give way to silence: 'The fable of one with you in the dark. The fable of one fabling of one with you in the dark.

And how better in the end labour lost and silence. And you as you always were. Alone.' (*Company*, 88–9). *Company* is divided into a voice speaking and a voice addressing the speaker, who is not only alone but also 'all-one'. Like *A Piece of Monologue* that invokes an unseen observer, it includes the presence of a narrating other, 'one fabling with you in the dark'. As Joseph Long has observed: 'Throughout *Company*, the reader of the English text is solicited by a third voice, largely inoperative in the French, a voice beyond the dark, a company of intertextual shades.'[20] Even though words and the fable finally expire, ending in 'labour lost and silence', *Company's* intertexts – *Hamlet*, *Macbeth* or *Love's Labour's Lost* – echo back into the novella. They are still alive, it seems, in spite of the text's programmatic solitude.

Beckett's late works such as *Company* examine the artistic process by exploring the mechanisms and conditions of perception and the imagination. They study the tension between the expansion, self-division and contraction of the imagination when the necessity to go beyond the self, to exceed its limitations in both mind and body, is counterbalanced by the inevitable condition to stay within the boundaries of the self.

In *Stirrings Still*, one of his last pieces of prose writing, Beckett scrutinizes the workings of the imagination. The first of the three parts of *Stirrings Still* presents a seated figure who sees himself rise and go, disappear and reappear. The figure is intrinsically divided, both hoping and fearing that time will come to a halt: 'Head on hands half hoping when the hour struck that the half-hour would not and half fearing that it would not' (*CSP*, 260). His longing for finitude, however, is not fulfilled, and instead, he finds himself doomed to patient waiting: 'And patience till the one true end to time and grief and self and second self his own' (*CSP*, 261). In the second part of the piece, the figure tries and fails to conjure in his mind images of boundless infinite space, and is time and again forced to return to the finitude of his vision: 'For he could recall no field of grass from even the very heart of which no limit of any kind was to be discovered but always in some quarter or another some end in sight such as a fence or other manner of bourne from which to return' (*CSP*, 263). Unlike Hamlet, whose hopes and fears are precipitated by 'The undiscovered country from whose bourn/No traveller returns' (*Ham* 3.1.79–80), Beckett's figure remains within the limits of his recursive imagination and decides to adopt a bodily posture that corresponds to his mental state: 'To this end for want of a stone on which to sit like Walther and cross his legs the best he could do was stop dead and stand stock still which after a moment of hesitation he did and of course sink his head as one deep in meditation which after another moment of hesitation he did also' (*CSP*, 263). Whereas for Walther von der Vogelweide, Beckett's narrator's medieval precursor, 'sitting on a stone, crossing his legs and resting his chin and cheek in his hand'[21] denotes a moment of contemplation about the state of the world, Beckett's protagonist for lack of stones being left to sit on, remains standing 'stock still'.

In the last part, he finally becomes aware of the faint appearance of a word that again he tries but fails to catch: '[SO ON TILL STAYED] when to his ears from deep within oh how and here a word he could not catch it were to end where never till then ... that missing word again it were to end where never till then' (*CSP*, 264).[22] The incessant pursuit of the elusive word prevents him from reaching the desired end.[23] Beckett's poem 'what is the word/Comment dire' traces a parallel course of forward and backward motion in trying to build a verse in search of a word. In *Stirrings Still*, bodily stasis, the concomitant wish to overcome it and the stirrings of the writer's mind in search of words create a paradoxical dynamic that describes the relentless movement of the imagination within and because of a given finitude.

The act of doubling in which the self perceives itself as both subject and object, at once lifeless and alive, is often associated with both Beckett's inquiry into the Cartesian subject, and with his variations on the Berkeleyan formula of 'esse est percipi': to be is to be perceived, even if only by the self, resulting in a doubling of the self that Beckett analyses in many variations in *Film*.[24] The idea of 'ghosting', of phantoms and spectral figures inhabiting indistinct territories of existence, is pervasive in Beckett's œuvre. As Porter Abbot and Ruby Cohn in her lecture on 'Ghosting through Beckett' have noted, in plays such as *Embers* or *Footfalls* the 'text as a representation of conjuring gives a special license to its complex unreadability'.[25] Secondary figures that haunt and reflect on the self through time and space appear prominently in *Krapp's Last Tape*, or in constellations of parallels and pairs of characters in *Mercier and Camier*, *Watt*, *Waiting for Godot*, *Happy Days* or *Endgame*. Lois Oppenheim summarizes that: '[d]oubling is so frequently employed by Beckett as to have become a platitude in the critical analyses of his work. Self-awareness, splitting, and twinning (such as we have in Vladimir/Estragon, Mercier/Camier, and Reader/Listener, for example) lend a palpable fragility to the Beckettian speaking subject.'[26] The restlessness of the Beckettian subject comes to resemble a still life that opposes stasis in continuously overcoming and reaffirming the boundaries of that self.

Winter Journeys: *What Where*, Beckett and Schubert

The uncanny necessity of seeing oneself as an other within the horizontal coordinates of motion and stasis, and the vertical ones of past and present, is a theme that Beckett not only explored in *Film* but also encountered in music, particularly in the lieder of Franz Schubert. Beckett once spoke of his own playing the piano as wandering within the sonatas of Haydn and Schubert.[27] He received a recording of Schubert's version of Heinrich Heine's poem 'Der Doppelgänger',[28] and planned to listen to it together with Avigdor Arikha. Schubert's song 'The Doppelganger' is about a lover who returns to the house of his former love during a 'still night'. The house from which the beloved has long departed has remained where it was and becomes a material memento of loss. The grief-stricken lover looks at it and becomes aware of a human figure lit by moonlight that he then suddenly recognizes as his former heartbroken self. The song expresses the horror of the self as it is mirrored by its own ghostly doppelganger in a moment of agony when he understands that the sorrow he felt in the past is still alive in the present, and helplessly accuses the spectre of mimicking his despair.

In the same letter to Avigdor Arikha of 17 December 1983 in which he suggests that they listen to 'The Doppelgänger' together, Beckett also mentions his latest play *What Where*, which was to be his last. He was commissioned to write a piece for a theatre festival in Graz in the autumn of 1983, and also intended to offer it to the German broadcasting station Süddeutscher Rundfunk in Stuttgart to be eventually turned into a television play. In a letter to the SDR-director Müller-Freienfels, Beckett describes 'ghostliness' as the main characteristic of the piece: 'Perhaps the clue to the whole affair is its ghostliness. The 4 are indistinguishable, visually & vocally, as ghosts are indistinguishable. Ghostly garments, ghostly speech.'[29] In the play, the four figures Bim, Bem, Bam and Bom are directed by a disembodied voice (V) offstage in a rectangular room that is marked by three points denoting east, north and west.

The play, at its very beginning, conveys the sense of an imminent ending: 'We are the last five' (*CDW*, 470). The ensuing, ongoing regress is underlined by imaginative lacunae such as the missing fifth figure in the vowel sequence of their names which would be 'Bum', or the lack of the south. Throughout its course, the play repeatedly rehearses versions of itself in which the alternation of the light being switched on and off, is paralleled by the action played with and without words. The temporal structure of the play moves through the seasons from spring to summer, autumn and winter, and refers repeatedly to a potentially violent action taking place offstage in which the single figures participate. They appear, reappear and are questioned by Voice if they have 'given somebody the works', but they have to admit that that somebody does not confess what or where. Gradually, the figures disappear one after the other until only Voice remains in a moment '[i]n the present as were I still' (*CDW*, 476).

As S.E. Gontarski observes, the play draws attention to its artistic virtuality: 'These are characters not there, the pattern of images coming and going, moving to and fro, to an off-stage fraught with possibility, to receive "the works".'[30] The play defies being tied down in representational categories. The characters are there and not there at the same time, which has prompted some of its performances to merely show the figures' heads without their bodies appearing against a dark background. They come and go, they act and yet they do not act to Voice's directorial satisfaction. Not unlike the supposedly tortured figure offstage, the audience confronted with this play would find it difficult to answer the questions of its title 'What, where'. What is taking place and where it happens remain hard to grasp in a play where the ghostly figures appear in an indistinct present over the course of a year somewhere between the cardinal points of west, north and east. The 'works' that Voice insistently enquires about remain equally obscure. While denoting some gruesome torture, they can also be taken as a reference to the works of an author or artist, not least the works of Samuel Beckett himself. The play therefore is also a commentary on its own representative properties as well as on the position of the viewer or reader, who after having been given this work along with many others of Beckett's is unable to 'make sense' of them in any conventional way. At the end, Voice describes its predicament as a paradoxical stasis in motion: 'It is winter./Without journey./Time passes./That is all./Make sense who may./I switch off (*CDW*, 476). This is arguably the last line that Beckett wrote for the theatre. James Knowlson aptly names the last chapter of his biography of Beckett 'Winter Journey', in which he describes Beckett's last years in Paris, and he is among the first to note Beckett's indebtedness to Schubert.[31] Not only can some of Beckett's spectral presences and 'doppelgangers' be seen as references to Schubert's 'swansong', but Beckett's last play, his own theatrical 'Winter Journey', alludes to Schubert's cycle as it ends in a motionless and frozen state: Winter without journey.

The notion of the still life here acquires an even more poignant dimension as a reflection on the vestiges of a life that is on the brink of vanishing and also as an inquiry into the question of what remains, of what precisely is or could be the vanishing point of life? What are the irrevocably residual qualities of something if it is still to be considered a form of life? In 'Texts for Nothing … 6', Beckett writes: 'Or to know it's life still, a form of life, ordained to end, as others ended and will end, till life ends, in all its forms' (*CSP*, 125). Beckett's works explore and perform such enduring forms of life in the face of their finitude in a continuous dialogue with other art forms and recurrently with music, exploring its immateriality and non-referential properties.

When Schubert, in 1827, composed *Winterreise*, his second cycle of songs for voice and piano that is based on the poems of Wilhelm Müller, he was aware of his imminent death and edited parts of *Winterreise* literally on his deathbed. In February 1956, Beckett attended a performance of *Winterreise*: 'I heard Fischer-Dieskau in the Salle Gaveau singing *Winterreise*. Marvellous.'[32] He describes his experience of revisiting *Winterreise* in a letter to his cousin on 11 May 1975 as one of 'shivering through the grim journey again'[33] perhaps alluding to the phrase 'zittr' ich, was ich zittern kann' (I shiver as much as I can) from the song 'Letzte Hoffnung'/'Last hope'.[34] The singer Ian Bostridge, who notes that 'there is something deeply Beckettian about the piece'[35], describes the alienation experienced by the speaker in many of the songs. Aimless wandering while moving towards one's death has been often identified as a thematic link between Beckett's plays, such as *Footfalls* or *Come and Go*, *Nacht und Träume*, and Schubert's lieder. Towards the end of the thirteen 'Texts for Nothing', the narrator embarks on a winter's journey as 'No. 12' begins: '[IT'S A WINTER NIGHT], where I was, where I'm going, remembered, imagined, no matter, believing in me, believing it's me, no, no need, so long as the others are there, where, in the world of the others, of the long mortal ways, under the sky, with a voice, no, no need, and the power to move' (*CSP*, 149).

Many of Schubert's speakers share with characters in Beckett's works the fate of being isolated outcasts, but *Winterreise* also conveys the idea of the still life, the simultaneity of beginning and end in a moment frozen in time. *Winterreise* begins with an ending as the first song 'Gute Nacht'/'Good night', resonant with 'Texts for Nothing', is the final goodbye of a lover who leaves the house of his beloved on a winter's night never to return. A number of songs express the desire Beckett had articulated about art to arrest time in representing it. 'Gefrorene Tränen'/'Frozen Tears' captures the moment of grief in which tears that spring from the burning heart of the speaker fall down his cheeks to his surprise like frozen drops of ice. 'Erstarrung'/'Frozen Stiff' traces the speaker's search for the image of the beloved in the snow and 'Auf dem Flusse'/'On the Stream' contrasts the summery jolliness of the river to its winter stillness under the ice onto which the speaker engraves the name of his beloved.[36] The transition between life and death and finality is implicit in 'Der Wegweiser'/'The Signpost', which Knowlson identifies as one of the songs most relevant to *What Where*.[37] 'The signpost' describes a moment of reflection in which the wanderer chooses to follow his own paths, away from towns and people and turns towards a road indicated by the signpost 'from which none has ever returned'.

Der last song of *Winterreise*, 'Der Leiermann'/'The Barrel Organ Player', suggests both repetitive movement and stasis when the desolate figure of the hurdy-gurdy man stands barefoot on the ice, moving to and fro, while endlessly turning his barrel-organ 'seine Leier steht ihm nimmer still' (his barrel organ never stands still).[38] Ian Bostridge explains that both the poverty and the resilience of the character are rendered in a destitute harmony: 'Our wanderer's existential misery is for the first time confronted with real material distress, unchosen and stoically borne. The world of Samuel Beckett collides with that of, say, Henry Mayhew.'[39] *Winterreise* ends with this eery, harmonically impoverished piece, presenting a fragment of humanity that carries on living despite its enduring existential misery.

'still living flesh': Trajectories of Dispossession in *King Lear*, *Timon of Athens*, *The End* and *Texts for Nothing*

Beckett's plays are known for their minimalist settings, their exploration of limitations, of spatial or bodily stasis and stagnant action. In his early essay on Proust, Beckett has defined this aesthetic idea: 'The artistic tendency is not expansive, but a contraction. And art is the apotheosis of solitude' (*Proust*, 47). Martin Esslin, early on, describes this trajectory of lessening, of self-impoverishment and increased formal rigidity in Beckett's works:

> In Beckett's most recent plays, this movement to stricter and stricter patterns seems to have carried him towards a new and far more austere form of drama: not only have his plays become more and more concise, they have also shed the notion of *characters in action* which is so often regarded as the basic minimum definition of drama itself.[40]

Apart from Beckett's dramatic works and also his prose, it is mainly his short stories that present forms of displacement and lessening, exploring the border between human being and animal, life and lifelessness.

'Lessness' (1969) is the title of a short narrative that Beckett translated into English from the French 'Sans' which conveys the sense of reduction and, not unlike the melancholic character Jacques in Shakespeare's *As You Like It*, describes the 'last scene of all/That ends this strange eventful history . . . Sans teeth, sans eyes, sans taste, sans everything' (*AYL* 2.7.163–6). In Beckett's text, however, the lessness of the scattered ash-grey ruins that his wanderer encounters is also an end-lessness of earth and sky becoming one in an issueless void.

Beckett had stated a dual imperative of his aesthetics in 'Assumption': 'To avoid the expansion of the commonplace is not enough; the highest art reduces significance in order to obtain that inexplicable bombshell perfection' (*CSP*, 4). Beckett works towards this 'inexplicable bombshell' in his many rather implosive still lifes, and his ventures are not only interwoven with his readings of Shakespeare but also reflect back on Shakespeare's treatment of the fine arts, painting, sculpture and music, in which drama becomes a generative form of art that relies on minimalist units and still lifes. Before many of Beckett's characters reach the condition of 'winter without journey', a paradoxical state of defiance of finitude in the face of it, they move towards this vanishing point in trajectories of dispossession, of shrinking, reduction and contraction, that can be associated with the predicament of *King Lear* and *Timon of Athens*. Analogous to some of the figures in Schubert's *Winterreise*, they are abandoned figures and homeless wanderers. Likewise, the narrators of pieces such as 'The Expelled', 'The End', and 'Texts for Nothing' are relentlessly on the move, unable to stay at a place for a longer period of time: 'I . . . Someone said, You can't stay here. I couldn't stay there and I couldn't go on. I'll describe the place, that's unimportant. The top, very flat, of a mountain, no, a hill, but so wild, so wild, enough. Quag, heath up to the knees . . . I could have stayed in my den, snug and dry, I couldn't' (*CSP*, 100).

In Beckett's short story 'The End' the nameless narrator who resembles both Christ and Everyman leads an existence on the margin between life and death and gradually retreats into solitude and death. He shares the fate of the outcast with many of Shakespeare's characters, most of all with King Lear who desires to '[u]nburdened crawl toward death' (*KL* 1.1.36) and also with Edgar who protects himself in '[taking] the basest and most poorest shape' (*KL* 2.3. 7). Shakespeare's *Timon of Athens* is perhaps the play that most unremittingly follows a Beckettian trajectory of lessening. After the last of his sycophantic friends have left him, Timon makes for the woods in impoverished bitterness. Abandoned by those false friends, he compares himself to a tree in winter, morphing into a withering vegetal creature like the nearly leafless tree in *Waiting for Godot*: '[My friends] That numberless upon me stuck, as leaves/Do on the oak, have with one winter's brush/Fell from their boughs, and left me open, bare,/For every storm that blows ...' (*Tim* 4.3.270–3). Timon's former servant Apemantus sarcastically compares Timon to such creatures 'whose bare unhousèd trunks/[are]To the conflicting elements exposed,/Answer mere nature; bid them flatter thee' (*Tim* 4.3.231–3). King Lear, when confronted with Edgar as poor Tom in the hovel rephrases Hamlet's statement 'what a piece of work is a man' in a more fundamental way: 'Thou wert better in a grave than to answer with thy uncovered body this extremity of the skies. Is man no more than this?' (*KL* 3.4.91–3) and he concludes: 'thou art the thing itself. Unaccomodated man is no more but such a poor, bare, forked animal as thou art' (*KL* 3.4.95–7). The human/animal border in both Beckett and Shakespeare is repeatedly evoked in order to be transgressed in the metamorphoses of Lear, Edgar and Gloucester, but also Regan and Goneril are called 'pelican daughters' (*KL* 3.4.70). Regan casts the blinded Gloucester out to 'let him smell/ His way to Dover' (*KL* 3.7.92–3), and King Lear's grief about the death of Cordelia surpasses words: 'Howl, howl, howl, howl!' (*KL* 5.3.231). Jean-Michel Rabaté considers Beckett a writer of 'the limits of the human',[41] and Joseph Anderton observes that 'Beckett's dehumanisation tests the elasticity and impermeability of the human ... until its discreteness comes into question',[42] describing Beckett's idea of the creature as: 'a vulnerable post-human state that resides within the human as a potential and is either actuated by other humans or manifest as an anachronistic performance of the human'.[43] Beckett's narrators approach the threshold between human being and animal, allowing both categories to mutually reflect upon one another and his works present both art and life in extremis.[44]

Unlike Timon, Beckett's narrator in 'The End' neither chooses to become an outcast nor does he fall from a tragic height in which family or friends, instead of saving him, betray him. When he, at the beginning of the story is released or rather expelled from a facility, a 'charitable institution', and told not to come back, he is already doomed, 'dressed in borrowed robes' that were formerly worn by deceased people and are still smelling of sulphur (*CSP*, 80). After he is then cheated by a landlady and once again evicted from his basement room, he sets out for the country and eventually meets a man he once knew who lives sheltered from the elements in a cave by the sea with his ass. The narrator mounts the ass and accompanies the man to his cave. The narrow winding path to a den by the sea is described in 'Texts for Nothing', where the scenario of an ending is evoked with reference to the scenes on Dover cliff from *King Lear*.

Like the dispossessed King Lear moving towards the hovel during the storm (*KL* 3.2.61; 78),[45] like Gloucester and Edgar on 'Both stile and gate, horseway and footpath' (*KL* 4.1.56), and also like Timon of Athens, who chooses death by the sea, the characters in 'The End' and 'Texts for Nothing' make their way to a den by the sea near the top of a cliff:

> 2... The way was long that led back to the den, over the fields, a winding way, it must still be there. When it comes to the top of the cliff it springs, some might think blindly, but no, wilily, like a goat, in hairpin zigzags towards the shore. Never had the sea so thundered from afar, the sea beneath the snow, though superlatives have lost most of their charm (*CSP*, 107).

Like Christ's entry into Jerusalem on the ass, which also marks the beginning of an end when the Passion and Crucifixion swiftly follow Palm Sunday, the narrator's journey in 'The End' inevitably becomes one of restricted movement and increased solitude. Out of the natural shelters, he travels back into town and finds himself out on the street, begging and exposed to the contempt of the passers-by. He is increasingly dehumanized, and when he is shouted at by a man as 'living corpse' (*CSP*, 94), 'Do you hear me, you crucified bastard!', the insult again cruelly invokes the parallel to the death of Christ since a crucifixion displays a living body that is eerily both dead and alive: 'still living flesh'. Paradoxically, his downfall is at the same time an exaltation, the lower he falls and the more he becomes degraded, the more Christlike he appears.

In a last phase of the story, the narrator moves to a derelict shed and sets up his bed in an abandoned boat, where he remains undisturbed by the rats. Stranded in this boat without water while being close to the sea, he finds himself in a predicament of stasis that latently recalls motion. He considers himself as 'still living flesh' in another allusion to the body of Christ in the Eucharist that commemorates a body both dead and alive, resuscitated by the sacramental act of continued remembrance. Molloy likewise invokes 'that unstable fugitive thing, still living flesh' (*Molloy*, 11), which in 'The End' is accompanied by a theatrical sense of the character: 'I knew it would soon be the end, so I played the part, you know, the part of – how shall I say, I don't know' (*CSP*, 96). This unknown part he decides to play involves imaginative journeys that recall Hamlet's disillusionment and Gloucester's attempted suicide. He looks up: 'I saw above me a vast trembling expanse without islands or promontories' (*CSP*, 88–9),[46] and decides to leave human company entirely, contemplating death: 'If I stayed here something awful would happen to me, I said, and a lot of good that would do me. You'd get drowned, he said. Yes, I said, or jump off the cliff' (*CSP*, 89).[47] His withdrawal from humankind also parallels the retreat into the woods of *Timon of Athens*, in which the trajectory of lessening akin to Jacques' speech is rendered in images of shrinking. Lucillius observes that Timon 'is shrunk indeed' (*Tim* 3.2.52), and that 'now Lord Timon's happy hours are done and past, and his estate shrinks from him' (*Tim* 3.2.5–6). Timon – like Edgar in *King Lear*, but more defiantly – leaves his home and his servants and shuns civilization altogether: 'Nothing I'll bear from thee/ But nakedness, thou detestable town!/Take thou that too, with multiplying bans!/ Timon will to the woods, where he shall find/Th'unkindest beast more kinder than mankind' (*Tim* 4.1.32–6).

In Beckett's 'The End', the narrator likewise feels close to some of the 'unkindest beasts': 'Just think of it, living flesh, for in spite of everything I was still living flesh. I had lived too long among rats, in my chance dwellings, to share the dread they inspire in the vulgar. I even had a soft spot in my heart for them' (*CSP*, 95–6). Like Timon who 'hath made his everlasting mansion/Upon the beachèd verge of the salt flood' (*Tim* 5.1.205–6) and is 'Entombed upon the very hem of the sea' (*Tim* 5.5.66), the narrator who had previously been in a cave near the sea now finds himself '[I was] very snug in my box' (*CSP*, 97) and thinks that he hears the sea, gulls, the lapping of water, the waves and the rain. Like Lear in the hovel, he braves wind and weather: 'All that composed a rather liquid world. And then of course there was the voice of the wind or rather those, so various, of its playthings. But what does it amount to? Howling, soughing, moaning, sighing' (*CSP*, 97). On his final imaginary journey, he thinks that he is in a boat with no oars drifting with the currents and tides until he finds a leak and realizes that he has reached the end. He takes his 'calmative', a drug to induce final stillness, and ultimately finds himself in the limbo of an impasse: 'story in the likeness of my life, I mean without the courage to end or the strength to go on' (*CSP*, 99). At the end, he reaches a point of no return, a 'Winter without journey', a still point from which there is no way forward and no way back.

'Texts for Nothing' explore a similar rest-lessness of an in-between state: 'Go then, no, better stay, for where would you go, now that you know? Back above? There are limits. Back in that kind of light. See the cliffs again, be again between the cliffs and the sea, reeling shrinking with your hands over your ears' (*CSP*, 105). Beckett's syntax and semantics quiver between motion and stillness as his texts juxtapose the longing for an end and the imperative to continue living: '12 ... Quick quick let us die, ... And this other now, obviously, what's to be said of this latest other, with his babble of homeless mes and untenanted hims, this other without number or person whose abandoned being we haunt, nothing' (*CSP*, 150). 'Texts for Nothing', at many instances, enter into a dialogue with *Timon of Athens* and *King Lear* while also recalling 'The End' as they explore nothingness as a still point towards which and again away from which their plots gravitate. In the 1980s, when Beckett wrote his last works, he reread *King Lear* and, on 7 October 1983, he writes to the American director and actor Joseph Chaikin: 'When I recently reread Lear I thought: unstageable. I know I'm wrong. All wishes to you for that formidable adventure.'[48]

Variations on the idea of nothingness in *King Lear* and elsewhere fascinated Beckett.[49] For both Beckett and Shakespeare 'nothingness' is also a productive kind of nothingness, a nothingness that remains a prerequisite for the imagination and holds possibilities for poetic creation. Beckett's engagement with nothingness, as has been shown, is by no means nihilistic, but rather an impetus to imagine the impossible, and to reach beyond the end of the imagination itself. In Beckett's prose, Molloy states: '*Nothing is more real than nothing*.' (*Malone Dies*, 193), and Watt observes what can be taken as a metanarrative comment: 'to elicit something from nothing requires a certain skill' (*Watt*, 77). Cordelia in *King Lear* preserves her true love for her father in a kind of nothing that is 'most rich being poor' (*KL* 1.1.245), and Edgar likewise preserves his life in reinventing himself out of nothing in order to become nothing: '"Poor Tom!"/That's something yet: Edgar I nothing am' (*KL* 2.2.20–1).

In *Timon*, after the plot enters its downward spiral that Philotus describes as "Tis deepest winter in Lord Timon's purse' (*Tim* 3.4.14), Timon stages his disgust in hosting a banquet of nothing to those he thinks nothing of, and dishes out water and stones to his former friends: 'For these my present friends, as they are to me nothing, so in nothing bless them, and to nothing they are welcome' (*Tim* 3.6.69–71). Whereas *Timon* ends with the protagonist wishing to be monumentalized in a gravestone to be an oracle (*Tim* 5, 1, 209), the final scene of *King Lear*, in which the desolate Lear enters the stage on which the bodies of Regan and Goneril have been arranged, holding the dead Cordelia in his arms, has often been compared to a still-life, an inverted pietà.[50] Lear's last words when he urges the bystanders and the audience to 'Look there, look there' (*KL* 5.3.285) express his futile hope that Cordelia might still be alive, and they point to the visual impact of the scene that will be retained in the audience's memory. Cordelia's refusal to play the game at the start of the play, her reply to Lear's question: 'Nothing' (*KL* 1.1.82) and Lear's rejoinder 'Nothing will come of nothing' (*KL* 1.1.85) harkens back to the audience at the end. *King Lear*, after its multiple forms of dispossession and displacement, ends in a still life that evokes the finality of death, its raw reality leaving the characters and the audience unconsoled in the absence of a sense of justice or the prospect of metaphysical gratification.

Winters's Tales, Breathing Statues and Poetic Still Lifes

In Shakespeare's poetry and plays, the power to produce lifelikenesses as still lifes that gesture towards the immortality of art is intensely explored in the sonnets and in *The Winter's Tale*. *The Winter's Tale* negotiates difference between opposites within the finite boundaries of a work of art, and in many respects engages the viewer in the process of seeing unity in difference, observing the self in relation to an other, and comparing art to life. '[Y]ou shall see, as I have said, great difference betwixt our Bohemia and your Sicilia' (*WT* 1.1.2–4) reasons Archidamus at the beginning of the play, addressing Bohemia as the heterotopic pastoral parallel to courtly Sicilia.[51] Polixenes and Leontes have since their childhood been 'together though absent, shook hands as over a vast, and embraced as it were from the ends of opposed winds' (*WT* 1.1.18–26). The audience is constantly encouraged to adopt this kind of synoptic vision. Leontes compares himself to his own son Mamilius – 'we are/Almost as like as eggs' (*WT* 1.2.128–129) – and he likens Polixenes' image to that of his son Florizel: 'Your father's image is so hit in you,/His very air, that I should call you brother' (*WT* 5.1.126–7). As characters like Leontes read others, the audience becomes aware of such opposites, which Leontes in his onesidedness deems impossible: 'Canst with thine eyes at once see good and evil,/ Inclining to them both' (*WT* 1.2.300–1). Unlike in *King Lear*, much of the dramatic impact of *The Winter's Tale* relies on romance trajectories of promise and desire pointing towards what is not there, or not there yet. Characters wait for the impossible: the return of the daughter and the wife, forgiveness through grace and the resurrection of the dead that Paulina prophesies: 'Unless another/As like Hermione as is her picture/Affront his eye' (*WT* 5.1.73–5).

Shakespeare's romance explores this kind of impossibility when it departs from its principal source, *Pandosto*, when at the end Hermione, Leontes' wife who had been thought dead for sixteen years, returns as a still life. Paulina reveals Hermione's statue in her 'chapel/gallery' in an intense moment, in which fine art, the theatre and music interact. The statue wondrously starts to move and produces the stage miracle that Hermione is still alive, an image coming to life through words.[52] Lifelikeness reflects life, the replica offers a new perspective on the original, art reflects on the processes of creating and artistic representation. In a prologue to her revelation Paulina addresses the audience and the characters on stage:

> As she lived peerless,
> So her dead likeness I do well believe
> Excels whatever yet you looked upon,
> Or hand of man hath done; therefore I keep it
> Lonely, apart. But here it is: prepare
> To see the life as lively mocked as ever
> Still sleep mocked death. Behold, and say 'tis well! (*WT* 5.3.14–20)

Hermione's theatrical resurrection trumps both life and death. The counterfeit mocks life in subverting the relation between the replica and the original when it is the supposed imitation of life that indeed is the thing itself. When Paulina calls for '[m]usic[ ][to] awake her' and urges the viewers to 'awake' their 'faith' (*WT* 5.3.95) so that Hermione may also awaken, she asks for faith in the power of the theatre to supersede itself and go beyond the very boundaries of the medium in creating life out of death.

The play is driven by the idea of longing for the impossible, longing to transgress death and defy time in the paradox of an eternal here and now. Early on, Polixenes had mused what it might be like 'to be boy eternal' (*WT* 1.2.64). And when Florizel gazes at Perdita, he wishes that her presence could last forever:

> What you do
> Still betters what is done. When you speak, sweet,
> I'd have you do it ever: . . .
> When you do dance, I wish you
> A wave o'th'sea, that you might ever do
> Nothing but that: move still, still so,
> And own no other function. Each your doing,
> So singular in each particular,
> Crowns what you are doing in the present deeds,
> That all your acts are queens (*WT* 4.4.135–46)

Florizel articulates the paradox of motion in standstill, a state in which the present moment seeks to perpetually surpass itself, and yet remains tied to its short-lived transience. He describes a creative mechanism of continuous self-enhancement in which being is never free from becoming, and his description of Hermione's daughter Perdita moving still anticipates the living statue of the final scene and the reunion of the revived mother and the lost child. The statue in *The Winter's Tale*, like any statue, realizes a moment frozen in time that endures in an eternal here and now. It fixes a transitional space in which death and immortality become inseparable – to become a work of art is both to die and to be immortal. The artwork, however, infinitely aspires towards lifelikeness and this desire also manifests itself in the very materiality of the sculpture. Marble, in this respect, was considered particularly apt to create a convincing, lifelike effect of soft surfaces and delicate tissues.[53]

As Perdita's return moves and vitalizes the onlookers – 'Who was most marble there changed color; some swooned, all sorrowed' (*WT* 5.2.76–7) – so the statue, when it does 'move indeed' (*WT* 5.3.88) bodily and emotionally, demonstrates the power of the object of art to animate the viewer. The ideas of resurrection and transubstantiation, of bringing the dead image to life, are revealed as a theatrical masterstroke. Hermione's still life both affirms the theatrical moment and reaches beyond it. Like *Antony and Cleopatra*, *The Winter's Tale* deflates binaries. It realizes the eternal in the sensuous here and now – 'Eternity was in our lips and eyes' (*AC* 1.3.35) – and, not unlike Cleopatra who can make 'defect perfection' (*AC* 2.2.241), Hermione is perfect in and through her imperfections.

The Winter's Tale offers a model of theatrical presence. It gestures towards perfection and immediacy and fulfils it in the finite moment of a scene on stage. The microcosm of the theatre creates a Beckettian 'bombshell' of perfection that lies in the imperfect and can be conceived as a process of transcending and, at the same time, affirming the very boundaries within which it operates. The theatre becomes a medium of transformation and the place where the impossible can be actualized as a possibility. A dialectical pervasion of opposites is part of its structure of meaning when Paulina, as Marjorie Garber writes: '[Paulina] re-creates art as life, and life as art.'[54] Beckett with Shakespeare, and as Shakespeare has done before him, casts his works into still lifes to explore the self-generating dynamics of a work of art that include taking its representational potential to the extreme, even if it entails the subversion of this potential.

Shakespeare presents still lifes as self-conscious theatricality in relation to the visual arts. This immanent configuration of poetic creation also emerges in many of his sonnets, which come to resemble poetic still lifes in that they trace their own process of becoming and both capture the moment and reach beyond it. Sonnet 55 'Not marble, nor the gilded monuments' invokes the ephemerality of static memorials that were built to last, but are indeed subject to 'sluttish time', to vanity and war by contrasting statues and marble to the liveliness of the sonnet.

> Not marble nor the gilded monuments
> Of princes shall outlive this pow'rful rhyme,
> But you shall shine more bright in these contènts
> Than unswept stone, besmeared with sluttish time.
> When wasteful war shall statues overturn,
> And broils root out the work of masonry,
> Nor Mars his sword nor war's quick fire shall burn
> The living record of your memory.
> 'Gainst death and all-oblivious enmity
> Shall you pace forth; your praise shall still find room
> Even in the eyes of all posterity
> That wear this world out to the ending doom.
> So, till the Judgement that yourself arise,
> You live in this, and dwell in lovers' eyes.

The speaker's love, which is tied to the sonnet itself, keeps 'the living record of your memory' and in 'powerful rhyme' moves, 'paces forth' against death, morphologically subverting 'ob-livi-on' until the edge of doom. This movement takes place and gains its dynamics within the boundaries of the sonnet form, its enjambements, its puns and its prosody. The living memory paces forth to 'praise [that] shall still find room', and in the sonnet, the poet creates such a living space for the memory of his beloved, who is continuously resurrected in the eyes of those who read it. The life of the sonnet and the beloved – 'you live in this' – continues as long as love itself exists and presents a stance '"[g]ainst death'.

Sonnet 18 'Shall I compare thee to a summer's day' presents itself as the opposite of the frozen winter moment and expands its subject, 'the summer's day' in 'eternal lines' affirming poetry as a reviving power that excels the temporality of physical existence and verges on immortality. This immortality, however, is created in the most delicate moments, the all-too brief 'lease' of a summer, and the transient beauty of the 'darling buds of May'.

> Shall I compare thee to a summer's day?
> Thou art more lovely and more temperate:
> Rough winds do shake the darling buds of May,
> And summer's lease hath all too short a date;
> Sometime too hot the eye of heaven shines,
> And often is his gold complexion dimmed;

And every fair from fair sometime declines,
By chance or nature's changing course untrimmed:
But thy eternal summer shall not fade,
Nor lose possession of that fair thou ow'st,
Nor shall Death brag thou wandr'st in his shade,
When in eternal lines to time thou grow'st.
So long as men can breathe or eyes can see,
So long lives this, and this gives life to thee.

The sonnet creates a distinct temporality that is at once evanescent and eternal, that paradoxically intertwines the eternity of art with the brevity of the moment when it grants to the beloved the continuity of a still life that lasts as long as human beings can breathe and eyes can see and read the sonnet: 'so long lives this and this gives life to thee'.

In Sonnet 81, the speaker's worry that he might not live to write the epitaph of his beloved is allayed by the sonnet itself that 'from hence' marks a stance against death and oblivion: 'your monument shall be my gentle verse'.

Or I shall live your epitaph to make,
Or you survive when I in earth am rotten,
From hence your memory death cannot take,
Although in me each part will be forgotten.
Your name from hence immortal life shall have,
Though I (once gone) to all the world must die;
The earth can yield me but a common grave,
When you intombèd in men's eyes shall lie:
Your monument shall be my gentle verse,
Which eyes not yet created shall o'er read,
And tongues to be your being shall rehearse,
When all the breathers of this world are dead;
You still shall live (such virtue hath my pen)
Where breath most breathes, even in the mouths of men.

Yet it is by invoking death, 'when I in earth am rotten, . . . I (once gone) to all the world must die' that the speaker immortalizes himself along with his beloved and the sonnet. It is his art that will continue to live in and through reading, in being recited, in 'tongues to be your being shall rehearse', perhaps even in singing. Helen Vendler notes the anagrammatical wordplays in which 'created' contains read, 'breathers' conceals earth and 'rehearse' contains 'hear'.[55] The being of the poem – the beloved – and with it that of the speaker will resonate in these readings, but it does not depend on them, because it resides in the poem itself by virtue of the poet's pen: 'where breath most breathes' is where the beloved still lives.

Sir Philip Sidney conceives of the artist in analogy to God when he describes poetry as being infused with a life that surpasses nature just as God endowed his creatures with divine breath in Gen 2.7: 'which in nothing he showeth so much as in poetry, when with the force of a divine breath he bringeth things forth surpassing her [nature's] doings'.[56] While the sonnets unfold the breadth of the poet's imagination and evince both his yearning for immortality and the fulfilment of that yearning in the poem, however, they also render his exasperation and despair in a way that is reminiscent of Schubert's barrel organ player. Stephen Orgel hence calls some of the sonnets 'monument[s] to frustration and loss'.[57]

Life and death, in many of Shakespeare's works, materialize in the onomatopoeic rhyme on death and breath that characterizes the paradoxical being of the still life as both creation and destruction. Lear desperately wishes to think that Cordelia is still alive and searches for a sign of life: 'If that her breath will mist or stain the stone,/Why then she lives' (*KL* 5.3.236–37), and deems it unjust that animals are alive and she is not: 'Why should a dog, a horse, a rat have life,/And thou no breath at all?' (*KL* 5.3.280–1). Beckett, in *Waiting for Godot*, deflates the pathos of this scene, when Vladimir and Estragon decide to kick the seemingly lifeless Lucky: 'Vladimir: Make sure he's alive before you start. No point in exerting yourself if he's dead./ Estragon: [*Bending over* Lucky]. He's breathing' (*CDW*, 82).

In *Antony and Cleopatra*, the statuesque Roman stoutness of Octavia is opposed to the sensuous liveliness of Cleopatra when the Messenger answers to Cleopatra's detailed inquiries about her:

> MESSENGER Madam, I heard her speak. She is low-voiced.
> CLEOPATRA That's not so good. He cannot like her long.
> CHARMIAN Like her? O Isis! 'Tis impossible.
> CLEOPATRA I think so, Charmian. Dull of tongue, and dwarfish. –
> What majesty is in her gait? Remember
> If e'er thou look'st on majesty.
> MESSENGER She creeps:
> Her motion and her station are as one.
> She shows a body rather than a life,
> A statue than a breather. (*AC* 3.3.13–21)

Whereas Octavia represents an inanimate still life in which the motion and station are one, the living statue of Hermione in *The Winter's Tale* breathes. Leontes notices this and wonders: 'What fine chisel/Could ever yet cut breath?' (*WT* 5.3.78–9), implying that this art would be impossible.

Beckett experiments with the simultaneity of breath and death in his many theatrical still lifes, but metonymically this opposition creates one of his most minute still lifes on stage. 'Breath', written in 1969,[58] can be seen as a culminating point of Beckett's still lifes in performance. The play starts with a faintly lit stage on which scattered remains of rubbish are spread. In the stage direction, Beckett explicitly notes that there should not be any verticals – 'all [should be] scattered and lying', conveying a two-dimensional space analogous to the condition of a painting. The pictorial silence of the setting is broken by a short recorded cry at the beginning and the end of the play that resembles the first cry of a child after birth, a vagitus, and echoes King Lear's lines referring to the position of human beings in a *teatrum mundi*: 'When we are born, we cry that we are come/ To this great stage of fools' (*KL* 4.5.174–5). The rising and falling action of a dramatic plot are rendered through the inspiration and expiration of a recorded inhale and exhale and the pause, the still point between them. Drama and life, the span of a lifetime from beginning to end, are cast into a theatrical still life in which the linearity of the plot is counterbalanced by the cyclical return suggested by the identical cry. The presence of a human being is substituted by stagecraft, light and sound. The entire play *Breath* lasts for about 35 seconds.

While, unlike in Shakespeare's sonnets, the words of the dramatist do not gesture towards eternity, they have been reduced to sound and the breath that produces them. *Breath* sets up an analogy between the play and a living, breathing being and shows that this being is produced by stagecraft. Life and the theatre converge inversely as Beckett creates art as life and life as art. Being is produced and presented in the condition of becoming and waning when the still life creates a winter without journey, which evokes its opposite through absence.

Notes

1 Samuel Beckett, *Selected Poems 1930–1989*, ed. by David Wheatley (London: Faber & Faber, 2009), 55. Cf. also *Letters*, IV, 653.
2 Walter Benjamin, *The Arcades Project*, ed. by Rolf Tiedemann, transl. by Howard Eiland and Kevin McLaughlin (Cambridge, MA: Belknap Press, 1999), 10.
3 Steven Connor, *Beckett, Modernism and the Material Imagination* (Cambridge University Press, 2014), 11.
4 S.E. Gontarski, 'Introduction' in S.E. Gontarski (ed.), *The Edinburgh Companion to Samuel Beckett and Art* (Edinburgh University Press, 2014), 10.

5 Lois Oppenheim, *The Painted Word: Samuel Beckett's Dialogue with Art* (Ann Arbor: University of Michigan Press, 2000), 5.
6 Ruby Cohn, *Just Play: Beckett's Theater* (Princeton University Press, 1980), 31
7 Mary Bryden, 'Beckett and the Dynamic Still', *Samuel Beckett Today/ Aujourd'hui*, 14 (2004), 179–92, 180.
8 Ibid., 180, 182.
9 Conor Carville, *Samuel Beckett and the Visual Arts* (Cambridge University Press, 2018) discusses Beckett's poetics of the image, 26–7, 35.
10 *Letters*, I, 222–3, 8.9.1934; Carville, *Samuel Beckett and the Visual Arts*, 182–3.
11 James Knowlson, 'Beckett and Seventeenth-Century Dutch and Flemish Art', *Samuel Beckett Today/Aujourd'hui*, 21 (2009), 27–44, 35.
12 David Lloyd, *Beckett's Thing* (Edinburgh University Press, 2016), 118–20.
13 Gottfried Boehm, 'Die Wiederkehr der Bilder', in Gottfried Boem (ed.), *Was ist ein Bild?* (München: Fink, 2006), 11–38, 35–6; Gottfried Boehm, Helmut Pfotenhauer, *Beschreibungskunst - Kunstbeschreibung: Ekphrasis von der Antike bis zur Gegenwart* (München: Fink, 1995), 38.
14 John Keats, *Selected Letters of John Keats*, ed. by Grant F. Scott, rev. ed. (Cambridge: Harvard University Press, 2005), 60. On 17 April, Keats writes to his friend, the poet J.H. Reynolds that he found a head of Shakespeare when unpacking his books, and hung it above his shelf. In the same letter, written on the Isle of Wight, Keats includes a poem 'On the Sea' and tells Reynolds that phrases from *King Lear* such as 'Do you not hear the Sea?' have been 'haunting' him. Ibid., 15–7.
15 Ruby Cohn describes Beckett's works in paradoxical terms such as stasis in motion, past present, word action; H. Porter Abbot, 'Consorting with Spirits: The Arcane Craft of Beckett's Later Drama', in Enoch Brater (ed.), *Theatrical Gamut: Notes for a Post-Beckettian Stage* (Ann Arbor: University of Michigan Press, 1995), 91–106, 100.
16 Ruby Cohn, 'Beckett's Theatre Resonance' in Morris Beja, S.E. Gontarski and Pierre Astier (eds.), *Samuel Beckett: Humanistic Perspectives* (Columbus: Ohio State University Press, 1983), 3–16, 11, 10: 'Words and music of *Footfalls* harmonize in an exquisite "cascando" of steps, chimes, and light. *A Piece of Monologue*, in contrast, is a still life unveiled by the parting of a curtain.'
17 Rosemary Pountney was among the first to address the shadowy non-presences in *Footfalls: Theatre of Shadows. Samuel Beckett's Drama, 1956–1976* (Gerrards Cross: Smythe, 1988), 166.
18 'O villain, villain, smiling damnèd villain!/. . ./That one may smile, and smile, and be a villain;/At least I'm sure it may be so in Denmark' (*Ham* 1.5.106–9).
19 'Thrift, thrift, Horatio. The funeral baked meats/Did coldly furnish forth the marriage tables' (*Ham* 1.2.180–1).
20 Joseph Long, 'Divine Intertextuality: Samuel Beckett, *Company*, *Le Dépeupleur*', *Samuel Beckett Today/Aujourd'hui*, 9 (2000), 145–57, 151.
21 Walther von der Vogelweide: 'Ich saz ûf einem steine/dô dahte ich bein mit beine./ dar ûf sazte ich mîn ellenbogen,/ ich hete in mîne hant gesmogen/ daz kinne und ein mîn wange./ dô dâhte ich mir vil ange,/ wie man zer welte solte

leben' (L 8,4–10). Walther von der Vogelweide, *Leich, Lieder, Sangsprüche*, ed. by Thomas Bein, 15th ed., (Berlin, Boston: de Gruyter, 2013), 12.

22 Dirk van Hulle, 'Undoing Dante: Samuel Beckett's Poetics from a Textual Perspective', *Text*, 16 (2006), 87–95; 87–88: 'In the last part of this late text (1989) the protagonist tries to find the right word describing (death, or) the place *'where never till then'* (Beckett 1995, 264)'.

23 Stanton B. Garner Jr., '"Still Living Flesh": Beckett, Merleau-Ponty, and the Phenomenological Body', *Theatre Journal*, 45 (1993), 443–60, 459: 'On the threshold of the body's disappearance into nothingness or its reversion to pure matter, there are stirrings still.'

24 Samuel Beckett, *Film: Complete Scenario, Illustrations, Production Shots* (New York: Grove Press, 1969), 11.

25 Porter Abbott, 'Consorting with Spirits', 91–107, 100. Ruby Cohn, 'Ghosting through Beckett' in Marius Buning and Lois Oppenheim (eds.), *Beckett in the 1990s* (Amsterdam: Rodopi, 1993), 1–11.

26 Lois Oppenheim, 'The Uncanny in Beckett' in Colleen Jaurretche (eds.) *Beckett, Joyce and the Art of the Negative*, European Joyce Studies 16 (Amsterdam, New York: Rodopi, 2005), 125–140, 129.

27 'The little piano is a great help. Have all Haydn Sonatas and all Schubert (from Avigdor) and wander therein. Have to memorize or it means playing with my hands behind my back.' (*Letters*, IV, 12.04.1966, 68–9); 'Also stood myself I fear a dull life & work of Schubert of bisexual Swiss authorship' (*Letters*, IV, 02.09.1969, 170) [Beckett was reading: Walter and Paula Rehberg, *Franz Schubert: Sein Leben und Werk* (Zürich: Artemis, 1946)]; 'Received from Stockholm cassette of the Doppelgänger sung by Ger[h]ard [edited in the text] Hüsch, piano Hans Müller. We'll listen to it together one of these days' (*Letters*, IV, 17.12.1983, 625). ('Stille ist die Nacht').

28 Still ist die Nacht, es ruhen die Gassen,
In diesem Hause wohnte mein Schatz;
Sie hat schon längst die Stadt verlassen,
Doch steht noch das Haus auf demselben Platz.
Da steht auch ein Mensch und starrt in die Höhe,
Und ringt die Hände, vor Schmerzensgewalt;
Mir graust es, wenn ich sein Antlitz sehe -
Der Mond zeigt mir meine eigne Gestalt.
Du Doppelgänger! du bleicher Geselle!
Was äffst du nach mein Liebesleid,
Das mich gequält auf dieser Stelle,
So manche Nacht, in alter Zeit?

29 Letter to Reinhart Müller-Freienfels, director at Süddeutscher Rundfunk, 5.3.1984, *Letters*, IV, 637.

30 Gontarski, 'Introduction' in S.E. Gontarski (ed.), *The Edinburgh Companion to Samuel Beckett and the Arts*, 7.

31 James Knowlson, *Damned to Fame: The Life of Samuel Beckett* (London: Bloomsbury, 1997), 685: Beckett was invited to write a stage play for the

Graz autumn festival in 1983 that was inspired by Schubert's *Winterreise*, particularly to 'Gute Nacht' and 'Der Wegweiser'; What Where, Quoi, où. (*Letters*, IV, 20.03.1983, 606–607). Beckett thought of offering the play to the Süddeutscher Rundfunk to be turned into a television play. (*Letters*, IV, 624; 631–632) Paul Lawley, '"The Grim Journey": Beckett Listens to Schubert', *Samuel Beckett Today/Aujourd'hui* 11 (2001), 255–66.

32 *Letters*, II, 605. Beckett acquired Fischer-Dieskau's recording of *Winterreise* (1955) in July 1956.

33 Knowlson, *Damned to Fame*, 626.

34 Franz Schubert, *Franz Schubert: Neue Ausgabe sämtlicher Werke*, ed. by Internationale Schubert-Gesellschaft, comp. by Walter Dürr (Kassel, Basel, Tours, London: Bärenreiter, 1979) vol. 4a [Lieder], 167.

35 Ian Bostridge, *Schubert's Winter Journey: Anatomy of an Obsession* (London: Faber & Faber, 2015), 25; Susan Youens, *Retracing a Winter's Journey: Schubert's 'Winterreise'* (Ithaca: Cornell University Press, 1991).

36 Bostridge, *Schubert's Winter Journey*, 180–1: 'The vocal phrases which relate the stillness and motionlessness of the frozen river ("Wie still bist du geworden," How still you've become, and "Liegst kalt und unbeweglich," You lie cold and unmoving) are marked "sehr leise" (very soft), and for me they seem to demand an inwardness and smoothness, as well as pianissimo, which contrasts with the hardness of the opening phrases ("Der du so lustig rauschtest," You who rushed along so heartily, and "Mit harter, starrer Rinde," With a hard, stiff crust).

37 Knowlson, *Damned to Fame*, 685.

38 Franz Schubert, *Franz Schubert: Neue Ausgabe sämtlicher Werke*, vol. 4a, 191.

39 Bostridge, *Schubert's Winter Journey*, 475. Cf. also Heinrich Heine, *Deutschland, ein Wintermärchen*, 1844.

40 Martin Esslin, 'A Theatre of Stasis – Beckett's Late Plays', *Critical Essays on Samuel Beckett*, 192–8, 193.

41 Jean-Michel Rabaté, *Think, Pig! Beckett at the Limit of the Human* (New York: Fordham, 2016), 17.

42 Joseph Anderton, '"Living Flesh": The Human–Nonhuman Proximity in Beckett's Four Stories', *Samuel Beckett Today/Aujourd'hui*, 32 (2020), 192–206, 195.

43 Joseph Anderton, *Beckett's Creatures: Art of Failure After the Holocaust* (London: Bloomsbury, 2016), 4.

44 Richard Carter Smith considers life on the verge of non-being as a starting point of Beckett's art: 'Beckett's fiction treats its perfect emptiness as a generative principle for art rather than a political ill to be rectified', 'Beckett and the Animal: Writing from "No-Man's land"', *ELH*, 79 (2012), 211–35, 221.

45 Kent: 'The wrathful skies/Gallow [in which] the very wanderers of the dark [,/And make them] keep their caves.' (*KL* 3.2.41–3); Lear: 'Expose thyself to feel what wretches feel' (*KL* 3.4.34).

46 Cf. *Ham* 2.2.281–6: 'it goes so heavily with my disposition that this goodly frame, the earth, seems to me a sterile promontory; this most excellent canopy

the air, look you, this brave o'erhanging firmament, this majestical roof fretted with golden fire – why, it appeareth no other thing to me than a foul and pestilent congregation of vapours.')

47 This passage is reiterated in 'Texts for Nothing', 3: 'I tried throwing me off a cliff, collapsing in the street in the midst of mortals, that led nowhere, I gave up' (*CSP*, 111).
48 *Letters*, IV, 620.
49 Dirk van Hulle, 'Beckett and Shakespeare on Nothing, or, Whatever Lurks behind the Veil', *Limit(e) Beckett*, 1 (2010), 196–217; cf. also *Beckett and Nothing: Trying to Understand Beckett*, ed. Daniela Caselli (Manchester University Press, 2010).
50 *KL* 5.3.230, note.
51 In hindsight, the performance of *The Winter's Tale* at the Palatine wedding of Elizabeth Stuart and Frederick of Palatine reflects uneasily on the events that made Frederick lose his crown and his Bohemian inheritance and to be known thereafter as the 'Winter king' because of the shortness of his reign. In *The Winter's Tale* it is Mamilius who whispers a story about a man who lives near a graveyard into his mother's ear and is going to be the first one to die. Cf. Sara Smart and Mara R. Wade (eds.), *The Palatine Wedding of 1613: Protestant Alliance and Court Festival* (Wiesbaden: Harrassowitz, 2013).
52 Claudia Olk, 'Vision and Desire in *Mary Magdalene* and *The Winter's Tale*' in Andrew James Johnston, Ethan Knapp and Margitta Rouse (eds.), *The Art of Vision: Ekphrasis in Medieval Literature and Culture* (Columbus: The Ohio State University Press, 2015), 79–100, 94.
53 Franz von Kutschera, *Ästhetik*, 2nd ed. (1998, repr. Berlin: de Gruyter, 2010), 327.
54 Marjorie Garber, *Shakespeare After All* (New York: Anchor Books, 2004), 851.
55 Helen Vendler, *The Art of Shakespeare's Sonnets* (Cambridge, MA: Harvard University Press, 1997), 361.
56 Sir Philip Sidney, *Miscellaneous Prose of Sir Philip Sidney*, ed. Katherine Duncan-Jones and Jan van Dorsten (Oxford: Clarendon Press, 1973), 79, l. 21–23.
57 G. Blakemore Evans (ed.), *The Sonnets. New Cambridge Shakespeare*, with a new introduction by Stephen Orgel (Cambridge University Press, 2006), 20.
58 *Breath* was performed at the Eden Theatre off-Broadway, and ran for a year. Graham Saunders, 'Contracts, Clauses and Nudes: *Breath, Oh! Calcutta!* and the Freedom of Authorship' in David Tucker and Trish McTighe (eds.), *Staging Beckett in Great Britain* (London: Bloomsbury, 2016), 176–92.

CHAPTER 6

Endgames

Clov: *[Imploringly.] Let's stop playing!*
Hamm: *Never! (CDW, 130)*

Infinite Finitude

When looking with Shakespeare at Beckett and with Beckett at Shakespeare, their works kaleidoscopically blend into each other in perpetually shifting combinations, where likenesses appear for a moment between seemingly unlike texts and then disappear with the next configuration. Reading sometimes resembles using an optical instrument: we find ourselves at both ends of the telescope, or rather looking through both a telescope and a microscope, where the closer we look the more we see. The finite and the infinite reciprocally define one another in a dialectics of contraction and expansion. Minute particles that compose an artistic universe expand and coalesce into metonymic configurations, in which representation constitutes itself through a reflection and a critique of representation. Among other aspects of their relationship, this chapter explores the altered ways of seeing brought about by constellational readings of Shakespeare with and through Beckett.

What is perceived as the abundance of Shakespeare's worlds often collides with the minimalist poverty of Beckett's stages. Beckett's works in turn reflect back on Shakespeare and provide a key to a more dissected, literal reading of single passages, which magnifies small scenes or single expressions. Hamm's reluctance to stop playing in *Endgame* not only resonates with Hamlet calling Yorick 'a fellow of infinite jest' (*Ham* 5.1.185) but also notions such as the one of an 'Endgame' acquire larger metonymic and compositional significance. Clov in *Endgame* performs this kind of metatheatrical critique when he looks at the auditorium through his telescope: 'Clov: I see ... a multitude ... in transports ... of joy. *[Pause.]* That's what I call a magnifier' (*CDW*, 106). The finite world of the stage that Hamm and Clov inhabit interacts with the larger world of the spectators in the auditorium. For a brief moment the roles of actor and spectator are reversed, as Clov becomes a spectator himself. He inverts the audience's view of the enclosed space of the stage and reciprocates their gaze by looking at them. Beckett's works negotiate this dialectic of perspective.

Shakespeare and many of his contemporaries shared a fascination with the seemingly finite and minute that could potentially unfold into infinite worlds. Unable to leave Denmark, Hamlet, who towards the end of the play sees 'special providence in the fall of a sparrow' (*Ham* 5.2.192–3) had earlier explained to Rosencrantz that dimensions are contingent upon one's perspective: 'I could be bounded in a nutshell, and count myself a king of infinite space, were it not that I have bad dreams' (*Ham* 2.2.243–4). Shakespeare often invokes the miniature world of faerie to inspire the audience's imagination. Mercutio in *Romeo and Juliet* surmises that Queen Mab, 'the faeries' midwife' in her chariot of an empty hazelnut '[d]rawn with a team of little atomi' (*RJ* 1.4.54; 57) has visited Romeo and made him dream of love. Celia in *As You Like It* knows that 'It is as easy to count atomies as to resolve the propositions of a lover' (*AYL* 3.2.194–5), and in *A Midsummer Night's Dream*, Puck reports that Oberon's and Titania's quarrel makes 'all their elves for fear/Creep into acorn-cups and hide them there' (*MND* 2.1.30–1).

In the early phase of microscopy around 1650–1750, from Henry Power's *Experimental Philosophy* (1664) and Richard Hooke's *Micrographia* (1665)[1] to Margaret Cavendish's *Observations upon Experimental Philosophy; to which is added, the Description of a New Blazing World* (1666), the subvisible world inaccessible to the senses provided models of creativity that acquired epistemological relevance. Seventeenth-century poetry, significantly the poems of Andrew Marvell, use the relativity of perspective to create multiple alternative worlds of language. The poem 'On a Drop of Dew' finds the human soul in a drop of dew, and juxtaposes contrasting notions of size that transcend conventional distinctions of space: 'Round in itself incloses:/And in its little globe's extent,/Frames as it can its native element.'[2]

The play with finitude, in which the sense of an ending opens up into potential infinity, characterizes Beckett's minimalist art. Small forms of narrative such as 'Fizzles', 'Texts for Nothing' and plays such as *Quad I* and *Quad II* exhibit their limitations and gesture beyond them when their formal and semantic contraction expands interpretive possibilities. Beginning and end, birth and death converge in many instances of

Beckett's works. Pozzo in *Waiting for Godot* describes the flickering moment of life: 'They give birth astride of a grave, the light gleams an instant, then it's night once more' (*CDW*, 83). Vladimir further illustrates the swift transition from birth to death: 'Astride of a grave and a difficult birth. Down in the hole, lingeringly, the grave-digger puts on the forceps' (*CDW*, 84), and the speaker in *A Piece of Monologue* starts the play with the statement: 'Birth was the death of him' (*CDW*, 425). Works like *Krapp's Last Tape*, 'Enough' or 'The End' explicitly refer to the end as their theme and record their own asymptotic movement towards it.

Endgame likewise presents itself as a dramatic form that captures the nexus between finitude and the idea of infinite play. As Stanley Gontarksi has shown, *Endgame*, which was completed in 1957 after a protracted composition process, became for Beckett a turning point in his writing, 'a new beginning for talking about the old ends'.[3] Beckett's experiments with longer fiction had come to an end with *The Unnamable* in 1953. From then on, he wrote his major dramatic works, but many of the narrative fragments and shorter fiction that he produced throughout his life continued to explore what Frank Kermode in *The Sense of an Ending* describes as 'fictions, whose ends are consonant with origins, and in concord, however unexpected, with their precedents'.[4]

Rather than the link between *Endgame* and *King Lear* that is addressed in Chapter 1, this chapter considers the many parallels, convergences and yet uncharted relations between Beckett's *Endgame* and one of Shakespeare's last works, his late romance *The Tempest*. Ruby Cohn has called *Endgame* 'Shakespearean in the metaphysics of its theatrical imagery',[5] and indeed, both plays, *Endgame* and *The Tempest*, use the notions of ending and finitude to explore and reflect on the nature of their medium.

The critics who have analysed *Endgame* in relation to Shakespeare, most prominently among them Theodor W. Adorno in his seminal essay 'Versuch, das Endspiel zu verstehen',[6] have, sometimes to Beckett's annoyance, euphorically pointed to the resemblance between Beckett's Hamm and Shakespeare's Hamlet, and those fewer scholars who have drawn a link between *The Tempest* and *Endgame* have relied on the direct allusion of Hamm's quotation from *The Tempest* 'Our revels now are ended' (*T* 4.1.148) after the lid of the dustbin in which his father vegetates has been finally closed for the rest of the play.

From Adorno's notion of a 'liquidation of the subject'[7] in Beckett to Ruby Cohn's observation that '*Endgame* mockingly reflects *The Tempest*',[8] the narrative of degeneration and loss is continuously present in considerations of Beckett's works themselves and their interaction with other authors. Habitually the scholarly endorsement of this trajectory of decline resorts to interpretive patterns in which Shakespeare remains superior and Beckett uses parody as a last resort with which to reveal the tragic as an obsolescent dramatic mode.[9] Rather than illustrating a hermeneutics of failure or merely offering a parody of *The Tempest*, Beckett's works such as *Endgame* present the anatomy of a generative structure of the theatre that creates new constellations of meaning and is developed through a critique of the very mode and medium of the theatre itself. This is most evident in Beckett's dialogue with *The Tempest*, Shakespeare's most ostentatiously metatheatrical play. Both plays bring those aspects of the theatre into focus that exhibit the dialectic of making and unmaking, creation and destruction, confinement and release.

Finitude is immanent in the theatre. It allows for a reflection of the theatre's dramatic possibilities and it initiates a logic of self-transcendence. Similar to Beckett, Shakespeare's works exhibit the poetic power of creation that lies within the limitations of theatrical means and the transgressive dynamics of the theatre that reach beyond the boundaries of the stage. To Peter Quince, trying to direct the mechanicals' play in *A Midsummer Night's Dream*, this presents a dilemma – he struggles to overcome the restrictions of the stage to make the audience believe that what they see is true: 'But there is two hard things: that is, to bring the moonlight into a chamber; for you know, Pyramus and Thisbe meet by moonlight' (*MND* 3.1.36–8). The Prologue of *Henry V* likewise alludes to the limitations of the theatrical space when he asks to be pardoned for bringing such a mighty personality as Henry V on this 'unworthy scaffold' (*H5* Prol.10), or when he challenges the audience: 'Can this cockpit hold/The vasty fields of France? Or may we cram/Within this wooden O the very casques/That did affright the air at Agincourt?' (*H5* Prol.11–14). Pointing out the confines of the theatre and the limits of representational practices is not merely a *captatio benevolentiae* of the audience but also an invitation to overcome these boundaries through the imagination, which is capable of compensating for potential faults and can perfect the impression of what is seen: '[p]iece out our imperfections with your thoughts' (*H5* Prol.23). Imperfections and shortcomings, failures and the limitations of a medium are not an end in themselves, but become the grounds on which plays like *The Tempest* and *Endgame* transcend the finitude of their art and reflect back on it, asserting its very finitude as a condition of possibility.

Insular Dominions and 'the full poor cell'

Endgame and *The Tempest* are set in the paradoxical space of a small, isolated world that, being richly allusive, becomes potentially boundless. Spatial limitation and the contraction of the dramatic plot simultaneously extend the plays' significance beyond the given boundaries and endow them with metonymical scope. Howard Felperin characterizes the spatial and temporal span of *The Tempest*:

> Shakespeare contains an action that stretches from 'the dark backward and abysm of time' to the dramatic present, from a lost Golden Age to a future Apocalypse, and that spans the Mediterranean from Italy to North Africa, and the Atlantic from the Old World to the New, to a single afternoon and a single place, an island brought forth from the sea by the kind of spontaneous generation Antonio goes on to ridicule.[10]

Prospero's island and the room that Beckett's characters inhabit in *Endgame* are experimental places that cannot be grasped with recourse to referential meaning.[11] As Jonathan Bate has shown, 'what is striking about *The Tempest* is its pointed absence of allusion to Spanish matter, its lack of referential anchorage'.[12] In spite of its reliance on numerous and diverse sources, *The Tempest* does not have any single or direct forerunner. It highlights possible rather than precise connections to geographic realities, and other than contemporary accounts of New World travel, *The Tempest*, like one of its sources, the *Aeneid*, is set in the Mediterranean. Compared to other Shakespearean 'romances' such as *The Winter's Tale* or *Pericles*, *The Tempest* is more tightly controlled, one of just two of Shakespeare's plays to observe the classical unities. And yet, as Christopher Pye illustrates, no Shakespeare play is so dispersed with its ambient voices, its projective relation between characters, its expansive web of specular correspondences, in which for instance the 'forward' and 'backward' voices of a monster can figure the self-divisions of the master and in which characters eerily anticipate themselves.[13] Lacking precise references to historical events and specific geographic places, the spaces of *Endgame* and *The Tempest* create theatrical worlds that reveal the ways in which the theatre reflects on its mechanisms of representation.

In *Endgame*, as many commentators have noted, the theatrical space appears as a world both upside down and inside out.[14] Apart from a ladder that Clov uses to open the curtains of two high-set windows and a picture that is facing the wall, the room is unfurnished. Sitting in a chair that rests on castor wheels, Hamm is in the centre of the room. At the front are two dustbins, in which Hamm's parents, Nagg and Nell, are kept, to be occasionally presented to quarrel or indulge in nostalgic musings. The four characters display different degrees of immobility and physical incapacity: Nagg and Nell have lost their legs. Hamm is blind, lame, bleeding and in need of medication, and Clov cannot sit down. The history of Beckett criticism has provided a broad range of options to read the characters' monosyllabic names. Hamm was seen as Hamlet, who is torn between two equally fatal options and procrastinating, putting an end to his dilemma, and indeed, the skull-like interior of *Endgame*, in which Hamm takes two turns around the world, recalls Hamlet's 'distracted globe', which refers both to his mind and to the theatre.'[15] Moreover, he has been seen as a ham actor or as Cham/Ham, the second son of Noah, either before, during or after the deluge and in anticipation of the endgame of apocalypse.

The play indeed starts with a prologue in what is either Heaven or Hell, and its very first line is already an ending: '*Fini, c'est fini, ça va finir, ça va peut-être finir* [Finished, it's finished, nearly finished, it must be nearly finished]' (*CDW*, 93). The play has just begun and already it is over, or perhaps only nearly over.[16] Clov's biblical pathos is at the same time undercut by irony, as he calls to mind both God's words at the end of creation and Christ's last words on the cross: 'It is finished, it will finish, it will perhaps finish.' The text balances a linear temporal pattern with a reiterative one, as the very beginning offers four different ways of imagining the end, none of which, however, suggests the fulfilment of a redemptive typology.

In Beckett's setting of *Endgame*, which in some productions is presented as an inverted skull, we find the two characters Hamm and Clov in a situation akin to the many shipwrecked in Shakespeare's *The Tempest*: stranded, marooned as it were, within a space that is their only shelter, a kind of 'post-apocalyptic bunker'[17]; 'Outside of here it's death' (*CDW*, 96), Hamm observes, pointing to a post-diluvian world that casts the stage set as a version of Noah's ark (*Gen* 8: 21–2, 11, 14–19). Beckett owned at least six Bibles, among them translations into English, Italian and French. In his copy of *The Comprehensive Teacher's Bible*, he marked the passage from Genesis 10:32: 'These *are* the families of the sons of Noah, after their generations, in their nations: and by these were the nations divided in the earth after the flood.'[18] *Endgame* is replete with water imagery and references to the sea. Yves Bonnefoy urges readers of Beckett that they 'should listen to his books only through the constant roll of waves, the intermittent drumming of rain'.[19]

Hamm repeatedly asks Clov to look at the sea,[20] Nagg and Nell reminisce about their boat trip on Lake Como: 'Nagg: You were in such fits that we capsized. By rights we should have been drowned' (*CDW*, 102), and fed up with Nagg and Nell's stories, Hamm asks Clov to '[c]lear away this muck! Chuck it in the sea' (*CDW*, 103). *Endgame* undergoes a sea-change when the sameness of the ocean and its 'leaden waves' that Clov observes at the beginning of the play, at the end are no longer discernible, and the outside world Clov looks at has become flooded: 'Under water! [...] Hamm: Whole thing' (*CDW*, 128).

Likewise, the watery world that surrounds the island in *The Tempest* is reflected in the play's imagery and its allusions to submersion and drowning. The shipwrecked Neapolitans express their fear of drowning as well as the hope that Ferdinand may be 'undrowned' (*T* 2.1.233; 235), and finally Prospero plans to abjure his magic and to 'drown his book': 'deeper than did ever plummet sound/I'll drown my book' (*T* 5.1.56–7).

The Tempest is an imaginary compound that combines elements of medieval romance, travel literature, aspects of colonialism and references to the ancient world.[21] Prospero's nameless island is sometimes read as a metonymy for a colonized world,[22] or rather a meeting place where old and new worlds interact, and where retrospection and projection coincide. The island is utopian and dystopian at once. It is a space of antagonistic dynamics where notions of mankind and monster, prelapsarian innocence and postlapsarian guilt are negotiated and interchange contingent upon one's perspective. *The Tempest*'s many allusions to ancient and mythological forebears and conceptions of ideal worlds such as the Golden Age collide with the penal environment instituted by Prospero's system of surveillance, which qualifies the island's promise of safe ground after shipwreck.

And yet, its rich, fanciful and elusive landscape is also a place of magic and illusion,[23] a place where discourses on sovereignty and aesthetic formation intersect:[24] 'rendering the island a pure conceptual space – or rather a purely theatrical space, for it is here that our sense of the resemblance between an island and the theatre is strongest'.[25] What fascinated Beckett about *The Tempest* was perhaps its engagement with the fantasy of political and artistic autogenesis – with a self-contained, insular world made from within itself that, at the same time, constitutes the world at large.

Beckett's aesthetics follows a similar hermeneutic trajectory in which holistic entities and fictions of totality are pared down to microscopic parts that in turn lay the foundations for new aesthetic configurations, worlds that are reinvented from inside a confinement. Beckett's plays, not least through their engagement with Shakespeare, become experimental spaces like Prospero's island where action can be observed and manipulated, where notions of order, power and humanity are explored and challenged.

The *'Bare interior'* (*CDW*, 92), Beckett's description of the stage for *Endgame*, forecloses mimetic options that rely on representation. In its world, the picture, one of the few props holding the promise of referential meaning, is turned against the wall as would be a mirror in the house of the deceased in Irish culture. Nature, birds, bicycles or coffins are only present through their absence. Wolfgang Iser describes negativity in Beckett's prose in similar terms: 'Negativity brings into being an endless potentiality, and it is this potentiality that forms the infrastructure of Beckett's writings. By negativity we mean the hidden motive for the many negations and deformations that condition the characters we meet in these works.'[26] Paradoxically, less is growing more as the play's semantic rhythm both elicits and then thwarts significance. *Endgame* stages trajectories of deprivation when Hamm's bitterly melancholic apprehension 'Nature has forgotten us' is coolly dismissed by Clov, 'There is no more nature' (*CDW*, 97); in the same way Nagg's stubborn request for 'Me sugar-plum!' is shushed by Hamm: 'There are no more sugar-plums!' (*CDW*, 119). Incredulously, Hamm and Clov wonder that the last vestiges of animal life still exist: 'A flea! Are there still fleas?' (*CDW*, 108); 'A rat! Are there still rats?' (*CDW*, 118).

Upon their flight from Milan, Prospero and Miranda had been left at sea on '[a] rotten carcass', which 'the very rats/Instinctively have quit' (*T* 1.2.146; 147–8), until they reached the 'bare island' (*T* Epilogue 8) '[b]y providence divine' (*T* 1.2.159). To some of the characters the island is a blank slate of floating signifiers, a newly found space that invites projections and enhances epic fantasies of natural abundance of resources and colonial fantasies about their exploitation; visions of imperial dominance vie with those of egalitarian governance. Prospero's island, however, remains a deeply ambiguous and unaccommodating place that is both life-giving and hostile. The newly ship-wrecked are divided in their opinions about the island space and contemplate its ambivalences:

> ADRIAN   The air breathes upon us here most sweetly.
> SEBASTIAN As if it had lungs, and rotten ones. . . .
> GONZALO   Here is everything advantageous to life.
> ANTONIO   True, save means to live. (*T* 2.1.45–9)

Gonzalo famously adumbrates his utopian vision of a perfect egalitarian, idle and innocent society that would 'excel the Golden Age' (*T* 2.1.165), but yet, as the others remind him, his projection is not entirely altruistic as he 'would be king on't' (*T* 2.1.153).

Before Antonio usurped his position, in Milan, Prospero had cultivated a life of learning in solitude and isolation: 'my library/Was dukedom large enough' (*T* 1.2.109–10), and once on the island, he again establishes a private world of art, which he governs from his cell: 'This cell's my court' (*T* 5.1.166). He introduces himself in paradoxical terms as the 'master of a full poor cell' (*T* 1.2.20), and repeatedly refers to the island and to his dwellings as the 'cell', denoting both his insular dominion, the limited space of the stage and the confinement of a monastic cell for contemplation.

Like the island in *The Tempest*, the space of *Endgame* resembles a space for thought and meditation; it can be likened to a skull, and yet, like Prospero's island or Hamlet's Denmark, it is a prison. Clov, like Prospero, therefore expresses his longing to leave the confinement of the 'cell': 'Then one day, suddenly, it ends, it changes ... I open the door of the cell and go. ... I say to myself that the earth is extinguished, though I never saw it lit' (*CDW*, 132).[27] Clov loves order and concentrates on the finite world that lies within his control. Prospero, likewise, was at ease in the kingdom of his library, and Clov feels at home in his cubic kitchen: 'Clov: ... I'll go now to my kitchen, ten feet by ten feet by ten feet, and wait for him to whistle me. [...] Nice dimensions, nice proportions' (*CDW*, 93). Clov entertains visions of order and final rest, and his dreamlike utopia is an apocalyptic scenario of the world ending in motionless silence: 'Clov: [*Straightening up.*] I love order. It's my dream. A world where all would be silent and still and each thing in its last place, under the last dust' (*CDW*, 120). The settings of both plays are confined, experimental spaces that release associations, exceeding physical and spatial limitations. *Endgame* and *The Tempest* become readable as metaphors for a theatrical world that generates its own condition of possibility and allows for a continuous expansion and transgression of the very boundaries within which it operates.

Contraction and expansion in both plays are rendered through the concomitant dialectic of confinement and liberation that structures *The Tempest* and *Endgame* on a number of levels. Prospero's confinement on the island is further reproduced in his self-division into his two similarly imprisoned servants that reflect on his dual powers. Ariel had been caged in the 'cloven pine' (*T* 1.2.277) by Sycorax and is liberated by Prospero only to enter into his service in return. One of the many tasks he accomplishes before his protracted release is to imprison the mariners, as well as the king and his followers: 'Confined together ... all prisoners, sir' (*T* 5.1.7–9). Caliban, Ariel's counterpart and Prospero's 'thing of darkness' (*T* 5.1.274), is 'styed' by Prospero and remains 'confined into this rock' (*T* 1.2.361) after his attempt to assault Miranda: 'In this hard rock, whiles you do keep from me/The rest o'th'Island' (*T* 1.2.344–5). And it is only when Ferdinand, who is himself taken prisoner, enters Prospero's service that Caliban is freed, or rather temporarily finds new masters in Stephano and Trinculo. Throughout the play, characters who are not imprisoned or held under a spell nevertheless remain isolated, either individually or in small groups.

In *Endgame*, confinement likewise occurs in the form of a *mise-en-abîme*. The very setting presents an enclosed space, within which Hamm cannot walk and remains tied to his wheelchair, where Clov cannot sit down and where Hamm's parents Nagg and Nell are kept like animals in their dustbins that are laid-out with 'sand from the shore': 'Nagg: It was sawdust once./Nell: Once!/Nagg: And now it's sand. [*Pause.*] From the shore. [*Pause. Impatiently.*] Now it's sand he fetches from the shore./Nell: Now it's sand' (*CDW*, 100). 'Sand from the shore' indicates the existence of a possible world elsewhere. It nurtures hope and nostalgia, but it also thwarts it when the sand that has not been changed ensures they remain trapped in their dustbin cages. Their confinement is further emphasized when it is acted out in farcical and tragic-comic terms, when Nagg and Nell reminisce about happier times in the past, and try to reach one another in vain:

> NELL   What is it, my pet? [*Pause*] Time for love?
> NAGG   Were you asleep?
> NELL   Oh no!
> NAGG   Kiss me.
> NELL   We can't.
> NAGG   Try. [*Their heads strain towards each other, fail to meet, fall apart again.*]
> NELL   Why this farce, day after day? (*CDW*, 99)

'Pet' is not only a term of endearment, but it also points to their animal-like existence, and Nell's comment about the farcical nature of their repeated fruitless efforts bitterly stresses the futility of their ritual.

In *The Tempest*, the 'yellow sands' onto which Ferdinand is lured by Ariel's song, like the sand in Nagg and Nell's dustbins, provide the material and geological base of the insular space, and they are associated with Ferdinand's falling in love with Miranda. Ariel's song that entices Ferdinand invites him to the island as if to a courtly dance: 'Come unto these yellow sands,/And then take hands./Curtsied when you have, and kissed,/The wild waves whist./Foot it featly here and there,/And sweet sprites the burden bear' (*T* 1.2.375–80). The world of *Endgame* is divested of magic, yet elements of romance are residually present in the play and enhance its tragicomic effect. Read with *Endgame*, Ariel's 'yellow sands' loose some of their temptation, and read with *The Tempest*, Nagg and Nell's sand gains a utopian dimension that reinforces the misery of their confinement.

Mastery and Meaning

In the course of *Endgame* and *The Tempest*, the power of control lies with the two ruler-figures. Hamm aligns himself with *Richard III* – 'My kingdom for a nightman!' (*CDW*, 103) – longing both for death and for a rubbish collector to empty the bins. He shares the pathos of an unaccommodated King Lear: 'But for me [*gesture towards himself*] no father. But for Hamm [*gesture towards surroundings*] no home' (*CDW*, 110–11), and like Prospero he is the sovereign at the centre of his world. Hamm's handkerchief, the 'old stauncher' that he takes off his face at the beginning of the play and puts on again at the end is a miniature version of the theatrical curtain. It is also reminiscent of the magic garment that Prospero takes off at the beginning of *The Tempest* (*T* 1.2. SD 24–5) and that he wears again at the end (*T* 5.1).

Hamm is fatigued but deprived of sleep, and longs for final rest: 'I feel rather drained. [*Pause.*] The prolonged creative effort. [*Pause.*] If I could drag myself down to the sea! I'd make a pillow of sand for my head and the tide would come. Clov: There's no more tide' (*CDW*, 122). Prospero, who at the end of the play is weary and seeks to retire to Milan 'where/ Every third thought shall be [his] grave' (*T* 5.1.308–9) had earlier compared the growing understanding of his adversaries to an 'approaching tide' that 'Will shortly fill the reasonable shore/That now lies foul and muddy' (*T* 5.1.81–2). Despite moments of wistfulness, Hamm despotically gives orders to his subaltern Clov, who, like Ariel, repeatedly reminds him that he wants to leave him, but cannot: 'Clov: There's one thing I'll never understand. [*He gets down.*] Why I always obey you' (*CDW*, 129).

In *Endgame* and in *The Tempest*, language and meaning are means of exerting power and authority. Miranda is kept ignorant about her past by Prospero, who delays his answer to her repeated inquiry: 'not yet' (*T* 1.2.36). When he decides to divulge the story of her origin, he asks Miranda to try to remember:

PROSPERO Obey, and be attentive. Canst thou remember
A time before we came unto this cell?
I do not think thou canst, for then thou wast not
Out three years old. ...
MIRANDA 'Tis far off;
And rather like a dream, than an assurance
That my remembrance warrants. (*T* 1.2.38–46)

Prospero teaches and preaches to his 'creature' Miranda and later in the play corrects her when she marvels at Alonso and his companions as 'goodly creatures': 'O wonder! How many goodly creatures are there here!/How beauteous mankind is! O brave new world/ That has such people in't!/Prospero:'Tis new to thee' (*T* 5.1.182–4).

Hamm also provides brief and fragmentary accounts of the past, fashions himself as a father-figure and repeatedly asks if Clov remembers how they met and came to stay where they are:

HAMM Do you remember when you came here?
CLOV No. Too small, you told me.
HAMM Do you remember your father?
CLOV [*Wearily.*] Same answer. [*Pause.*] You've asked me these questions millions of times.
HAMM I love the old questions. [*With fervour.*] Ah the old questions, the old answers, there's nothing like them! [*Pause.*] It was I was a father to you.
CLOV Yes. [*He looks at* HAMM *fixedly.*] You were that to me. (*CDW*, 110)

Like Miranda, who struggles to stay awake during Prospero's story, Clov is weary of listening to Hamm and continues to wonder why he allows himself to be ordered around: 'Do this, do that, and I do it. I never refuse. Why?' (*CDW*, 113), until Hamm exasperatedly exclaims: 'Ah the creatures, the creatures, everything has to be explained to them' (*CDW*, 113). Clov and Miranda, the next generation of creatures, are reluctant to be part of the history into which the narrative of their father-figures places them. Clov is a creature who is obliging and defiant at the same time, and he epitomizes characteristics of all three of Prospero's minions: Miranda, Ariel and Caliban. Ruby Cohn summarizes the ways in which Clov acts out some of Ariel's and Caliban's tasks, if on a homelier scale:

Clov serves as Ariel and Caliban to Prospero. Resembling Caliban in clumsiness and surliness, Clov performs trivial but necessary tasks. Raising a tempest is beyond his wildest dreams, but he speaks of building a raft to cross the seas. Clov cannot prepare a banquet, but he can get a dog-biscuit from the cupboard. Clov cannot arouse alarm in a Harpy disguise, but he can set an alarm-clock to ring. Clov cannot summon hunting-hounds, but he can make a three-legged, sexless, ribbonless toy dog. Clov lends himself to Hamm's fantasies, as Ariel does to Prospero's, and he attends to Hamm's material needs, as Caliban does to Prospero's.[28]

Like Ariel, he is ready to oblige, but nevertheless he desires his freedom. Like Clov's actions, Ariel's swiftness in carrying out his tasks 'Before you can say 'come' and 'go',/And breathe twice, and cry "so, so"' (*T* 4.1.44–5) is governed by the rhythm of coming and going, expansion and contraction: 'Clov: I come…and go' (*CDW*, 109). Beckett's later play *Come and Go* (1965) refers to the beginning of *Macbeth* when it opens with Vi, one of the three female characters of the play asking: 'When did we three last meet?' (*CDW*, 354). It also recalls Psalm 121:8: 'The Lord shall preserve your going out and your coming in from this day forth, for evermore' that is in some congregations used as a blessing at the end of a church service, and gestures towards the circular repetition of an action in the face of endless eternity. Clov's comings and goings cyclically structure the play and become themselves a game about theatrical exits and entrances when Hamm and Clov, at the end of the play, rehearse Clov's leave-taking:

> CLOV   This is what we call making an exit.
> HAMM   I'm obliged to you, Clov. For your services.
> CLOV   [*Turning sharply.*] Ah pardon, it's I am obliged to you.
> HAMM   It's we are obliged to each other. (*CDW*, 132)

Yet Clov remains, standing motionless by the door. The play repeatedly re-enacts these endgames of their relationship, which do not end until the play itself finishes in the same tableau in which it began. From the beginning of his life, Clov has been trying to leave Hamm: 'Hamm: I thought I told you to be off./Clov: I'm trying [*He goes to door, halts.*] Ever since I was whelped' (*CDW*, 98). His 'whelping' associates him with Caliban, whom Prospero describes as 'A freckled whelp, hag-born – not honoured with/A human shape' (*T* 1.2.283–4). Like Prospero, Miranda refers to Caliban's once inhuman and cultureless state when she chides him:[29] 'When thou didst not, savage,/Know thine own meaning, but wouldst gabble like/A thing most brutish, I endowed thy purposes/With words that made them known' (*T* 1.2.355–8). Miranda's language teaches Caliban to ascribe conventional meaning to his utterances. He replies and stresses that he is able to master 'her language' to use it for his own purposes: 'You taught me language, and my profit on't/Is, I know how to curse. The red plague rid you/For learning me your language!'

(*T* 1.2.363–5). Clov directly aligns himself to Caliban, when he replies to Hamm: 'I use the words you taught me. If they don't mean anything any more, teach me others. Or let me be silent' (*CDW*, 113).

Like Caliban, Clov speaks an acquired language that reflects on ways in which structures of power and dominance become naturalized through speech;[30] unlike Caliban, who knows how to turn the words against his master, Clov realizes that apart from silence there is no escape from the words he has been taught. In *Waiting for Godot* Lucky, not unlike Clov, is a creature domesticated and drilled by Pozzo. When Pozzo commands him: 'Think, pig!' (*CDW*, 41), he delivers his monologue, which contains references to some of Shakespeare's plays and mentions 'the divine Miranda' (*CDW*, 42). The perspective of Lucky, the subaltern, the pig, verges on meaninglessness and suspends the boundary between human being and animal. Jean-Michel Rabaté notes that Lucky's 'botched performance joins the bestial and the divine in a self-canceling obliteration of human rationality'.[31] Difference and resemblance are continuously at play as language denotes a trace of humanity in both Lucky and Caliban. Whereas in Caliban, who had previously been 'styed', it surfaces in the curse as a counter-action, Lucky's speech exhibits endgames of conventionally coded meaning.[32]

In both plays, meaning is described as dependent on ascription; it is presented as a product of interpretation that refers to the incongruence between the thing and what it signifies. This incongruence also operates on a metatheatrical level as Beckett's characters both affirm their embeddedness in prior structures of significance and supersede them at the same time:

> HAMM We're not beginning to ... to... mean something?
> CLOV Mean something! You and I, mean something! [*Brief laugh.*] Ah that's a good one! (*CDW*, 108)

References to patterns of signification create distance through a process of self-reflection that is at once destructive and creative. Meaning is both absent and ubiquitously present in the ways in which the characters evoke its absence. Stanley Cavell reads *Endgame* in similar terms, as performing the impossibility of non-meaning: 'The discovery of *Endgame*, both in topic and technique, is not the failure of meaning (if that means the lack of meaning) but its total, even totalitarian success – our inability *not* to mean what we are given to mean.'[33]

In both plays, the struggle for meaning and the release from it are experienced simultaneously.

Fundamental Sounds and Elementary Matter

Beckett, in a letter to Alan Schneider, describes *Endgame* as 'a matter of fundamental sounds'.[34] He conceives of the foundational elements of his dramatic composition as musical and considers his play as an acoustic phenomenon in which every 'fundamental' or lower frequency generates a variety of higher frequencies. Fundamental sounds first of all create something that without them would not exist. The musicality of *Endgame* does not so much consist in the material and medial presence of sound, but rather in the inaudible music that emerges in the play's structures and arrangements. Instead of modelling *Endgame* on any particular musical form or genre, Beckett explored the musicality of language and of patterns of movement and sound. Roger Blin notes that Beckett looked at *Fin de partie* 'as a kind of musical score'.[35] Music, or rather the absence of it, refers to his method of aspiring to music's non-referentiality as a source and a goal of aesthetic creation.

Similarly, Prospero's island is created aurally, through sounds, and also through silences when Prospero insists on the masque being silent: 'Such shapes, such gesture, and such sound, expressing –/Although they want the use of tongue – a kind/Of excellent dumb discourse' (*T* 3.3.37–9). In *The Tempest*, form and formlessness interact in onomatopoetic discourse and build a language out of pre-linguistic sounds and noises. Ariel's songs entice the mariners, and Alonso is taken aback by the sounds of the island that remind him of his usurpation: 'The winds did sing it to me, and the thunder,/That deep and dreadful organ-pipe, pronounced/The name of Prosper. It did bass my trespass' (*T* 3.3.97–9).

Beckett alludes to the songs in *The Tempest* when he takes the title of his short story 'Yellow' in *More Pricks Than Kicks* from Ariel's song 'Come unto these yellow sands', and 'Ding-Dong' in the same collection from the dirge: 'Full fathom five thy father lies, ... Sea-nymphs hourly ring his knell./Hark, now I hear them, ding dong bell' (*T* 1.2.396–403). In 'Ding-Dong', which – referring to *Antony and Cleopatra* – describes 'the old story of the salad days' (*MPTK*, 39), a Hamm-like character appears when the narrator observes a 'blind paralytic' in a wheelchair who is pushed by an assiduous chairman and the narrator remarks that 'this beggar was a power in the Coombe' (*MPTK*, 42). Read with *Endgame*, Ariel's songs create parallels to Hamm's father Nagg lying buried in his trashcan, evoke Clov ringing the alarm clock and accentuate the homophonic and semantic link between a 'knell' and the moribund 'Nell'.

Stephen Greenblatt has shown that accounts of the New World often attributed ancient forms of poetry to the language and songs of Indigenous people,[36] and as Julia Lupton has observed, it is through Caliban that *The Tempest* voices 'the re-creative resources of poetic language'.[37] Noises and natural fundamental sounds are part of the island's enchanting soundscape that Caliban describes:

> Be not afeared; the isle is full of noises,
> Sounds, and sweet airs, that give delight and hurt not.
> Sometimes a thousand twangling instruments
> Will hum about mine ears; and sometime voices,
> That if I then had waked after long sleep,
> Will make me sleep again; and then in dreaming,
> The clouds methought would open, and show riches
> Ready to drop upon me, that when I waked
> I cried to dream again (*T* 3.2.127–35).[38]

Caliban's benign version of the island coexists with the world under Prospero's rule and resembles an orchestral arrangement. The noises, sounds and 'sweet airs' that compose the music of the island enthral Caliban, who, as Simon Palfrey has argued, 'takes metaphors back to a manner of inaugurative or formative principle'.[39]

When Ferdinand asks 'Where should this music be? I'th'air, or th'earth?' (*T* 1.2.387), he refers to one of the play's compositional dichotomies, which is related to the elements of air and earth. Shakespeare condenses the macrocosm of the elements in Prospero's two servants Ariel and Caliban, who symbolize mind and body, air and earth, materiality and the immaterial. Prospero wonders that Ariel can feel human empathy with the shipwrecked party 'thou, which art but air' (*T* 5.1.21) and scolds Caliban: 'Thou earth, thou!' (*T* 1.2.315), perhaps inadvertently aligning his creaturely existence to Adam, the first human, created out of clay. Stephano and Trinculo find him in his muddy abode and view him as a subhuman monster, the epitome of primeval desire, neither flesh nor fish – and yet both.

Air and earth become material and immaterial principles of creation and destruction. To the melancholic Hamlet, who considers himself a 'fellow ... crawling between earth and heaven' (*Ham* 3.1.124–5), earth and sky have lost their lustre: 'this goodly frame, the earth, seems to me a sterile promontory; this most excellent canopy the air, look you, this brave o'erhanging firmament ... it appeareth no other thing to me but a foul and pestilent congregation of vapours' (*Ham* 2.2.282–6).[40] Beckett ironically alludes to this languor in *Watt*: 'If there were two things that Watt loathed,' we are told, 'one was the earth, and the other was the sky' (*Watt*, 28).

Mud and earth are a mythological as well as a natural habitat for many of Beckett's works. He subtitles his essay on *Proust* with Leopardi's line 'E fango è il mondo' from his poem 'A se stesso' (1833), expressing the vanity of earthly doings; Hamm repeatedly asks Clov to '[l]ook at the earth' (*CDW*, 127); and H. Porter Abbot claims that Beckett 'recycles both the mud out of which God made Adam and the Word by which God gave life to the mud'.[41] Early works such as 'Echo's Bones' begin 'in the muck' (3), with the protagonist 'flat on my face in the mud under the moon' (First Love). In *Waiting for Godot*, Estragon states 'All my lousy life I've crawled about in the mud! And you talk to me about scenery!' (*CDW*, 57). Mud is indeed the malleable metamorphic substance to which Beckett's works such as *How It Is*, his 'epic of mud', are continuously drawn.[42]

From his early poetry up to his late plays such as *Breath*, Beckett's works are preoccupied with air, with its immaterial materiality, its organic and artistic rhythms of repetition and pause that provide his plays with a kind of systolic and diastolic pulse. The narrator of *Texts for Nothing* wonders, 'Is this stuff air…',[43] and Hamm observes, 'we breathe, we change' (*CDW*, 97). To him, however, Clov is not the gentle spirit that Ariel is to Prospero; he accuses him, 'You pollute the air!' (*CDW*, 93). In Shakespeare's plays, as Werner Habicht has shown, 'air is a potential source of dramatic illusion'.[44] Air is essential for the imagination when Theseus in *A Midsummer Night's Dream* acknowledges that the poet's pen gives 'to airy nothing/a local habitation and a name' (*MND* 5.1.15–17). Air is integral to the medium of the theatre and to performance when the dissimulating Hamlet feeds on the 'chameleon's dish' (*Ham* 3.2.83) or when he advises the players not to 'saw the air too much' (*Ham* 3.2.3–4).[45]

In *The Tempest*, air, the very metaphor of the title, is the play's principle of creation. Air is both the substance of Ariel's songs that accompany Prospero, and it is the breath from which they are created. As the source of the tempest that sets off the play, air inspires the entire action. Prospero's tempest is both nature and art, both creative and destructive, both cause and effect of the play as a whole.

When Prospero ends the masque of Ceres, Juno and Iris that he had staged to distract the lovers, saying 'Our revels now are ended', he describes the airy effects of the theatre on the audience and illustrates the elusive imaginary quality of what they have seen:

> these our actors,/As I foretold you, were all spirits, and/Are melted into air, into thin air;/And like the baseless fabric of this vision, … the great globe itself,/Yea, all which it inherit, shall dissolve,/And like this insubstantial pageant faded/Leave not a rack behind. We are such stuff/As dreams are made on; and our little life/Is rounded with a sleep (*T* 4.1.148–59).

Prospero twice uses theatrical spectacle as punishment and retribution, both when he stages apparitions like the magic banquet that vanishes as soon as the Neapolitans try to reach it, with Ariel descending upon them in the shape of a Harpy, and when he confronts Caliban, Trinculo and Stephano with a vision of shining garments. The conspirators appear gullible and pompous when 'they smote the air/For breathing in their faces' (*T* 4.1.172–3). Air, thin or thick, is ambiguous in that it creates illusion and disenchantment at the same time.

Like things and material objects that in *Endgame* are present through their absence, *The Tempest* offers visions of something supremely beautiful and desirable only to withdraw them. The individual interlaced romance plots in *The Tempest* are guided by the search for an ideal, even utopian, goal that remains notoriously elusive and exceptionally difficult to reach. Utopian visions such as the masque that impresses Ferdinand as '[h]armonious charmingly' (*T* 4.1.119), do not go unchallenged in Shakespeare – not least because while the masque displays an ideal world, Caliban, Trinculo and Stephano plot to murder Prospero. In *Endgame*, Hamm similarly both invokes and deflates utopian notions of the masque's pastoral idyll: 'Hamm: That here we're down in a hole. [*Pause.*] But beyond the hills? Eh? Perhaps it's still green. Eh? [*Pause.*] Flora! Pomona! [*Ecstatically.*] Ceres! [*Pause.*] Perhaps you won't need to go very far. Clov: I can't go very far' (*CDW*, 111). Beckett's explicit reference to *The Tempest* underlines the insubstantial character of Prospero's spectacle as an ideal that cannot be reached, and reinforces the tragicomic situation in which Hamm and Clov find themselves. Hamm stylizes himself as Prospero: after Nagg has reminded him that he used to listen to Hamm when he was a little boy, he knocks on Nell's bin in vain and disappears back into his own: 'Hamm: Our revels now are ended!' (*CDW*, 120). Prospero's spirits perform the masque of the ancient goddesses that celebrates '[a] contract of true love' (*T* 4.1.84) and which promises Arcadian abundance, where 'Scarcity and want shall shun you' (*T* 4.1.116). In *Endgame*, this vision is contrasted by the dearth and the impossibility of love that Nagg and Nell's farcical play in the play represents.

Foul Play

One of the configurations in which the two plays blend into one another is when they converge on the game of chess. Whereas *Endgame* alludes to an endgame in chess and creates an analogy to chess as one of the play's principles of construction, in *The Tempest*, which, even though it is not Shakespeare's last play, has been interpreted by some scholars as his farewell to the stage, chess occurs in a brief scene between Ferdinand and Miranda. Prospero's famous and poignant equation of life and the theatre 'We are such stuff/As dreams are made on; and our little life/Is rounded with a sleep' (*T* 4.1.156–8) encapsulates the nexus between the finite materiality of the theatrical performance and the 'stuff of dreams'. Immaterial matter and potentially infinite creation find a metatheatrical parallel in the play's reference to chess as a particular kind of endgame. While Prospero is busy haunting the buffoons, confronting the Neapolitans and pondering whether he should resign his magic, Ferdinand and Miranda have retired to play a game of chess. Prospero, who intends to 'bring forth a wonder' (*T* 5.1.170) strives to stage-manage the reunion between Alonso and his lost son. Like all the other apparitions presented by Prospero, the chess game between Miranda and Ferdinand is interrupted and remains unfinished.

The brief scene in which Prospero discovers Ferdinand and Miranda playing chess is one of the few occasions on which Shakespeare refers to chess.[46] Prospero's discovering the lovers at play multiplies the experience of watching characters engage in a game that becomes a metaphor for the play itself. The scene functions as a *mise-en-abîme*, as a play-within-the-play. Chess traditionally presents a political and romantic world *en miniature*, in which opposition and union, war and peace are negotiated.[47] Ferdinand and Miranda's game casts their newly found love into this chivalrous and strategic frame, and also reflects back on the opposition between brothers, the initial 'foul play' of Antonio, and the strategies later employed by Prospero to manipulate others to his own ends:

> MIRANDA   What foul play had we, that we came from thence?
> (*T* 1.2.60)
> PROSPERO   By foul play, as thou say'st, were we heaved thence
> (*T* 1.2.62).

Loughrey and Taylor have argued that 'the game of chess contributes to the play's discussion of its own aesthetic nature',[48] and indeed, it is in the game of chess that the political, courtly and romantic spheres of the play intersect to comment on the fictional nature and principles of construction of *The Tempest*.

The courtly context of the game has been described by many critics, who refer to chess as an aristocratic pastime and a part of the education of the nobility.[49] In Act I, Prospero elaborates that he had educated Miranda in courtly fashion 'Have I, thy schoolmaster, made thee more profit/Than other princes can, that have more time' (*T* 1.2.172–3), and apparently her upbringing included training in how to play chess.

From its origins, chess was a game of strategy and a game of war. In Europe, from early dream allegories such as *Les eschez amoureux* (1370–80) to William Caxton's English translation of the French translations of Jacobus de Cessolis' Latin treatise on chess, *De Ludo Scaccorum* – which was the second book to be printed in English – *The Game and Playe of Chesse* (1474), chess was a central feature in Medieval literature. It was used as an allegory of the state and society and praised for its civilizing and educational function. Murray, in his *History of Chess*, lists numerous references to romances such as *Guy of Warwick*,[50] and contemporaries of Shakespeare such as Thomas Middleton in *A Game at Chesse* (1624) further expound the analogy between chess and politics.[51] In Chaucer's *The Book of the Duchess*, chess is played between Dame Fortune and 'the man in blak', who accuses fortune: 'For fals Fortune hath pleyd a game/ Atte ches with me, allaes the while! The trayteresse fals and ful of gyle' (618–20).[52] In the brief episode in *The Tempest*, Miranda likewise accuses Ferdinand of cheating:

> MIRANDA   Sweet lord, you play me false.
> FERDINAND No, my dearest love, I would not for the world.
> MIRANDA   Yes, for a score of kingdoms you should wrangle,
>   And I would call it fair play (*T* 5.1.172–5)

The Tempest draws on the tradition of medieval romance, in which the orderly world of the chessboard becomes a matrix in which love and betrayal are encoded and negotiated. In Thomas Malory's *Le Morte D'Arthur*, the story of Tristan and Isolde contains many references to chess, and prominently in Gottfried's von Straßburg *Tristan und Isolde* (written around 1210), Tristan steals away from his sleeping companion Marjodo and makes for Isolde's chamber. To protect the lovers, Brangaene, Isolde's maid, places a chessboard in front of the chamber, to keep the light out, but she leaves the door open and goes to bed herself: 'nu er in die kemenâten kam,/Brangæne ein schâhzabel nam:/vür daz lieht leinde s'daz./nune weiz ich, wie si des vergaz,/daz si die tür offen lie/und si wider slâfen gie' (20, 29–36).[53] Marjodo awakes and, as is his habit, wishes to tell Tristan about his dream but finds him gone. He follows his traces in the snow and looks for him, until he approaches Isolde's chamber, finds the door open with the chessboard leaning against it, and he stealthily enters the room where, much to his chagrin, he sees the two lovers. The chessboard at the door occupies an ambivalent space in that it both conceals and reveals the lovers' union that in itself is tinged with love and betrayal. It becomes an emblem of a multiplicity that is spatially confined and a synecdoche representing the creative and destructive forces in the relationship of the lovers and society at large.

The chess scene in *The Tempest* condenses many elements of romance, and it connects Ferdinand and Miranda to Tristan and Isolde. Structurally, the scene is an instance of revelation and reunion between two brothers, between fathers and children and between past and future. Gina Bloom describes the recursive temporality of *The Tempest*:

> The chess scene invites theatregoers to approach history as they would a game of chess, wherein players and spectators inhabit multiple temporal frames simultaneously during a game, their perspective on the present informed by their recollections of prior moments of play and anticipation of possible outcomes.[54]

The chess game also reflects on Prospero's masterly arrangement of the plot in which he has anticipated the many moves of the play, the Neapolitan ship nearing his shores, the union between Miranda and Ferdinand and the conspiracy against him. He has laid out a game in which all those who try to play against him will inevitably lose. Yet the theme of falsehood and deceit also takes Prospero back to his own past and his defeat by Antonio, who was master of the game in Milan.

The allusion to chess in medieval allegory and romance in *The Tempest* not only casts the play itself within the mode of romance but also functions as a two-way mirror that confronts Prospero and Antonio with their past actions and at the same time is a projection into the future of the next generation. Ferdinand and Miranda will be the new rulers, and this future of the play is envisaged in terms of Arthurian romance – a romance, however, that, like that of Tristan and Isolde, is not free from destructive forces inside and out. Miranda accusing Ferdinand of playing false and her willingness to cover it up can be read as an anticipation of potential betrayal, taking some of the shine off the formerly pure romance of their love.

As a social allegory, a symbol of power relations, strategy and stratagems that prominently include an erotic dimension, chess is never unambiguous. In *The Tempest*, chess refers to the power relations within the play. It is a metonymical recapitulation of Prospero's artistry and his strategy to marry his daughter to Alonso's son instead of killing the usurper, but chess also functions as a self-reflexive comment on the art of the playwright.

Beckett explicitly associated his play with an endgame in chess. Jeevan Kumar reads chess as a central organizing element of *Endgame*: 'the chess metaphor in *Endgame* functions as a unifying element, linking the other symbols with it and integrating movements and decor in the play'.[55] Ruby

Cohn has argued that *Endgame* is Shakespearean in referring to the death of kings, where 'Hamm and Clov derive from tragedy as king and fool, king and rebel, king and retainer.'[56] Hugh Kenner regards Hamm as an endangered King, Nagg and Nell as pawns and Clov 'with his arbitrarily restricted movements . . . and his equestrian background . . . resembles the Knight'.[57] Beckett had learned how to play chess from his brother and his uncle Howard, 'who once defeated the world chess champion from 1921 to 1927'.[58] He took part in chess matches at Trinity College, and in the summer of 1940, he played with Marcel Duchamp and others, who took refuge in Arcachon during the German occupation of many parts of France. He also owned Alexander Alekhine's *My Best Games of Chess 1924–1937*.[59]

References to chess appear in many of Beckett's works. In *Dream of Fair to Middling Women*, Belacqua's lover the Smeraldina-Rima is accosted by a chess champion (*Dream*, 89). A passing reference to chess is given in *Rough for Theatre II* where an 'unfinished game of chess with a correspondent in Tasmania' (*CDW*, 242) is mentioned. Chess becomes the endgame of Murphy since visiting the self-contained Mr. Endon in his cell at the MMM to play chess is one of the last things he does. The novel meticulously records the chess moves of both players and describes the regal attire of Mr. Endon, who resembles both a magician and a chess figure: 'Mr. Endon, an impeccable and brilliant figurine in his scarlet gown' (*Murphy*, 241). Whereas chess with Mr. Endon grants Murphy peace and the freedom of nothingness, this fascination is not reciprocated: 'the sad truth was, that while Mr. Endon for Murphy was no less than bliss, Murphy for Mr. Endon was no more than chess' (*Murphy*, 242).

Chess presents a matrix of multiplicity that remains tied to form. What is intriguing about chess as a paradigm for Beckett's and Shakespeare's theatre, is, as Derek Alsop has observed for Beckett, that it presents a 'closed, perfect, abstract system that is theoretically finite but practically inexhaustible. . . . chess offers both the temptation of something exhaustible (Murphy's biscuits on a cosmic scale) and the opportunity of practically infinite continuation.'[60] Endings in chess, as well as in *Endgame*, where Hamm hesitates to end, can be delayed and protracted for a long time. To pass the time rather than end straightaway, Hamm and Clov engage in language games and theatrical roleplay, and Prospero charms his opponents or executes retribution to ward off an early ending. Like a game of chess, both plays play with an end that is to be kept at bay.

Endgames in chess provide room for variation, for new moves and new beginnings, and Beckett's *Endgame* plays on these variations in its repeated scenes and in the conflation of its beginning and end. *The Tempest*, apart from the small scene between Ferdinand and Miranda, also introduces a prolonged temporality that is both a backward- and a forward-looking experiment, where reminiscences about the end are paralleled by a thrust towards the future: 'to perform an act/Whereof what's past is prologue; what to come/In yours and my discharge' (*T* 2.1.248–50).[61] The possibility that past events, including the play itself, are only a prologue to another play to come, counters the received notion of *The Tempest* as Shakespeare's farewell to the stage, and Prospero's Epilogue as Shakespeare's final gesture of aesthetic relinquishment, retirement and abdication of his theatrical magic.

Beginning to End

Beckett's narrative 'The Lost Ones'[62] is set in an 'abode' where lost bodies search for other lost ones not unlike the shipwrecked in *The Tempest*. The piece, in which two storms appear, is structured by repetition: 'The more so as the two storms have this in common that when one is cut off as though by magic then in the same breath the other also as though again the two were connected somewhere to a single commutator' (*CSP*, 216). *The Tempest* follows a similarly reflexive structure in which two tempests mark decisive points of the action, where the second storm answers the first, and where history seemingly repeats itself after the twelve years that Prospero has spent on the island. As Marjorie Garber observes: 'Once again a cycle seems about to repeat itself – a second storm, and a second usurpation. Shakespeare's craftsmanship in this play is superbly evocative and economical, so that such doublings and repetitions become an intrinsic, almost uncanny, part of the structure and effect of the play.'[63]

Like *Endgame*, which from the beginning ends in different ways and postpones finality, 'Finished, it's finished, nearly finished, it must be nearly finished' (*CDW*, 93), *The Tempest* delays finality and introduces a number of different endings. Prospero's 'Our revels now are ended' (*T* 4.1.148) interrupts and ends the masque that he and Ariel have staged and he sets out to thwart Caliban's plot to kill him.[64] A further sense of an ending occurs when he, prompted by Ariel, renounces his revenge and resorts to his 'nobler reason' (*T* 5.1.26) to offer mercy to his opponents, and when, finally, in his epilogue, Prospero directly addresses the audience, and, like Ariel, asks for freedom from bondage and confinement, acknowledges his guilt, and demands some poetic justice: 'let me not,/Since I have my dukedom got/And pardoned the deceiver, dwell/In this bare island, by

Beginning to End 175

your spell' (*T* Epilogue. 5–8). Having renounced his magic, he finds himself under the spell of the audience instead, and virtually puts himself in their hands: 'I must be here confined by you, ... But release me from my bands/With the help of your good hands' (*T* Epilogue 4; 9–10).

In both plays, this dynamic of confinement and release is not merely a motif that occurs on various levels of the plays; it also transcends the inner world of the play when both Prospero and Hamm seek final release from their audience. Searching for comfort, Hamm similarly beseeches a defiant Clov: 'Give me your hand at least. [*Pause.*] Will you not give me your hand?' (*CDW*, 125). When Prospero forgives Alonso and the others, 'I do forgive thee,/Unnatural though thou art' (*T* 5.1.78–79), his words are directed at the audience while the characters whom they concern remain charmed and cannot hear him.[65] Clov, by contrast, hears Hamm's repeated plea for forgiveness, but remains nonplussed:

HAMM Forgive me. [*Pause. Louder.*] I said, Forgive me.
CLOV I heard you. (*CDW*, 95; 98)

Like Prospero, Hamm divests himself of some of the paraphernalia that define his role, such as his gaff, and at the end, he also plans to leave their confinement and thinks about embarking on a sea voyage: 'Let's go from here, the two of us! South! You can make a raft and the currents will carry us away, far away, to other ... mammals!' (*CDW*, 109).

Freedom or redemption are not offered by the plays themselves, but ultimately lie in the hands of the audience. For the audience, the applause by their 'gentle hands' is the only means to release themselves from the endless endings of Shakespeare's and Beckett's unredeemed worlds, yet this is a response that is already anticipated by Prospero's metatheatrical reference to a new journey and possibly a new performance. The ending that Prospero desires when he asks for the '[g]entle breath' (*T* Epilogue 11) of the audience 'to fill his sails or else his project fails' appeals to breath as an immaterial force outside the play that can potentially repeat the tempest with which the play began and thus return to the beginning.

It is part of the nature of a game that it supersedes what it has previously established. The audience is always already included, their breath is needed for Prospero and Hamm to set sail again, to embark on a new journey, a new performance, a new beginning. It is also in this way that both *Endgame* and *The Tempest* are about the impossibility of ending. In referring back to the impossible, Beckett's theatre in engaging with Shakespeare creates an ontology of the possible in which meaning is both erased and maintained in multiple combinations. Jean-Michel Rabaté remarks about Beckett: 'His sense of the *impossible*, ... , made him an exception that turned into the norm.'[66] The narrator in *The Unnamable* seems to corroborate this when he confidently asserts 'That the impossible should be asked of me, good, what else could be asked of me' (*The Unnamable*, 70).[67] And also Antonio in *The Tempest* wonders at Gonzalo: 'What impossible matter will he make easy next?' (*T* 2.1.84), a notion that also applies to the playwright who is able to create a utopian world in the finitude of the theatre.

Tom Stoppard, whose plays reconfigure many elements of both Beckett and Shakespeare, continues this inquiry into the endlessness of ending when Rosencrantz in *Rosencrantz and Guildenstern Are Dead* ventures to ask 'Eternity is a terrible thought. I mean, where's it going to end?'[68]

Notes

1 Catherine Wilson, *The Invisible World: Early Modern Philosophy and the Invention of the Microscope* (Princeton University Press, 1995), 12.
2 Andrew Marvell, 'On a Drop of Dew' in Nigel Smith (ed.), *The Poems of Andrew Marvell* (London: Longman, 2003), 39–42, 41.
3 S.E. Gontarski, 'A Sense of Unending: Samuel Beckett's Eschatological Turn', *Samuel Beckett Today/Aujourd'hui*, 21 (2009), 135–49, 138.
4 Frank Kermode, *The Sense of an Ending: Studies in the Theory of Fiction with a New Epilogue* (Oxford University Press, 2000), 5.
5 Ruby Cohn, *Modern Shakespeare Offshoots* (Princeton University Press, 1976), 378.
6 Theodor W. Adorno, 'Versuch, das Endspiel zu verstehen' in Theodor Adorno, *Versuch, das Endspiel zu verstehen. Aufsätze zur Literatur des 20. Jahrhunderts* (Frankfurt a.M.: Suhrkamp, 1973), 167–214; cf. also Dirk van Hulle, 'Adorno's Notes on Endgame', *Journal of Beckett Studies*, 19.2 (2010), 196–217, 204: 'Adorno's reference to Hamlet could all too easily be interpreted as an invitation to reduce *Endgame* to the line "to be or not to be".'
7 Theodor W. Adorno, 'Versuch, das Endspiel zu verstehen', 174.
8 Ruby Cohn, '*The Tempest* of an Endgame', *Symposion*, XIX 4 (Winter 1965), 328–34.
9 Paul Stewart, 'But Why Shakespeare? Dickens in *Endgame*' in Mark S. Byron (ed.), *Samuel Beckett's Endgame* (Amsterdam: Rodopi, 2007), 220–1.
10 Howard Felperin, *Shakespearean Romance* (Princeton University Press, 1972), 247.
11 Gabriele Schwab, 'On the Dialectic of Closing and Opening in *Endgame*' in Steven Connor (ed.), *New Casebooks:* Waiting for Godot *and* Endgame (Houndmills: Macmillan, 1996), 88.

12 Jonathan Bate, 'Shakespeare's Islands' in Tom Clayton, Susan Brock and Vicente Forés (eds.), *Shakespeare and the Mediterranean* (Newark: University of Delaware Press, 2004), 289–308, 301.
13 Christopher Pye, *Storm at Sea: Political Aesthetics in the Time of Shakespeare* (New York: Fordham University Press, 2015), 147.
14 Hugh Kenner, '"Life in the Box", Twentieth-Century Interpretations of *Endgame*' in Bell Gale Chevigny (ed. and introd.), *A Collection of Critical Essays* (Englewood Cliffs: Prentice Hall, 1969), 53–60, 53.
15 Ruby Cohn, 'Beckett and Shakespeare', *Modern Drama* 15 (1972), 223–30, 225.
16 In a letter to Alan Schneider, Beckett writes: 'One purpose of the image throughout the play is to suggest the impossibility logically, i.e. eristically, of the "thing" ever coming to an end. "The end is in the beginning and yet we go on." In other words, the impossibility of catastrophe. Ended at its inception, and at every subsequent instant, it continues, ergo can never end. Don't mention any of this to your actors!,' *Letters*, III, 73. Beckett here alludes to the beginning of T.S. Eliot's 'East Coker' from *Four Quartets*.
17 Stewart, 'But Why Shakespeare?', 212.
18 *Holy Bible. The Comprehensive Teacher's Bible* (London: Bagster and Sons, n.d.), *Samuel Beckett Digital Manuscript Project*.
19 Yves Bonnefoy, 'A Seascape, a Landscape', *New England Review*, 31.1 (2010), 99–102, 100.
20 HAMM: Look at the sea.
   CLOV: It's the same.
   HAMM: Look at the ocean! (*CDW*, 106)
21 *The Tempest*'s projection of its insular setting is informed by classical epics of expansion and colonization such as the *Aeneid*, and also more contemporary travel narratives like William Strachey's *A True Reportory of the Wreck and Redemption of Sir Thomas Gates, Knight* (1610), Silvester Jourdain's *A Discovery of the Barmudas, otherwise Called the Isle of Divels* (1610), or Montaigne's essays such as 'Des Cannibales'.
22 For interpretations of *The Tempest* in the context of postcolonial theory see Stephen J. Greenblatt, 'Learning to Curse: Aspects of Linguistic Colonisation in the Sixteenth Century' in Fredi Chiappelli (ed.), *First Images of America: The Impact of the New World on the Old* (Berkeley: University of California Press, 1976), 561–80; Paul Brown, '"This thing of darkness I acknowledge mine": *The Tempest* and the Discourse of Colonialism' in Jonathan Dollimore and Alan Sinfield (eds.), *Political Shakespeare: New Essays in Cultural Materialism* (Manchester University Press, 1994), 48–71; Tobias Döring and Virginia Mason Vaughan (eds.), *Critical and Cultural Transformations: Shakespeare's* The Tempest *– 1611 to the Present* (Tübingen: Narr, 2013); Ania Loomba, 'Shakespeare and Cultural Difference' in Terence Hawkes (ed.), *Alternative Shakespeares*, vol. 2 (London: Routledge, 1996), 164–91.
23 Marjorie Garber, *Shakespeare After All* (New York: Anchor, 2004), 856: 'Prospero's enchanted island, while drawn from real explorations and published accounts, is ultimately a country of the mind.'

24 Cf. Pye, *Storm at Sea*, 142.
25 Bate, 'Shakespeare's Islands', 304.
26 Wolfgang Iser, 'The Pattern of Negativity in Beckett's Prose' in Harold Bloom (ed.), *Samuel Beckett. Modern Critical Views* (Philadelphia: Chelsea House Publishers, 1985), 140–51, 127.
27 Murphy describes the ward at the MMM in terms of church architecture: 'in the south transept, off which opened the padded cells, known to the wittier as the "quiet rooms", "rubber rooms" or, in a notable clip, "pads"' (*Murphy*, 167).
28 Cohn, *Modern Shakespeare Offshoots*, 382.
29 Stephen J. Greenblatt discusses the views of European colonists regarding American Indians in similar terms. Stephen Greenblatt, *Learning to Curse: Essays in Early Modern Culture* (London: Routledge, 2006), 24.
30 On linguistic colonialism in the sixteenth century cf. Greenblatt, *Learning to Curse*, 23f. As Simon Palfrey has argued, language becomes a powerful tool of colonisation: 'the processes through which structures of dominance and subservience become canonized and naturalized in language'. Simon Palfrey, *Late Shakespeare: A New World of Words* (Oxford: Clarendon, 2000 [1997]), 151.
31 Jean-Michel Rabaté, *Think, Pig! Beckett at the Limit of the Human* (New York: Fordham University Press, 2016), 12.
32 In the story 'Yellow', which can be seen as Belacqua's endgame, before he is resurrected in 'Echo's Bones', he is awaiting an operation and comments on the numerous women in the hospital who look after the patients. A woman Belacqua calls Aschenputtel sees to the fire, and Miranda becomes part of the fairy-tale world he imagines himself to be in when he is prepared for his operation by a nurse of the same name. Before Belacqua is taken into the operating theatre, he calls her 'The divine creature! He would assault her in another minute!' (*MPTK*, 186), echoing both Ferdinand and Caliban. Cf. also *Dream of Fair to Middling Women*: 'Miranda had not been in his class at all' (*Dream*, 11).
33 Stanley Cavell, *Must We Mean What We Say?* (Cambridge University Press, 2002), 117.
34 Samuel Beckett, *Disjecta: Miscellaneous Writings and a Dramatic Fragment by Samuel Beckett*, ed. with a foreword by Ruby Cohn (London: Calder, 1983), 108.
35 Tom Bishop, 'Blin on Beckett: Interviewed by Tom Bishop' in S.E. Gontarski (ed. and introd.), *On Beckett: Essays and Criticism* (New York: Grove, 1986), 226–35, 223.
36 Stephen Greenblatt, *Learning to Curse*, 28–9.
37 Julia Lupton, 'Creature Caliban', *Shakespeare Quarterly*, 51 (2000), 1–23, 13.
38 In 'Yellow', Belacqua imagines a nurse trying to sleep: 'The place was too full of noise' (*MPTK*, 177); and Vladimir in *Waiting for Godot* reminisces: 'The air is full of our cries' (*CDW*, 84).
39 Like Beckett's theatre, 'Caliban takes metaphors back to a manner of inaugurative or formative principle. They become inherently reflexive, reliving the processes or relationships which make language, and the social priorities they

Beginning to End 179

frame and then control, simultaneously so unstable and once learned, so easily assumed.' Palfrey, *Late Shakespeare*, 163.
40 In Renaissance philosophy and physiology, air has both physical and figurative meanings. The chapter 'Digression of Air' of Robert Burton's *The Anatomy of Melancholy* distinguishes between fair and foul air and discusses the salutary effects of a change of air and of music as a remedy for melancholy. Robert Burton, *The Anatomy of Melancholy*, ed. by Floyd Dell and Paul Jordan-Smith (New York: Tudor, 1931), 412–13.
41 H. Porter Abbott, 'Beginning Again: The Post-Narrative Art of *Texts for Nothing* and *How It Is*' in John Pilling (ed.), *The Cambridge Companion to Beckett* (Cambridge University Press, 1994), 106–23, 116.
42 Leland de la Durantaye, *Beckett's Art of Mismaking* (Cambridge, London: Harvard University Press, 2016), 93.
Cf. Ackerley and Gontarski: 'Sometimes a shelter is just a shelter, a road a road, and mud mud', Ackerley and Gontarski (eds.), *The Grove Companion to Samuel Beckett* (New York: Grove, 2004), 207.
43 *Texts for Nothing* 2: 'Is this stuff air that permits you to suffocate still, almost audibly at times, it's possible, a kind of air' (*CSP*, 107).
44 Werner Habicht, '"And Mock Our Eyes With Air": Air and Stage Illusion in Shakespearean Drama' in Frederick Burwick and Walter Pape (eds.), *Aesthetic Illusion: Theoretical and Historical Approaches* (Berlin: de Gruyter, 1990), 301–12, 304.
45 Carla Mazzio, 'The History of Air: *Hamlet* and the Trouble with Instruments', *South Central Review*, 26.1–2 (2009), 153–96, 157–8.
46 Bryan Loughrey and Neil Taylor, 'Ferdinand and Miranda at Chess', *Shakespeare Survey*, 35 (1982), 113–18.
47 From its origins, chess and the skills of playing it were expressive of social rank: 'Chess was after all the royal game.' 'SchaTrandJ' C.E. Bosworth, E. van Donzel, W.P. Heinrichs (eds.), *Encyclopedia of Islam*, Vol. IX (Leiden: Brill, 1997), 367.
48 Loughrey and Taylor, 'Ferdinand and Miranda at Chess', 117.
49 Loughrey and Taylor, 'Ferdinand and Miranda at Chess', 114; William Poole, 'False Play: Shakespeare and Chess', *Shakespeare Quarterly*, 55 (2004), 50–70, 50.
50 H.J.R. Murray, *A History of Chess* (Oxford: Clarendon Press, 1962 [1913]), 434–7.
51 For the use of subterfuge and fraud in the chess scene in Middleton's *Women Beware Women* (1654), cf. Neil Taylor and Bryan Loughrey, 'Middleton's Chess Strategies in *Women Beware Women*', *SEL*, 24. 2 (1984), 341–54.
52 Geoffrey Chaucer, 'The Book of the Duchess', Larry D. Benson (ed.), *The Riverside Chaucer* (Boston: Houghton Mifflin, 1987), 329–46, 618–20.
53 Gottfried von Straßburg, *Gottfried's von Strassburg Tristan*, ed. by Reinhold Bechstein (Leipzig: F.A. Brockhaus, 1873).
54 Gina Bloom, 'Time to Cheat. Chess and *The Tempest*'s Performative History of Dynastic Marriage' in Valerie Traub (ed.), *The Oxford Handbook of*

Shakespeare and Embodiment: Gender, Sexuality, and Race (Oxford University Press, 2016), 419–34, 420.
55 Jeevan K. Kumar, 'The Chess Metaphor in Samuel Beckett's *Endgame*', *Modern Drama*, 40.4 (1997), 540–52, 540.
56 Cohn, *Modern Shakespeare Offshoots*, 379–80.
57 Hugh Kenner, *Samuel Beckett. A Critical Study* (London: Calder, 1962), 156.
58 Harry Vandervlist, 'Beckett, Duchamp and Chess: A Crossroads at Arcachon in the Summer of 1940', *Caliban* 33 (2013), 173–82, 180.
59 Alexander Alekhine, *My Best Games of Chess 1924–1937* (London: G. Bell and Sons, 1949 [1939]).
60 Derek Aslop, 'Playing On: Chess and its Metaphors in the Life and Work of Samuel Beckett', *Critical Quarterly* 54 (2012), 26–40, 37–8.
61 Simon Palfrey, *Late Shakespeare*, 142: 'past events share their teleology with a prologue to a play'.
62 'The Lost Ones': 'Abode Where Lost bodies roam each searching for its lost one' (*CSP*, 202); 'The more so as the two storms have this in common that when one is cut off as though by magic then in the same breath the other also as though again the two were connected somewhere to a single commutator' (*CSP*, 216).
63 Garber, *Shakespeare After All*, 865.
64 'Our revels now are ended ... The solemn temples, the great globe itself,/Yea, all which it inherit, shall dissolve,/And like this insubstantial pageant faded/Leave not a rack behind. We are such stuff/As dreams are made on; and our little life/Is rounded with a sleep' (*T* 4.1.148–58).
65 Pye, *Storm at Sea*, 152.
66 Rabaté, *Think, Pig! Beckett at the Limit of the Human*, 2.
67 Cf. Gilles Deleuze, *Essays Clinical and Critical*, 'The Exhausted', 152; 'That the impossible should be asked of me, good, what else could be asked of me' (*The Unnamable*, 70). 'There is no longer any possible: a relentless Spinozism. Does he exhaust the possible because he is himself exhausted, or is he exhausted because he has exhausted the possible? He exhausts himself in exhausting the possible, and vice-versa. He exhausts that, which, in the possible, is not realized. He has had done with the possible, beyond all tiredness, "For to end yet again".' (*CSP*, 179–81)
68 Tom Stoppard, *Rosencrantz and Guildenstern Are Dead* (London: Faber & Faber, 2000), 51.

CHAPTER 7

Theatres of Sleep

Prospero's poignant comparison between the short span of the actor's 'little life' on stage and human life at large draws on the ancient analogy between sleep and death: 'We are such stuff/As dreams are made on; and our little life/Is rounded with a sleep' (*T* 4.1.156–8). Sleep not only surrounds the time of waking and the action of a play, it becomes an intrinsic part of Shakespeare's and Beckett's plays, where the performance of sleep also reflects on the theatrical medium, on the presence of the actor's body and on the experience of watching a play. Scarcely any state of being could be less dramatic than sleep. A sleeping protagonist seems oddly out of place in the theatre, which from its origins has been mainly defined by action, plot and development. The 'involuntary form of "in-action"' that sleep presents[1] hence seems rather remote from drama as such: 'Sleep may strike us as the action farthest removed from thinking, speaking, writing or indeed acting – as such, perhaps the most unpromising state of all dramatic representation,' notes William Sherman.[2]

Inertia, motionlessness and half-waking, half-sleeping states of consciousness seem to be the default position of many of Beckett's characters, and Shakespeare's œuvre stages sleep in such a number of ways that this at seemingly passive state merits particular attention. Whether it is the beast-like sleep of Falstaff, the potion-induced sleep of Juliet or Imogen,[3] the fatal sleep of sovereigns like old King Hamlet and King Duncan in *Macbeth*,[4] the sleep of Hermione that gives way to a theatrical form of awakening and resurrection or the deathlike yet restorative sleep of King Lear (*KL* 4.6.38), Shakespeare's concern with this seemingly inconspicuous constant of human life threads its way through his entire work: 'No dramatist represents the act of sleep more frequently or graphically than he does,'[5] confirms David Roberts, and Sherman also observes, 'Shakespeare's entire corpus testifies to a deep and enduring preoccupation with sleep.'[6] This preoccupation often manifests itself in the interplay between allusions to sleep and its performance on stage.

Shakespeare's and Beckett's plays approach sleep as a liminal bodily state that blurs the distinctions between presence and absence, familiarity and the unfamiliar, appearance and essence. Sleep, moreover, becomes a productive meta-dramatic state, in which the theatre foregrounds its own mode of being. Staged sleep both creates and dissolves the illusion of an action unfolding as if unseen by and independent from the audience that is watching it. Dramatic distance is at the same time reduced by watching the seemingly familiar experience of sleep as well as established because the sleep the spectators observe is part of the play they see.

Placing sleeping characters on stage multiplies the experience of watching and observing, particularly at those moments in which characters deem themselves unobserved. It introduces a further level to the theatrical experience of seeing and being seen, of active and passive characters. Jennifer Lewin notes: 'When sleep overtakes a character onstage, it turns waking characters into an audience of sorts and can arouse strange, and even menacing, emotions or temptations in them.'[7] The audience is watching characters watching other characters sleep, and the passivity of the audience hence becomes part of the theatrical experience to the degree in which passivity on stage dominates.

Beckett's familiarity with contemporary psychoanalytical research on sleep and the unconscious is widely discussed,[8] and also Shakespeare's interest in sleep is not singular in the Renaissance. In recent years, a number of important works on sleep in Shakespeare have appeared, along with many cultural, historical and sociological studies on sleep in early modern discourse that describe sleep as 'one of the great unattended driving forces in the mapping of early modern culture'.[9] As Maria Ruvoldt has shown, in the Renaissance, drawing on classical sources, sleep and dreams were valued for providing access to divination and knowledge that is not linked to corporeal and empirical experience, and yet dreams were also considered as mere meaningless trifles.[10] Renaissance culture, however, also knew the other side of sleep, the debilitating effects of insomnia and the sinister uses of enforced sleep deprivation. Plays such as *The Taming of the Shrew*, *Macbeth* and *Othello*[11] poignantly show how sleeplessness affects the characters' psychosomatic states.

In the sixteenth century, sleep was widely discussed as a foundation for bodily and spiritual health. It featured in many popular medical treatises such as Thomas Elyot's *The Castell of Health* (1536), Andrew Boorde's *A Compendious Regiment, or Dyetary of the Regyment of Health* (1547), William Bullein's *The Government of Health* (1558) or Thomas Cogan's *The Haven of Health* (1584). Cogan's chapter 'Of sleepe' engages with

Aristotle, St Paul, Ovid and Seneca, lists the salutary effects of rest and provides detailed guidance as to the duration of sleep, the sleeper's position and types of bedding. Cogan also recommends sleep in moderation, warning against an excess of sleep that may lead to sloth and lethargy: 'And as moderate sleepe doth help digestion and confirme the body, and comfort the minde: So contrariwise, immoderate sleepe maketh the body slow, and unapt to honest exercises, and subject to many diseases, and the wit dull and unable either to conceive or to retaine.'[12] Works such as Cogan's mainly relied on Aristotle's investigation into sleep in *De somno et vigilia* and the development of Aristotelian thought by Hippocrates' *Prognostic* and Avicenna's *Canon of Medicine*.[13]

As Sasha Handley has demonstrated: 'Sleep was understood as a state of transition between day and night, between degrees of consciousness, between the earthly and spiritual realms, and between life and death.'[14] Not only were sleep and death considered siblings, but night was held to be a period of peaceful repose subject to danger and evil. Thomas Nashe's *Terrors of the Night. Or, a Discourse of Apparitions* (1594) studies unsettling nocturnal encounters with a demonic realm and the ensuing despair and desolation that afflict a conscience troubled by introspection. The spiritually vulnerable state of the sleeper is extensively treated by James I in the *Daemonologie*, in which the King cautions his readers against shape-changing devils that may enter their dreams to deceive them:

> For hee [the devil] being a spirite, may hee not so rauish their thoughts, and dull their sences, that their bodie lying as dead, hee may obiect to their spirites, as it were in a dreame, and (as the Poets write of *Morpheus*) represent such formes of persons, of places, and other circumstances, as hee pleases to illude them with.[15]

To avert spiritual and bodily harm, the 'Collect for aid against Perils' held a firm place in the 'Order For Evening Prayer' which was also part of *The Book of Common Prayer*: 'Lighten our darkness, we beseech thee, O Lord, and by thy great mercy defend us from all perils and dangers of this night, for the love of thy only Son, our Saviour Jesus Christ. *Amen*.'[16] Imogen in *Cymbeline* loosely quotes from this passage before she falls asleep: 'To your protection I commend me, gods./From fairies and the tempters of the night/Guard me, beseech ye' (*Cym* 2.2.8–10).

From classical antiquity onwards, texts such as Plato's *Timaios* explore states of consciousness during sleep, in which physical inactivity gives way to inspiration and generates pre-rational, subconscious forms of knowledge.[17] Sigmund Freud repeatedly discusses symbolic interpretations of 'artificial' dreams in poetry and literature and their prophetic functions.[18] Biblical sources such as Jacob's dream of the gate of heaven (Genesis 28), the dream of the Pharaoh of Egypt (Genesis 41) or the apocryphal dream of Pilate's wife acknowledge the prophetic power of dreams as a means of communicating with the divine. Macrobius' important treatise on the *Dream of Scipio* in the fifth century links dreaming to poetic invention, configuring the text as a dream. Medieval dream visions such as the prologue to Geoffrey Chaucer's *Legend of Good Women* (around 1386) from which Beckett draws in *Dream of Fair to Middling Women*,[19] the fourteenth-century alliterative poem *Pearl* (around 1392) and William Langland's dream vision *Piers Plowman* (c.1360–99) explore the narrative functions of sleep and dreams as ways of entering into the fictional world of a text.

In Shakespeare's plays, sleep is not merely a recurrent literary motif; rather, the dramatization of sleep grants insights into their poetic structure and generates moments of reflection in which the theatre refers to its own condition as theatre. Sleep in the theatre offers a double vision of presence and absence, of actors and spectators and of states of being that take place within linear time and yet are exempt from it. Sleep, and the fragile ontology it presents, becomes a metaphor for watching a play and partaking in the theatrical experience. According to David Bevington, Shakespeare's sleepers are different from those 'canonic' sleepers on the medieval stage of the mystery and morality plays because they are more complex and less univocally encoded. Sleep on Shakespeare's stage is, as Bevington notes, 'an ambiguous state uncertain in its meaning'.[20] Sleep is a fragile and ambivalent condition in that it refers to more than merely bodily rest and indeed highlights the inscrutable activity of the mind. The bodily presence of the sleeper hence simultaneously conveys a mental distance. Sleeping characters are withdrawn from the world around them, and their motionless bodies become opaque material signifiers that undermine notions of presence by performing a presence that is at the same time an absence. To the audience, the sleepers on stage are there and yet not fully there.

Sleep on stage introduces a presence that is suspended. Part of the action and yet remote from it, sleeping characters retreat into the safety of a space in which they believe they are alone. Yet sleep renders them all the more exposed and vulnerable. Shakespeare reveals this vulnerability when he introduces sleeping rulers and monarchs in *Hamlet*, *Macbeth* and *The Tempest*. In *Hamlet*, King Hamlet's habit of seeking a moment's private repose remote from his public kingly duties – 'Sleeping within my orchard,/My custom always of the afternoon,/Upon my secure hour' (*Ham* 1.5.59–61) – proves a fatal mistake as his assassin breaches the sanctity of the king's sheltered space and time. In *The Tempest*, Caliban and co. likewise plan to murder Prospero during his afternoon sleep: "'tis, a custom with him/I'th'afternoon to sleep. There thou mayst brain him' (*T* 3.2.79–80). Furthermore, the regicide committed by Macbeth is not only a sacrilege and a breach of the right of hospitality but the deed is also all the more heinous and shameful because King Duncan is killed while he is defenceless in his sleep. Sleep and awakening are not only a theme of many of Shakespeare's plays but they also frame the action and create a tension that Hamlet investigates in 'The Mousetrap': 'For some must watch while some must sleep,/Thus runs the world away' (*Ham* 3.2.248–9). The use of sleep and dream in the theatre explores the creation of theatrical presence, a process that foregrounds, draws and suspends the fine line between reality and illusion. Sleeping characters create liminal states in which sleep and waking become indistinguishable.

Sleeping Presences in *The Tempest*

The 'little life' of the stage on which Prospero comments also refers to the structure of *The Tempest*, where sleep forms a parenthesis for the entire play, which itself becomes 'such stuff', technically 'rounded with a sleep'. After the spectacularly theatrical beginning of *The Tempest*, miraculously, no one is harmed during the storm. Prospero wreaks shipwreck but eventually saves everyone on board. After the tempest, Ariel puts those mariners who are not dispersed around the island into a sleep that is going to last until Act V of the play: 'The mariners all under hatches stowed,/Who, with a charm joined to their suffered labour, I've left asleep' (*T* 1.2.230–2). The sleeping sailors frame the entire play, and also characters such as Miranda (*T* 1.2.185–6) and Gonzalo (*T* 2.1.185) recurrently succumb to drowsiness. Creating a background for the plot, the sleeping mariners are not visually present. Yet their sleep takes place for the entire duration of the play and their falling asleep and waking up mark its beginning and end: 'Boatswain: We were dead of sleep. ... We were awaked, straightway at liberty' (*T* 5.1.230–5). The play remains within this curious in-between-state that is topographically presented by the island, where sleep both stands for the continuity of life and the proximity of death.

During the storm, the boatswain rebels against death, 'Have you a mind to sink?' (*T* 1.1.34), whereas Antonio resigns to surrender to his fate: 'Let's all sink wi'th' king' (*T* 1.1.55). Sasha Handley notes that the metaphor of sinking often characterizes the experience of falling asleep: 'Feelings of submersion, sinking and loss of control surface time and time again in people's descriptions of falling asleep, which mark its distinctiveness from all other sensory experiences.'[21] Sinking in *The Tempest* parallels drowning and drowsiness: 'Doth it not then our eyelids sink?' (*T* 2.1.196). The play lets some of the shipwrecked sink into sleep when their almost inevitable death by water is transformed into a lasting sleep on the island, and it is only towards the end of the play that Prospero commends Ariel to one of his final tasks, to wake the sailors.

Part of Prospero's magic and power is to put characters to sleep and to awake them at his will. None of the sleepers in *The Tempest* awake by themselves, but they have to be woken up from a sleep that is frequently characterized as '[w]onderous heavy' (*T* 2.1.193). After the shipwreck, Ariel plays music and its narcotic charm sends the stranded party, except for Antonio and Sebastian, to sleep:

> SEBASTIAN What a strange drowsiness possesses them?
> ANTONIO It is the quality o'th'climate. ...
> SEBASTIAN What? Art thou waking?
> ANTONIO Do you not hear me speak?
> SEBASTIAN I do, and surely
> It is a sleepy language, and thou speak'st
> Out of thy sleep. What is it thou didst say?
> This is a strange repose, to be asleep
> With eyes wide open; standing, speaking, moving,
> And yet so fast asleep (*T* 2.1.193–4; 205–11)

Although Prospero is presented as the ruler over the sleep of others, his human need to sleep makes him vulnerable: 'Caliban: Yea, yea, my lord, I'll yield him thee asleep' (*T* 3.2.54). Prospero escapes the danger, and when he brings his former opponents together, he not only frees them from a short-term charm but also awakens them from the longer and morally depraved sleeplike state in which they have found themselves since they arrived on the island. Their enlightened awakening is paralleled by Prospero's farewell to his magic: 'The charm dissolves apace,/And as the morning steals upon the night,/Melting the darkness, so their rising senses/ Begin to chase the ignorant fumes that mantle/Their clearer reason' (*T* 5.1.64–8). When Prospero finally forgives his enemies and renounces his magic powers, these two last gestures are intricately interwoven. It seems as though to perform the act of forgiveness, Prospero is still in need of his magic, and hence his last act as a magus is to transport the traitors and Gonzalo into a sleeplike state, while he grants them forgiveness and thanks Gonzalo. This act of forgiveness, however, takes place without them being conscious of it.

Prospero's field of action is the sphere of sleep, and his turning away from illusion and magic gives way to a waking up to reality, reason and mortality that is to form the end of the play and the end of the time on stage. For the duration of the play, however, the characters do not escape from this in-between realm in which magic continues to work.[22] Similar to the awakening of the lovers in *A Midsummer Night's Dream*, characters in *The Tempest* find it difficult to distinguish between reality and dream: 'Whether this be/Or be not, I'll not swear' (*T* 5.1.122–3) remarks Gonzalo. And yet, the dreamlike quality of their existence remains, and Prospero himself abides between presence and absence.

Towards the end of the play, he is tired, aged and weary, and the play once again juxtaposes sleep and imminent death when he plans to retire to Milan 'where/Every third thought shall be [his] grave' (*T* 5.1.308–09). Like the sailors who were at his mercy during the storm at the beginning of the play, he, at the end, places his fate into the 'good hands' (*T* Epilogue 10) of the audience, whom he needs to release him from his staged presence.

Dreamscapes in *A Midsummer Night's Dream*

In *A Midsummer Night's Dream*, staging sleep is linked to the experience of change, transformation and metamorphosis. The play draws and redraws the fine line between an audience's reality and the dreamlike illusion on stage as it investigates non-conscious states of mind. The main acts of *A Midsummer Night's Dream* are pervaded by the continual falling asleep and waking up of its various characters. In no other play of Shakespeare, are sleep, dream and awakening such key elements of the plot. Yet in *A Midsummer Night's Dream* sleep is not merely a major plot device; it also creates a metatheatrical constellation that includes the experience of the audience. Peter Holland observes:

> In most plays by Shakespeare – and indeed by most playwrights – characters not directly involved in the action are usually left off-stage; in *A Midsummer Night's Dream*, they are just as likely to lie down on stage in full view of the audience and fall asleep. This has the double effect of removing characters from the action while keeping them in the eye of the audience: they are both there and not there.[23]

The simultaneity of waking and sleeping on stage allows for both states of consciousness to drift into one another. The sleeping bodies in *A Midsummer Night's Dream* remind the audience of the existence of a reality in which the boundary between waking and dreaming becomes permeable.

The ambivalence of characters and the changes they undergo between one world and another is one of the play's guiding paradoxes, and it is explored through the use of contrast and symmetry. Not only do Athens and Fairyland resemble one another but the dramatic structure of *A Midsummer Night's Dream* also follows the three phases of falling asleep, sleeping and waking up. The play creates a trajectory of transformation from the world of apparent reality, law and order to an interior or inverted middle place of wilderness, magic, night and potentially chaos and confusion, and then back, or out again into the exterior world of Athens that is commonly held as reality. The middle place, the 'wood near Athens' into which the lovers flee, is a place of sleep and transformation of body and mind, a place of enchantment, night and dreams, but also of disenchantment, where the lovers are to experience the transition between various degrees and kinds of love.

The middle world of *A Midsummer Night's Dream* is the 'mazèd world' (*MND* 1.2.113) that Titania describes, a world of transition and confusion. Likewise, the three parallel worlds of the play – Athens, Fairyland and the meta-theatrical world created in the amateur performance – pervade and define one another and grant the audience a position from which to compare them and to simultaneously see analogies and differences between them. Next to Athens and the enchanted realm of Fairyland, the third world of *A Midsummer Night's Dream* is the world of the mechanicals, the play-within-the-play. Peter Quince, who like Theseus and Oberon tries and fails to rule his realm, first inspects the place in the wood and notes that it is 'a marvellous convenient place for our rehearsal. This green plot shall be our stage, this hawthorn brake our tiring-house' (*MND* 3.1.2–4). He favours the open-air stage of the forest that, like Shakespeare's globe, collapses the illusion of a fourth wall and elides distinctions between actors and spectators. The 'green plot' becomes a playground for the imagination, for change and transformation. As an outdoor place, located at the crossroads of nature and artifice, the stage both refers to the theatre's ritual roots and allows the present, such as Bottom's translation, into the performance. The 'green plot' denotes an in-between place that challenges a univocal notion of locality and time and is at once the rehearsal stage of Peter Quince's troop, the alluring Athenian wood, Theseus' hunting ground and

Dreamscapes in A Midsummer Night's Dream 189

the enchanted realm of Fairyland, a zone of transformation between parallel worlds that relies on constant shifts of perspective between them.

The use of sleep and waking in *A Midsummer Night's Dream* inspires the notion of metaphorical difference in which something is seen in terms of an other. It constantly invites the audience to observe how different, even contrasting, elements are at play. Whereas the mechanicals highlight the difference between the actor and his role, Peter Quince faithfully adheres to the realistic similarity between the world of the play and that of the audience.[24] It is in these first scenes of Act III, when the mechanicals discuss the difficulty of how much imagination they can ask of their audience and relinquish theatrical illusion, that the play relies most heavily on this very illusion. In the scene, in which Bottom asks for a prologue that explains that no harm will be done with the swords and that he is in fact not Pyramus but Bottom the weaver (*MND* 3.1.15–20), the sleeping Fairy Queen Titania, who can only be seen by the audience, subtly undermines the words of the mechanicals.

Titania's presence likewise unites different roles. It alludes to the mythological Fairy Queen and to Queen Elizabeth I[25] and also points to the world of the imagination, of dream and immortality, over which she presides, and which the mechanicals find so hard to imagine. In her sleep, these different strands of reference come together and mark the sleeping body as a performative event that suggests the conflation and identity of such differences. The sleeping Titania becomes an epitome of theatrical illusion, saturated with allusions that exceed the presence of the sleeping body. Her sleep, in this scene, supports the interweaving of parallel plots in providing the place where their boundaries become permeable.

Sleep and dream present the simultaneity of different identities and different worlds, and the play also stages their momentary intersection in the realm of love as a dream that is dreamt together. From Act II scene ii until well into Act IV, the spheres of worldly Athens and the fantastic realm of faerie are held simultaneously present through sleeping characters onstage who complicate questions of whose dream is presented, who dreams and who is being dreamt of. Sleep becomes a shared experience and it only disintegrates when the sleepers awake, and when the distance between two possible states of consciousness and two kinds of reality is re-established.

Oberon wakes Titania, who is startled and incredulous that her dream was not a dream at all: 'Tell me how it came this night/That I sleeping here was found/With these mortals on the ground' (*MND* 4.1.97–9). Awakening is an irreversible act, and so is the change that was brought about by sleep.

One of the most drastic scenes in the play is the moment of Titania's disenchanting awakening when she realizes that she has spent the night with an ass-monster. The lovers' awakening, by contrast, is more benign when Demetrius and Lysander reciprocate the love of Hermia and Helena that had remained constant throughout the play. Awakening is at the same time a change of state and in the case of characters such as Gregor Samsa in Franz Kafka's 'Die Verwandlung', it brings with it the uncanny certainty that one is no longer the same person one was when one went to sleep.[26] Sleep once again is a phase of transition or metamorphosis in which an old identity is modified or even destroyed and a new one is created.

Even though some characters in *A Midsummer Night's Dream* are eager to embrace the world of daylight as the only possible reality and suppress the reality of the night, the latter proves resilient. Theseus tries to belittle the reports of the lovers, 'I never may believe/These antique fables, nor these fairy toys' (*MND* 5.1.2–3), but, in contrast to him, the audience has witnessed the presence of Fairyland and can therefore reasonably doubt Theseus' view. To them, the seemingly fixed opposition between day and dream, reality and the world of shadows, gradually starts to dissolve. Even if Oberon had casually noted that 'When they next wake, all this derision/ Shall seem a dream and fruitless vision' (*MND* 3.2.370–1), waking up becomes ambivalent as a line of demarcation between the spheres: 'Are you sure/That we are awake?' – Demetrius asks – 'It seems to me/That yet we sleep, we dream' (*MND* 4.1.189–91). Theatrical performance turns a dream into reality. Awakening becomes a reflecting device in which the dream that is reality and the reality that is a dream converge.

The mental isolation of the sleeper underlined by treatises on sleep since antiquity is suspended in *A Midsummer Night's Dream*. The play challenges the solitude and incommunicability of sleep and instead makes the state of sleep productive for a shared theatrical experience. As David Marshall notes, this is part of the appeal of the play: 'The magic of the play is that separate minds appear to be transfigured together; dreams (or what seem like dreams) appear to be shared.'[27] Through staging this shared experience of sleep, Shakespeare engages the audience in the dynamic of fluid identities and visions, and makes them partake in Hermia's double vision when she 'see[s] these things with parted eye,/When everything seems double' (*MND* 4.1.186–7).

Bottom conceives of sleep in theatrical terms – 'I have an exposition of sleep come upon me' (*MND* 4.1.35–36) – and wakes from his dream as if for him time had stood still and he was still taking part in the rehearsal; only gradually does he realize that he had been left asleep. Recalling his dream, he plans: 'I will get Peter Quince to write a ballad of this dream; it shall be called "Bottom's Dream", because it hath no bottom' (*MND* 4.1.207–9). The dream into which the play has transported the audience is indeed without a bottom as it lacks a firm point of reference in a clearly determinable reality. For a play in which so much depends on the imagination to stage its faerie dreamworld, sleep becomes a productive metaphor to unfold what otherwise cannot be presented: 'We are not here' (*MND* 5.1.115), Peter Quince's prologue reminds both the audience of 'Pyramus and Thisbe' and that of *A Midsummer Night's Dream*.

After the mechanicals' play and the retreat of the wedding party, Puck's epilogue directly addresses the audience: 'If we shadows have offended,/ Think but this, and all is mended:/That you have but slumbered here/ While these visions did appear;/And this weak and idle theme,/No more yielding but a dream' (*MND* 5.1.401–6). The play, the dream on stage, becomes the audience's dream. Not only does Puck carry Oberon's explanation to a metatheatrical level, but the epilogue also prolongs Bottom's interweaving of dream, vision and inspiration. What appears as a final apologetic gesture partakes in the tradition of poetic invention that regards a text as a dream. Puck's epilogue inverts the prologue of the play-within-a-play in that it does not seek to reconnect the theatre to any given reality, but rather asserts the theatre as an aesthetic reality on its own and appeals to an imagination that rests on sleep.

Night Pieces – *Nacht und Träume, Rockaby* and *The Winter's Tale*

Sleep and dream present what is distant, absent even, and introduce states in which two selves or remnants of them are at play: 'Sleep, in its guises of dream, trance, ghostliness and unconsciousness, is a corporeal trace of the void and the inaccessibility of pure interiority.'[28] Beckett's dreamlike stages and the sleeping non-presences of his fragmented characters examine notions of theatrical presence and explore the medial properties of the theatre, radio and television. Paul Sheehan observes a dramaturgical shift in Beckett's works for the stage that increasingly move away from the corporeal 'into the ethereal realm of disembodied drama'.[29] Sheehan characterizes this drama in terms similar to Prospero's in *The Tempest*: 'a theatre of shadows, traces, impressions and phantoms, whose fleeting qualities belie their material underpinnings'.[30]

Beckett's 'nightpiece', as he initially called his last television play *Nacht und Träume* (1982) stages nightfall and a character's drifting into a dreamlike state in a cyclical and synesthetic manner. The setting of the play is reminiscent of a religious painting,[31] its soundscape is created by the diminishing of the last seven bars of Franz Schubert's song 'Nacht und Träume', which is paralleled by the lights fading out. The dreaming consciousness of the dreamer, who himself is only faintly lit, is presented by a procession of visions appearing from above him: his dreamt self, the apparition of hands as if bestowing a benediction on him, a chalice providing communion and a cloth that wipes the brow of the dreamer, reminiscent of the legendary sudary of Veronica. The visions appear and disappear like double exposures and invoke central Christian rites of salvation, evoking faith in an entity that is only presented in a mediated way. Each of the apparitions that visit the dreamer captures a reflection on presence: the presence of the Holy Spirit summoned in a blessing, the real or symbolic presence of God in the act of communion and the imprint of Christ's face on the sudary.

The dreamer and the dreamt self are separated by these externalized apparitions, but they also remain connected, in touch, through the self-reflexive mediality of the hands, the chalice and the cloth, which like relics promise an enduring connection with the divine. The final words of Schubert's song, 'Holde Träume kehret wieder', urge the dreams to return, because it is only for the duration of the dream that the dreamer is able to experience this connection through the potentially salutary signs, before the play, at its end, returns to his seated figure. Sleeplike states do not present the self as a self-contained, opaque unit, but rather negotiate difference and similarity within the self and question the relation between an original and versions of it.

The recursive rhythm of motion and standstill, beginning and end, in which a sleeping, dreamlike state manifests itself and releases reflections on secondary presences beyond the self, is staged in *Rockaby* (1980). In this dramaticule, the movement of the figure of a mother[32] seated in a rocking chair is synchronized with her recorded voice reciting a poem. Like Murphy, who exhibits the dualism of mind and body when he ties himself to his rocking chair, *Rockaby* both divides and connects the exterior of the actress' body and the interior of her voice. The to and fro movement of the chair also evokes the movement of a cradle, and encompasses the beginning, the continuation and the end of life. The title 'Rockaby' suggests a lullaby as the text casts itself into the timeframe of a long day coming to an end. The play anticipates the ending of the woman's life and the continuation of life in 'another creature like herself': 'till in the end/the day came/ in the end came/close of a long day [...] for another/another like herself/

another creature like herself/a little like/going to and fro' (*CDW*, 435). The mother's desire to stop is counterbalanced by the desire to continue moving, and the play is structured by three instances in which the rocking comes to a halt at the words 'time she stopped' and then resumes its momentum, until at the end of the play the rocking finally stops on the echo of 'rock her off' (*CDW*, 442).

Next to *A Midsummer Night's Dream*, Shakespeare's *The Winter's Tale* centres on synoptic vision, in which the coexistence of two modes of being enables resemblance and difference to be negotiated. The chorus of Time at the beginning of Act IV refers to this construction of the play, and compares its two parts to the turning of an hourglass. Time's monologue describes itself as the night between two days, and this contraction of time is meant to have happened while the audience was asleep: 'Your patience this allowing,/I turn my glass, and give my scene such growing/As you had slept between' (*WT* 4.1.15–17).

The audience eventually awakes to the court of Polixenes in Bohemia as the play establishes parallel worlds – Sicily and Bohemia – in which characters assume double identities such as shepherd and Prince. The play creates constant shifts of perspective between these worlds that engage the viewer in a process of seeing that both creates and suspends the distance between father and son, mother and daughter, nature and artifice. When Paulina brings the baby Perdita to the sleepless Leontes and urges him to acknowledge the child as his own: 'Although the print be little, the whole matter/And copy of the father' (*WT* 2.3.98–9), she announces: 'I come to bring him sleep' (*WT* 2.3.33). Later, in Act V of *The Winter's Tale*, Paulina makes Leontes swear not to marry until she gives him leave to do so: 'Unless another,/As like Hermione as is her picture/Affront his eye' (*WT* 5.1.73–5).

In *Rockaby*, the promise of the return of 'another creature' remains unfulfilled, and early in Act V of *The Winter's Tale*, Paulina's prophecy seems equally unlikely to come true. Yet, similar to *Rockaby*, the story of the lost daughter creates the temporal arc of the plot, and throughout *The Winter's Tale*, the mother's, Hermione's, real and her spectral identity are kept at play. When Paulina's husband Antigonus and the banished child Perdita find themselves cast off in the wilderness of the seacoast of Bohemia, he addresses Perdita, stating that he thinks that something impossible has happened, that he may have seen her dead mother in a dream, although he is not sure exactly what he 'saw', nor even whether it was definitely a dream: 'Antigonus: Come, poor babe./I have heard, but not believed, the spirits o'th'dead/May walk again. If such thing be, thy mother/Appeared to me last night, for ne'er was dream/So like a waking' (*WT* 3.3.14–18). Antigonus' dream is so lively that in it, the boundaries between reality and dream have become penetrable. His awakening also refers to the final awakening of the play when Hermione transitions into life from being a statue. Antigonus leaves the child as he is ordered to do and, shortly after, leaves the stage forever as one of Shakespeare's most famous stage directions succinctly states: '*Exit pursued by a bear*' (*WT* 3.3.57). Perdita, the lost likeness of Hermione, however, returns to Sicily sixteen years later to witness the Pygmalion-like resurrection of her mother. In the performance of Hermione's ekphrastic resurrection, which needs the onlookers to 'awake' their 'faith' (*WT* 5.3.95), *The Winter's Tale* recasts a religious poetics into an aesthetics of theatrical immanence, one in which the work of art generates its own condition in its bodily materiality.

In the final awakening that figures an immanent resurrection in which a lifelike work of art comes to life in the microcosm of the theatre, *The Winter's Tale* offers a model of aesthetic experience. It includes the audience in a process in which theatrical presence is created. The scene evokes the binaries of art and nature, dream and reality, presence and absence, sleep and death, and challenges the validity of representational practices that rely on them. Paulina's staging affirms the theatre as a medium of transformation and the place in which the impossible can be actualized as a possibility: 'To see the life as lively mocked as ever/Still sleep mocked death' (*WT* 5.3.19–20). The reunion at the end of the play, however, does more than merely celebrate the redemptive magic of the theatre. Not much is well. The element of difference between two presences remains when the restitution of the family comes at a price of sixteen years' absence as well as the loss of a husband and a son. Whereas *The Winter's Tale* stages the resurrection of Hermione and the return of Perdita, *Rockaby* gestures towards the arrival of a likeness, yet leaves the mother in an undead, ghostly state.

Deep Sleep in *Footfalls* and *Endgame*

The technical and medial possibilities, as well as limitations, of stagecraft, light, voice and music to create stage presence are central to Beckett's theatre when it negotiates inside and outside, similarity and difference, continuation and discontinuity in relation to his dramatic selves. The dreamlike immateriality of Beckett's plays is further enhanced by his writing and producing them for the radio and television, where the concentration on sounds and voices, the angle of the camera and the

Deep Sleep in Footfalls and Endgame

distant presence of a recorded production emphasize the medial constitution of presence. The liminal, sleeplike state of plays such as *Rockaby* or *Nacht und Träume* epitomizes this paradoxical similarity in difference.

Antigonus' premonition in *The Winter's Tale* that 'the spirits o'th'dead/ May walk again' is almost literalized in the mother-daughter likenesses that pervade Beckett's late play *Footfalls*. *Footfalls* presents the relation between a mother and her daughter who is named May. The mother is only present through her voice coming from above in the womblike interior of the stage that May has not been out of 'since girlhood' (*CDW*, 401). Imprisoned, protected and entombed, unborn or undead, May restlessly paces to and fro along a central line, in a timespan of exactly nine seconds. The metronome-like rhythm of her nine steps forward and her nine steps back is a self-cancelling mechanism of progress into the future and a return to the past. Perpetuity and standstill become one, inside and outside merge, as her mind 'revolves' around unresolved issues that remain unspoken. Each of the four parts of the play opens with a faint chime echoing, a sign of awakening as May summons the ghostly presence of her mother:

M   Mother. [*Pause. No louder.*] Mother.
    [*Pause.*]
V   Yes, May.
M   Were you asleep?
V   Deep asleep. [*Pause.*] I heard you in my deep sleep. [*Pause.*]
    There is no sleep so deep I would not hear you there. (*CDW*, 399)

The bond between mother and daughter that is maintained aurally cannot be severed. May, who does not share her mother's deep sleep, but only 'sleep[s] [. . .] in snatches' (*CDW*, 401) with her head against the wall, remains dependent on her mother. The play further reproduces the constellation between May and her mother in the parallel story about a character Amy – (A me), an inverted version of May's self – and a Mrs Winter. At the end of this 'Winter's tale', May's presence merges into non-presence when the mother calls her 'Amy' instead of May and a disembodied voice answers: 'Yes, Mother' (*CDW*, 403). At the end, May, like her mother, assumes a ghostlike presence. No trace of her is to be seen on stage any more, and their last piece of dialogue inversely repeats the beginning. The final chime sounds, but it does not introduce another part of the play, and the fade up of light on the strip remains the only residue of a presence that has disappeared. As if in waiting, the final tableau is to last ten seconds.

The deep sleep of the mother that could also be death, the unborn state of a child or the undead state of a revenant is referred to by Hamm in

Endgame, when he tells the unfinished story about the man asking for bread: 'Hamm: Three whole days. Good. In what condition he had left the child. Deep in sleep. [*Forcibly.*] But deep in what sleep, deep in what sleep already?' (*CDW*, 118). *Endgame*, and also *Happy Days*, begin with an awakening. Clov removes the sheets that cover Hamm and the ashbins. Hamm 'seems to be asleep' (*CDW*, 93), and begins to stir and yawn under his handkerchief until he takes it from his face like a blanket. His first words and sentences are interrupted by yawns. Musing about his dreams, 'What dreams! Those forests!' (*CDW*, 93), makes him want to return to sleep, 'God, I'm tired, I'd be better off in bed' (*CDW*, 93), and he orders Clov, 'Get me ready, I'm going to bed. Clov: I've just got you up' (*CDW*, 93–4). His longing for sleep surfaces again when he ponders, 'If I could sleep I might make love. I'd go into the woods' (*CDW*, 100). Sleep for Hamm is a desired yet impossible form of closure, and it is a constant part of the performative present of *Endgame*. Throughout the play, Nagg and Nell in their dustbins – in spite of their brief appearances – remain a sleeping or dying presence.

Waking in *Endgame* is waking up to being on stage in front of an audience or waking up to be part of an audience. In needing to be seen and heard, Hamm needs Nagg to be awake and listen to his story: 'Hamm: Ask my father if he wants to listen to my story. [. . .]/Clov: He's asleep./Hamm: Wake him' (*CDW*, 115–16). Clov wakes him with the alarm that is '[f]it to wake the dead' (*CDW*, 115), and Nagg complains that this was unnecessary and refuses to play his role as a listener: 'Nagg: I was asleep, as happy as a king, and you woke me up to have me listen to you. It wasn't indispensable, you didn't really need to have me listen to you. Besides I didn't listen to you' (*CDW*, 119). During the play in which characters play for and with each other, waking up and falling asleep become miniature forms of making theatrical entrances and exits.

Watching, Waiting and Sleeping in *Happy Days* and *Waiting for Godot*

Sleep and waking, the longing for sleep and the inability to fall asleep coincide in *Endgame* and *Happy Days* and structure both plays, in which sleeping characters are paralleled by their not-sleeping playmates. Prompted by the inexorable bell, Act I of *Happy Days* starts with Winnie's awakening into '[a]nother heavenly day' (*CDW*, 138), Act II with her Miltonic greeting of the light, 'Hail, holy light' (*CDW*, 160). Whereas Winnie is unable to sleep, Willie remains a body more or less visible and more or less awake during the entire play. Winnie's ceaseless chatter is paralleled by Willie's inert, silent presence. Winnie begs Willie not to 'curl up on [her] again' (*CDW*, 141) and expresses sleep envy:

[P]oor Willie – [...] – no zest – [...] – for anything – [...] no interest – [...] – in life – [...] – poor dear Willie – [...] – sleep for ever – [...] – marvellous gift – [...] – nothing to touch it – [...] – in my opinion – [...] – always said so – [...] – wish I had it. (*CDW*, 139)

Winnie needs the reassuring presence of Willie as a sounding board: 'when two are gathered together – [*faltering*] – in this way – [*normal*] – that because one sees the other the other sees the one' (*CDW*, 149).

The more her bodily presence diminishes, the deeper she sinks into the ground, the more she needs to be seen and heard by someone and therefore cannot be alone: 'Would I had let you sleep on. [...] Ah yes, if only I could bear to be alone, I mean prattle away with not a soul to hear' (*CDW*, 145). Like the relentless bell that wakes her, she inexorably tries to wake Willie to reassure herself that he is still alive: 'Willie? [*Pause*.] Have you gone off on me again? [...] Your eyes appear to be closed, but that has no particular significance we know. [*Pause*.] Raise a finger, dear, will you please, if you are not quite senseless. [*Pause*.] Do that for me, Willie please, just the little finger, if you are still conscious' (*CDW*, 153–4).

In the blazing light of the sun that is created by the lighting on stage, Winnie senses that she is being watched by someone: 'Strange feeling that someone is looking at me. I am clear, then dim, then gone, then dim again, then clear again, and so on, back and forth, in and out of someone's eye' (*CDW*, 155). Her life on stage is made possible by the footlights, and she further reflects on her theatrical being through her story about the 'shower' and the 'cooker'.[33] 'To be is to be seen' is what fosters Winnie's resilience. Waking up, to Winnie, is being awake on a stage where she gains reassurance by being looked at by an audience: 'Someone is looking at me still. [*Pause*.] Caring for me still. [*Pause*.] That is what I find so wonderful. [*Pause*.] Eyes on my eyes' (*CDW*, 160).

Both acts of *Waiting for Godot* begin in the evening, and the rhythm of sleeping and waking pervades the play's diurnal structure when night falls and the moon rises at the end of each act. The ability to sleep is equally distributed between the four main characters. While Estragon and Lucky are either sleeping or continuously about to fall asleep,[34] Pozzo and Vladimir, who yearns for nightfall (*CDW* 33, 35, 74), remain awake and keep waking up their companions:

[[...] ESTRAGON *falls asleep.* VLADIMIR *halts before* ESTRAGON.]
Gogo! ... Gogo! ... GOGO!
[ESTRAGON *wakes with a start.*]
ESTRAGON: [*Restored to the horror of his situation.*] I was asleep!
[*Despairingly.*] Why will you never let me sleep? (*CDW*, 17)

Whereas Estragon's states of sleeping and waking can be distinguished from one another, for Lucky they become increasingly blurred. Not only does he instantaneously fall asleep when he falls down – Pozzo: 'Every time he drops he falls asleep' (*CDW*, 24) – but he also appears to be asleep while standing: '[[...] Lucky *sags slowly, until bag and basket touch the ground, then straightens up with a start and begins to sag again. Rhythm of one sleeping on his feet.*]' (*CDW*, 26).

Lucky, who is mostly '*half asleep*' (*CDW*, 36), or continuously dozing off, is a silent, indeterminate and unpredictable presence on stage, standing asleep while holding on to his bags. His sleep could be recreational or deadly as his being becomes a dramatic lacuna that causes speculation and wonder. Vladimir and Estragon timidly approach him, curiously examine his appearance and register the sore on his neck and his facial expression. Throughout the play, their feelings towards him alternate between pity and hatred. When Lucky is prompted by Pozzo to 'Think!' (*CDW*, 41), his fragmented speech also resembles a person talking in his sleep, with references to Shakespeare's plays – such as 'love's labour's lost'; from *Hamlet*, 'the skull the skull the skull the skull' (*CDW*, 43); and, from *The Tempest*, 'the divine Miranda' (*CDW*, 42)[35] – surfacing from a half-sleeping, half-awake consciousness.

Sleep and waking in *Waiting for Godot* indicate the blurring of distinctions between dream and reality, past and present. Vladimir seems to be the only character in the entire play who possesses a sense of time. He is oriented towards the future, constantly reminding Estragon that they are waiting for Godot and thereby endowing their situation with a sense of purpose. Whereas Estragon has forgotten most of what happened the day before, Vladimir remembers the immediate past and also recalls former times when he and Estragon worked in the Macon country picking grapes. Upon his return in Act II, Pozzo does not remember having met the two before, and Estragon, when prompted, only faintly remembers, and rather suggests that Vladimir has only dreamt what went on:

VLADIMIR   [...] Do you not remember? [...]
ESTRAGON   You dreamt it.
VLADIMIR   Is it possible that you've forgotten already?
ESTRAGON   That's the way I am. Either I forget immediately or I never forget. [...]
VLADIMIR   He's forgotten everything! (*CDW*, 56)

Watching, Waiting and Sleeping 199

To Estragon, dreams are just as valid as present reality. He insists that he is 'not a historian' (*CDW*, 61), is not interested in past events and prefers to go to sleep:

ESTRAGON   What about a little snooze?
VLADIMIR   Did you hear him? He wants to know what happened!
ESTRAGON   Don't mind him. Sleep. (*CDW*, 77)

Dreams and nightmares increasingly pervade the play, and characters become less certain whether someone is asleep or awake. Vladimir and Estragon ruminate about the dead voices rustling like leaves, ashes or sand in a state between life and death that is reminiscent of the souls in Dante's Purgatory.[36] Vladimir's nightmares are repeatedly mentioned, and when Estragon falls asleep he wakes from his nightmare with a start and is comforted by Vladimir, who does not want to be told the dream:

ESTRAGON   I was falling –
VLADIMIR   It's all over, it's all over.
ESTRAGON   I was on top of a –
VLADIMIR   Don't tell me! Come, we'll walk it off. (*CDW*, 66)

When Pozzo and Lucky re-enter, fall and remain stretched out motionless among their scattered baggage, their helpless bodies become ambivalent signs. They might or might not be asleep, they might be unconscious or dying. Like Caliban, Vladimir and Estragon contemplate whether they should attack Pozzo in his sleep:

VLADIMIR   For the moment he is inert. But he might run amuck any minute. [. . .]
VLADIMIR   You mean if we fell on him in his sleep?
ESTRAGON   Yes.
VLADIMIR   That seems a good idea all right. But could we do it? Is he really asleep? (*CDW*, 73–4)

Pozzo himself also intermittently doubts whether he is awake: 'Pozzo: I woke up one fine day as blind as Fortune. [*Pause*.] Sometimes I wonder if I'm not still asleep' (*CDW*, 80). Lucky's state of being is even more uncertain, and Vladimir even suggests that he might be dead:

POZZO   Where is my menial?
VLADIMIR   He's about somewhere.
POZZO   Why doesn't he answer when I call?
VLADIMIR   I don't know. He seems to be sleeping. Perhaps he's dead. (*CDW*, 81)

The reality that dreams and nightmares acquire for the characters challenges the ontology of a play that is increasingly perceived as a dream.

Estragon suggests that Vladimir has only dreamt that Pozzo was blind, and feels much more comfortable sleeping and reproaches Vladimir for waking him:

> ESTRAGON Why will you never let me sleep?
> VLADIMIR I felt lonely. (*CDW*, 83)

Vladimir is denied the 'gift of sleep' that Winnie praises. Towards the end of the play, he is himself not sure whether he is awake, and compares himself to one of the disciples of Christ who went to sleep rather than stayed awake with him in the night before his arrest:

> Was I sleeping, while the others suffered? Am I sleeping now? Tomorrow, when I wake, or think I do, what shall I say of today? That with Estragon my friend, at this place until the fall of night, I waited for Godot? That Pozzo passed, with his carrier, and that he spoke to us? Probably. But in all that what truth will there be? [ESTRAGON, *having struggled with his boots in vain, is dozing off again.* VLADIMIR *stares at him.*] He'll know nothing. (*CDW*, 84)

Past, present and future to Vladimir have become contingent as he asks himself if what he experiences is not rather a dream. He summarizes the play that the audience has witnessed in retrospect and questions as well as affirms the truth of what has happened on stage. Sleep and dream make visible the limits of theatrical representation and Beckett's waking sleepers perform this critique of their dramatic medium. The play assumes a dual quality: it becomes both an inscrutable, non-referential, absent entity, and yet it is present as a material and performative reality.

Vladimir watches the sleeping Estragon and considers the possibility that he, like him, is in a sleeplike state being watched by someone: '[*He looks again at* Estragon.] At me too someone is looking, of me too someone is saying, he is sleeping, he knows nothing, let him sleep on. [*Pause.*] I can't go on! [*Pause.*] What have I said?' (*CDW*, 84–5).[37] Equating his sleeplike state with that of an actor on stage, who is being looked at by an audience, Vladimir suggests that what the audience has witnessed is what goes on in the mind of a sleeping body. The audience therefore not only watches a character sleeping but also partakes in the dream of the characters that constitutes the play, which is analogous to what is happening while somebody is asleep. Other than Estragon, Vladimir, like Winnie, momentarily steps out of his role, acknowledges that he is being watched by someone and that he possibly finds himself in somebody else's play. He also expresses the need to be seen and remembered when he urges the boy: 'You're sure you saw me, you won't come and tell me tomorrow that you never saw me!' (*CDW*, 86). He asserts his presence as an actor to whom being is being on stage, and not to be seen by someone would mean to acquire a ghostly existence. As night falls towards the end of *Waiting for Godot*, Estragon awakes and asks:

ESTRAGON Was I long asleep?
VLADIMIR I don't know. (*CDW*, 86)

Their final dialogue casts the play into a place between day and night, between sleep and waking, lingering restlessly between the desire to leave and the inability to do so.

'Sleep no more': 'restless ecstasy' in *Macbeth* and *Cascando*

Whereas the sleeper in *Nacht und Träume* is asleep and dreaming during the entire play, Woburn, the main character in *Cascando* is prompted by Voice to finish a story after which he will be able to rest. The piece is set in the month of May: 'Opener: Yes, correct, the month of May./You know, the reawakening' (*CDW*, 301). Rather than embracing the cheerfulness of springtime, however, Woburn waits for night to fall, gets up and struggles to stay awake on his way to his destination, an island. Encouraged by Voice, he is determined to end his journey and to find a story: 'Voice: [*Low, panting.*] –story ... if you could finish it ... you could rest ... sleep ... not before ... oh I know ... the ones I've finished ... thousands and one ... all I ever did ... in my life' (*CDW*, 297). Rest and sleep are desirable states and the journey towards them is presented in structural oscillation between crescendo and decrescendo, opening and closing, as well as the alternating rhythm of speech and silence that structures his journey to the island.

Woburn's stop-and-go movement towards the shore, his rising up and falling down, is described by Voice, which is not only a disembodied external observer but also becomes an interior narrative voice. Intermittently, Voice is joined by Music, another invisible and bodiless character, and both urge Woburn to endure in a restless journey towards sleep. They gesture towards closure, rest and sleep: '–rest ... sleep ... no more stories ... no more words' (*CDW*, 299), and yet they make him go on. Finality and sleep become a promised end never to be reached as the play ends on Voice and Music pressing him to continue. Woburn's restless state echoes Hamlet's longing for sleep: 'To die, to sleep – /No more; and by a sleep to say we end/The heart-ache and the thousand natural shocks/That flesh is heir to – 'tis a consummation/Devoutly to be wished.

To die, to sleep – /To sleep, perchance to dream. Ay, there's the rub' (*Ham* 3.1.60–5).

Similar to *Waiting for Godot*, the piece ends hovering, with Voice starting in mid-sentence, without a beginning and unable to stop. The longing for closure and rest, for finding the story to finish all stories, is undermined by the restless search for the right story and the fear of ending prematurely. Woburn's woe finds its performative equivalent in a process of writing and speaking that can never reach an end, leaving the character in a trancelike, sleepless state.

Shakespeare's interest in sleep as a constant of human life is poignantly evident in *Macbeth* where sleep is almost entirely lacking. The great number of images of and allusions to sleep stands in contrast to the absence of a sleeping body on stage. The bodies of the few characters that do find sleep in the tragedy, the king and his two chamberlains, are not shown on stage. In *Macbeth*, sleep is not tied to the presence of the sleeping body, but it is created in metaphors and images that configure it as a bodily experience. Whereas in *A Midsummer Night's Dream* the boundary between sleep and waking is staged as a world of the imagination, similar and yet distinct from the world of Athens, *Macbeth* is positioned on the other side of sleep, in a state of waking that does not find rest. This state of being becomes a destructive sphere of madness into which the audience, which no longer finds rest in comfortably watching a sleeping body, is included.

The first two acts of *Macbeth* provide the most intense concentration of sleep-imagery in all of Shakespeare's works. The First Witch promises that she will afflict the sailor whose wife has turned her away so direly that 'Sleep shall neither night nor day/Hang upon his penthouse lid' (*Mac* 1.3.18–19). Also Banquo is tormented by sombre premonitions: 'A heavy summons lies like lead upon me,/And yet I would not sleep; merciful powers,/Restrain in me the cursèd thoughts that nature/Gives way to in repose' (*Mac* 2.1.6–9).[38] The sailor's fate foreshadows that of Macbeth as these early scenes circle around the regicide in which they culminate. As much as the action gravitates towards the body of the sleeping sovereign, King Duncan is withheld from the audience's gaze. His absent presence is created by the dialogue of the Macbeths when Lady Macbeth muses: 'Had he not resembled/My father as he slept, I had done't' (*Mac* 2.2.12–13). Even if this dramaturgical decision is in keeping with the requirements of decorum, Shakespeare in *Macbeth* preserves the body of the king as untouchable. In removing the deed from the audience's sight, Shakespeare emphasizes the scale of an event that cannot be presented and increases the severity of the crime.

The transition from victim to perpetrator is metonymically performed when Macbeth returns with bloodied hands and the daggers, and at the same time the scene prefigures the unnatural line from Duncan to Macbeth: Not only will the blood of his victim forever stay with Macbeth, who eventually does become king, but the sleep of the sovereign that is violently ended will be the end of any sleep for Macbeth. Deprived of the restorative function of sleep, Macbeth enters a horrid and hallucinatory world: 'Methought I heard a voice cry, "Sleep no more:/Macbeth does murder Sleep" – the innocent sleep' (*Mac* 2.2.38–9). Even though Lady Macbeth dismisses his despair as 'brain-sickly' (*Mac* 2.2.49), and chides him for being 'Infirm of purpose' (*Mac* 2.2.55), trying to reassure him and herself that 'The sleeping and the dead/Are but as pictures;'tis the eye of childhood/That fears a painted devil' (*Mac* 2.2.56–8), Macbeth is not to be consoled and the rift between him and his former 'dearest partner of greatness' (*Mac* 1.5.9–10) starts to widen, never to be healed. He still hears the voice crying relentlessly, affecting all levels of him as a subject: '"Sleep no more" to all the house;/"Glamis hath murdered sleep, and therefore Cawdor/Shall sleep no more: Macbeth shall sleep no more"' (*Mac* 2.2.44–6).

The Macbeths' crime against the lifegiving force of sleep results in inner excesses of restlessness and dehumanizing insomnia: 'You lack the season of all natures, sleep' (*Mac* 3.4.141). The play's many allusions to sleep give way to the performance of sleeplessness. At first, the Macbeths pretend to have slept, 'Get on your night-gown, lest occasion call us/And show us to be watchers' (*Mac* 2.2.73–4), and manage to mingle with '[t]he sleepers of the house' (*Mac* 2.3.76) without raising suspicion. However, it is not Macbeth but Macduff who finally defeats him, who summons the household to a dismal awakening: 'Macduff: . . . Awake, awake! . . . Banquo and Donaldbain! Malcolm, awake,/Shake off this downy sleep, death's counterfeit,/And look on death itself' (*Mac* 2.3.67–71). The characters, unlike the audience, are made witnesses to Duncan's death.

Beset by the fear that his deed will become known, Macbeth becomes entangled in a downward spiral of murders that precipitate one another. After the murder of Banquo, Macbeth mentions that he sleeps 'In the affliction of . . . terrible dreams/That shake us nightly' (*Mac* 3.2.18–19). In *Macbeth*, the desire to find rest and the impossibility of doing so is constitutive for the character and the world at large. Agonizingly,

Macbeth, who lacks sleep, knows about its soothing and life-preserving powers:

> Sleep that knits up the ravelled sleeve of care,
> The death of each day's life, sore labour's bath,
> Balm of hurt minds, great nature's second course,
> Chief nourisher in life's feast (*Mac* 2.2.40–3).

Beckett, in a less poignant way, alludes to this passage in *Murphy*, when Murphy on his nightshift wanders through his ward at the MMM as through a gallery and when looking at the sleeping or waking patients is reminded of ancient Greek sculptors, whose statues represent either peaceful repose or violent unrest: 'Murphy's first round had shown him what a mere phrase was Neary's "Sleep and Insomnia, the Phidias and Scopas of Fatigue". [...] Here those that slept and those that did not were quite palpably by the same hand, that of some rather later artist whose work could by no means have come down to us, say the Pergamene Barlach' (*Murphy*, 238).

To Murphy, the spectator, the figures, the quiet sleepers and the convulsive insomniacs, like sculptures, resemble mere material bodies. The sleepers seem lifeless, as if interrupted in their ways by some abrupt calamity:

> Those that slept did so in the frozen attitudes of Herculaneum, as though sleep had pounced upon them like an act of God. And those that did not did not by the obvious grace of the same authority. The contortions of the resistive in particular seemed to Murphy not so much an entreaty to nature's soft nurse as a recoil from her solicitations. The economy of care was better served, in the experience of the resistive, when they knit up the sleeve by day (*Murphy*, 239).

Murphy literalizes the imagery of restoration and cure that is used by Macbeth and transports it to the reality of the asylum where the 'sleeve of care' more prosaically resembles the sleeve of a straitjacket.

Macbeth longs for death but realizes that he will not find peace: 'Better be with the dead/Whom we, to gain our peace, have sent to peace,/Than on the torture of the mind to lie/In restless ecstasy. Duncan is in his grave./ After life's fitful fever, he sleeps well' (*Mac* 3.2.19–23). In the course of the play, Macbeth is consumed by restless ecstasy and wakes sleepless, while Lady Macbeth sleeps waking. The Doctor witnesses her paradoxical 'slumbery agitation': 'A great perturbation in nature, to receive at once the benefit of sleep and do the effects of watching' (*Mac* 5.1.8–9). Macbeth's hallucinating sleeplessness is complemented by the sleepwalking fantasies of his wife. It is in this interaction between two modes of perception restlessly oscillating between waking and sleeping that the play's oppositions of human and supernatural, manly and womanly power, good and evil, life and death, day and night, illusion and reality are upheld. This in-between state, at the end of the tragedy, is equated with sleeplessness and the theatre when upon hearing that his wife has died, Macbeth turns the sleepwalking figure of his wife into an image of life itself as an actor: 'a walking shadow, a poor player/That struts and frets his hour upon the stage/And then is heard no more' (*Mac* 5.5.23–5).

Macbeth's reflection on his shadowy existence as an actor is paralleled by Beckett's Molloy, who fashions himself as a sleepless writer. Like Lady Macbeth, who twice hears the owl shriek after the murder (*Mac* 2.2.3; 15), he is summoned to his desk by the night owl: 'All is sleeping. Nevertheless I get up and go to my desk. I can't sleep. My lamp sheds a soft and steady light. I have trimmed it. It will last till morning. I hear the eagle-owl. What a terrible battle-cry!' (*Molloy*, 92).

Sleep and sleeplessness are crucial to the metadramatic framework of Beckett's and Shakespeare's plays. Sleep is used a principle of form that shapes the structure of plays such as *The Tempest* and relates to its treatment of magic and mortality. It introduces a twofold perspective on dramatic selves and staged presences, in which the permeable boundary between sleep and waking also includes the experience of the audience, making it part of the play in *Happy Days* and *Waiting for Godot*. In *Cascando*, sleeplessness refers to the tantalizing process of artistic creation, and in *Macbeth* sleep and its absence constitute the increasingly fragile ontology of the world of the theatre.

Notes

1 Simon J. Williams, *Sleep and Society: Sociological Ventures into the (Un)Known* (London, New York: Routledge, 2005), 3.
2 William Sherman, 'Shakespearean Somnilogy: Sleepy Language in *The Tempest*' in Tom Healy and Margaret Healy (eds.), *Renaissance Transformations: The Making of English Writing* (Edinburgh University Press, 2009), 177–91, 180.
3 IACHIMO: O sleep, thou ape of death, lie dull upon her (*Cym* 2.2.31).
4 Benjamin Parris argues that: 'These tragedies hinge on the violent deaths of sleeping kings and a politically chaotic aftermath, both of which resist the highly wrought fictions of constant vigilance, immortality, and stately perfection that help to legitimate the doctrine of the King's Two Bodies.' Benjamin Parris, '"The Body is with the King, but the King is not with the Body":

Sovereign Sleep in *Hamlet* and *Macbeth*', *Shakespeare Studies*, 40 (2012), 101–42, 102.
5 David Roberts, 'Sleeping Beauties. Shakespeare, Sleep and the Stage', *The Cambridge Quarterly*, 35.3 (2006), 231–54, 235.
6 Sherman, 'Shakespearean Somnilogy', 179.
7 Jennifer Lewin, '"Your Actions are My Dreams": Sleepy Minds in Shakespeare's Last Plays', *Shakespeare Studies*, 31 (2003), 184–204, 190.
8 Cf. e.g. James Knowlson, *Damned to Fame. The Life of Samuel Beckett* (London: Bloomsbury, 1997), 64. S.E. Gontarski, *The Intent of Undoing in Samuel Beckett's Dramatic Texts* (Bloomington: University of Indiana Press, 1985), 1.
9 Simon C. Estok, 'The Ecocritical Unconscious: Early Modern Sleep as "Go-Between"', *Ecocriticism and Shakespeare: Reading Ecophobia* (New York: Palgrave, 2011), 111–21, 111.
10 Maria Ruvoldt, *The Renaissance Imagery of Inspiration: Metaphors of Sex, Sleep and Dreams* (Cambridge University Press, 2004), 14.
11 Timothy A. Turner, 'Making the Moor: Torture, Sleep Deprivation, and Race in *Othello*' in Nancy L. Simpson-Younger and Margaret Simon (eds.), *Forming Sleep. Representing Consciousness in the English Renaissance* (University Park: The Pennsylvania State University Press, 2020), 89–109, 100.
12 Thomas Cogan, *The Haven of Health: Chiefly Gathered for the Comfort of Students and Consequences of All Those that Have a Care of Their Health, Amplified upon Five Words of Hippocrates* (London: Anne Griffin, 1636), 275: 'it recovereth strength, it refresheth the body, it reviveth the mind, it pacifieth anger, it driveth away sorrow, & finally, if it be moderate, it bringeth the whole man to good state and temperature' (270). He, however, advises against afternoon sleep: 'For afternoone sleepe maketh undigested and raw humours, whereof groweth oppilations, which oppilations ingender Fevers. Also it maketh a man slothfull, by reason that superfluous humours, remaine still in the muskles, veines and ioynts' (271).
13 Garrett Sullivan Jr., *Sleep, Romance, and Human Embodiment: Vitality from Spenser to Milton* (Cambridge University Press, 2012), 1–26. Sullivan emphasizes the importance of Aristotle's tripartite conception of the soul in *De anima* for English Renaissance discourses of the human, particularly in epic and romance where sleep blurs the boundaries between human, plant and animal lives.
14 Sasha Handley, *Sleep in Early Modern England* (New Haven: Yale University Press, 2016), 7.
15 *Daemonologie, in Forme of a Dialogue, Diuided into three bookes. Written by the high and mightie Prince Iames by the grace of God King of England, Scotland, France, and Ireland, Defender of the faith. & c.* (Printed for William Cotton, and Will. Aspley, according to the copie printed at Edenburgh [1597] (London: 1603), 41.

16 *The Book of Common Prayer: The Texts of 1549, 1559, and 1662*, ed. by Brian Cummings (Oxford University Press, 2011), 16, 114, 256. [The citation used in the text is from the 1662 version (256)]
17 On early modern dream theories cf. also: S.J. Wiseman 'Introduction' in Katharina Hidgkin, Michelle O'Callaghan and S.J. Wiseman (eds.), *Reading the Early Modern Dream: Terrors of the Night* (New York, London: Routledge, 2008), 1–13, 1–6.
18 Sigmund Freud, *Die Traumdeutung*, 8th ed. (Frankfurt a.M.: Fischer, 2001), 110–11.
19 Cf. Chapter 2 of this study.
20 David Bevington, 'Asleep Onstage' in John A. Alford (ed.), *From Page to Performance: Essays in Early English Drama* (East Lansing: Michigan State University Press, 1995), 51–83, 68.
21 Handley, *Sleep in Early Modern England*, 6–7.
22 Lewin, '"Your Actions Are My Dreams"', 199.
23 Peter Holland, 'Dreams and the Play's Structure' in Stephen P. Thomason (ed.), *Readings on* A Midsummer Night's Dream (San Diego: Greenhaven Press, 2011), 84–90, 88.
24 R.W. Dent, 'Imagination in *A Midsummer Night's Dream*', *SQ* 15:2 (1964), 115–29, 125–26.
25 For the many layers of mythological, folkoric and erotic epithets connected to Elizabeth I in dream-visions in general and particularly in *MND* cf.: Helen Hackett, 'Dream-Visions of Elizabeth I' in Hidgkin, O'Callaghan and Wiseman (eds.), *Reading the Early Modern Dream*, 58–61.
26 Andreas Höfele, 'Erwachen in Shakespeares *A Midsummer Night's Dream*', *Archiv für das Studium der Neueren Sprachen und Literaturen*, 228 (1991), 41–51.
27 David Marshall, 'Exchanging Visions: Reading *A Midsummer Night's Dream*' in Harold Bloom (ed.), *William Shakespeare's* A Midsummer Night's Dream*: Modern Critical Interpretations* (New York: Chelsea House), 87–115, 111.
28 Corey Wakeling, 'Sleeplessness in Sleep: Beckett's Gestures of Dream', *Performance Research*, 21.1 (2016), 42–8, 42. Wakeling analyses Beckett's materialist, anatomical view of sleep's gestures as a map of the human figure's proximity to the void in *Happy Days* and *Nacht und Träume*, drawing on Agamben's theory of gesture.
29 Paul Sheehan, 'Beckett's Ghost Dramas: Monitoring a Phenomenology of Sleep' in Ulrika Maude and Matthew Feldmann (eds.), *Beckett and Phenomenology* (London: Continuum, 2009), 158–77, 159.
30 Ibid.
31 Knowlson specifically mentions Albrecht Dürer's etching of praying hands, a reproduction of which Beckett kept in his room in his childhood home in Cooldrinagh. Knowlson, *Damned to Fame*, 682.
32 Knowlson lists Whistler's painting 'Mother', van Gogh's 'La Berceuse' and Rembrandt's 'Margaretha Trip (de Geer)' as possible analogues. Knowlson,

Damned to Fame, 662–3: 'Jack Yeats' painting of an old woman sitting by the window, with her head drooped low onto her chest, has something of the ambiguity of *Rockaby*'s closing moments. The picture, reproduced in the Yeats exhibition catalogue that was in Beckett's library, is entitled Sleep.' Jack B. Yeats, *The Charmed Life* (London: George Routledge & Sons, Ltd, 1938). Dirk van Hulle and Mark Nixon (directors), *Beckett Digital Manuscript Project*, technical realization Vincent Neyt, Centre for Manuscript Genetics University of Antwerp: beckettarchive.org.
33 Both words refer to the German words for watching: *schauen* and *gucken*.
34 ESTRAGON: If I could only sleep.
   VLADIMIR: Yesterday you slept. (*CDW*, 65)
35 The phrase conflates Ferdinand's address to Miranda, 'Admired Miranda,/ Indeed the top of admiration' (*T* 3.1.38–9), and Miranda's view of Ferdinand, 'I might call him/A thing divine, for nothing natural/I ever saw so noble' (*T* 1.2.416-18).
36 Cf. Chapter 4.
37 Ruby Cohn connects this phrase to Prospero's lines, 'We are such stuff as dreams are made on/And our little life is rounded by a sleep.' Ruby Cohn, *Modern Shakespeare Offshoots* (Princeton University Press), 377.
38 Sleeplessness is a fate shared by many of Shakespeare's tyrants like Richard III, who is cursed by Margaret, 'No sleep close up that deadly eye of thine' (*R III* 1.3.223), and who, contrary to Richmond, does not find rest in the night before the battle (*R III* 5.3).

Conclusion

Restlessness is a resistance to finality. Shakespeare and Beckett were restless writers. 'Parfois tu sais, [...] c'est pire de ne pas écrire que d'écrire',[1] Beckett told Raymond Federman in one of their last conversations. The necessity to write that is accompanied by a profound scepticism about the success story of an enlightened, humanist modernity is a stance shared by both Beckett and Shakespeare. Written on the edges of modernity, their works create and reflect on the very thresholds they represent. They articulate a restlessness between representation and what happens when representation becomes impossible.

Tragedies such as *King Lear*, which Beckett understatedly deemed 'unstageable',[2] foreground the limits of representation not only as a thematic part of the plot but also as structural and conceptual concerns of the entire play. In Beckett's plays, borders and edges acquire further metonymic significance. Many of them concentrate on central scenes in *King Lear*, prominently those on Dover cliff in Act IV, to elaborate on the experience of standing on a precipice, of blindness and of rising and falling. More than in Shakespeare, Beckett's variations on crawling and falling also metaphorically comment on the compositional process, the writer's desire to stop and his inability to do so. With Shakespeare, Beckett explores a theatre that verges on the worst, takes its medium to the edge of its capacities and then goes a step further, a theatre that presents and exceeds the very boundaries within which it operates.

The audience is included in the theatrical experience of encountering limits, when radio plays such as *Cascando* or *All That Fall* first of all create the uncertainty linked to the restriction of sensory perception but subsequently emphasize the importance of sound to constitute dramatic reality and unfold the potentiality of an imagination that relies on hearing. In the light of Beckett's experiments with 'voices coming from the dark' in his radio plays and in pieces such as *Company*, Edgar's staging of Gloucester's fall gains further significance as a critique of the reliance on the visual, as does Lear's advice to 'look with thine ears' (*KL* 4.1.145).

Beckett's dialogue with Shakespeare is often guided by the dialectical impulses of reduction and expansion. Single phrases such as '[t]he worst is not/So long as we can say "this is the worst"' (*KL* 4.1.27–8), or seemingly minor and inconspicuous moments such as Lear struggling with his boots, are used as metaphors to reflect on larger tragicomic predicaments such as Vladimir and Estragon's inability to move in *Waiting for Godot*. Beckett extracts minute scenes such as these and decontextualizes them to then reflect back on Shakespeare's lines, at times deflating some of their pathos: 'We are all born mad. Some remain so' (*CDW*, 75). This process both defamiliarizes readers and audiences with Shakespeare's text and offers them a synoptic view on the incongruences between the two versions, expanding the scope of their meaning. Vladimir's: 'What are we doing here, *that* is the question' (*CDW*, 74), extends Hamlet's dilemma to include a meta-theatrical reflection on their act of waiting for Godot and links it to Hamlet's procrastination and inability to act. In Beckett's dialogue with Shakespeare, words often become concepts, and are then translated into the dramatic reality of the plays and in turn grant new perspectives on Shakespeare's use of language.

Beckett works through Shakespeare, not around him. The process of inventing one's predecessors while also competing with them, is what he found in Joyce's creative interaction with Shakespeare. Joyce's command of language and his immanent aesthetics of reduction and re-composition inspired Beckett, who also read Shakespeare through these refigurations. In the 'Scylla and Charybdis' episode of *Ulysses*, Stephen Dedalus relates himself to Hamlet, and in examining the generation of literary afterlives the episode exhibits the very intertextual tradition into which it emphatically inserts itself. The excavations and dissections at work in the creative and destructive acts of inquiring into authorship, patrilineality and literary heritage are encapsulated in the metaphorical and metaleptic uses of the mole. The mole not only turns the attention to the miniature, as it were mole-cular level of language, but it also configures the relation of a text to its antecedent. The mole is both a birthmark and a marker of filial connection in *Cymbeline* and *Twelfth Night* and it also characterizes old Hamlet's ghost in its underground dwelling (*Ham* 1.5.164). Unlike Stephen Dedalus' 'mole on [his] right breast' (*U*, 159) in *Ulysses*, the mole in Beckett's *Murphy* is both a 'birthmark and a deathmark' (*Murphy*, 267), installing its own circular demise. In later works of Beckett, it becomes an epithet of the author, the 'crawling creator' (*Company*, 52), exemplifying and creating his own heritage.

In Shakespeare's and Beckett's art, the echo is central to a notion of poetry that is concerned with its own making. It also describes Shakespeare's metamorphoses in Beckett's works, which are configured by oppositional pairs that depend on and define one another. Ovid's metamorphosis of 'Echo and Narcissus' serves as a metaphor for textual processes of reverberation and reflection as well as for the creation of material and immaterial presences. Beckett's *Happy Days* and *Play* present characters who are, or are about to be, buried alive. In *Happy Days*, the increase of matter, of stones and earth, correlates with the fading of Winnie's immaterial voice into silence. Drawing on *Romeo and Juliet* and *Cymbeline*, Beckett metonymically creates tragic inevitability by means of theatrical materiality. His plays condense Shakespeare's plots into elementary components and subsequently extend them by way of a self-materialization of the text in the performance: a couple that cannot be united and characters that are paralysed by conventions and circumstances. Form and content converge as the play becomes what it is about. 'Happy days' also resonates back to our reading of Shakespeare's works, where his many uses of the phrase, especially in *Romeo and Juliet* and *Richard III*, obtain more sinister and ironical overtones.

Plays such as *Happy Days* not only combine spatial expanse and confinement but themselves are cast into an in-between state. Many of Beckett's plays, above all *Waiting for Godot*, create spaces of waiting and expectation. Among the many fictional topographies of these plays, it is the idea of purgatory that links them to both Dante and to Shakespeare. The invention of purgatory as a place of transcendence, by both Shakespeare and Beckett, in plays such as *Hamlet* or *The Lost Ones*, is transformed into textual immanence. On a conceptual level, the space of purgatory as an in-between realm also configures intertextual exchange, and presents a way of reflecting on the processes by which literary space is constructed. Purgatory invokes binarisms only to undermine them by leaving them in limbo, in a textual purgatory. Beckett's story 'Dante and the Lobster', which was not only inspired by Dante's *La Divina Commedia*, but also by Thomas McGreevy's poems and *Hamlet*, centres on the notions of paradox and pause. In bringing together a major poet, and a seemingly minor creature, pity and piety, life and death, it fashions itself into a liminal, purgatorial place in between the extremes – in a dialectics without synthesis.

Still lifes occupy liminal spaces in the visual arts, as well as in poetry and drama. They present and are set on the threshold between life and death, motion and standstill. Beckett, most of all in his later prose and drama, uses the still life as a reflection on the creation of a work of art while simultaneously performing the creative process as it were *in vivo*. In his dramatic *tableaux vivants*, the boundaries between life and death and self and other are permeable, giving way to a restless oscillation between the two. Prose pieces such as *Stirrings Still* explore this double-connectedness. Stasis in motion, a 'ghostly' stance of 'winter/Without journey' (*CDW*, 476) echoes Franz Schubert's song cycle *Winterreise* in Beckett's last play *What Where*. In treating doppelgangers, likenesses and faint resonances that dwell in the difference between the original and its replica, Beckett's texts partake in these very resonances.

Beckett's processes of reduction, in which texts are made to resemble still lifes, draws attention to Shakespeare's trajectories of regress. Forms of dispossession and displacement that approximate nothingness and death constitute the dramatic structure of *Timon of Athens* and *King Lear*. Lifelikeness that includes the ambivalence of an artistic still life is vital to *The Winter's Tale*, in which the boundary between life and death is transformed into one between life and art, manifesting itself in the theatrical resurrection of Hermione's statue. The minimalism of Beckett's shortest play, *Breath*, resonates with those sonnets of Shakespeare that, in reaching beyond their time and form, create poetic still lifes that evolve the notion of similarity in difference, of breath and death, and assert an infinity that resides in the ephemeral.

The interdependence of finitude and the infinite is pertinent to the 'sense of ending' in Shakespeare's and Beckett's 'endgames'. *The Tempest*, one of Shakepeare's latest plays, and Beckett's *Endgame* converge on a number of levels. The insularity and confinement of Prospero's 'cell' and the more abstract 'cell' of Beckett's upside-down and inside-out stage set present minimal worlds that gain metonymical scope for the plays as a whole. In its language games, its role play between characters, and its shifting master-and-servant-constellations, Beckett's *Endgame* creates many explicit links to *The Tempest*. Both plays produce variations on the idea of ending: in *The Tempest* it is protracted and in *Endgame* it becomes a performative, temporary and potentially repeatable act. Reading *The Tempest* through Beckett's central allusion to an endgame in chess, Shakespeare's play does not conform to the traditional view of it as his farewell to the stage; rather, Beckett's emphasis on chess invites us to review the chess scene between Miranda and Ferdinand – the new rulers playing, and cheating, at chess anticipates a somewhat chequered future, and chess also provides a backward-looking perspective that aligns their romance to the fate of their medieval forebears Tristan and Isolde. In both plays, the reference to chess has further conceptual and compositional significance because it indexes a closed symmetrical matrix that generates multiple moves.

Sleeping and waking not only structure plays such as *The Tempest* or *Waiting for Godot*, providing a frame and recurrent theme but sleep also reflects on forms of closure and on the staging of dramatic presence as a state between bodily presence and mental distance. Shakespeare, more extensively than Beckett, adheres to the poetic convention of figuring the play as a dream. The analogy of sleeping and dreaming to the act of watching a play further emphasizes the theatrical experience as transitional and creates viewing situations that engage and comment on the role of the audience. In *Happy Days* and *Waiting for Godot*, characters mention that they are being watched by someone, adding both reassuring and uncanny overtones to the Berkleyan hypothesis of *esse est percipi*. In *A Midsummer Night's Dream*, sleep and waking foregrounds the co-presence of different worlds and the simultaneity of different selves to introduce a double-vision in which something can be seen in terms of an other. Beckett's 'night-pieces' – *Nacht und Träume*, *Rockaby* or *Footfalls* – present likenesses and unquiet revenants in a theatre that resembles unconscious, dreamlike states of deep sleep. The bond between mother and daughter on which both *Rockaby* and *Footfalls* dwell reflects on the relation between secondary presences and the original in *The Winter's Tale*, where Hermione reappears as her own likeness to be united with her daughter. The eerie world of claustrophobic insomnia, in which Beckett's characters are neither dead nor alive finds a precedent in the sleepless world of *Macbeth*, a play in which the vulnerability of the sleeping monarch precipitates the nightmarish downward spiral of the protagonists, turning them into 'walking shadows' (*Mac* 5.5.23). Beckett's piece *Cascando* draws on Shakespeare's sleep imagery in *Macbeth* and *Hamlet* to perform the writer's sleepless efforts to finish a story. Insomnia characterizes the world of the text, and is seen as a permitting condition for its composition.

Beckett's texts, frequently at their endings, produce narratives that are self-effacing, pointing to their fictional construction. 'Dante and the Lobster' famously ends: '[I]t's a quick death. ...It is not' (*MPTK*, 21), and *Molloy* retracts the scene it had previously established: 'It is midnight. The rain is beating on the windows. It was not midnight. It was not raining' (*Molloy*, 176). Moving towards representation and away from it, implanting the element of difference into the text that, as a consequence, is and is not the same coherent entity, finds a parallel in instances where Shakespeare highlights the difference between actor and character. King Lear proclaims: 'This is not Lear' (*KL* 1.4.185), and only the fool, his shadow, a term that also refers to the actor playing Lear, can tell him who he is. '[T]hink this not Cressid' (*TC* 5.2.132), Troilus laments, and when both Iago in *Othello* and Viola in *Twelfth Night* confess: 'I am not what I am' (*Oth*, 1.1.66; *TN* 3.1.126) they speak a truth that only the audience can know. Likewise, in *All That Fall*, Mrs Rooney states: 'Don't take any notice of me. I do not exist. The fact is well known' (*CDW*, 179). Summarizing the actor's presence as simultaneously a non-presence, Peter Quince in *A Midsummer Night's Dream* deftly confirms: 'We are not here' (*MND* 5.1.115). In instances such as these, Shakespeare's and Beckett's texts install an element of self-differentiation that questions the nature of their very medium. This also implies writers' freedom to retreat from their creation and reminds audiences and readers that what we commonly consider well known and familiar can indeed never be unfamiliar enough.

The dialogue between Shakespeare and Beckett is an invitation to alterity and experiment that inspired many poets and dramatists after Beckett. The poems of Ann Carson take the afterlives of Shakespeare and Beckett into the twenty-first century. In the volume *Decreation*, the poem 'Her Beckett' begins 'Going to visit my mother is like starting in on a piece by Beckett'[3] and her 'Beckett's Theory of Tragedy' compresses single observations from Beckett's works and combines them with an allusion to *King Lear*: '(living moving mourning lamenting and howling incessantly)'.[4] 'Decreation' for Carson, similar to Beckett, becomes a creative act that reconsiders the categories with which we traditionally approach drama: 'What do we learn we learn to notice everything now'.

Harold Pinter and Tom Stoppard are the two dramatists best-known for drawing inspiration from Shakespeare and Beckett, reappropriating their works to create new meaning and dramatic form. Stoppard's *Dogg's Hamlet* and *Cahoot's Macbeth*, and most notably *Rosencrantz and Guildenstern Are Dead* engage with Shakespeare on many levels that are decidedly Beckettian. Stoppard thus creates further echoing effects when he takes Hamlet's most famous lines via Vladimir's meta-theatrical observation in *Waiting for Godot* – 'What are we doing here, *that* is the question?' (*CDW*, 74) – and reinserts them into his own recreation of Shakespeare's play from the point of view of two protagonists:

ROS   [...] Where's it going to end?
GUIL   That's the question.⁵

Shakespeare's plays often end and not much is well, yet they reach closure, however protracted, unfulfilled and far from promised their endings may be. Beckett's plays, by contrast, often end in the quivering restlessness of still lifes. While to some this presents the nightmare of an issueless world without end, to others it is a source of infinite play: 'VLADIMIR You're right, we're inexhaustible' (*CDW*, 58).

Notes

1 James and Elizabeth Knowlson (eds.), *Beckett Remembering, Remembering Beckett* (New York: Arcade, 2006), 304. In a letter to Alex Kaun, Beckett criticizes the poetry of Ringelnatz and voices a similar opinion: 'As a poet, however, he seemed to have been of Goethe's opinion: *better to write NOTHING than not to write*'. *Letters*, I, 9.7.1937, 517.
2 *Letters*, IV, 620, 07.10.1983 to Joseph Chaikin: 'When recently I reread Lear I thought: unstageable. I know I'm wrong.'
3 Anne Carson, *Decreation. Poetry, Essays, Opera* (New York: Knopf, 2005), 14.
4 Beckett's Theory of Tragedy
   Hegel on sacrifice. The animal dies. The man becomes alert.
   What do we learn we learn to notice everything now.
   We learn to say he is a hero let him do it.
   O is shown moving to the window.
   What a rustling what an evening. *Oh little actor*
   (living moving mourning lamenting and howling incessantly)
   Time to fly back to where they keep your skin.
   Frail was it.
   Sound of oar drawing away from shore.
   That tang of dogshit in darkness.
   That's your starry crown,
   Off with his hood.
   Anne Carson, *Decreation*, 15.
5 Tom Stoppard, *Rosencrantz and Guildenstern Are Dead* (London: Faber & Faber, 2000), 35.

Bibliography

Texts and Editions

Augustinus, Aurelius. *Confessiones Libri XIII. Corpus Christianorum Series Latina XXVI.* Turnhout: Brepols, 1981.
Alighieri, Dante. *La Commedia Secondo L'Antica Vulgata*, 4 vols., ed. Giorgio Petrocchi. Florence: Casa Ed. Le Lettere, 1994 [1966–1967].
The Divine Comedy Being the Vision of Dante Alighieri, transl. Henry Francis Cary. Oxford University Press, 1950.
The Divine Comedy, transl. C.H: Sisson. Oxford University Press, 2008.
Arnold, Matthew. *The Poems of Matthew Arnold*. London: Longman, 1979.
Beckett Digital Manuscript Project. ed. Dirk van Hulle, Mark Nixon and Vincent Neyt, (student library ed.) Veronica Bălă. Centre for Manuscript Genetics University of Antwerp: beckettarchive.org.
Beckett, Samuel. *Company*. London: Calder, 1980.
Company. Ill Seen Ill Said. Worstward Ho. Stirrings Still, ed. Dirk van Hulle. London: Faber & Faber, 2009.
The Complete Dramatic Works. London: Faber & Faber, 2006.
The Complete Shorter Prose 1929–1989, ed. S.E. Gontarski. New York: Grove, 1995.
Disjecta: Miscellaneous Writings and a Dramatic Fragment. London: John Calder, 1983.
Dream of Fair to Middling Women, ed. Eoin O'Brien and Edith Fournier. New York: Arcade, 1992.
Echo's Bones, ed. Mark Nixon. New York: Grove, 2014.
Echo's Bones, ed. Mark Nixon. London: Faber & Faber, 2014.
Endspiel. Fin de Partie. Endgame, transl. Elmar Tophoven, 16th ed. Frankfurt a. M.: Suhrkamp, 2013.
Film: Complete Scenario, Illustrations, Production Shots. New York: Grove Press, 1969.
How It Is, ed. Édouard Magessa O'Reilly. London: Faber & Faber, 2009.
Molloy, Malone Dies, The Unnamable. London, New York: John Calder, 1994.
More Pricks than Kicks, ed. Cassandra Nelson. London: Faber & Faber, 2010.
Murphy. New York: Grove, 1957.

Bibliography

Poems 1930–1989. London: John Calder, 2002.
Selected Poems 1930–1989. London: Faber & Faber, 2009.
Proust. New York, London: Grove, 1957.
Samuel Beckett's German Diaries 1936–1937, ed. Mark Nixon. New York: Continuum, 2011.
The Letters of Samuel Beckett, 4 vols., ed. Martha Dow Fehsenfeld et al. Cambridge University Press, 2009–2016.
The Theatrical Notebooks of Samuel Beckett: Volume II, Endgame, ed. S.E. Gontarski. London: Faber & Faber, 1992.
Watt. New York: Grove, 1953.
'Commentaries: Denis Devlin'. *transition,* 27 (April–May 1938), 289–94.
Book of Common Prayer, The. The Texts of 1549, 1559, and 1662, ed. Brian Cummings. Oxford University Press, 2011.
Borges, Jorge Luis. *Labyrinths: Selected Stories and Other Writings.* Harmondsworth: Penguin, 1970.
Burton, Robert. *The Anatomy of Melancholy,* ed. Floy Dell and Paul Jordan-Smith. New York: Tudor, 1931.
Carson, Anne. *Decreation: Poetry, Essays, Opera.* New York: Knopf, 2005.
Chaucer, Geoffrey. 'The Legend of Good Women' in Larry Benson (ed.), *The Riverside Chaucer,* 3rd ed. Oxford: Oxford University Press, 1998. 587–630.
'The Book of the Duchess' in Larry Benson (ed.), *The Riverside Chaucer,* 3rd ed. Oxford: Oxford University Press, 1998. 329–46.
'The Knight's Tale' in Larry Benson (ed.), *The Riverside Chaucer,* 3rd ed. Oxford: Oxford University Press, 1998. 37–66.
Cogan, Thomas. *The Haven of Health. Chiefly Gathered for the Comfort of Students and Consequences of All Those that Have a Care of Their Health, Amplified upon Five Words of Hippocrates.* London: Anne Griffin, 1636.
Denzinger, Heinrich. *Enchiridion Symbolorum et Deinitionum, que de Rebus Fidei et Morum A Conciliis Oecomenicis et summis Pontificibus emanarunt,* 7th ed. Würzburg, 1895.
Eliot, T.S. *Collected Poems 1909–1962.* London: Faber & Faber, 2002.
Dante. London: Faber & Faber, 1929.
Elizabethan Essays. New York: Haskel House, 1964.
'Hamlet and his Problems', in *The Sacred Wood: Essays on Poetry and Criticism.* London: Faber & Faber, 1920. 95–104.
Selected Prose of T.S. Eliot, ed. and intr. by Frank Kermode. London: Faber & Faber, 1975.
'Tradition and the Individual Talent', in *The Sacred Wood: Essays on Poetry and Criticism.* London: Faber & Faber, 1920. 47–59.
Freud, Sigmund. *Die Traumdeutung,* 8th ed. Frankfurt a. M.: Fischer, 2001.
Goethe, Johann Wolfgang. *Prometheus,* in *Goethes Werke. Hamburger Ausgabe.* 14 vols. ed. Erich Trunz. Hamburg: Wegener, 1948. 176–81.
'Shakespear und kein Ende!', in *Sämtliche Werke nach Epochen seines Schaffens.* ed. Karl Richter et al., vol. XI.ii, ed. Johannes John et al. Munich: Hanser, 1998. 173–86.

Wilhelm Meisters Lehrjahre, in *Sämtliche Werke nach Epochen seines Schaffens*. ed. Karl Richter et al., vol. V, ed. Hans-Jürgen Schings. Munich: Hanser, 2006.
'Zwischen beiden Welten', in *Ästhetische Schriften: 1816-1820. Über Kunst und Altertum I-II*. ed. Hendrik Birus. Frankfurt a. M.: Deutscher Klassiker Verlag, 1999.
Gottfried von Straßburg. *Gottfried's von Straßburg Tristan*, ed. Reinhold Bechstein. Leipzig: F.A. Brockhaus, 1893.
Hall, Peter. *Peter Hall's Diaries: The Story of a Dramatic Battle*, ed. John Goodwin. London: Hamish Hamilton, 1983.
Heine, Heinrich. *Buch der Lieder*. Hamburg: Hoffmann und Campe, 1827.
Herder, Johann Gottfried. 'Shakespear' in Hansjürgen Blinn (ed.), *Shakespeare-Rezeption. Die Diskussion um Shakespeare in Deutschland 1. Ausgewählte Texte von 1741-1788*. Berlin: Erich Schmidt, 1982. 104–19.
Von Deutscher Art und Kunst. Einige fliegende Blätter. Hamburg: Bode, 1773.
Holinshed, Raphael. *Holinshed's Chronicles of England, Scotland, and Ireland*, vol. IV. London: J. Johnson et al., 1807–1808.
Holy Bible. The Comprehensive Teacher's Bible. London: Bagster and Sons, n.d.
King James VI of Scotland and I of England. *Daemonologie in Forme of a Dialogue, Diuided into Three Books. Written by the High and Mightie Prince Iames by the Grace of God King of England, Scotland, France, and Ireland, Defender of the faith. & c.* London: William Cotton and Will Aspley, 1603.
Jolas, Eugène. 'The Revolution of Language and James Joyce'. *transition*, 11 (February 1928), 109–16.
Joyce, James. *A Portrait of the Artist as a Young Man*. London: Penguin, 1996.
Finnegans Wake. New York: Viking, 1959.
Occasional, Critical and Political Writings, ed. Kevin Barry. Oxford University Press, 2000.
The James Joyce Archive, 63 vols., ed. Michael Groden, Hans Walter Gabler, Walton Litz and Danis Rose. New York: Garland, 1977–1979.
The Letters of James Joyce, ed. Stuart Gilbert, vol. I. London: Faber & Faber, 1957.
Ulysses, ed. Jeri Johnson. Oxford University Press, 2008.
Ulysses, ed. Hans Walter Gabler. London: Bodley Head, 1986.
Keats, John. *Selected Letters of John Keats*, ed. Grant F. Scott. rev. ed. Cambridge, MA: Harvard University Press, 2005.
Léhar, Franz. *The Merry Widow*. London: Glocken, 2016.
Marvell, Andrew. 'On a Drop of Dew' in Nigel Smith (ed.). *The Poems of Andrew Marvell*. London: Longman, 2003, 39–42.
McGreevy, Thomas. 'A Note on Work in Progress'. *transition*, 12 (September 1928), 216–19.
Nicolas Poussin. Dublin: The Dolmen Press, 1960.
Poems. London: William Heinemann, 1934.
Milton, John. *Paradise Lost*, ed. Gordon Tesky. New York, London: Norton, 2005.

Bibliography

Schubert, Franz. *Franz Schubert: Neue Ausgabe sämtlicher Werke*, ed. Internationale Schubert-Gesellschaft, comp. by Walter Dürr. Kassel, Basel, Tours, London: Bärenreiter, 1979, vol. IVa [Lieder].
Shakespeare, William. *A Midsummer Night's Dream*, ed. R.A. Foakes. Cambridge University Press, 2003.
Antony and Cleopatra, ed. David Bevington. Cambridge University Press, 2005.
As You Like It, ed. Michael Hattaway. Cambridge University Press, 2021.
Cymbeline, ed. Martin Butler. Cambridge University Press, 2006.
Hamlet, Prince of Denmark, ed. Philip Edwards. Cambridge University Press, 2003.
King Henry V, ed. Andrew Gurr. Cambridge University Press, 2005.
King Richard II, ed. Andrew Gurr. Cambridge University Press, 2003.
King Richard III, ed. Janis Lull. Cambridge University Press, 2009.
Macbeth, ed. A.R. Braunmuller. Cambridge University Press, 2008.
Macbeth, ed. A.W. Verity, M.A. Cambridge University Press, 1922.
Measure for Measure, ed. Brian Gibbons. Cambridge University Press, 2006.
The Merchant of Venice, ed. M.M. Mahood. Cambridge University Press, 2003.
Othello, ed. Norman Sanders. Cambridge University Press, 2003.
Romeo and Juliet, ed. G. Blakemore Evans. Cambridge University Press, 2003.
The Sonnets, ed. G. Blakemore Evans. Cambridge University Press, 2006.
The Tempest, ed. David Lindley. Cambridge University Press, 2002.
The Tragedy of King Lear, ed. Jay L. Halio. Cambridge University Press, 2005.
The Winter's Tale, ed. Susan Snyder and Deborah T. Curren-Aquino. Cambridge University Press, 2007.
Timon of Athens, ed. Karl Klein. Cambridge University Press, 2001.
Troilus and Cressida, ed. Anthony B. Dawson. Cambridge University Press, 2003.
Twelfth Night, or What You Will, ed. Elizabeth Story Donno, intr. Penny Gay. Cambridge University Press, 2004.
Sidney, Philip. 'An Apology for Poetry' in G. Gregory (ed.), *Elizabethan Critical Essays I*. Oxford University Press, 1971. 148–207.
Miscellaneous Prose of Sir Philip Sidney, ed. Katherine Duncan-Jones and Jan van Dorsten. Oxford: Clarendon Press, 1973.
Stoppard, Tom. *Rosencrantz and Guildenstern Are Dead*. London: Faber & Faber, 2000.
Walter von der Vogelweide. *Leich, Lieder, Sangsprüche*, ed. Karl Lachmann, rev. Thomas Bein, 15th ed. Berlin, Boston: de Gruyter, 2013.
Woolf, Virginia. *Mrs. Dalloway*. London: Penguin, 1992.
The Diary of Virginia Woolf V, ed. Anne Olivier Bell and Andrew McNeillie. New York: Harcourt Brace Jovanovich, 1980.
To the Lighthouse. New York, London: Harcourt Brace Jovanovich, 1989.
'Craftsmanship' in *The Death of the Moth and Other Essays*. London: The Hogarth Press, 1942. 126–32.
Yeats, Jack B. *The Charmed Life*. London: George Routledge & Sons, Ltd, 1938.

Secondary Sources

Abbott, Porter H. *Beckett Writing Beckett: The Author in the Autograph*. Ithaca: Cornell University Press, 1996.
  'Beginning Again: The Post-Narrative Art of *Texts for Nothing* and *How It Is*' in John Pilling (ed.), *The Cambridge Companion to Beckett*. Cambridge University Press, 1994. 106–23.
Ackerley, Chris J. *Demented Particulars: The Annotated Murphy*. Edinburgh University Press [Journal of Beckett Studies Books], 2010 [2004].
  'The Uncertainty of Self: Samuel Beckett and the Location of Voice'. *Samuel Beckett Today/Aujourd'hui*, 14 (2004), 39–51.
Ackerley, Chris J. and Gontarski, S.E. (eds.). *The Grove Companion to Beckett*. New York: Grove, 2004.
Ackerman, Alan. *Seeing Things: From Shakespeare to Pixar*. University of Toronto Press, 2011.
Adler, Tony. 'Waiting for Hamlet: Tom Stoppard's Early, Beckettian Play at Writers' Theatre'. *Chicago Reader*, 5 November 2009.
Adorno, Theodor W. 'Trying to Understand *Endgame*' in Harold Bloom (ed.), *Modern Critical Interpretations: Samuel Beckett's* Endgame. New York: Chelsea House, 1988. 9–40.
  'Versuch, das Endspiel zu verstehen' in Theodor Adorno, *Versuch, das Endspiel zu verstehen. Aufsätze zur Literatur des 20. Jahrhunderts*. Frankfurt a. M.: Suhrkamp, 1973. 167–214.
Albright, Daniel. *Beckett and Aesthetics*. Cambridge University Press, 2003.
  Representation and the Imagination: Beckett, Kafka, Nabokov, and Schoenberg. University of Chicago Press, 1981.
Alekhine, Alexander. *My Best Games of Chess 1924–1937*. London: G. Bell and Sons, 1949 [1939].
Alsop, Derek. 'Playing on: Chess and its Metaphors in the Life and Work of Samuel Beckett'. *Critical Quarterly*, 54 (2012), 26–40.
Althaus, Peter. 'Luthers Gedanken über die Letzten Dinge'. *Luther Jahrbuch*, 23 (1941), 9–34.
Anderton, Joseph. *Beckett's Creatures: Art of Failure After the Holocaust*. London: Bloomsbury, 2016.
  '"Living Flesh": The Human–Nonhuman Proximity in Beckett's Four Stories'. *Samuel Beckett Today/Aujourd'hui*, 32 (2020), 192–206.
Anspaugh, Kelly. '"Faith, Hope and – What is it?": Beckett Reading Joyce Reading Dante'. *Journal of Beckett Studies*, (n.s.) 5.1 & 2 (1995/1996), 19–38.
Atik, Anne. *How It Was: A Memoir of Samuel Beckett*. London: Faber & Faber, 2001.
Badiou, Alain. *On Beckett*, ed. Nina Power and Alberto Toscano. Manchester: Clinamen, 2003.
Barale, Michèle Aina and Rubin Rabinovitz. *A KWIC Concordance to Samuel Beckett's Murphy*. New York, London: Garland, 1990.

Barthes, Roland. 'The Death of the Author' in Roland Barthes (ed.), *Image – Music – Text*, selected and trans. by Stephen Heath. London: Fontana Press, 1982. 142–8.
Roland Barthes, trans. by Richard Howard. New York: Hill and Wang, 1977.
Barone, Rosangela. 'On the Route of a Walking Shadow: Samuel Beckett's *Come and Go*'. *Études Irlandaises: Revue Française d'Histoire, Civilisation et Litterature de l'Irelande*, 10 (1985), 117–28.
Barton, Anne. 'Shakespeare and the Limits of Language'. *Shakespeare Survey*, 24 (1971), 19–30.
Bate, Jonathan. *Shakespeare and Ovid*. Oxford University Press, 1993.
'Shakespeare's Islands' in Tom Clayton, Susan Brock and Vicente Forés (eds.), *Shakespeare and the Mediterranean*. Newark: University of Delaware Press, 2004. 289–308.
Bates, Julie. *Samuel Beckett and the Art of Salvage*. Cambridge University Press, 2017.
Begam, Richard. *Samuel Beckett and the End of Modernity*. Stanford University Press, 1996.
Benn, Tony. *Years of Hope: Diaries, Paper and Letters 1940–1962*, ed. Ruth Winstone. London: Hutchinson, 1994.
Benjamin, Walter. 'Central Park', Selected Writings, vol. IV [1938–1940], ed. Howard Eiland and Michael W. Jennings. Cambridge, MA: Belknap, 2003. 161–99.
The Arcades Project, ed. Rolf Tiedemann, trans. Howard Eiland and Kevin McLaughlin. Cambridge, MA: Belknap Press, 1999.
Ben-Zvi, Linda. 'Samuel Beckett, Fritz Mautner, and the Limits of Language'. *PMLA*, 95.2 (1980), 183–200.
Women in Beckett: Performance and Critical Perspectives. Urbana: University of Illinois Press, 1990.
Berlin, Normand. 'Beckett and Shakespeare'. *French Review*, 40.5 (1967), 647–51.
'Beyond Beckett = Before Beckett' in Bruce Stewart (ed.), *Beckett and Beyond*. Gerrards Cross, England: Smythe, 1999. 16–22.
'Traffic of Our Stage: Why *Waiting for Godot*?'. *Massachusetts Review*, 40.3 (1999), 420–34.
Bevington, David. 'Asleep Onstage' in John A. Alford (ed.), *From Page to Performance: Essays in Early English Drama*. East Lansing: Michigan State University Press, 1995. 51–83.
'Conclusion. The Evil of "Medieval"' in Ruth Morse, Helen Cooper and Peter Holland (eds.), *Medieval Shakespeare: Pasts and Presents*. Cambridge University Press, 2013. 232–7.
Bies, Frank. *Republik der Angst. Eine andere Geschichte der Bundesrepublik*. Reinbek: Rowohlt, 2019.
Bishop, Tom. 'Blin on Beckett: Interviewed by Tom Bishop' in Stanley E. Gontarski (ed. and introd.), *On Beckett: Essays and Criticism*. New York: Grove, 1986. 226–35.

Bizub, Edward. 'Beckett's Boots: The Crux of Meaning'. *Samuel Beckett Today/ Aujourd'hui*, 25 (2013), 267–78.
Blau, Herbert. *Sails of the Herring Fleet: Essays on Beckett*. Ann Arbor: University of Michigan Press, 2000.
Bloom, Gina. 'Time to Cheat: Chess and *The Tempest*'s Performative History of Dynastic Marriage' in Valeria Traub (ed.), *The Oxford Handbook of Shakespeare and Embodiment: Gender, Sexuality and Race*. Oxford University Press, 2016. 419–34.
Blumenberg, Hans. *Die Legitimität der Neuzeit*. Frankfurt a. M.: Suhrkamp, 1988.
Boehm, Gottfried. *Was ist ein Bild?* Munich: Fink, 2006.
Boehm, Gottfried and Helmut Pfotenhauer. *Beschreibungskunst, Kunstbeschreibung: Ekphrasis von der Antike bis zur Gegenwart*. Munich: Fink, 1995.
Boitani, Piero. 'Irish Dante: Yeats, Joyce, Beckett' in Manuele Gragnolati, Fabio Camilletti and Fabian Lampart (eds.), *Metamorphosing Dante: Approximations, Manipulations and Rewritings in the Twentieth and Twenty-First Centuries [Cultural Inquiry 2]*. Vienna: Turia + Kant, 2011. 37–59.
Bonnefoy, Yves. 'A Seascape, a Landscape'. *New England Review*, 31.1 (2010), 99–102.
Bostridge, Ian. *Schubert's Winter Journey: Anatomy of an Obsession*. London: Faber & Faber, 2015.
Bosworth, C.E., E. Donzel and W.P. Heinrichs (eds.). *Encyclopedia of Islam*, vol. IX. Leiden: Brill, 1997.
Bradley, A.C. *Shakespearean Tragedy*. London: Macmillan, 1904.
Brater, Enoch. 'Beckett's Shades of the Color Gray'. *Samuel Beckett Today/ Aujourd'hui*, 21 (2010), 103–16.
  'Fragments and Beckett's Form in *That Time* and *Footfalls*'. *Journal of Beckett Studies*, 2 (1977), 70–81.
  'The Company Beckett Keeps: The Shape of Memory and One Fabulist's Decay of Lying' in Morris Beja, S.E. Gontarski and Pierre Astier (eds.), *Samuel Beckett: Humanistic Perspectives*. Columbus: Ohio State University Press, 1983. 157–71.
  'The Seated Figure on Beckett's Stage' in S.E. Gontarski (ed.), *A Companion to Samuel Beckett*. Chichester: Wiley-Blackwell, 2010. 346–57.
  (ed.) *The Theatrical Gamut: Notes for a Post-Beckettian Stage*. Ann Arbor: University of Michigan Press, 1995.
Breuer, Horst. 'Disintegration of Time in Macbeth's Soliloquy "Tomorrow, and Tomorrow, and Tomorrow"'. *Modern Language Review*, 71 (1976), 256–71.
Bronfen, Elizabeth. 'Afterword', in Tobias Döring and Ewan Fernie (eds.), *Thomas Mann and Shakespeare: Something Rich and Strange*. London: Bloomsbury, 2015. 246–56.
Brook, Peter. '*Endgame* as *King Lear*, or How to Stop Worrying and Love Beckett'. *Encore*, 12.1 (Jan–Feb 1965), 8–12.
  'For Jan Kott'. *New Theatre Quarterly*, 10 (1994), 303–4.

The Shifting Point: Forty Years of Theatrical Exploration 1946–1987. London: Bloomsbury Methuen Drama, 1989.
Brown, John Russell. 'Mr. Beckett's Shakespeare'. *Critical Quarterly*, 5 (1963), 310–26.
Brown, Paul. '"This thing of darkness I acknowledge mine": *The Tempest* and the Discourse of Colonialism' in Jonathan Dollimore and Alan Sinfield (eds.), *Political Shakespeare: New Essays in Cultural Materialism*. Manchester University Press, 1994. 48–71.
Bryden, Mary. 'Beckett and the Dynamic Still' in Anthony Uhlmann, Sjief Houppermans and Bruno Clément (eds.), *Samuel Beckett Today/Aujourd'hui*, (1994), 179–92.
Byron, Mark. 'English Literature' in Anthony Uhlmann (ed.), *Samuel Beckett in Context*. Cambridge University Press, 2013. 218–28.
Campbell, Julie. 'Allegories of Clarity and Obscurity: Bunyan's *The Pilgrim's Progress* and Beckett's *Molloy*'. *Samuel Beckett Today/Aujourd'hui*, 24 (2012), 89–103.
Carey, Phyllis. 'Stephen Dedalus, Belacqua Shuah, and Dante's Pietà' in Phyllis Carey and Ed Jewinski (eds.), *RE: Joyce'n Beckett*. New York: Fordham University Press, 1992. 104–16.
Carville, Conor. *Samuel Beckett and the Visual Arts*. Cambridge University Press, 2018.
Caselli, Daniela. *Beckett's Dantes: Intertextuality in the Fiction and Criticism*. Manchester University Press, 2005.
(ed.), *Beckett and Nothing: Trying to Understand Beckett*. Manchester University Press, 2010.
Cavell, Stanley. *Disowning Knowledge: Seven Plays of Shakespeare*. Cambridge University Press, 2003.
'Ending the Waiting Game: A Reading of Beckett's *Endgame*' in *Must We Mean What We Say?* Cambridge University Press, 2015. 115–62.
Cerrato, Laura. 'Postmodernism and Beckett's Aesthetics of Failure'. *Samuel Beckett Today/Aujourd'hui*, 2 (1993), 21–30.
Chattopadhyay, Arka. '"Worst in Need of Worse": *King Lear*, *Worstward Ho* and the Trajectory of Worsening'. *Samuel Beckett Today/Aujourd'hui*, 24 (2012), 73–87.
Clare, Janet, *Shakespeare's Stage Traffic: Imitation, Borrowing and Competition in Renaissance Theatre*. Cambridge University Press, 2014.
Cohn, Ruby. *A Beckett Canon*. Ann Arbor: University of Michigan Press, 2001.
Back to Beckett. Princeton University Press, 1973.
'Beckett and Shakespeare'. *Modern Drama*, 15 (1972), 223–30.
'Beckett's Theater Resonance' in Morris Beja, S.E. Gontarski and Pierre Astier (eds.), *Samuel Beckett: Humanistic Perspectives*. Columbus: Ohio State University Press, 1983. 3–16.
Ghosting through Beckett, Beckett in the 1990s, ed. Marius Buning and Lois Oppenheim. Amsterdam: Rodopi, 1993, 1–11.
Just Play: Beckett's Theater. Princeton University Press, 1980.

Modern Shakespeare Offshoots. Princeton University Press, 1976.
Samuel Beckett: The Comic Gamut. New Brunswick: Rutgers University Press, 1962.
'The Tempest of an *Endgame*'. *Symposion* XIX 4 (Winter 1965), 328–34.
Connor, Steven. 'Beckett's Atmospheres' in S.E. Gontarski and Anthony Uhlmann (eds.), *Beckett After Beckett*. Gainesville: University of Florida Press, 2006. 52–65.
Beckett, Modernism and the Material Imagination. Cambridge University Press, 2014.
Samuel Beckett: Repetition, Theory and the Text. Oxford: Blackwell, 1988.
Critchley, Simon. *Very Little . . . Almost Nothing: Death, Philosophy, Literature*. London, New York: Routledge, 1997.
Cronin, Anthony. *Samuel Beckett: The Last Modernist*. London: HarperCollins, 1996.
DaSilva, Gregorio. *Intersections between Shakespeare and Beckett on Stage, Screen and Page*. Dissertation, University of Birmingham, 2017.
De Grazia, Margareta. Hamlet *without Hamlet*. Cambridge University Press, 2008.
Deleuze, Gilles. *Essays Clinical and Critical*, transl. Daniel W. Smith and Michael A. Greco. London, New York: Verso, 1998.
Dent, R.W. 'Imagination in *A Midsummer Night's Dream*'. *Shakespeare Quarterly*, 15.2 (1964), 115–29.
Derrida, Jacques. *Acts of Literature*, ed. Derek Attridge. London, New York: Routledge, 1992.
Writing and Difference, transl., introd. and add. notes by Alan Bass. London: Routledge and Kegan Paul, 1978.
Döring, Tobias and Virginia Mason Vaughan (eds.). *Critical and Cultural Transformations: Shakespeare's* The Tempest *– 1611 to the Present*. Tübingen: Narr, 2013.
Drew, Anne Marie (ed.), *Past Crimson, Past Woe: The Shakespeare-Beckett Connection*. New York, London: Garland, 1993.
Tragicomic Fools in Shakespeare and Beckett. *DAI*, 1987.
Durantave, Leland de la. *Beckett's Art of Mismaking*. Cambridge, MA, London: Harvard University Press, 2016.
Ellmann, Richard. *James Joyce*. New York: Oxford University Press, 1982.
Elsom, John. *Cold War Theatre*. London, New York: Routledge, 1992.
Eltis, Sos. '"It's All Symbiosis": Peter Gall Directing Beckett' in David Tucker and Trish McTighe (eds.), *Staging Beckett in Great Britain*. London, Oxford, New York, New Delphi, Sydney: Bloomsbury Methuen Drama, 2016. 87–104.
Encyclopedia Britannica: britannica.com.
Esslin, Martin. 'Introduction' in Martin Esslin (ed.), *Samuel Beckett: A Collection of Critical Essays*. Englewood Cliffs: Prentice Hall, 1965. 1–15.
The Theatre of the Absurd. Harmondsworth: Penguin, 1961.

Estok, Simon C. 'The Ecocritical Unconscious: Early Modern Sleep as "Go-Between"' in *Ecocriticism and Shakespeare: Reading Ecophobia*. New York: Palgrave, 2011. 111–21.
Federman, R. 'Beckett's Belacqua and the Inferno of Society'. *Arizona Quarterly*, 20 (1964), 231–41.
Feldman, Matthew. *Beckett's Books: A Cultural History of the Interwar Notes*. London: Continuum, 2006.
Felperin, Howard. *Shakespearean Romance*. Princeton University Press, 1972.
Ferrell, Lori Anne. 'Religion' in Bruce R. Smith (ed.), *The Cambridge Guide to the Worlds of Shakespeare*, vol. I. Cambridge University Press, 2016. 681–760.
Fitzsimons, Andrew. '"What Wretches Feel": Lear, Edgar and Samuel Beckett's *Worstward Ho*' in Graham Bradshaw and Tom Bishop (eds.), *The Shakespearean International Yearbook 7. Special Section, Updating Shakespeare*. Aldershot: Ashgate, 2007. 256–71.
Foakes, R.A. '*King Lear* and *Endgame*'. *Shakespeare Survey*, 55 (2002), 153–8.
Foster, Verna. 'Beckett's Winter's Tale: Tragicomic Transformation in Ohio Impromptu'. *Journal of Beckett Studies*, 1.1–2 (1992), 67–75.
Foucault, Michel. 'What is an Author?' in James D. Faubion (ed.), *Aesthetics, Method and Epistemology*, trans. by Robert Hurley et al. New York: The New Press, 1999. 205–22.
Fowlie, Wallace. 'Dante and Beckett' in Stuart McDougal (ed.), *Dante Among the Moderns*. Chapel Hill: University of North Carolina Press, 1985. 129–52.
Furbank, P.N. 'Beckett's Purgatory'. *Encounter*, 22 (1964), 69–72.
Garber, Marjorie. *Shakespeare After All*. New York: Anchor Books, 2004.
'"The rest is silence". Ineffability and the "Unscene" in Shakespeare's Plays' in Peter S. Hawkins, Anne Howland Schotter and Allen Mandelbaum (eds.), *Ineffability: Naming the Unnamable from Dante to Beckett*. New York: AMS, 1984. 35–50.
Garner, Stanton B. Jr. '"Still Living Flesh": Beckett, Merleau-Ponty, and the Phenomenological Body'. *Theatre Journal*, 45.4 (1993), 443–60.
Giles, Jana Maria. 'The Aesthetics of Relinquishment: Natural and Social Contracts in Beckett's *The End*'. *Samuel Beckett Today/Samuel Beckett Aujourd'hui*, 20 (2008), 175–88.
Gluck, Barbara Reich. *Beckett and Joyce: Friendship and Fiction*. Lewisburg, London: Bucknell University Press/Associated University Press, 1979.
Gontarski, S.E. 'A Sense of Unending: Samuel Beckett's Eschatological Turn'. *Samuel Beckett Today/Samuel Beckett Aujourd'hui*, 21 (2009), 135–49.
Beckett Matters: Essays on Beckett's Late Modernism. Edinburgh University Press, 2017.
Creative Involution: Bergson, Beckett, Deleuze. Edinburgh University Press, 2015.
'"I Think This does Call for a Firm Stand." Beckett at the Royal Court' in David Tucker and Trish McTighe (eds.), *Staging Beckett in Great Britain*. London, Oxford, New York, New Delphi, Sydney: Bloomsbury Methuen Drama, 2016. 21–36.

'Literary Allusions in *Happy Days*' in S.E. Gontarski (ed. and intr.), *On Beckett*. London: Anthem Press, 2012. 232–44.
The Intent of Undoing in Samuel Beckett's Dramatic Texts. Bloomington: University of Indiana Press, 1985.
(ed.) *A Companion to Samuel Beckett*. Oxford: Wiley Blackwell, 2010.
(ed.) *The Beckett Critical Reader: Archives, Theories and Translations*. Edinburgh University Press, 2012.
(ed.) *The Edinburgh Companion to Samuel Beckett and the Arts*. Edinburgh University Press, 2014.
Gontarski, S.E. and Uhlmann, Anthony (eds.). *Beckett after Beckett*. Gainesville: University of Florida Press, 2006.
Grady, Hugh. *Shakespeare and Modernity*. London: Routledge, 2000.
Graver, Lawrence. *Waiting for Godot*. Cambridge University Press, 2004.
Greenblatt, Stephen. *Hamlet in Purgatory*. Princeton University Press, 2001.
'Learning to Curse: Aspects of Linguistic Colonisation in the Sixteenth Century' in Fredi Chiappelli (ed.), *First Images of America: The Impact of the New World on the Old*. Berkeley: University of California Press, 1976. 561–80.
Learning to Curse: Essays in Early Modern Culture. London: Routledge, 2006.
Goldberg, Jonathan. *Voice Terminal Echo: Postmodernism and English Renaissance Texts*. New York: Methuen, 1986.
Guggenheim, Peggy. *Out of this Century: Confessions of an Art Addict*. London: Deutsch, 2005.
Gunn, Dan. 'Samuel Beckett' in Adrian Poole (ed. and intr.), *Joyce, T.S. Eliot, Auden, Beckett: Great Shakespeareans Volume XII*. New York: Continuum, 2012. 149–97.
Habermas, Jürgen. 'Das Zeitbewußtsein der Moderne und ihr Bedürfnis nach Selbstvergewisserung' in *Der Philosophische Diskurs der Moderne: Zwölf Vorlesungen*. Frankfurt a. M.: Suhrkamp, 1989. 9–33.
'Hegels Begriff der Moderne' in *Der Philosophische Diskurs der Moderne: Zwölf Vorlesungen*. Frankfurt a. M.: Suhrkamp, 1989. 34–58.
Habicht, Werner. '"And Mock Our Eyes with Air": Air and Stage Illusion in Shakespearean Drama' in Frederick Burwick and Walter Paper (Eds.), *Aesthetic Illusion: Theoretical and Historical Approaches*. Berlin: de Gruyter, 1990. 301–12.
'Becketts Baum und Shakespeares Wälder'. *Shakespeare-Jahrbuch*, 106 (1970), 77–98.
Hackett, Helen. 'Dream-Visions of Elizabeth I' in Katharina Hidgkin, Michelle O'Callaghan and S.J. Wiseman (eds.), *Reading the Early Modern Dream: The Terrors of the Night*. New York: Routledge, 2008. 58–61.
Hainsworth, J.D. 'Shakespeare, Son of Beckett?' *Modern Language Quarterly*, 25 (1964), 346–55.
Hall, A. 'Tycho Brahe's New Star'. *Science* 1, 23 (1880), 271–5.
Hall, Peter. *Exposed by the Mask: Form and Language in Drama*. London: Oberon Books, 2010.

Hall, Ronald. 'Sleeping through Shakespeare'. *Shakespeare in Southern Africa*, 12 (1999/2000), 24-32.
Halpern, Richard. 'After Beckett' in Richard Halpern (ed.), *Eclipse of Action. Tragedy and Political Economy*. University of Chicago Press, 2017, 255-73.
'Beckett's Tragic Pantry', in Richard Halpern (ed.), *Eclipse of Action: Tragedy and Political Economy*. University of Chicago Press, 2017. 226-55.
Shakespeare among the Moderns. Ithaca, London: Cornell University Press, 1997.
Handley, Sasha. *Sleep in Early Modern England*. New Haven: Yale University Press, 2016.
Harmon, Maurice (ed.). *No Author Better Served: The Correspondence of Samuel Beckett and Alan Schneider*. Cambridge, MA: Harvard University Press, 1998.
Harries, Martin. *Scare Quotes from Shakespeare: Marx, Keynes, and the Language of Reenchantment*. Stanford University Press, 2000.
Harris, T.J.G. '*Lear, Godot, Waste* and Other Plays'. *PN Review*, 24.4 [120] (1998), 55-58.
Harvey, Lawrence. *Samuel Beckett: Poet and Critic*. Princeton University Press, 1970.
Hennessy, Peter. *Having It So Good: Britain in the Fifties*. London: Penguin, 2007 [2006].
Hill, Leslie. *Beckett's Fiction: In Different Words*. Cambridge University Press, 1990.
Hinden, Michael. 'After Beckett: The Plays of Pinter, Stoppard, and Shepard'. *Contemporary Literature*, 27.3 (1986), 400-8.
Hird, Alastair. '"What does it Matter Who is Speaking": Beckett, Foucault, Barthes'. *Samuel Beckett Today/Aujourd'hui*, 22 (2010), 289-99.
Höfele, Andreas. 'Erwachen in Shakespeares *A Midsummer Night's Dream*'. *Archiv für das Studium der Neueren Sprachen und Literaturen*, 228 (1991), 41-51.
No Hamlets: German Shakespeare from Nietzsche to Carl Schmitt. Oxford University Press, 2016.
Hollander, John. *The Figure of Echo: A Mode of Allusion in Milton and After*. Berkeley: University of California Press, 1981.
Holland, Peter. 'Dreams and the Play's Structure' in Stephen P. Thomason (ed.), *Readings on* A Midsummer Night's Dream. San Diego: Greenhaven Press, 2011. 84-90.
Hulle, Dirk van. 'Adorno's Notes on *Endgame*'. *Journal of Beckett Studies*, 19.2 (2010), 196-217.
'Beckett and Shakespeare on Nothing, or, Whatever Lurks behind the Veil'. *Limit(e) Beckett*, 1 (2010), 123-36.
'Beckett's Principle of Reversibility: Chiasmus and the "Shape of Ideas"'. *Samuel Beckett Today/Aujourd'hui*, 21 (2009), 179-93.
'Undoing Dante: Samuel Beckett's Poetics from a Textual Perspective'. *Text*, 16 (2006), 87-95.
Hulle, Dirk van and Nixon, Mark. *Samuel Beckett's Library*. Cambridge University Press, 2013.

Hulle, van, Dirk and Pim Verhulst. *The Making of Beckett's* En attendant Godot/ Waiting for Godot. London: Bloomsbury, 2017.
Iser, Wolfgang. 'Counter-Sensical Comedy and Audience Response in Beckett's Waiting for Godot' in Steven Connor (ed.), *New Casebooks: Waiting for Godot and* Endgame. Basingstoke: Macmillan, 1992. 55–70.
  The Implied Reader: Patterns of Communication in Prose Fiction from Bunyan to Beckett. Baltimore: Johns Hopkins University Press, 1974.
  'The Pattern of Negativity in Beckett's Prose' in Harold Bloom (ed.), *Samuel Beckett: Modern Critical Views*. Philadelphia: Chelsea House Publishers, 1985. 140–51.
Judt, Tony. *Postwar: A History of Germany since 1945*. London: Random House Vintage, 2010 [2005].
Juliet, Charles. *Conversations with Samuel Beckett and Bram van Velde*, transl. Tracy Cooke and Axel Nesme. London: Dalkey, 2009.
  Rencontre avec Beckett. Paris: Fata Morgana, 1986.
Katz, Daniel. 'What Remains of Beckett: Evasion and History' in Ulrika Maude and Matthew Feldman (eds.), *Beckett and Phenomenology*. London: Continuum, 2009. 144–57.
Kenner, Hugh. *A Reader's Guide to Samuel Beckett*. London: Thames and Hudson, 1973.
  Flaubert, Joyce and Beckett: The Stoic Comedians. London: W.H. Allen, 1964.
  '"Life in the Box": Twentieth-Century Interpretations of *Endgame*' in Bell Gale Chevigny (ed. and introd.), *A Collection of Critical Essays*. Englewood Cliffs: Prentice Hall, 1969. 53–60.
  Samuel Beckett: A Critical Study. London: Calder, 1962.
Kermode, Frank. *The Sense of an Ending: Studies in the Theory of Fiction with a New Epilogue.* Oxford University Press, 2000.
Kiberd, Declan. 'Shakespeare and Company: *Hamlet* in Kildare Street', in Janet Clare (ed.), *Shakespeare and the Irish Writer*. University College Dublin Press, 2010. 95–106.
Knight, Wilson G., *Shakespearian Dimensions*. Brighton: Harvester, 1984.
  The Wheel of Fire. London: Routledge, 2001 [1930].
Knowlson, James. 'Beckett and Seventeenth-Century Dutch and Flemish Art'. *Samuel Beckett Today/Aujourd'hui*, 21 (2009), 27–44.
  Damned to Fame. The Life of Samuel Beckett. London: Bloomsbury, 1997.
  Happy Days: Samuel Beckett's Production Notebook. New York: Grove, 1957.
  Light and Darkness in the Theatre of Samuel Beckett: Text of a Public Lecture Delivered at Trinity College, Dublin, on February 7th, 1972. London: Turret, 1972.
  'Practical Aspects of Theatre, Radio, and Television: Extracts from an Unscripted Interview with Billie Whitelaw'. *Journal of Beckett Studies*, 3 (1978), 85–91.
Knowlson, James and John Pilling. *Frescoes of the Skull: The Late Prose and Drama of Samuel Beckett.* London: John Calder, 1979.
Knowlson, James, and Elizabeth Knowlson (eds.). *Beckett Remembering, Remembering Beckett.* New York: Arcade, 2006.

Kott, Jan. *Shakespeare our Contemporary*, transl. Boleslaw Taborski, pref. by Peter Brook. London: Methuen, 1965.
Kristeva, Julia. 'Bakhtine, le Mot, le Dialogue et le Roman'. *Critique*, 23.4 (Avril 1967), 438–65.
'Postmodernism?' *Bucknell Review*, 25 (1980), 136–41.
'Word, Dialogue and Novel' in Toril Moi (ed.), *The Kristeva Reader*. New York: Columbia University Press, 1986. 34–61.
Kumar, Jeevan K. 'The Chess Metaphor in Samuel Beckett's *Endgame*'. *Modern Drama*, 40.4 (1997), 540–52.
Kutschera, Franz, *Ästhetik*, 2nd ed. repr. Berlin: de Gruyter, 2010 [1998].
Loughrey, Bryan and Neil Taylor. 'Ferdinand and Miranda at Chess'. *Shakespeare Survey*, 35 (1982), 113–18.
Lawly, Paul. '"The Grim Journey": Beckett Listens to Schubert'. *Samuel Beckett Today/Aujourd'hui*, 11 (2001), 255–66.
Lehmann, Hans-Thies. *Postdramatisches Theater*. Frankfurt a. M.: Verlag der Autoren, 1999.
LeGoff, Jaques. *La Naissance du Purgatoire*. Paris: Gallimard, 1981.
Un autre Moyen Âge. Paris: Gallimard, 1999.
Levenson, Jill L. 'Stoppard's Shakespeare' in Katherine E. Kelly (ed.), *The Cambridge Companion to Stoppard*. Cambridge University Press, 2006. 154–70.
Lewin, Jennifer. '"Your Actions are My Dreams": Sleepy Minds in Shakespeare's Last Plays'. *Shakespeare Studies*, 31 (2003), 184–204.
Liebow, Cynthia. 'Shakespeare, Beckett and Pinter' in Brigitte Gauthier (ed.), *Viva Pinter: Harold Pinter's Spirit of Resistance*. Oxford: Peter Lang, 2009, 111–18.
Lloyd, David. *Beckett's Thing*. Edinburgh University Press, 2016.
Lobsien, Eckhard. *Der Alltag des Ulysses. Die Vermittlung von Ästhetischer und Lebensweltlicher Erfahrung*. Stuttgart: J.B. Metzler, 1978.
Long, Joseph. 'Divine Intertextuality: Samuel Beckett, *Company*, *Le Dépeupleur*'. *Samuel Beckett Today/Aujourd'hui*, 9 (2000), 145–57.
Loomba, Anja. 'Shakespeare and Cultural Difference' in Terence Hawkes (ed.), *Alternative Shakespeares*, vol. II. London: Routledge, 1996, 164–91.
Lupton, Julia. 'Creature Caliban'. *Shakespeare Quarterly*, 51 (2000), 1–23.
Lyons, Charles R. 'Beckett, Shakespeare, and the Making of Theory' in Enoch Brater and Ruby Cohn (eds.), *Around the Absurd: Essays on Modern and Postmodern Drama*. Ann Arbor: University of Michigan Press, 1990. 97–127.
MacGregor, Neil. *Shakespeare's Restless World*. London: Allen Lane, 2012.
Marshall, David. 'Exchanging Visions: Reading *A Midsummer Night's Dream*' in Harold Bloom (ed.), *William Shakespeare's* A Midsummer's Night's Dream: *Modern Critical Interpretations*. New York: Chelsea House. 87–115.
Marshall, Peter. *Beliefs and the Dead in Reformation England*. Oxford University Press, 2002.
'The Reformation of Hell? Protestant and Catholic Infernalism in England c.1560–1640'. *Journal of Ecclesiastical History*, 61 (2010), 279–98.

Matthews, Steven. 'Beckett's Late Style' in Steven Barfield, Matthew Feldman and Philip Tew (eds.), *Beckett and Death*. London: Continuum, 2009. 188–205.
Mayer, Hans. 'Shakespeare – von Beckett her verstanden', *Die Zeit*, 1 May 1964.
Mayoux, Jean Jacques. 'The Theatre of Samuel Beckett'. *Perspective*, (1959), 142–55.
Mazzio, Carla. 'The History of Air. *Hamlet* and the Trouble with Instruments'. *South Central Review*, 26.1–2 (2009), 153–96.
McCarthy, Patrick A. (ed.). *Critical Essays on Samuel Beckett*. Boston: Hall, 1986.
McCourt, John. 'Joyce's Shakespeare. A View from Trieste' in Laura Pelaschiar (ed.), *Joyce/Shakespeare*. New York: Syracuse University Press, 2015. 72–88.
McMullan, Anna and S.E. Wilmer (eds.). *Reflections on Beckett: A Centenary Celebration*. Ann Arbor: University of Michigan Press, 2009.
Menke, Christoph. 'Tragödie und Skeptizismus. Zu *Hamlet*'. *DVJS*, 75/4 (2001), 561–86.
Moorjani, Angela. 'Beckett's Racinian Fictions: "Racine and the Modern Novel" Revisited'. *Samuel Beckett Today/Aujourd'hui*, 24 (2012), 41–55.
'Peau de Chagrin. Beckett and Bion on Looking not to See'. *Samuel Beckett Today/Aujourd'hui*, 14 (2004), 25–38.
Morse, Ruth, Helen Cooper and Peter Holland (eds.). *Medieval Shakespeare: Pasts and Presents*. Cambridge University Press, 2013.
Murphy, John L. 'Beckett's Pugatories' in Colleen Jaurretche (ed.), *Beckett, Joyce and the Art of the Negative*. Amsterdam, New York: Rodopi, 2005. 109–24.
Murphy, Peter J. *Beckett's Dedalus: Dialogic Encounters with Joyce in Beckett's Fiction*. University of Toronto Press, 2009.
'Reincarnations of Joyce in Beckett's Fiction'. *Samuel Beckett Today/Aujourd'hui*, 22 (2010), 67–77.
Murray, H.J.R. *A History of Chess*. Oxford: Clarendon Press, 1962 [1913].
Neumann, Gerhard. 'Inszenierung und Destruktion. Zum Problem der Intertextualität in Samuel Becketts Erzählung *Dante and the Lobster*'. *Poetica*, 19 (1987), 278–301.
Nixon, Mark. *Beckett's German Diaries 1936-1937*. London: Continuum, 2011.
Olk, Claudia. '"Ah the soap": Objekt und Materie im *Ulysses*'. *Poetica*, 40 (2008), 169–88.
'"A matter of fundamental sounds": The Music of Beckett's *Endgame*'. *Poetica*, 43 (2011), 391–411.
'*Prinz Friedrich von Homburg*: Kleists Märkischer *Hamlet*'. *Kleist Jahrbuch*, (2017), 23–37.
Reisen und Erzählen: Studien zur Entwicklung von Fiktionalität in Narrativen Reisedarstellungen des Englischen Spätmittelalters und der Frühen Neuzeit. Trier: WVT, 1999.
'The Musicality of *The Merchant of Venice*', in Christina Wald (ed.), *Medieval Shakespeare*. London, New York: Routledge, 2012. 386–97.

'Vision and Desire in Mary Magdalene and *The Winter's Tale*' in Andrew James Johnston, Ethan Knapp and Margitta Rouse (eds.), *The Art of Vision: Ekphrasis in Medieval Literature and Culture*. Columbus: The Ohio State University Press, 2015. 79–100.
Oppenheim, Lois. *The Painted Word: Samuel Beckett's Dialogue with Art*. Ann Arbor: University of Michigan Press, 2000.
'The Uncanny in Beckett' in Colleen Jaurretche (ed.), *Beckett, Joyce and the Art of the Negative*. Amsterdam, New York: Rodopi, 2005, 125–40.
Palfrey, Simon. *Late Shakespeare: A New World of Words*. Oxford: Clarendon Press, 2000 [1997].
Parris, Benjamin. '"The Body is with the King, but the King is not with the Body": Sovereign Sleep in *Hamlet* and *Macbeth*'. *Shakespeare Studies*, 40 (2012), 101–42.
Patey, Caroline. 'Beckett's Shakespeare, or, Silencing the Bard' in Giovanni Cianci (ed. and intr.) and Caroline Patey (ed.), *Will the Modernist: Shakespeare and the European Historical Avant-Gardes*. Oxford: Lang, 2014. 223–50.
Pattie, David. 'The Arrival of Godot: Beckett, Cultural Memory and 1950s British Theatre' in David Tucker and Trish McTighe (eds.), *Staging Beckett in Great Britain*. London, Oxford, New York, New Delphi, Sydney: Bloomsbury Methuen Drama, 2016. 3–20.
Paulin, Roger. *The Critical Reception of Shakespeare in Germany 1682–1914: Native Literature and Foreign Genius*. Hildesheim: Olms, 2003.
Pavese, Michael. 'On the Five Nevers'. *High Plains Literary Review*, 9.3 (1994), 47–61.
Peat, Derek. '"And that's true too": *King Lear* and the Tension of Uncertainty'. *Shakespeare Survey*, 33 (1980), 43–53.
Pelaschiar, Laura (ed.). *Joyce/Shakespeare*. New York: Syracuse University Press, 2015.
Pfister, Manfred. 'Beckett, Barker, and Other Grim Laughter' in Manfred Pfister (ed.), *A History of English Laughter – Laughter from Beowulf to Beckett and Beyond*. New York: Rodopi, 2002. 175–89.
Pilling, John. *Beckett Before Godot*. Cambridge University Press, 1997.
'Dates and Difficulties in Beckett's *Whoroscope Notebook*'. *Journal of Beckett Studies*, 3 (2004), 39–48.
'From a (W)horoscope to Murphy' in John Pilling and Mary Bryden (eds.), *'The Ideal Core of the Onion': Reading Beckett Archives*. Reading: Beckett International Foundation, 1992. 1–20.
Plock, Vike Martina. 'Made in Germany. Why Goethe's Hamlet Mattered to Joyce' in Laura Pelaschiar (ed.), *Joyce/Shakespeare*. New York: Syracuse University Press, 2015. 89–106.
Poole, William. 'False Play: Shakespeare and Chess'. *Shakespeare Quarterly*, 55 (2004), 50–70.
Pountney, Rosemary. *Theatre of Shadows: Samuel Beckett's Drama, 1956–1976*. Gerrards Cross: Smythe, 1988.

Poussin, Nicolas. *Lettres et Propos sur l'Art*. Textes réunis et présentés par Anthony Blunt. Paris: Hermann, 1964.
Pye, Christopher. *Storm at Sea: Political Aesthetics in the Time of Shakespeare*. New York: Fordham University Press, 2015.
Rabaté, Jean-Michel. *1913: The Cradle of Modernism*. London: Wiley, 2007.
The Pathos of Distance. Affects of the Moderns. New York, London: Bloomsbury, 2016.
Think, Pig! Beckett at the Limit of the Human. New York: Fordham, 2016.
Rabinovitz, Ruben. *The Development of Samuel Beckett's Fiction*. Urbana: University of Illinois Press, 1984.
Ratcliffe, Sophie. 'Savage Loving: Beckett, Browning and *The Tempest*'. *Samuel Beckett Today/Aujourd'hui*, 12 (2002), 147–62.
Rebellato, Dan. *1956 and All That: The Making of Modern British Drama*. London: Routledge, 1999.
Rehberg, Walter and Paula Rehberg. *Franz Schubert. Sein Leben und Werk*. Zürich: Artemis, 1946.
Reichert, Klaus. 'Endlose Enden. Zu Apokalyptischen Figuren bei Beckett und Shakespeare' in Karlheinz Stierle and Rainer Warning (eds.), *Das Ende. Figuren einer Denkform*. Munich: Fink, 1996. 495–514.
Restivo, Giuseppina. 'Caliban/Clov and Leopardi's Boy: Beckett and Postmodernism' in Bruce Stewart (ed.), *Beckett and Beyond*. Gerrards Cross: Smythe, 1999, 217–30.
Ricks, Christopher. *Beckett's Dying Words*. Oxford: Clarendon, 1993.
Robbe-Grillet, Alain. 'Samuel Beckett, or "Presence" in the Theatre' in Martin Esslin (ed.), *Samuel Beckett: A Collection of Critical Essays*. Englewood Cliffs: Prentice Hall, 1965. 108–16.
Roberts, David. 'Sleeping Beauties: Shakespeare, Sleep and the Stage'. *The Cambridge Quarterly*, 35.3 (2006), 231–54.
Robinson, Michael. 'From Purgatory to Inferno: Beckett and Dante Revisited'. *Journal of Beckettian Studies*, 5 (1979), 69–82.
Russel Taylor, John. *Anger and After: A Guide to the New British Drama*. London: Methuen, 1962.
Ruvoldt, Maria. *The Renaissance Imagery of Inspiration: Metaphors of Sex, Sleep and Dreams*. Cambridge University Press, 2004.
Ruyter, Danièle de. 'Facination de la Tragédie Racinienne: Resonances dans *Oh les beaux jours*'. *Samuel Beckett Today/Aujourd'hui*, 24 (2012), 57–71.
Salisbury, Laura. *Samuel Beckett: Laughing Matters, Comic Timing*. Edinburgh University Press, 2012.
Saunders, Graham. 'Contracts, Clauses and Nudes: *Breath, Oh! Calcutta!* and the Freedom of Authorship' in David Tucker and Trish McTighe (eds.), *Staging Beckett in Great Britain*. London, Oxford, New York, New Delphi, Sydney: Bloomsbury Methuen Drama, 2016. 177–92.
Schmidt-Biggemann, Wilhelm. 'Tradition und Legitimation' in Andreas Höfele, Jan-Dirk Müller and Wulf Oesterreicher (eds.), *Die Frühe Neuzeit: Revisionen einer Epoche*. Berlin, Boston: De Gruyter, 2013. 47–83.

Schneider, Alan. 'Waiting for Beckett: A Personal Chronicle'. *Chelsea Review*, 2 (September 1958), 3–20.
Schwab, Gabriele. 'On the Dialectic of Closing and Opening in Samuel Beckett's *Endgame*' in Steven Connor (ed.), *New Casebooks: Waiting for Godot and Endgame*. Houndmills: Macmillan, 1996. 87–99.
Sheehan, Paul. 'Beckett's Ghost Dramas: Monitoring a Phenomenology of Sleep' in Ulrika Maude and Matthew Feldmann (eds.), *Beckett and Phenomenology*. London: Continuum, 2009. 158–76.
Shenker, Israel. 'An Interview with Beckett' in Raymond Federman and Lawrence Graver (eds.), *Samuel Beckett: The Critical Heritage*. London: Routledge, 1979. 160–3.
Sherman, William H. 'Shakespearean Somniloquy: Sleep and Transformation in *The Tempest*' in Tom Healy and Margaret Healy (eds.), *Renaissance Transformations: The Making of English Writing*. Edinburgh University Press, 2009. 177–91.
Slote, Sam. 'The Joyce Circle' in Anthony Uhlmann (ed.), *Samuel Beckett in Context*. Cambridge University Press, 2013. 150–9.
  'Stuck in Translation: Beckett and Borges on Dante'. *Journal of Beckett Studies*, 19.1 (2010), 15–28.
Smart, Sara and Mara R. Wade (eds.). *The Palatine Wedding of 1613: Protestant Alliance and Court Festival*. Wiesbaden: Harrassowitz, 2013.
Smith, Frederik N. *Beckett's Eighteenth Century*. Houndmills: Palgrave, 2002.
  'Fiction as Composing Process: *How It Is*' in Morris Beja, S.E. Gontarski and Pierre Astier (eds.), *Samuel Beckett: Humanistic Perspectives*. Columbus: Ohio State University Press, 1983. 107–21.
Smith, Richard Carter. 'Beckett and the Animal: Writing from "No-Man's Land"'. *ELH*, 79 (2012), 211–35.
Sontag, Susan. 'Waiting for Godot in Sarajevo'. *Performing Arts Journal*, 16.2 (1994), 87–106.
Spurr, David. *Joyce and the Scene of Modernity*. Gainesville: University Press of Florida, 2002.
Stewart, Paul. 'But Why Shakespeare? The Muted Role of Dickens in *Endgame*' in Mark S. Byron and Michael J. Meyer (eds.), *Samuel Beckett's* Endgame. Amsterdam: Rodopi, 2007. 207–25.
  'Stages of Influence. Shakespeare, Joyce; Joyce, Beckett'. *In-Between: Essays and Studies in Literary Criticism*, 12.1–2 (2003), 99-111.
Strauss, Walter. 'Dante's Belacqua and Beckett's Tramps'. *Comparative Literature*, 11.3 (1959), 250–61.
Sullivan, Garrett Jr. *Sleep, Romance, and Human Embodiment: Vitality from Spenser to Milton*. Cambridge University Press, 2012.
Swander, Homer. 'Shakespeare and Beckett: What the Words Know' in Marvin Thompson, Ruth Thompson, and Jay L. Halio (eds.), *Shakespeare and the Sense of Performance: Essays in the Tradition of Performance Criticism in Honor of Bernard Beckerman*. Newark: University of Delaware Press, 1989. 60–78.

Tassi, Marguerite. 'Shakespeare and Beckett Revisited: A Phenomenology of Theater'. *Comparative Drama*, 31.2 (1997), 248–76.
Taylor, Neil and Bryan Loughrey. 'Middleton's Chess Strategies in *Women Beware Women*'. *SEL*, 24.2 (1984), 341–54.
Tophoven, Erika. *Becketts Berlin*. Berlin: Nicolai, 2005.
Trezise, Thomas. *Into the Breach: Samuel Beckett and the Ends of Literature*. Princeton University Press, 1990.
Tucker, David and Trish McTighe (eds.). *Staging Beckett in Great Britain*. London, Oxford, New York, New Delphi, Sydney: Bloomsbury, 2016.
Turner, Timothy A. 'Making the Moor: Torture, Sleep Deprivation, and Race in *Othello*' in Nancy L. Simpson-Younger and Margaret Simon (eds.), *Forming Sleep: Representing Consciousness in the English Renaissance*. University Park: The Pennsylvania State University Press, 2020. 89–109.
Tynan, Kenneth. 'New Writing'. *The Observer*, 7 August 1955.
Uhlmann, Anthony. *Beckett and Poststructuralism*. Cambridge University Press, 1999.
 (ed.). *Samuel Beckett in Context*. Cambridge University Press, 2013.
Unglaub, Jonathan. *Poussin and the Poetics of Painting: Pictorial Narrative and the Legative of Tasso*. Cambridge University Press, 2006.
Vandervlist, Harry. 'Beckett, Duchamp and Chess: A Crossroads at Arcachon in the Summer of 1940'. *Caliban*, 33 (2013), 173–82.
Vendler, Helen. *The Art of Shakespeare's Sonnets*. Cambridge, MA: Harvard University Press, 1997.
Wakeling, Corey. 'Sleeplessness in Sleep'. *Performance Research*, 21.1 (2016), 42–8.
Wallace, David Foster. 'Consider the Lobster'. *Gourmet Magazine*, August 2004, 50–64.
Weidle, Roland. '"If man were porter of hell gate": Dante in der Englischen Frühen Neuzeit und Shakespeares Hölle' in Stephanie Heimgartner and Monika Schmitz-Emans (eds.), *Komparatistische Perspektiven auf Dantes 'Divina Commedia'. Lektüren, Transformationen und Visualisierungen*. Berlin, Boston: de Gruyter, 2017. 183–205.
Weller, Shane. *A Taste for the Negative: Beckett and Nihilism*. Leeds: Legenda, 2005.
 Literature, Philosophy, Nihilism: The Uncanniest of Guests. London, New York: Continuum, 2008.
 'Phenomenologies of the Nothing: Democritus, Heidegger, Beckett' in Ulrika Maude and Matthew Feldmann (eds.), *Beckett and Phenomenology*. London, New York: Continuum, 2009, 39–55.
Wells, Stanley. 'My Name is Will: Shakespeare's Sonnets and Autobiography'. *Shakespeare Survey*, 68 (2015), 99–108.
Wells, Stanley and Paul Edmondson. *Shakespeare's Sonnets*. Oxford University Press, 2004.
Wheatley, David. '"Nothing Will Come of Nothing": Zero-Sum Games in Shakespeare's *King Lear* and Beckett's *Endgame*' in Janet Clare (ed.), *Shakespeare and the Irish Writer*. University College Dublin Press, 2010. 166–79.

Whitelaw, Billie. *Billie Whitelaw ... Who He?* New York: St. Martin's Press, 1996.
Williams, Simon J. *Sleep and Society: Sociological Ventures into the (Un)Known.* London, New York: Routledge, 2005.
Wilson, Catherine. *The Invisible World: Early Modern Philosophy and the Invention of the Microscope.* Princeton University Press, 1995.
Wiseman, S.J. 'Introduction' in Katharina Hidgkin, Michelle O'Callaghan and S.J. Wiseman (eds.), *Reading the Early Modern Dream: Terrors of the Night.* New York, London: Routledge, 2008. 1–13.
Wolosky, Shira. 'The Negative Way Negated: Samuel Beckett's *Texts for Nothing*'. *NLH*, 22.1 (199), 213–30.
Worthen, W.B. *Drama: Between Poetry and Performance.* Malden: Wiley-Blackwell, 2010.
Youens, Susan. *Retracing a Winter's Journey: Schubert's 'Winterreise'.* Ithaca: Cornell University Press, 1991.
Zeifman, Hersh. 'Come and Go: A Criticule', in Morris Beja, S.E. Gontarski and Pierre Astier (eds.), *Samuel Beckett: Humanistic Perspectives.* Columbus: Ohio State University Press, 1983, 137–44.
Žižek, Slavoj. 'The Minimal Event: Subjective Destitution in Shakespeare and Beckett' in Russell Sbriglia (ed.), *Everything You Always Wanted to Know about Literature but were Afraid to Ask Žižek.* Durham: Duke University Press, 2017. 290–316.

Index

Adorno, Theodor, 3, 81–2, 154–5
"analogy-mongering," for Beckett, 2–3
Arikha, Avigdor, 125, 132
Arnold, Matthew, 22
Ashcroft, Dame Peggy, 21, 33, 90
Atik, Anne, 5
Avicenna, 183

Bakhtin, Mikhail, 3–4
Barthes, Roland, 3–4, 10
Beckett, Samuel
  academic education
    at Portora Royal School, 41
    at Trinity College, 1, 41
  All that Fall, 29–31, 209–10
  "Assumption," 97, 136
  Breath, 147
  "Capital of the Ruins," 65
  Cascando, 201–5, 209–10, 213
  "Casket of Pralinen for the Daughter of a Dissipated Mandarin," 112
  Catastrophe, 18
  Come and Go, 134
  Company), 23–5, 58, 63–4, 73, 129–30, 210–11
  Complete Dramatic Works of Samuel Beckett, 81–4, 90–2
  "Dante and the Lobster," 106–18
  Dante as influence on, 105–6
  Divina Commedia, 105–18
  "Dante...Bruno..Vico.Joyce," 97, 105–6
  Disjecta, 1–3, 39–41, 105–6, 125
  Dream of Fair to Middling Women, 58–9, 61–3, 87, 97–8, 107–8, 173, 183–4
  "Echo's Bones," 64, 74–5, 78–81
  Echo's Bones and Other Precipitates, 74–6
  Embers, 28–31, 131
  "The End," 135–41
  Endgame, 18, 26, 73, 131
  "The Expelled," 136
  Film, 132
  "Fizzles," 153
  Footfalls, 131, 134, 194–6, 213
  Happy Days, 5, 18, 20–1, 64, 81–6, 92, 131, 196–201, 211, 213
  "Her Beckett," 214
  How It Is, 63–4, 106
  "Imagination Dead Imagine," 26
  Joyce and, 39–40
  Krapps Last Tape, 73, 131, 154
  "Lessness," 135–6
  "The Lost Ones," 106, 174, 180, 211
  Malone Dies, 140
  Mercier and Camier, 131
  Molloy, 57–8
  More Pricks Than Kicks, 78, 85, 106, 108, 114–15, 166, 178
  Murphy, 58–61, 71, 83, 173, 204, 210–11
  Nacht und Träume, 134, 191–2, 213
  Not I, 25
  Piece, 129–30
  A Piece of Monologue, 127–30
  Play, 126–7
  Proust, 39, 62, 97, 135, 168
  Quad I, 153
  Quad II, 153
  Rockaby, 126–7, 191–4, 213
  Rough for Theatre II, 27–8, 30–1, 173
  Schubert and, 132–5
  Stirrings Still, 130–1, 212
  at Stratford-upon-Avon, 1
  "Texts for Nothing," 3–4, 134–41, 153, 168
  The Unnamable, 153, 175–6
  "Vive morte," 123–4
  Waiting for Godot, 24, 58, 131, 165, 168, 210
  Watt, 131
  What where, 132–5
  "Whoroscope," 97
  Worstward Ho, 20
Blinn, Roger, 20, 166
Blumenberg, Hans, 13
The Book of Common Prayer, 82, 183

Index

The Book of the Duchess (Chaucer), 171
Borges, Jorge Luis, 13
Bostridge, Ian, 134–5, 150
Bradley, A. C., 24, 104
Brahe, Tycho, 53
Breath (Beckett), 147
Brook, Peter, 20
Brown, John Russell, 5
Bruno, Giordano, 40–1
Bunyan, John, 15

Carson, Ann, 214–15
Caselli, Daniela, 105
The Castell of Health (Elyot), 182–3
Cavell, Stanley, 15, 33, 165
Cavendish, Margaret, 153
Caxton, William, 171
Cessolis, Jacobus de, 171
Chaucer, Geoffrey, 79, 100
    The Book of the Duchess, 171
    The House of Fame, 78–9
    The Legend of Good Women, 97–8, 107, 183–4
chess imagery, 169–74
clowns and comics, 5
Coetzee, J. M., 104–5
Cogan, Thomas, 182–3, 206
Complete Dramatic Works of Samuel Beckett, 81–4, 90–2
The Comprehensive Teacher's Bible, 157
contraction, 160–1
Corneille, Pierre, 15
Council of Trent, 100
Creative Devolution (Gontarski), 56
Creative Involution (Gontarski), 5
cross-mapping, 4

Daemonologie, 183
Damned to Fame (Knowlson), 5
Dante Alighieri (Dante), 38, 74, 78–9. *See also* Divina Commedia
La *Divina Commedia*, 105–18
DaSilva, Gregorio, 35
"De civitate hominum" (McGreevy), 116–17
De Ludo Scaccorum (Cessolis), 171
Decreation (Carson), 214
Deleuze, Gilles, 56, 180
Derrida, Jacques, 15, 32
Descartes, René, 15
Devine, George, 20–1
Devlin, Denis, 55–6
dispossession, trajectories of, 135–41
Divina Commedia (Dante), 74, 78–9
    Beckett influenced by, 105–18
    "Inferno," 108, 110–11, 114
    "Paradiso," 108, 114, 120–1

"Purgatorio," 78–9, 100, 108, 114, 120
    purgatory as intermediary space in, 98–101
Doctrinal Treatises (Tyndale), 100
"Der Doppelgänger" (Heine), 132
Dover Beach (Arnold), 22
dreamscapes, sleep and, 187–91
Duthuit, Georges, 125

Echo and Narcissus (Poussin), 76–7
echoes, as literary theme
    in Beckett's works, 74, 211
    conceptual approach to, 4, 74–5
    in *Cymbeline*, 88–91
    Metamorphosis, 74–8
    in Shakespeare's works, 211
    in Woolf's works, 74
Eliot, T. S., 41, 104
    Dante as influence on, 98–101
    Four Quartets, 14, 73
    "Tradition and the Individual Talent," 13–14
    The Waste Land, 1, 41–2
Eltis, Sol, 21–2, 35–7
Elyot, Thomas, 182–3
Les eschez amoureux, 171
Esslin, Martin, 19, 135
Experimental Philosophy (Power), 153

Florio, John, 100
Foucault, Michel, 10, 15, 32
"Fragments" (McGreevy), 121–2
Freud, Sigmund, 183–4

The Game and Playe of Chesse, 171
A Game at Chesse (Middleton), 171
German classicism
    Shakespeare and, 44–5
    Sturm und Drang, 44
Germany. *See* German classicism; Weimar Germany
Geulincx, Arnold, 15
ghosts
    in Beckett's works, 131
    in *Hamlet*, 128
Gielgud, John, 90
Goethe, Johann Wolfgang von, 44, 54–5
Goldberg, Jonathan, 75
Golding, Arthur, 91
Gottfried, von Straßburg, 171
Gower, John, 100
Greenblatt, Stephen, 100–2, 167
Gregory the Great (Pope), 99
Guggenheim, Peggy, 39

Habermas, Jürgen, on modernity, 12–14, 32
Hall, Peter, 20–2, 36, 41, 90

Halpern, Richard, 10, 41–2
Hamlet in Purgatory (Greenblatt), 100, 102
happiness
  in *Macbeth*, 85–6
  in *A Midsummer Night's Dream*, 85–6
  in *Happy Days*, 84–6
  in *Romeo and Juliet*, 86
Havel, Václav, 18
The Haven of Health (Cogan), 182–3, 206
Hegel, Georg Wilhelm Friedrich, 32
Heine, Heinrich, 132
"Holde Träume kehret wieder" (Schubert), 192
Holinshed, Raphael, 53, 69
Holinshed's Chronicles of England (Holinshed), 53, 69
Hooke, Richard, 153
How It Was. A Memoir of Samuel Beckett (Atik), 5
humanism, 12–13
  Shakespeare and, 15
"humanity in ruins," 65

Iser, Wolfgang, 159

Jolas, Eugène, 40
Joyce, James, 1
  Beckett and, 39–40
  Joyce as literary influence on, 41–55
  Finnegan's Wake, 39–40, 105–6
  poetics of, 40
  The Portrait of the Artist as a Young Man, 104
  purgatory themes, 104–6
  The Portrait of the Artist as a Young Man, 104
  Renaissance texts as influence on, 14
  Shakespearean influences on, 41–55
  Hamlet, 43–50
  in *Ulysses*, 41–55
  Ulysses, 1, 69, 210–11
  use of language by, 40–1, 46–7, 210–11
  hieroglyphic, 56–7
  Work in Progress, 105–6
Juliet, Charles, 63–4

Kafka, Franz, 190
"Kafka and his Precursors" (Borges), 13
Keats, John, 126, 148
Kepler, Johannes, 53
Knight, G. Wilson, 24, 104
Knowlson, James, 1, 3, 5, 25, 67, 95, 122
Kott, Jan, 4–5
  on *King Lear*, 19
Kristeva, Julia, 3–4

Langland, William, 184
Leavis, F.R., 104

Léhar, Franz, 92
Leibniz, Gottfried Wilhelm, 15
Lieder (Schubert), 132–5
Life of Goethe (Dunster), 45
Lodge, Thomas, 100
Luther, Martin, 100
Lyotard, Jean-François, 13–14

Malory, Thomas, 171
Mandeville, Bernard de, 79
Marvell, Andrew, 153
Marx, Karl, 47
Mayhew, Henry, 135
McGreevy, Thomas, 7–8, 39, 95, 116–17, 121–2, 211
meanings
  as dependent on ascription, 165
  exertion of power through, 162–5
Meredith, George, 51
The Merry Widow (Léhar), 92
metamorphosis
  in *Romeo and Juliet*, 86–8
  sleep as, 187–91
Metamorphosis (Ovid), 74–8
The Metamorphosis (Kafka), 190
Micrographia (Hooke), 153
Middleton, Thomas, 171
Milton, John, 15, 100
Molière, 15
monologues, 128–9
Le Morte D'Arthur (Malory), 171

"Nacht und Träume" (musical piece) (Schubert), 191–2
Nashe, Thomas, 183

Observations upon Experimental Philosophy (Cavendish), 153
"On a Drop of Dew" (Marvell), 153
Ovid, 74–8
Oxford English Dictionary, 1–2

Paradise Lost (Milton), 100
"Paradiso" (Dante), 108, 114, 120–1
Pascal, Blaise, 15
pause. *See also* waiting
  in *Hamlet*, 101–4
Pearl, 183–4
Péron, Alfred, 39
Piers Plowman (Langland), 184
Pinter, Harold, 35–6, 214
Plato, 183–4
  in Joyce's works, 42–3
Plurabelle, Anna Livia, 39

Index

Pound, Ezra, 14, 42
Poussin, Nicolas, 76–7, 95
Power, Henry, 153
Prentice, Charles, 78
Prognostic (Hippocrates), 183
"Prometheus" (Goethe), 55
Proust, Marcel, 14, 20–2, 38
"Purgatorio" (Dante), 78–9, 100, 108, 114, 120
purgatory, as intermediary space, 98–101
  in Becket's works, 104–6
  in England, 100
  in *Hamlet*, 100–1
  invention of, 100
  in Joyce works, *The Portrait of the Artist as a Young Man*, 104
  in *The Portrait of the Artist as a Young Man*, 104

Rabelais, François, 15
Racine, Louis, 15
Recherche (Proust), 20–2
reflection, as conceptual process, 75–8
Ronsard, Pierre de, 15
Rosencrantz and Guildenstern are Dead (Stoppard), 104, 175–6, 214–15
Rudmose-Brown, Thomas, 67

Samuel Beckett Archive, 5
Samuel Beckett Digital Manuscript Project, 5
Schneider, Alan, 20–1, 166, 177
Schubert, Franz, 191–2
  Beckett and, 132–5
  Winterreise, 8, 121, 134–6, 212
Schubert's Winter Journey (Bostridge), 150
Shakespeare, William
  Antony and Cleopatra, 50, 143, 146, 166
  Cymbeline, 47–8, 88–91, 210–11
  Hamlet, 20–1, 23–5, 63–5, 79–81
    Beckett's works and, referential themes in, 61–6
    corruption in, 40
    "Dante and the Lobster" and, 110
    finitude in, 153
    ghosts in, 128
    imaginary third spaces in, 117
    melting flesh in, 91–2
    pause in, 101–4
    purgatory in, 100–1
    sleep in, 184–5, 213
    waiting in, 101–4
  Henry V, 80, 155
  King Lear, 5, 19–20, 35, 209
    Brook's production of, 20
    dispossession trajectories in, 135–41
    Dover cliff setting, 22–5, 30–1
    existentialist themes in, 19
    Hall's production of, 21–2
    horizontal movement in, 30
    imaginary third space in, 117–18
    inescapability in, 26–7
    Kott on, 19
    as Theatre of the Absurd, 20
  Love's Labour's Lost, 50
  Macbeth, 85–6, 201–5, 213
  Measure for Measure, 54, 110–11
  The Merchant of Venice, 50, 62
  The Merry Wives of Windsor, 92
  A Midsummer Night's Dream, 50, 59, 61–6, 79–80, 85–6, 153, 155, 168, 187–91, 213
  Richard III, 85–6
  Romeo and Juliet, 30, 60–6, 85–8
  "Sonnet 18," 144–5
  "Sonnet 55," 143–4
  "Sonnet 71," 93–4
  "Sonnet 81," 145
  "Sonnet 135," 52
  The Tempest, 154
  Timon of Athens, 8, 135–41
  Twelfth Night, 47–8, 210–11
  The Winter's Tale, 8, 49–50, 141–7, 191–4, 213
  As You Like It, 135–6, 153
Sidney, Sir Philip, 146
Stoppard, Tom, 104, 175–6, 214–15
Sturm und Drang, 44

tableaux vivants, in Beckett works, 126–31
Terrors of the Night (Nashe), 183
Timaios (Plato), 183–4
Tristan und Isolde (Gottfried), 171
Tynan, Kenneth, 16–17
Tyndale, William, 100

Unglaub, Jonathan, 77
Unseld, Siegfried, 3

van Velde, Bram, 125
Vico, Giambattista, 39–40
Voice Terminal Echo (Goldberg), 75

Waiting for the Barbarians (Coetzee), 104–5
Warrilow, David, 127–9
Weimar Germany, Beckett in, 55–6
Wells, Stanley, 36
Whitelaw, Billie, 25

Wilhelm Meisters Lehrjahre (Goethe), 44
Williams, Tennessee, 35–6
Winterreise (Schubert), 8, 121, 134–6, 212
Woolf, Virginia
　"Craftsmanship," 74
　Jacob's Room, 1

　To the Lighthouse, 125–6
　Mrs. Dalloway, 89

Yeats, W. B., 104

Žižek, Slavoj, 13, 32

For EU product safety concerns, contact us at Calle de José Abascal, 56–1°, 28003 Madrid, Spain or eugpsr@cambridge.org.

www.ingramcontent.com/pod-product-compliance
Ingram Content Group UK Ltd.
Pitfield, Milton Keynes, MK11 3LW, UK
UKHW021501220625
459949UK00018B/530